T0332717

Big Data, Political Campaigning and the Law

In this multidisciplinary book, experts from around the globe examine how data-driven political campaigning works, what challenges it poses for personal privacy and democracy, and how emerging practices should be regulated.

The rise of big data analytics in the political process has triggered official investigations in many countries around the world, and become the subject of broad and intense debate. Political parties increasingly rely on data analytics to profile the electorate and to target specific voter groups with individualised messages based on their demographic attributes. Political micro-targeting has become a major factor in modern campaigning, because of its potential to influence opinions, to mobilise supporters and to get out votes. The book explores the legal, philosophical and political dimensions of big data analytics in the electoral process. It demonstrates that the unregulated use of big personal data for political purposes not only infringes voters' privacy rights, but also has the potential to jeopardise the future of the democratic process, and proposes reforms to address the key regulatory and ethical questions arising from the mining, use and storage of massive amounts of voter data.

Providing an interdisciplinary assessment of the use and regulation of big data in the political process, this book will appeal to scholars from law, political science, political philosophy and media studies, policy makers and anyone who cares about democracy in the age of data-driven political campaigning.

Normann Witzleb, Moira Paterson and Janice Richardson all work at the Faculty of Law, Monash University, Australia.

Big Data, Political Campaigning and the Law

Democracy and Privacy in the Age of Micro-Targeting

Edited by
Normann Witzleb, Moira Paterson and
Janice Richardson

Routledge
Taylor & Francis Group

a GlassHouse book

First published
by Routledge
2 Park Square, Milton Park, Abingdon, Oxon OX14 4RN

and by Routledge
52 Vanderbilt Avenue, New York, NY 10017

A GlassHouse book

Routledge is an imprint of the Taylor & Francis Group, an informa business

British Library Cataloguing in Publication Data
A catalogue record for this book is available from the British Library

Library of Congress Cataloging-in-Publication Data
A catalog record has been requested for this book

ISBN: 978-0-367-23054-8 (hbk)
ISBN: 978-0-429-28865-4 (ebk)

Typeset in Galliard
by Taylor & Francis Books

Contents

List of contributors   vii

1 Political micro-targeting in an era of big data analytics: An overview
   of the regulatory issue   1
   JANICE RICHARDSON, NORMANN WITZLEB AND MOIRA PATERSON

PART I
The need for a civic disposition   15

2 From mass to automated media: Revisiting the 'filter bubble'   17
   MARK ANDREJEVIC AND ZALA VOLCIC

3 Filter bubbles, democracy and conceptions of self: A brief genealogy
   and a Spinozist perspective   34
   JANICE RICHARDSON

4 Voting public: Leveraging personal information to construct voter
   preference   47
   JACQUELYN BURKELL AND PRISCILLA M. REGAN

PART II
Public international and European law   69

5 International law and new challenges to democracy in the digital age:
   Big data, privacy and interferences with the political process   71
   DOMINIK STEIGER

6 Social media in election campaigns: Free speech or a danger for
   democracy?   99
   UDO FINK

7 Freedom of processing of personal data for the purpose of electoral
activities after the GDPR   114
MAEVE MCDONAGH

PART III
**Domestic laws in Canada, Australia, the United States and
the United Kingdom**   139

8 From the doorstep to the database: Political parties, campaigns, and
personal privacy protection in Canada   141
COLIN J. BENNETT AND MICHAEL MCDONALD

9 Voter privacy in an era of big data: Time to abolish the political
exemption in the Australian Privacy Act   164
MOIRA PATERSON AND NORMANN WITZLEB

10 Big Data and the electoral process in the United States:
Constitutional constraint and limited data privacy regulations   186
RONALD J. KROTOSZYNSKI JR

11 Data and political campaigning in the era of big data – the UK
experience   214
STEPHANIE HANKEY, RAVI NAIK AND GARY WRIGHT

Index   236

Contributors

Mark Andrejevic is Professor of Media and Communication in the School of Media, Film and Journalism at Monash University. He is the author of *Reality TV: The Work of Being Watched*; *iSpy: Surveillance and Power in the Digital Era*; and *Infoglut: How Too Much Information is Changing the Way We Think and Know*. He is also the author of more than 75 journal articles and academic book chapters on surveillance, digital media and popular culture, as well as a co-editor of *Commercial Nationalism* and *What's Become of Australian Cultural Studies?*

Colin J. Bennett received his Bachelor's and Master's degrees from the University of Wales, and his PhD from the University of Illinois at Urbana-Champaign. Since 1986 he has taught in the Department of Political Science at the University of Victoria, where he is now Professor. He has enjoyed Visiting Professorships at Harvard's Kennedy School of Government, the Center for the Study of Law and Society at University of California, Berkeley, the School of Law, University of New South Wales, the Law, Science, Technology and Society Centre at the Vrije Universiteit in Brussels and at the University of Toronto. His research has focused on the comparative analysis of surveillance technologies and privacy protection policies at the domestic and international levels. In addition to numerous scholarly and newspaper articles, he has written or edited seven books, including *The Governance of Privacy* (MIT Press, 2006, with Charles Raab) and *The Privacy Advocates: Resisting the Spread of Surveillance* (MIT Press, 2008), and policy reports on privacy protection for Canadian and international agencies. He was co-investigator of a large SSHRC Major Collaborative Research Initiative grant entitled 'The New Transparency: Surveillance and Social Sorting' which culminated in the report: *Transparent Lives: Surveillance in Canada*. Through a SSHRC Partnership Grant on 'Big Data Surveillance', he is currently researching the capture and use of personal data by political parties in Western democracies.

Jacquelyn Burkell is an Associate Professor in the Faculty of Information and Media Studies at the University of Western Ontario. She holds a PhD in Cognitive Science from the University of Western Ontario. This background, including a focus on behavioural decision making, informs her research, which examines how technological mediation changes social interaction and information behaviour. She co-leads a working group on AI governance and policies in the Autonomy Through Cyberjustice Technologies SSHRC Partnership grant (led by Karim Benyekhlef of the University of Montreal), where her research focuses on accountability (explanatory mechanisms) and algorithmic bias. She is a co-investigator on the eQuality project (a SSHRC Partnership Grant led by Valerie Steeves and Jane Bailey, University of Ottawa), where her work focuses on empirical examinations of attitudes toward and experiences of behavioural tracking.

Udo Fink is a Professor of Law at the Johannes Gutenberg University Mainz (Germany). He holds a Chair in Public Law, European Law, International Public Law and International Trade Law. From 1990 to 1996 he was an Assistant Professor at the Institute of Public International Law, University of Cologne, where he obtained his Habilitation (post-doctoral degree). From 1996 to 2000 he was an Associate Professor for Public International Law, International Commercial Law at the University Göttingen (Germany). He has been visiting professor *inter alia* at the Lewis & Clarke Law School, Portland, Oregon, the University of Louisville, Kentucky, and Trinity College Dublin, Ireland. Since 2002 he has been the Director of the School of German Law and School of Polish Law, at the University of Krakow, Poland, and since 2011 has been the Co-Director of Mainz Media Institute. His research interests are in the area of the law of the United Nations, international media law, the European Convention on Human Rights and constitutional law.

Stephanie Hankey is a designer, technologist and activist who has been working internationally at the intersection of technology, human rights and civil liberties for the past 20 years. Her work combines her art, design and technology background with her focus on privacy, personal data and ethics. She is the Executive Director of the Berlin-based NGO the Tactical Technology Collective, which she co-founded in 2003. She has been awarded an Ashoka Fellowship for her work as a social entrepreneur. In 2016/17 she was an affiliate at the Berkman Klein Center for Internet and Society at Harvard University, and in 2017 she was made a Visiting Industry Associate at the Oxford Internet Institute at the University of Oxford. She has a degree in the History of Design and Art from Manchester Metropolitan University and a Master's in Computer-Related Design from the Royal College of Art, London.

Ronald J. Krotoszynski Jr is the John S. Stone Chair, Director of Faculty Research and Professor of Law at the University of Alabama School of Law. Before embarking on his academic career, he practised law as an associate with Covington & Burling, in Washington, DC. Prior to joining the faculty at the University of Alabama School of Law, he served on the law faculties at the Washington and Lee University School of Law and the Indiana University

McKinney School of Law. He has also taught as a visiting professor at Washington and Lee University School of Law, William and Mary School of Law, Brooklyn Law School, Florida State University School of Law, Seattle University School of Law, Texas A&M University School of Law and Syracuse University College of Law. He writes and teaches in the areas of constitutional law, administrative law, First Amendment law and comparative constitutional law. He is the author of *The Disappearing First Amendment* (Cambridge University Press, 2019), *Privacy Revisited: A Global Perspective on the Right to Be Left Alone* (Oxford University Press, 2016), *Reclaiming the Petition Clause: Seditious Libel, "Offensive" Protest, and the Right to Petition the Government for a Redress of Grievances* (Yale University Press, 2012), and *The First Amendment in Cross-Cultural Perspective: A Comparative Legal Analysis of the Freedom of Speech* (New York University Press, 2006). His law review articles have appeared in leading national law reviews and journals, including the *Yale Law Journal*, the *Michigan Law Review*, the *Duke Law Journal*, the *Northwestern University Law Review*, the *Georgetown Law Journal* and the *Texas Law Review*. Krotoszynski is also the co-author of casebooks in administrative law and First Amendment law.

Maeve McDonagh is a Professor at the Law School, University College Cork, Ireland. She specialises in information law and is the author of *Freedom of Information Law* (Thomson Round Hall, 3rd edition, 2015) and *Cyber Law* (with M. O'Dowd) (International Encyclopaedia of Laws Series, Kluwer Law, 2nd edition, 2015). She has published widely in the field of information law and has advised various governments on the drafting and implementation of FOI legislation. She has been engaged as an expert on information law matters by the Organisation for Security and Cooperation in Europe (OSCE) and by the European Commission. She has taught law at National University of Ireland Galway, La Trobe University, Melbourne, Australia, and University College Cork, and has served as Dean of the Faculty and Head of the Department of Law at University College Cork. She has been a visiting Professor at the University of Melbourne, University College London, Monash University, La Trobe University and Queensland University of Technology. She was Deputy Chair of the inaugural Press Council of Ireland from 2007 to 2013. In 2012, she was one of three international experts on freedom of information law appointed as members of the newly established Independent Appeals Panel on access to information of the Asian Development Bank. Her appointment has been renewed twice. In 2013, she was appointed by the Irish government to the FOI Implementation Review Group. In 2015, she was appointed to the board of the Broadcasting Authority of Ireland.

Michael McDonald holds an MA from the University of Victoria where he researched the Canadian government's 2017 apology to LGBTQ2+ communities in Canada. Specifically, he examined the pre-apology process, the government's substantive post-apology policy initiatives, and queer and trans community reactions to the apology in an effort to understand how governments use political apologies to renegotiate relationships with marginalised communities. He also worked as a research assistant for Dr Colin Bennett, and is interested in the privacy risks associated with political parties and data-driven campaigns. He is an alumnus of the BC Legislative Internship Program, has volunteered on many political campaigns and has previously worked with a federal political party. He is currently pursuing a JD at the University of Ottawa Faculty of Law.

Ravi Naik, the Law Society's 2018 Human Rights Lawyer of the Year, is a multi-award winning solicitor with a ground-breaking practice at the forefront of data rights and technology. He represents clients in some of the most high-profile data rights cases. These include the case against Cambridge Analytica for political profiling, claims against Facebook for their privacy policies and data practices, challenges to financial profiling companies and the leading regulatory complaint against the Advertising Technology industry. He is a well-known advocate and speaker on developing rights in technology and has written extensively on the new data rights movement. He is also often sought for his commentary in the media on a range of data rights issues.

Moira Paterson is a Professor at the Faculty of Law of Monash University Australia. She teaches, researches and publishes in information law, including privacy and data protection. She was a member of the Privacy Advisory Committee to the Office of the Australian Information Commissioner and has been a member of advisory committees to the Australian Law Reform Commission in relation to its inquiry into the Commonwealth Privacy Act and to the Victorian Law Reform Commission in relation to its Surveillance in Public Places report. Her current research focuses on the regulation of Big Data.

Priscilla M. Regan is a Professor in the Schar School of Policy and Government at George Mason University. Prior to joining that faculty in 1989, she was a Senior Analyst in the Congressional Office of Technology Assessment (1984–1989). Since the mid-1970s, her primary research interests have focused on the analysis of the social, policy and legal implications of organisational use of new information and communications technologies. She is currently a co-investigator on a Social Sciences and Humanities Research Council of Canada's eQuality grant exploring big data, discrimination and youth. She has published more than 70 articles or book chapters, as well as *Legislating Privacy: Technology, Social Values, and Public Policy* (University of North Carolina Press, 1995). She was a member of the National Academy of Sciences, Computer Science and Telecommunications Board, Committee on Authentication Technologies and their Privacy Implications. She received her PhD in Government from Cornell University and her BA from Mount Holyoke College.

Janice Richardson is an Associate Professor at the Faculty of Law of Monash University. She is author of the following three single-authored books: *Selves, Persons, Individuals: Philosophical Perspectives on Women and Legal Obligations*

(Ashgate, 2004), *The Classic Social Contractarians: Critical Perspectives from Feminist Philosophy and Law* (Ashgate, 2009) and *Law and the Philosophy of Privacy* (Routledge, 2016). She is co-editor of Routledge's *Feminist Perspectives on Tort Law* and *Feminist Perspectives on Law and Theory* and has published extensively in journals, including *Feminist Legal Studies, Law and Critique, Angelaki: Journal of the Theoretical Humanities, Minds and Machines: Journal for Artificial Intelligence, Philosophy and Cognitive Science.*

Dominik Steiger holds the chair of Public International Law, European Law and Public Law at Technische Universität Dresden and is the director of its Center for International Studies. From 2004 to 2009 he worked at the University of Potsdam, where he also obtained his PhD. He was a visiting fellow/professor at the University of Stellenbosch in 2012, at the University of Leipzig in 2016, at Monash University in 2018, at Auckland University of Technology in 2019 and an Emile Noël Fellow at New York University in the academic year 2014/ 2015. In 2016 he completed his Habilitation and was named Associate Professor for Public International Law at KU Leuven in Belgium as well as Hoogeleraar (Full Professor) at the Open Universiteit of the Netherlands. His research and publications focus *inter alia* on digitalisation and international law, democracy, international human rights law, international criminal law, international humanitarian law and United Nations law.

Zala Volcic is a Senior Lecturer at the School of Media, Film and Journalism, Monash University. Her scholarship, research and creative works are all manifestations of her commitment to a deeper understanding of the relationships between media, nationalism, gender, collective memory and politics. Her research has focused on a critical cultural studies based approach to popular media. She is the author and editor of several books and many of her articles have appeared in scholarly journals including *Critical Studies of Media Communication, International Journal of Cultural Studies* and *Feminist Media Studies.*

Normann Witzleb is an Associate Professor at the Faculty of Law of Monash University, Australia, and a Deputy Director of its Centre for Commercial Law and Regulation, leading its Privacy, Media and Communication Law Group. Prior to joining Monash University in 2008, he worked at the University of Western Australia (2001–2007) and the European University Viadrina Frankfurt (Oder) (1996–2000), where he also obtained his PhD. He has published widely on Australian and European privacy law, torts law and remedies. His publications include *Emerging Challenges in Privacy Law: Comparative Perspectives* (Cambridge University Press, 2014), co-edited with David Lindsay, Moira Paterson and Sharon Rodrick.

Gary Wright is the co-project lead at Tactical Tech's Data and Politics project, researching the uses of personal and voter data in political processes by political campaigns and the digital campaigning industry around the world. His previous work revolved around the use of information technology and technology innovation in the international development sector and he was an organiser and part of the founding team behind the Global Innovation Gathering (GIG) – a network of innovation hub, maker- and hackerspace managers based primarily in the global south. He also spent several years working in the communications team for the Berlin-based re:publica tech-festival. Gary's academic background lies in International Relations at the University of Edinburgh.

Chapter 1

Political micro-targeting in an era of big data analytics

An overview of the regulatory issue

Janice Richardson, Normann Witzleb and Moira Paterson

In March 2018, *The New York Times* and *The Observer* revealed that the data analytics company Cambridge Analytica (CA) had obtained data from more than 50 million Facebook profiles in its quest to develop techniques for predicting and shaping the behaviour of individual American voters.[1] The data was harvested through a Facebook app containing a personality quiz, which was developed by a contracted researcher, Aleksandr Kogan. Around 320,000 users who downloaded the quiz not only provided their own personal information but also granted the app permission to access the personal information of many millions of other users who were their friends. Neither the individuals who completed the quiz nor their Facebook friends were aware that their information was being harvested, and commercially and possibly politically exploited.

These events, which Facebook acknowledged to constitute a 'major breach of trust',[2] have revealed significant weaknesses in the way the social media giant manages and protects the vast troves of personal information it holds on its users. The incident also dramatically increased the concerns that had first arisen in relation to the role of data analytics in the Trump election and Brexit referendum

---

1 Carole Cadwalladr and Emma Graham-Harrison, 'Revealed: 50 million Facebook profiles harvested for Cambridge Analytica in major data breach' *The Guardian* (17 March 2018) www.theguardian.com/news/2018/mar/17/cambridge-analytica-fa cebook-influence-us-election, accessed 19 February 2019; Matthew Rosenberg, Nicholas Confessore and Carole Cadwalladr, 'How Trump Consultants Exploited the Facebook Data of Millions' *The New York Times* (17 March 2018) www.nytimes. com/2018/03/17/us/politics/cambridge-analytica-trump-campaign.html, accessed 19 February 2019. Facebook has since revised this figure upwards to up to 87 million users: Cecilia Kang and Sheera Frenkel, 'Facebook Says Cambridge Analytica Harvested Data of Up to 87 Million Users' *The New York Times* (4 April 2018) www. nytimes.com/2018/04/04/technology/mark-zuckerberg-testify-congress.html, accessed 19 February 2019.
2 David Ingram, 'Zuckerberg apologizes for Facebook mistakes with user data, vows curbs' *Reuters* (21 March 2018) www.reuters.com/article/us-facebook-cambridge-a nalytica/zuckerberg-apologizes-for-facebook-mistakes-with-user-data-vows-curbs-i dUSKBN1GX0OG, accessed 19 February 2019.

results.[3] Prior to its demise, Cambridge Analytica boasted that it has collected up to 4,000 personal data points on people, including 240 million Americans.[4] It claimed to have developed models for sophisticated 'psychographic' profiling that allowed political parties to target potential voters with specifically tailored advertisements. A related issue that arose in this context was related to the use of 'fake news' and, specifically, the use of so-called 'bots'[5] to flood social networks with false information in order to influence election results.

The topic of disinformation and the Cambridge Analytica scandal were the subject of an 18-months-long, ground-breaking enquiry by the United Kingdom House of Commons Digital, Culture, Media and Sport (DCMS) Committee. The DCMS Committee relied upon voluminous evidence from witnesses, submissions and internal documents, and collaborated with other domestic and international agencies and organisations. Its Final Report[6] found that Facebook intentionally and knowingly violated UK data privacy and competition laws, and recommended greater regulatory control of social media companies through a compulsory Code of Ethics to be enforced by an independent regulator, reforms to electoral communications laws and improved transparency.

The Cambridge Analytica scandal also prompted the UK Information Commissioner's Office (ICO) to launch an investigation into whether Cambridge Analytica or Facebook had committed any breaches of privacy legislation. As part of its investigation, it examined the practices of 30 organisations in the context of political campaigning with a view to developing recommendations on enhanced disclosure rules for political advertising.[7] The ICO published two reports. Its first report[8] contains a detailed account of its findings concerning how social media platforms were used for micro-

3   See e.g. Jamie Doward and Alice Gibbs, 'Did Cambridge Analytica influence the Brexit vote and the US election?' *The Guardian* (4 March 2017) www.theguardian.com/politics/2017/mar/04/nigel-oakes-cambridge-analytica-what-role-brexit-trump, accessed 19 February 2019.
4   David Carroll, 'Cambridge Analytica Is Dead, Long Live Our Data: Were data crimes perpetrated against U.S. voters? We are about to know a lot more' *Boston Review* (24 May 2018) http://bostonreview.net/law-justice-david-carroll-cambridge-analytica, accessed 19 February 2019.
5   Otherwise known as internet robots – i.e. software applications that runs automated tasks, including, in the case of chat bots/social media bots, simulations of human activity.
6   UK Parliament, Digital, Culture, Media and Sport Committee, *Disinformation and 'fake news': Final Report* (HC 2017–19, 1791). See also UK Parliament, Digital, Culture, Media and Sport Committee, *Disinformation and "fake news": Interim Report* (HC 2017–19, 363).
7   UK Information Commissioner's Office, 'Investigation into the use of data analytics in political campaigns: A report to Parliament' (6 November 2018) https://ico.org.uk/media/action-weve-taken/2260271/investigation-into-the-use-of-data-analytics-in-political-campaigns-final-20181105.pdf, accessed 19 February 2019, 5–6.
8   Information Commissioner's Office, 'Democracy disrupted? Personal information and political influence' (11 July 2018) https://ico.org.uk/media/2259369/democracy-disrupted-110718.pdf, accessed 19 February 2019.

targeting by UK political parties and a set of policy recommendations in respect of the transparent and lawful use of data analytics in future political campaigns. The second, a report to the UK Parliament that was also considered by the DCMS Committee,[9] summarised the results of the ICO's investigations and the regulatory enforcement actions that it has taken in response to its findings. As part of its enforcement action, the ICO fined Facebook £500,000[10] for failing to sufficiently protect the privacy of its users before, during and after the unlawful processing of their data. In the US, Facebook agreed to pay a record US$5 billion fine and to upgrade its privacy procedures and protections, in order to settle a long-running privacy investigation by the Federal Trade Commission and resolve its involvement the Cambridge Analytica data scandal.[11]

Taken together, these developments shine a stark light on emerging data-driven practices that present a major shift in the operation of the democratic process. Big data analytics represents a new frontier in the way in which information is processed and used to affect individuals. While the use of elector databases by political parties is not a new development,[12] it is important to understand the transformative effect of big data analytics and artificial intelligence. What is significant about the new 'big data' phenomenon is not just the size, variety and complexity of the datasets available for analysis but also that new tools harness the power of artificial intelligence to find 'small patterns'[13] and provide new insights concerning data subjects. While much recent research focused on the potentially discriminatory effects of decisions based on big data analytics[14] and the issue of consumer manipulation,[15] an aspect that is now emerging as at least equally important is the extent to which it makes voters more vulnerable to illegitimate manipulation, thereby undermining the democratic process.

There have recently been major advances in assessing psychological traits derived from the digital footprints of large groups of individuals, and putting them to use for mass persuasion.[16] The ubiquity of social media is central to many of

9   Information Commissioner's Office (n 7).
10 This was the maximum allowable under the former Data Protection Act 1998 (UK).
11 David McLaughlin and Daniel Stoller, 'Facebook $5 Billion U.S. Privacy Settlement Approved by FTC' *Bloomberg* (13 July 2019) www.bloomberg.com/news/articles/ 2019-07-12/ftc-approves-facebook-privacy-settlement-worth-about-5-billion, accessed 29 July 2019.
12 See e.g. the Resolution on the Use of Personal Data for Political Communication (adopted at the 27th International Conference on Privacy and Personal Data Protection, Montreux, 14–16 September 2005).
13 Luciano Floridi, 'The Search for Small Patterns in Big Data' (2012) 59 The Philosophers' Magazine 17–18.
14 See e.g. Jenifer Winter, 'Algorithmic Discrimination: Big Data Analytics and the Future of the Internet' in Jenifer Winter and Ryota Ono (eds), *The Future Internet: Alternative Visions* (Springer International Publishing 2015) 125.
15 See e.g. Max N Helveston, 'Consumer Protection in the Age of Big Data' (2016) 93 (4) Washington University Law Review 859; Nir Kshetri, 'Big data's impact on privacy, security and consumer welfare' (2014) 38(11) Telecommunications Policy 1134.
16 Sandra C Matz et al., 'Psychological Targeting as an Effective Approach to Digital Mass Persuasion' (2017) 114(48) Proceedings of the National Academy of Sciences 12714–12719.

these practices. The digital footprints of social media users are utilised not only as a data source for their psychographic assessment but also to influence the behaviours of users. Given the increased public reliance on social media as a source of ideas and information, these platforms are increasingly used for behavioural targeting with messages that are devised to resonate with populations that share distinct personal characteristics or persuasions. With growing awareness of the opportunities offered by social media, political campaigns increasingly make use of them to combine data-driven voter research with personalised political advertising, a practice known as political micro-targeting. Through micro-targeting, a political party can identify the individual voters whom it is most likely to convince and match its message to the specific interests and vulnerabilities of these voters. Micro-targeting activities may be accompanied by other practices, including the use of bots to spread ideas and information, including fake information.

These developments have increased the efficiency of political campaigning but raise a number of issues that go to the heart of democratic systems of government: To what extent do micro-targeting practices, in particular when they are not made transparent, involve unacceptable manipulation? Does the crafting of personalised messages exacerbate the issue of 'filter bubbles' and does this undermine some of the inherently collective processes underpinning democratic governance?

The profiling practices that underlie these campaigns also raise profound privacy issues. To what extent is it acceptable for personal information disclosed for other purposes to be repurposed and used for political gain? Are our regulatory systems sufficiently robust to address this issue? Is there some need for broader group privacy protection, given that much of modern data analytics relies on classification and the analysis of defined groups for the purpose of making predictions about them or seeking to influence their behaviour?

The vast accumulations of data on voters and politicians in the computer networks of political parties have also made them increasingly attractive targets for malicious hacking. Over the last few years, there have been reports from a number of countries that their parliamentary IT infrastructure, or the computer systems of political parties, had been attacked and compromised.[17] While it is notoriously difficult to confirm the origin of such attacks, there are many indications that sophisticated state actors have been involved.[18] These attacks have led to increased

---

17   See e.g. Rohan Pearce, 'Government says "state actor" hacked Australian political parties' networks' *Computer World*, 18 February 2019, www.computerworld.com. au/article/657853/government-says-state-actor-hacked-australian-political-parties-networks, accessed 21 July 2019; Danny Palmer, 'Cyber-espionage warning: Russian hacking groups step up attacks ahead of European elections' *ZDNet* (21 March 2019) www.zdnet.com/article/cyber-espionage-warning-russian-hacking-groups-step-up -attacks-ahead-of-european-elections, accessed 21 July 2019.

18   See e.g. Brett Worthington, 'Scott Morrison reveals foreign government hackers targeted Liberal, Labor and National parties in attack on Parliament's servers' *ABC News* (18 February 2019) www.abc.net.au/news/2019-02-18/prime-minister-scott-morri son-cyber-attack-hackers/10821170, accessed 21 July 2019.

attempts to secure these networks against cyber threats. The connections between privacy and cybersafety lie in the requirement of data protection laws to keep data secure.

Many of the arising issues are complex and interrelated, and it is not possible to deal with them all in a single volume. In particular, this book does not consider in detail the broader challenges posed by the new big data environment to data protection regimes that focus on data relating to identifiable individuals. The new big data environment challenges the focus on individual privacy because it facilitates the targeting of individuals on the basis of analyses of group data gleaned from studies of the groups to which an individual belongs.[19] It also challenges the assumption that there is a sharp line between identifiable and non-identifiable information, given that modern data analytics increasingly facilitates the re-identification of data that has been ostensibly de-identified.[20]

The focus of this book is the exploration of issues raised by the use of personal information in the electoral process. The chapters that follow provide a variety of perspectives drawn from multiple disciplines and countries on the effect of the rise of big data analytics in politics and election campaigns on voter privacy and democracy. It incorporates a number of papers that were discussed at a Roundtable on Big Data, Privacy and the Political Process held in Prato, Italy, on 18 and 19 June 2018. The papers presented at the Roundtable, which was financially supported by the Strategic Initiatives Fund of the Faculty of Law at Monash University, have been revised and updated to keep up with events in this fast-moving field. A number of papers have also been especially commissioned for this volume.

Part I: The need for a civic disposition

The first part of this book entitled 'The need for a civic disposition' provides an overview of the political and ethical issues raised by filter bubbles, political microtargeting and fake news. The contributors to this part recognise the need to facilitate a 'civic disposition', a willingness to listen to another party's perspective, and to draw on different experiences in order to inform debate and decision making. The reasons why such communication is important and how democracy came to be vulnerable to a particular type of political manipulation are analysed in the first two chapters, drawing from media theory and political philosophy. While the arguments in these first two chapters are not reliant upon the success of Cambridge Analytica (and the many companies that continue their work globally), they diagnose the problems that made Cambridge Analytica possible. The third chapter continues this theme but shifts from theoretical analyses to examine empirical work in psychology to ask about the methods and conditions of such

---

19 See, generally, Linnet Taylor, Luciano Floridi and Bart van der Sloot (eds), *Group Privacy: New Challenges of Data Technologies* (Springer 2016).
20 See the useful discussion in Office of the Victorian Information Commissioner, *De-identification and privacy: Considerations for the Victorian public sector* (OVIC 2018).

political manipulation – the opposite of a civic disposition. The legal mechanisms through which our democracy could be protected against such threats are then further explored in the rest of the book, which investigates law and regulation from a range of international and domestic perspectives.

In Chapter 2, 'From mass to automated media: Revisiting the filter bubble', Mark Andrejevic and Zala Volcic argue that the problem with filter bubbles is not simply that individuals are limited in the news that they receive such that their own political positions are reinforced. Instead, they posit that the ability to form a 'civic disposition' – to be willing to listen to and assimilate others' points of view as part of a reasoned attempted to find solutions to a problem – is undermined today. We no longer envisage ourselves as part of an imagined community while reading the daily newspaper, for example. This imagined community, so vividly described by Benedict Anderson, was a repeated daily occurrence that prompted a feeling of a bond with others whom we would never meet but who were viewed as part of 'us'. Anderson makes this striking point by citing Hegel:

> The significance of this mass ceremony – Hegel observed that newspapers serve modern man as a substitute for morning prayers – is paradoxical. It is performed in silent privacy, in the lair of the skull. Yet each communicant is well aware that the ceremony he performs is being replicated simultaneously by thousands (or millions) of others of whose existence he is confident, yet of whose identity he has not the slightest notion.[21]

In contrast, political positions now appear polarised, particularly in the US. Andrejevic and Volcic warn that the evolution of a population with a civic disposition was an historical achievement that may be lost with the erosion of the institutions and practices that underpinned it. The next chapter employs arguments from political philosophy to show how the civic disposition, which is vital for a thriving democracy, is threatened in the big data era.

In Chapter 3, 'Filter bubbles, democracy and concepts of self: A brief genealogy and a Spinozist perspective', Janice Richardson asks how we arrived at a position where our democracy is viewed as involving nothing more than the marketing of politicians, employing the same methods as commercial advertising. She answers that it fits within the conceptual framework of neo-liberalism in which privacy and other human abilities are treated as if they were mere commodities. Drawing on the work of Carole Pateman,[22] Richardson compares this weakened image of 'democracy' with the ideals of a participative democracy in which everyone has a say in decisions that affect their lives, which includes the workplace as well as the

---

21   Benedict Anderson, *Imagined Communities* (2nd edn, Verso Books 2006).
22   Carole Pateman, *The Sexual Contract* (Polity Press 1988); Carole Pateman, 'Self-Ownership and Property in the Person: Democratization and a Tale of Two Concepts' (2002) 10(1) The Journal of Political Philosophy 20.

polis. A more robust democracy would not be so easily undermined by micro-targeting and fake news.

Such attempts at political manipulation rely upon a diminished view not only of democracy but also of ourselves in relation to each other. To uncover what needed to be in place for such attempts to be possible, Richardson draws a genealogy of our self-image by tracing the pivotal position of John Locke. Janet Coleman[23] has cited both Locke's *Two Treatises of Government*[24] and *An Essay on Human Understanding*[25] to argue that Locke envisaged a self that was able to appropriate both property and ideas into itself. Richardson contrasts this image of an 'internal self' with Spinoza's alternative description of how we are changed by interactions with others (humans and other things in the world) and considers the politics that would arise if Spinoza's more radical enlightenment thought were more influential than that of his contemporary, Locke.

As the key figure in Europe's Radical Enlightenment, Spinoza's *Ethics* addresses questions that are relevant today: Why is civic discourse dominated by hatred and confused ideas? How can we do better? It is central to Spinoza's *Ethics* that to live a good life involves our own self-interest but that central to this is our ability to increase our understanding of the world. This is necessarily a collective endeavour that allows us to be active. Improvements in communication are therefore of central importance to us because communication (of adequate knowledge rather than passions) allows us to pool our powers of understanding. This is why Spinoza has been described as 'the philosopher of communication'.[26] Richardson points to the ways in which subordination undermines our ability to communicate, thereby diminishing both individuals and cultures. Some of the emerging practices in data-driven political campaigning that impede our ability for democratic engagement are assessed in the next chapter.

In Chapter 4, 'Voting public: Leveraging personal information to construct voter preference', Jacquelyn Burkell and Priscilla Regan explore the possible effects of micro-targeted information, which can be highly selective or even manipulative, on voter preferences and thus on the electoral processes that underlie democratic government. The authors synthesise the findings of political science on why people vote as they do and what motivates their political behaviour with insights from empirical studies into behavioural psychology. Burkell and Regan conclude from this research that the most effective political messaging is both *targeted* to specific subsets of the population and *tailored* in its content so that it affects the attitudes and behaviour of the selected audience. This is clearly a conclusion shared by

23   Janet Coleman, 'Pre-Modern Property and Self-Ownership Before and After Locke: Or, When Did Common Decency Become a Private Rather than a Public Virtue?' (2005) 4(2) European Journal of Political Theory 125.

24   Roger S Woolhouse (ed), *John Locke: An Essay Concerning Human Understanding* (Penguin 1997).

25   Peter Laslett (ed), *Locke: Two Treatises of Government* (Cambridge University Press 1988).

26   Étienne Balibar, *Spinoza and Politics* (Peter Snowdon tr, Verso 1998) 101.

political parties who invest in companies such as Cambridge Analytica globally. Burkell and Regan's examination of the conditions in which voter manipulation is possible, and of the increasingly scientific attempts to profile voters and micro-target political messaging, shows that we are moving away from a civic disposition, as discussed in the previous two chapters. In the final section of their chapter, Burkell and Regan analyse the implications of these developments for democracy and the importance of privacy in protecting voter autonomy and fostering partici-pation in decisions affecting the body politic. They conclude that the problems arising from the political data-sharing industry and their activities for democratic government are 'profound and have arguably reached something of a crisis' and that effective regulation requires dealing with the 'infrastructure of the online information economy as a whole'.

The rest of the book then explores how data protection laws currently respond to these challenges and how they could be reformed to better promote privacy and the democratic process. The second part considers public international as well as supranational European law and the third and final part focuses upon the domestic laws in Canada, Australia, US and UK.

Part II: Public international and European law

The second part of the book entitled 'Public international and European law' starts with Chapter 5 by Dominik Steiger, 'International law and new challenges to democracy in the digital age: Big data, privacy and interferences with the poli-tical process'. In this chapter, Steiger analyses to what extent democracy is actually threatened by big data operations – such as US mass surveillance, Cambridge Analytica and the Russian troll farms – and what role international law can play to respond to these threats. While there has been reference to the importance of democracy by the European Court of Human Rights, for example, the emphasis of international courts has tended to be on the right to privacy as a human right. Steiger argues that a concern to safeguard democracy in the context of public international law could strengthen and reinforce the existing human rights approach. He discusses seven constitutive elements of a democracy: anonymity, the electorate's freedom of forming a political will, openness to discourse, demo-cratic control and accountability, the acceptance of the majority position, pluralism and transparency. The reference to 'openness to discourse' picks up concerns that a civic disposition is being lost, discussed in the first section of this collection, and translates them into a legal argument.

Steiger illustrates how such a legal argument based upon the interest of the State in furthering democracy could be employed to strengthen arguments based on the right to privacy. To do so, he points out the role that achieving 'pro-portionality' – the need to weigh up competing values – plays in the European Convention on Human Rights. For example, a case could arise in which the Eur-opean Court of Human Rights would be asked to consider the question of whe-ther the State's use of mass surveillance could be justified by balancing the need to protect citizens against terrorism and citizens' rights to privacy. The question would be framed in the following terms: Would mass surveillance be proportionate to its aim of protecting citizens against terrorist threats? Steiger argues that, in this example, the additional need to safeguard democratic values would weigh in on the side of the citizens' privacy rights, strengthening the argument in favour of a restriction of mass surveillance.

In Chapter 6, 'Social media in election campaigns: Free speech or a danger for democracy?', Udo Fink focuses on the law of the European Union and the jurisprudence of the European Court of Human Rights. He situates his legal analysis by considering the background to the problems of online social media campaigns that have come to light, including the Cambridge Analytica scandal and fake news. He then outlines the European Commission's 2018 campaign Tackling Online Disinformation, which was based on the view that disinformation has the potential to manipulate and undermine democracy and so the EU has a duty to prevent this from occurring. Tackling Online Disinformation proposes a number of measures: an EU-wide Code of Practice on Disinformation, support for an independent network of fact-checkers, and tools to stimulate quality journalism.

Fink also outlines the approach to free speech and privacy rights in arts 10 and 8 of the European Convention on Human Rights. In addition, art. 3 of Additional Protocol No. 1 to the Convention states that free elections should be ensured, 'under conditions which will ensure the free expression of the opinion of the people in the choice of the legislature'. He goes on to examine the European jurisprudence on journalism and blogs. Here, the same type of test applies – in particular, whether standards of reasonable journalism are maintained. In addition to European law, the chapter details how some member states – such as Germany and France – have passed their own legislation to allow them to deal with social media content.

The last chapter in Part II is Maeve McDonagh's 'Freedom of processing of personal data for the purpose of electoral activities after the GDPR' (Chapter 7). In this chapter, McDonagh provides a detailed summary and evaluation of the European General Data Protection Regulation (GDPR) and its role in the context of processing personal data in elections. She puts particular emphasis on analysing the grounds that make such processing lawful, which – apart from consent – depend on establishing a public interest and legitimate interests of the processor. McDonagh demonstrates that this framework provides greater scope for data processing by political parties and candidates than by social media platforms, data brokers and data analytics companies. The chapter also contains detailed discussions of how the transparency requirements, the right to object to data processing and the new right not to be subject to a decision based solely on automated processing, including profiling, operate in the context of personal data processing for the purpose of electoral activities. McDonagh concludes that, despite considerable constraints provided for in the GDPR, there are also significant gaps in the protection afforded to the processing of personal data in this context and that there is some lack of clarity concerning the operation of some of the provisions. Her chapter further notes that the GDPR allows for derogations and significant variation in the application by Member States of the provisions relevant to the processing of personal data for electoral purposes. The interplay between European data protection rules and domestic implementation is further explored in Part III, which includes a discussion of the position in the United Kingdom.

Part III: Domestic laws in Canada, Australia, the United States and the United Kingdom

The third and final part of the book considers the problem of voter manipulation and privacy invasion from the perspective of selected domestic laws, detailing the legal position in Canada, Australia, the United States and the United Kingdom respectively. In Chapter 8, 'From the doorstep to the database: Political parties, campaigns, and personal privacy protection in Canada', Colin Bennett and Michael McDonald point out that Canada has more in common with the US than with Europe. It has few regulations protecting voter privacy against political parties. While the legal context differs, the Canadian position shares some of the shortcomings of Australian law, discussed in Chapter 9. Bennett and McDonald illustrate how these shortcomings have resulted in Canada being influenced by voter analytics from US, entailing the widespread use of voter relationship management platforms. Bennett and McDonald start by outlining the constitutional rules that govern the processing of personal data by political parties and candidates. This includes the Charter of Rights and Freedoms, the Canadian Elections Act and its provincial equivalents, as well as the telemarketing rules, and the Canada Anti-Spam legislation. They also consider the only provincial law to cover political parties: British Columbia's Personal Information Protection Act. Bennett and McDonald thereby produce a comprehensive survey of Canada's position and argue that the Canadian experience offers useful insights and lessons for other democracies about what can happen without sufficient regulation. This includes an exploration of how political parties end up competing with each other to renew their platforms, accompanied by their increased dependence on companies who produce data analytics.

Bennett and McDonald then turn to current attempts to regulate political parties' collection of data. The Canadian Government has introduced provisions in the Election Modernization Act (Bill C-76) to ensure that political parties publish a policy that describes their collection, protection and sale of personal information, procedures for staff training, and the identity of a designated person to whom privacy concerns can be addressed. Bennett and McDonald note that these proposals have been almost universally criticised for their incompleteness, vagueness and lack of enforcement mechanism. In a point that underlines Steiger's concerns in Part II, Bennett and McDonald point out that 'the inappropriate capture, use and disclosure of personal data by political actors does not only implicate privacy, but it may also affect electoral outcomes, and damage the credibility of democratic institutions'.

In Chapter 9, 'Voter privacy in an era of big data: Time to abolish the political exemption in the Australian Privacy Act', Moira Paterson and Normann Witzleb examine an issue that has become controversial in Australia: the fact that registered political parties and the political acts and practices of specified organisations are exempt from Australia's Privacy Act 1988 (Cth). The Privacy Act 1988 (Cth) provides a number of fundamental privacy principles, such as a requirement to let individuals know that their personal data has been collected, giving them rights of access and correction, and an obligation on organisations to safeguard the privacy of the data collected. As a result of the exemptions, these basic protections do not apply vis-à-vis political parties, and the Privacy Commissioner has no jurisdiction over the use of personal data for political purposes. Given that there is also no common law right to privacy in Australia, this exemption means that citizens generally lack any redress against the collection and use of their data in the political process. The current position has been criticised over the years by the Australian Law Reform Commission, former Privacy Commissioners and some of the minor parties, but continuously upheld by federal governments of both persuasions.

Paterson and Witzleb give a detailed analysis of the interaction between the implied constitutional freedom of political communication and the data protection obligations that the Privacy Act would impose if it were applicable. They conclude that the original reason for the exemption, that it is necessary to protect the freedom of political communication, is no longer valid in an era of big data analytics and political micro-targeting. In light of the increased risk to citizens' privacy and the need to create a binding regulatory framework that obliges all political actors to use personal data fairly and transparently, Paterson and Witzleb argue that the exemptions applying to political parties should be removed.

In Chapter 10, 'Big data and the electoral process in the United States: Constitutional constraint and limited data privacy regulations', Ronald Krotoszynski Jr. analyses the influence of big data analytics in the context of US elections. Sophisticated data techniques to predict voter behaviour are not only used to micro-target voters but also increasingly to rig electoral districts in favour of incumbents. Krotoszynski shows that the particular design of the electoral process in the US, such as voting in districts rather than proportional representation, currently exacerbates the risk of voter manipulation. Despite the serious problems that these processes cause for the democratic process, Krotoszynski is sceptical about the prospects of effective regulation. He views the strict protection of free speech in the First Amendment as a serious obstacle to greater regulation of the collection, storage and transfer of personal data in the political process. He also advises caution in regulatory attempts to suppress fake news, arguing instead for greater transparency and disclosure requirements so that voters have a clearer picture of the information that is held about them and of the uses that it is being put to by political parties and candidates.

Krotoszynski argues that structural reforms aimed at increasing the competitiveness of elections present the most promising avenue for reform, which in light of the deep political divisions would need to emanate from the courts. However, the hope that there will be greater judicial scrutiny of malapportioned electoral districts recently suffered a serious setback when the US Supreme Court held by a narrow majority that partisan gerrymanders present non-justiciable 'political' questions that the federal courts may not address on the merits. Krotoszynski's chapter demonstrates that the design of the electoral process and the specific human rights context are significant variables that need to be carefully examined before recommendations for reform of the use of personal data in the political process can be formulated.

In Chapter 11, 'Data and political campaigning in the era of big data – the UK experience', Stephanie Hankey, Ravi Naik and Gary Wright explore the rise of the data-driven political campaigns, with a particular emphasis on developments in the United Kingdom. As a result of concerns about Cambridge Analytica's influence on the Brexit referendum, both the UK Information Commissioner and the Parliamentary Committee on Digital, Culture, Media and Sport have engaged in detailed inquiries, and the chapter summarises the findings and evaluates the recommendations made. Hankey, Naik and Wright also analyse the current regulation of data use in election campaigns, focusing on the impact of the EU's General Data Protection Regulation, the UK Data Protection Act (DPA) 2018 and the Privacy and Electronic Communications Regulations. These regulations have also opened up the possibility of litigation by citizens outside the EU. This is illustrated by the case of David Carroll, a US citizen who, represented by Ravi Naik, has sued Cambridge Analytica in the UK courts.

Hankey, Naik and Wright outline the European data protection regime as it applies to the political processing of data and targeted marketing. While political parties are generally subject to the GDPR, it does not apply to anonymised data and has no role in the restriction of fake news. Therefore, while the means by which communications are targeted to individuals or groups may be covered by the GDPR and DPA, the content may not be because it is not classified as 'personal data'. The DPA 2018 furthermore provides that the processing of personal data that is necessary for 'an activity that supports or promotes democratic engagement' is processing for a task carried out in the public interest, thereby making such processing lawful under the GDPR. Hankey, Naik and Wright conclude that, despite these significant limitations, the current UK data protection rules represent a considerable step forward in ensuring the right to privacy, but call for better resourcing of the ICO so that it can properly exercise its important regulatory functions.

Hankey, Naik and Wright conclude with an analysis that dovetails with the initial theoretical analysis discussed in Part I: that it would miss the point to view data as merely a commodity. The importance of individual data rights does not lie in being financially compensated for their breach, but in the protection of such rights because they are 'intrinsic to our humanity'. Hankey, Naik and Wright end on a positive note and express the expectation that if data flows and uses are made more transparent, individuals will be able to assert more control over their data, provided this is backed up by the possibility of collective enforcement. In their view, the real shift that is required is not a need for new rights in the UK but a shift in culture.

Conclusion

This book is about democracy in our time. It examines how big data operations in the electoral process undermine the enlightenment values of democracy and equality and how, in different ways and with differing degrees of success, this challenge is being, or could be, met. At this moment of transition, it is some European governments – rather than, for example, the US, Canada or Australia, also discussed in the book – that are more actively defending democratic participation in our data-driven world. These governments recognise that political debates are increasingly held – and election campaigns are fought and won – on platforms managed by US billion-dollar corporations. On these platforms, citizens are predominantly seen as users, and opaque algorithms rather than responsible journalism decide on which information and opinions are made available, giving prominence to 'clickbait' and exposing readers to fake news disseminated by disruptive bots. By dominating the fora in which much of the public discourse occurs, the private tech giants have particular responsibilities, but they seem slow to respond adequately to the risks for democracy that arise from the pursuit of their commercial interests.

The Enlightenment political theories of Kant and Habermas stress the importance of a public sphere in which someone's ideas, rather than class (if not gender and race), are what matters. The image is of citizens who try to understand each other's viewpoints in order to solve problems, creating an 'enlarged mentality'. This ideal of an active citizenry is a historical achievement that is threatened by the dominance of a market view of ourselves as atomistic individuals holding on to narrow, selfish interests. It is only when democracy is weak, and citizens are disconnected from decisions over their everyday lives, that politics can be reduced to a cynical appeal to fear and politicians are inclined to market themselves rather than competing visions of the public interest. The possibility of common concerns is undermined by hate speech and great disparities of wealth, both of which countenance the idea that some persons are to be treated as less worthy of respect.

This is a transitional period, and there is a great deal at stake. The US – and similarly Canada and Australia – have been reluctant to develop further privacy rights to restrain the 'influence industry'.[27] This industry of over 300 companies, of which the most infamous was Cambridge Analytica, uses personal data as its

---

27 A detailed examination of the 'influence industry' is contained in a report produced by Tactical Tech, an international NGO that explores the impacts of technology on society: Tactical Tech, *Personal Data: Political Persuasion – Inside the Influence Industry. How it works.* https://cdn.ttc.io/s/tacticaltech.org/Personal-Data-Politica l-Persuasion-How-it-works.pdf, accessed 23 July 2019.

resource and the techniques of the marketing industry as tools for political persuasion. In contrast to North America and Australia, the European courts and legislators are more alert to these new dangers. They are undertaking greater efforts to protect their citizens from fake news and misuse of their personal information in the political process and to safeguard democratic values more broadly. In doing so, they have been able to draw from their vast jurisprudence on human rights. Apart from democratic rights, the most relevant human rights values in the context of big data and the political process are the right to free speech and the right to privacy. Unlike the US, which has prioritised free speech to the point of condoning hate speech, European courts have grappled with the areas of conflict, employing the principle of proportionality to balance competing human rights.

This book focuses upon political micro-targeting in the age of big data analytics. It demonstrates that enhanced regulation of the use of personal data in the political process is needed not only to safeguard individual privacy but also for the protection of public discourse and democratic participation more broadly. But the problems examined in this book, and the solutions proposed, are situated within the wider global concern of how to regulate platforms. The United Nations Special Rapporteur on the promotion and protection of the right to freedom of opinion and expression, David Kaye, recently argued[28] for human rights standards to become the norms by which platforms such as Facebook and Twitter are moderated. In our view, and confirmed by the contributions to this volume, it is no longer acceptable that political parties and movements, the ecosystem of advisors and consultants that has developed around them and the platforms on which they engage with the electorate can make largely unregulated use of personal information for their respective purposes. Citizens must be able to trust that the important data protection values of accountability, transparency, accuracy, security and fairness also guide the information-handling practices of political actors. Our democracy will suffer if we do not address the new threats to privacy arising from data-driven political discourse.

---

28   David Kaye, *Speech Police: The Global Struggle to Govern the Internet* (Columbia Global Reports 2019) 118.

Part I

The need for a civic disposition

From mass to automated media

Revisiting the 'filter bubble'

Mark Andrejevic and Zala Volcic

In the face of social media's problems with fake news and political polarisation, the ready response has been to propose economic, technical, and educational fixes. Reacting to US concerns about Russian disinformation campaigns, for example, Facebook executive Rob Goldman tweeted: 'There are easy ways to fight this. [...] Finland, Sweden and Holland have all taught digital literacy and critical thinking about misinformation to great effect.'[1] A recent report by the Data & Society Research Institute considered a range of possible solutions, including fortified fact-checking and verification services and incentives for de-emphasising fake content and closing down the accounts of those who circulate it.[2] The hope embedded in such responses is that the overarching commercial model we have developed for circulating news and information online can be salvaged for the purposes of informed communication and democratic deliberation. Some combination of self-regulation by platform giants, public pressure to reconfigure economic incentives, anti-trust measures, and increased media literacy on the part of users has been advanced as a strategy for curbing the flood of politically polarised misinformation online.

This chapter argues that the concerns raised by commercial social media are significant and structural, which means the commercial model we have developed is not salvageable solely through education and self-regulation. Rather we need to critically examine the broader connections between media infrastructures and social policies that erode the resources for mutual recognition and collective deliberation. The question is not just what kind of information people receive online, but the conditions under which they receive it, and the disposition these foster. Diverse content and perspectives are necessary but not sufficient for democratic deliberation. Meaningful deliberative processes rely equally upon the formation of a 'discourse ethics', which, 'by requiring that perspective-taking be

1   Sheera Frenkel, 'Fact-Checking a Facebook Executive's Comments on Russian Inter-ference' *The New York Times* (19 February 2018) www.nytimes.com/2018/02/19/technology/facebook-executive-russia-tweets-fact-check.html, accessed 30 August 2019.
2   Robyn Caplan, Lauren Hanson and Joan Donovan, *Dead Reckoning: Navigating Content Moderation After 'Fake News'* (Data & Society Report, 21 February 2018) https://datasociety.net/output/dead-reckoning, accessed 30 August 2019.

general and reciprocal, builds the moment of empathy into the procedure of coming to a reasoned agreement'.[3] The critique of online 'filter bubbles'[4] can have the misleading effect of diverting attention away from the context and material conditions of news reception and the broader societal conditions within which these are embedded, including the ongoing regulatory assault on 'social bonds and obligations, social conscience, and social welfare'.[5] The shift in the news environment associated with the platform economy coincides with a political assault on the conditions that enable citizens to take into consideration the needs, perspectives, and values of others, including those whom they do not know and may never meet, but who nevertheless form part of their shared communities.

I. 'Everyone's got their goons'

Many of the proposed solutions to the pathologies of commercial media platforms assume a shared understanding of the problem and the civic will to solve it. It is possible to discern quite different subject positions from those that share civic good will – indeed, ones that are cultivated by and thrive on the logics of polarisation. Consider, for example, the conservative businessman interviewed by the *New York Times* who views right-wing conspiracy theories as a form of entertainment: 'I just like the satisfaction [...] It's like a hockey game. Everyone's got their goons. Their goons are pushing our guys around, and it's great to see our goons push back.'[6] The subject position here is one that seeks out fake news as a form of politicised entertainment because it confirms one's prejudices and preconceptions.

There is another subject position that is worth taking into consideration: that which questions the efficacy of fact-checking itself. Consider the example of Florine Goldfarb, one of the 'unwitting' Americans who promoted events orchestrated by Russian Internet trolls during the 2016 presidential campaign.[7] When confronted with the fact that she had posted information generated by a Russian propaganda organisation on her pro-Trump Facebook page, her response was dismissive: 'I don't believe that. That's bulls—.'[8] Such responses highlight the impasse of media

3   Jürgen Habermas, *Moral Consciousness and Communicative Action* (MIT Press 1990) 11.
4   Eli Pariser, *The Filter Bubble: How the New Personalized Web is Changing What We Read and How We Think* (Penguin 2011).
5   Jo Littler, 'Where the files are: Wendy Brown Talks to Jo Littler' (2018) 68 Soundings 14, 14.
6   Sabrina Tavernise, 'As Fake News Spreads Lies, More Readers Shrug at the Truth' *The New York Times* (6 December 2016) www.nytimes.com/2016/12/06/us/fake-news-partisan-republican-democrat.html, accessed 30 August 2019.
7   Scott Shane, 'How Unwitting Americans Encountered Russian Operatives Online' *The New York Times* (18 February 2018) www.nytimes.com/2018/02/18/us/politics/russian-operatives-facebook-twitter.html, accessed 30 August 2019.
8   Bryan Logan, 'CNN interview with a Trump supporter goes sideways after she learns she unknowingly touted pro-Trump events coordinated by Russian trolls' *Business Insider* (21 February 2018) www.businessinsider.com/cnn-interviews-woman-unknowingly-manipulated-by-russian-trolls-2018-2, accessed 30 August 2019.

education: it runs the danger of simply pushing the problem of fact-checking back a level. The philosopher Slavoj Žižek has described this vertiginous infinite recess of credibility as the retreat of 'symbolic efficiency', suggesting that in the contemporary information environment, 'what is increasingly undermined is precisely the symbolic trust which persists against all skeptical data'.[9]

II. The role of a 'civic disposition'

The issues raised by political polarisation thus reach beyond the circulation of content to the ways in which information is experienced, and the concrete practices that materialise this experience. Keeping this claim in mind, this chapter argues for a reconsideration of arguments about media customisation, suggesting that the critiques they raise are relevant but that the mechanism they posit needs to be revisited. Specifically, it argues that while the notion of a 'filter bubble'[10] has captured much of the research attention in the field, additional emphasis needs to be placed on the conditions available for the formation of a 'civic disposition' in the platform economy.[11] The central concern from the perspective of fostering democratic deliberation is not (only) whether people are exposed to a narrower range of news and information online (a claim that seems increasingly implausible in the contemporary media environment), but whether social media undermine the civic purchase of diverse information streams. In other words, it may be that, in a context of media surfeit, people find themselves both exposed to a broader range of information and less inclined to take into consideration the larger community of which they are part and the perspectives of those unknown others who comprise it. The point here is not simply that confirmation bias[12] might contribute to how people navigate a flood of information, but that a combination of platform logics and communicative practices with broader social policies undermines the background conditions for democratic deliberation. The problem of the 'filter bubble' may really be one of the declining efficacy of the conditions that make deliberation meaningful. If, as Benedict Anderson argued,[13] the rise of print capitalism resulted in media technologies and artefacts that helped people form a sense of imagined community at the national level, the shift toward platform media in the era of 'statist neo-liberalism'[14] undoes this achievement. Growing resistance to countervailing facts and opinions may not be due to echo chambering, but rather to the degradation of people's ability to see themselves as part of an

---

9   Slavoj Žižek, *The Ticklish Subject: The Absent Centre of Political Ontology* (Verso 1999) 332.
10   Pariser (n 4).
11   Richard Pratte, *The Civic Imperative: Examining the Need for Civic Education* (Teachers College Press 1988).
12   Pariser (n 4).
13   Benedict Anderson, *Imagined Communities: Reflections on the Origin and Spread of Nationalism* (Verso 1983).
14   Littler (n 5).

imagined community in which the concerns and interests of others, both individually and collectively, matter to one's own thriving and thus to one's deliberative decision-making processes. This is a large claim that reaches beyond the limits of a book chapter, so the goal of this piece is to establish the importance of revisiting the filter bubble argument by moving beyond its focus on the range of available content and perspectives. The chapter discerns in pioneering work on the filter bubble the resources for considering the overarching question of the formation of a civic disposition and the conditions that threaten it.

The two most influential writers positing a connection between online news and political fragmentation, Eli Pariser[15] and Cass Sunstein,[16] both develop arguments that have a dual focus: the range of content to which users are exposed and the resulting shift in civic dispositions. However, it tends to be the content side of the argument that gets the most attention in recent research, perhaps because of the keywords with which their work is associated: 'The Daily Me' (Sunstein, borrowing from Negroponte) and the 'Filter Bubble' (Pariser's term) both refer to the automated tailoring of content to particular users. As Sunstein puts it in his first book on the topic

> [T]here are serious dangers in a system in which individuals bypass general interest intermediaries [mass circulation newspapers and electronic mass media] and restrict themselves to opinions and topics of their own choosing [...] A situation of this kind is likely to produce far worse than mere fragmentation.[17]

Pariser uses Sunstein's book as a jumping-off point for his own exploration of online filtering, coming to much the same conclusion: 'Together, these engines create a unique universe of information for each of us – what I've come to call a filter bubble – which fundamentally alters the way we encounter ideas and information'.[18] He notes the inevitability of filtering in an increasingly saturated information environment, while also critiquing its tendency toward individualisation: 'Left to their own devices, personalization filters serve up a kind of invisible autopropaganda, indoctrinating us with our own ideas.'[19] The concerns here have to do with a shifting information environment in which the broadening of available information coincides with increasing information nichification.

III. Finding filter bubbles

One result of this argument, which has regained attention in the wake of recent events, has been a spate of research seeking to empirically verify the existence of 'filter bubbles' – customised information environments that reflect a narrowing of perspectives despite the proliferation of online content. However, the empirical

---

15   Pariser (n 4).
16   Cass Sunstein, *Republic.com* (Princeton University Press 2001).
17   Ibid 16.
18   Pariser (n 4) 12.
19   Ibid 13.

evidence in this regard remains contested. Fletcher and Nielsen draw on the *Reuters Institute Digital News Report* to argue that, '[c]ontrary to conventional wisdom, our analysis shows that social media use is clearly associated with incidental exposure to additional sources of news that people otherwise wouldn't use – and with more politically diverse news diets'.[20] Similarly, Flaxman and colleagues found that the use of social media and search engines is 'associated with an increase in an individual's exposure to material from his or her less preferred side of the political spectrum'.[21] Alternatively, a review essay by Borgesius and colleagues concludes that, 'at present, there is no empirical evidence that warrants any strong worries about filter bubbles'.[22]

In the era of high-volume social media sharing, it seems increasingly plausible that those who spend more time online are likely to encounter diverse perspectives – even if these are simply shared in the form of critique or indignation. *Wired* magazine reported, for example, that those who most strenuously critiqued conspiracy theories about school shootings in the United States contributed to their prominence on social networking platforms since 'people outraged by the conspiracy helped to promote it – in some cases far more than the promoters of the story'.[23] The communicative economy of outrage and sensationalism that characterises so much of the online information helps circulate a broad range of perspectives – if only to allow people to critique and deride those with whom they disagree.

The focus on content that characterises the recent reception of the filter bubble argument gives rise to the assumption that exposure to a broader range of perspectives could ameliorate the problem of fragmentation and polarisation. However, even if the evidence regarding the extent of 'autopropaganda' remains in dispute, the evidence of increasing polarisation is less controversial. A large-scale survey by the Pew Research Center found that, by a number of measures, the level of political polarisation in the United States has increased dramatically in the previous two decades.[24] According to these findings, the number of Americans who

20   Richard Fletcher and Rasmus K. Nielsen, 'Using social media appears to diversify your news diet, not narrow it' *NiemanLab* (21 June 2017) www.niemanlab.org/2017/06/using-social-media-appears-to-diversify-your-news-diet-not-narrow-it/comment-page-1, accessed 30 August 2019.
21   Seth Flaxman, Sharad Goel and Justin M Rao, 'Filter Bubbles, Echo Chambers, and Online New Consumption' (2016) 18(S1) Public Opinion Quarterly, 298, 303.
22   Frederik J Zuiderveen Borgesius et al., 'Should we worry about filter bubbles?' (2016) 5(1) Internet Policy Review DOI: 10.14763/2016.1.401.
23   Molly McKew, 'How liberals amped up a Parkland shooting conspiracy theory' *WIRED* (27 February 2018) www.wired.com/story/how-liberals-amped-up-a-parkland-shooting-conspiracy-theory, accessed 30 August 2019.
24   Pew Research Center, *Political Polarization in the American Public: How Increasing Ideological Uniformity and Partisan Antipathy Affect Politics, Compromise and Everyday Life* (Pew Research Center, 12 June 2014) http://assets.pewresearch.org/wp-content/uploads/sites/5/2014/06/6-12-2014-Political-Polarization-Release.pdf, accessed 30 August 2019.

expressed consistently conservative or consistently liberal views doubled – that is, people seemed to be more 'dug into' a partisan political perspective. At the same time, Pew researchers reported:

> Partisan animosity has increased substantially. [...] In each party, the share with a highly negative view of the opposing party has more than doubled since 1994. Most of these intense partisans believe the opposing party's policies 'are so misguided that they threaten the nation's well-being'.[25]

Although levels of polarisation vary internationally, the Reuters Institute has discovered growing perceptions of media bias and increasing political polarisation in the countries it surveyed: 'People cluster to media organisations that fit their belief, and dismiss other outlets. The internet, once thought to open the world up to all the information possible and bring people together, has instead drawn people into their own corners.'[26] A variety of other factors come into play in discussions of political polarisation, including media deregulation and levels of economic inequality; however, the media remain an important realm in which these tensions are played out.[27]

IV. Beyond content

Further consideration of the filter bubble arguments provides resources for considering the ways in which increased exposure to diverse content might coincide with increasing political polarisation. Attempts to verify the existence of filter bubbles shift attention away from ancillary concerns raised by both Pariser and Sunstein about shifting civic dispositions, because the latter are viewed simply as a consequence of the former. However, their work provides some openings for considering the possibility that content alone is not the issue. Indeed, there are openings in their arguments for approaching the question of how even greater exposure to a range of perspectives might coincide with increasing political polarisation. Both authors supplement their concerns about customisation with criticism of the impact that media have on the disposition of users. For Sunstein, the operative distinction is between what he describes as 'consumer sovereignty' and 'political sovereignty'.[28] The former prioritises individual tastes and defines freedom as their expression within the constraints set by the price system (and available resources). From the perspective of consumer sovereignty, consuming the news is indistinguishable from shopping for clothes or cars. Political sovereignty,

---

25   Ibid.
26   Nic Newman et al., *Reuters Institute Digital News Report 2017* (Reuters Institute for the Study of Journalism, 2017) 30 https://reutersinstitute.politics.ox.ac.uk/sites/default/files/Digital%20News%20Report%202017%20web_0.pdf, accessed 30 August 2019.
27   Ibid.
28   Sunstein (n 16) 86.

by contrast, 'does not take individual tastes as fixed or given. It prizes democratic self-government, understood as a requirement of "government by discussion," accompanied by reason-giving in the public domain'.[29] In other words, political sovereignty requires the practices of recognition that make it possible to form preferences in discussion with others, taking into consideration their perspectives and claims. It relies on the recognition that the conditions for the formation of individual tastes rely on underlying forms of sociality and community that enable a perceived commonality of interests.

Similarly, Pariser argues that filter bubbles collapse citizenship into consumerist individualism: 'The filter bubble [...] creates the impression that our narrow self-interest is all that exists. And while this is great for getting people to shop online, it's not great for getting people to make better decisions together.'[30] Beyond his concern with a potential narrowing of the range of content, Pariser is targeting the ways in which automated curation helps erode the social foundation upon which meaningful deliberation relies: 'Personalization has given us something very different: a public sphere sorted and manipulated by algorithms, fragmented by design, and hostile to dialogue.'[31] At the same time, Pariser's concern over the fate of the public and the social suggests the possibility that recalibrating algorithms for serendipity and breadth may not, on its own, address the pathologies of fragmentation. As he puts it, the problem must also be countered by 'a more humanistic and nuanced sense of identity, and an active promotion of public issues and cultivation of citizenship'.[32]

Tellingly, in this regard, both Pariser and Sunstein invoke the importance of what we might describe as a 'civic disposition' that recognises the claims and concerns of others as playing an important role in one's own political calculus. Such a disposition is difficult to achieve without the community resources that allow for the imagined possibility of a shared, public interest. As Pratte puts it, '[c]ivic virtue is not a matter of mere behavior; it is a matter of forming a civic disposition, a willingness to act in behalf of the public good while being attentive to and considerate of the feelings, needs, and attitudes of others'.[33] For Habermas, such a disposition is the result of concrete social practice and conscious forms of social cultivation. As McCarthy puts it, practical discourse features 'moral agents trying to put themselves in each other's shoes [...] And this must be done publicly; arguments played out in the individual consciousness or in the theoretician's mind are no substitute for real discourse.'[34] Viewed as a concrete social practice, the formation of such a disposition relies upon materialised practices that foster

29   Ibid 45.
30   Pariser (n 4) 90.
31   Ibid 91.
32   Ibid 127.
33   Pratte (n 11) 308.
34   Thomas McCarthy, Introduction, in Jürgen Habermas, *Moral Consciousness and Communication Action* (Shierry Weber Nicholsen and Christian Lenhardt tr, MIT Press 1990) 12.

turn taking, the ability to place oneself in the position of others, and a sense of a community in common with them.

Pariser and Sunstein closely associate customisation of content with the fragmentation of a shared media sphere and thus with the erosion of conditions for the formation of a civic disposition, which is displaced by abstract conceptions of primary individualism and the concrete practices of consumerism. Their own arguments suggest that the core problem is not just a question of information, but also one of a civic disposition toward that information, in which case we might consider what factors beyond content are implicated in the erosion of such dispositions online (and off). It may be the fact of customisation itself and the concrete technologies and practices with which it is associated, rather than the alleged narrowing of content, that plays the more decisive role – accompanied as it is with broader shifts in the social, cultural, and political environment.

It is nice to imagine that diverse ideas and perspectives, on their own, would bring into being an openness to considering competing claims and putting one's own preconceptions to the test, but history has disproven this over and over. The development of a civic disposition is an historical achievement that requires the development of societal and institutional resources and practices. It is an achievement that can be undone if the reservoir of public commitment and social practices that impel people toward good faith engagement and public deliberation are reconfigured. The philosopher J.M. Bernstein highlights the underlying issues in his discussion of Jürgen Habermas's version of communicative reason – a core attribute of deliberation in the public sphere: 'The ground for orienting ourselves toward establishing validity claims through intersubjective recognition is intersubjective recognition.'[35] Much as we might like them to do so, arguments do not command recognition on their own. The deeper question at work in critiques of media fragmentation, then, is the extent to which the rise of customised commercial platforms does more than simply reproduce niche world views (a contested claim) by helping to reconfigure the practices and dispositions that serve as the underlying conditions for meaningful public deliberation. One crucial task for addressing contemporary concerns about the relationship of platform media to democracy is to identify some starting points for moving the discussion beyond an overly narrow focus on content customisation. The remainder of this chapter considers, in turn, the shift from mass to automated media and the dismantling of imagined community and sociality associated with statist neoliberalism.

V. From mass to automated media

The 20th-century era of mass circulation media represents, for Sunstein, a significant if relatively brief historical period that played an important democratic role at the national level. The mainstream mass media – what he describes as 'general

35   J M Bernstein, *Recovering Ethical Life: Jürgen Habermas and the Future of Critical Theory* (Routledge 1995) 180.

interest intermediaries'[36] – provide a mediated sociality that serves as the social glue that enables shared deliberation. As he puts it, '[p]eople who rely on such intermediaries have a range of chance encounters, involving shared experience with diverse others and exposure to material that they did not specifically choose'.[37] The emphasis in this formulation, as in much of Sunstein's writing on the topic, is, unsurprisingly, on content: a common set of stories contributes to the formation of shared world views that provide common ground for deliberation. Sunstein compares these media to public spaces in which people encounter perspectives and viewpoints that differ from their own but that are nevertheless contained within a shared set of reference points.[38] The advantage of mass media is that they can extend this sense of a shared informational space beyond the limits of physical space: '[I]ntermediaries of this sort have large advantages over streets and parks precisely because they tend to be national, even international. Typically they expose people to questions and problems in other areas, even other countries.'[39] Sunstein is moving beyond content in this formulation: he is articulating the role that the mass media play in forming a sense of what Benedict Anderson has described as an 'imagined community'.[40] Anderson draws on the example of one of the first mass production technologies, the commercial printing press, to explore the relationship between the rise of the concept of the nation state and of the mass audience for newspapers and novels. The novel, he argues, ushers in the notion of 'a sociological organism moving calendrically through homogeneous, empty time'[41] – a notion that parallels 'the idea of the nation' as a container that holds together people who will never know each other but who nonetheless are conceptually assembled into a shared sense of community. As he puts it:

> An American will never meet, or even know the names of more than a handful of his 240,000,000-odd fellow Americans [Anderson was writing 80 million people ago]. He has no idea of what they are up to at any one time. But he has complete confidence in their steady, anonymous, simultaneous activity.[42]

He describes the daily newspaper – Sunstein's general interest intermediary – as the basis of a rhythmic ritual of reading that reinforces a sense of community:

> The significance of this mass ceremony – Hegel observed that newspapers serve modern man as a substitute for morning prayers – is paradoxical. It is performed in silent privacy, in the lair of the skull. Yet each communicant is

36   Sunstein (n 16) 3.
37   Ibid 11.
38   Ibid 12.
39   Cass Sunstein, 'The Daily We: Is the Internet really a blessing for democracy' (2001) 26 Boston Review 3, 6.
40   Benedict Anderson, *Imagined Communities* (2nd edn, Verso Books 2006).
41   Ibid 26.
42   Ibid.

well aware that the ceremony he performs is being replicated simultaneously by thousands (or millions) of others of whose existence he is confident, yet of whose identity he has not the slightest notion.[43]

This awareness is a true achievement insofar as it calls into being the sense of a shared, common, existence with unknown, remote, but imagined others. Dwelling on the power of this achievement, we might consider the practical and material components that underwrite a sense of simultaneity as community. The news comes according to a rhythm – morning edition, late edition, evening edition – that synchronises reading patterns across space. Readers know the stories they are reading are simultaneously being consumed by unknown others in their regional or national sphere. The papers themselves circulate as discrete sharable items whether in the home or on the commuter train, where a discarded paper might be retrieved and re-read by many, marking an informational bond between readers. Mass media homogenise and unify the informational community – a process that has both its benefits and its pathologies (the latter of which provided the impetus for undermining the former). Like mass transport, mass media assemble people into groups and provide them with a collective sense of movement through time.

Anderson's formulation is suggestive because it highlights the role that media infrastructures, artefacts, and practices play in providing the imagined community that contributes to the formation of a civic disposition. As Bernstein suggests, recognising the claims of unknown others requires that some sense of a shared community interest must already be in place.[44] Anderson provides us with some ways of thinking about the role played by media practices and technologies in building this sense of community (which is not to say that the media are the sole contributor, but surely they have an important role to play). The mass reproduction enabled by the printing press standardised a national language and provided those who spoke it with shared informational resources. Mass circulation newspapers helped to build a shared sense of mediated experiences and rituals at the regional and eventually the national level. People watched the same shows at the same times (more or less); they read stories about the same issues, and the mass market gave rise to conventions of objectivity that set the boundaries for what counted as mainstream perspectives. The subsequent critique of the 'mainstream' media was enabled by the fact that there *was* a palpable mainstream, largely built around the consensus of political and media elites and those who depended on these for information and access.[45] The limitations of mass media meant that there was an 'outside' to the media environment – people were not immersed in the endless flow of customised information and entertainment that characterises

---

43 Ibid 35.
44 Bernstein (n 35).
45 See e.g. Robert W. McChesney, *The Political Economy of Media: Enduring Issues, Emerging Dilemmas* (NYU Press 2008); Edward S. Herman and Noam Chomsky, *Manufacturing Consent: The Political Economy of the Mass Media* (Random House 2010).

always-on media. There is no need to romanticise the era of the general interest intermediary (from its inception riven by commercial pressures – at least in the US – and constrained by power and convention), to trace the role it might play in the formation of an imagined community that could gesture toward something like a shared public interest.

The rise of the commercial model for information provision online offers some telling contrasts to the era of the general interest intermediary – beyond the differences in content identified by Sunstein and Pariser. The notion of homogenous time gives way to mass customisation and the rhythm of media consumption becomes disaggregated and reconfigured. The evening newscast is replaced, for many, by the constant flow of customised information. We dig into our own worlds not simply by drawing on customised content, but by reconfiguring our spatial and temporal relationships to information, to the world around us, and to each other. The TV room in the dorm gives way to roommates watching separate Netflix shows in adjoining rooms on their personal devices. Local newspapers dry up and blow away, leaving a vacuum to be filled by local Facebook groups created by, among others, civilian militias and right-wing hate groups. The rhythm of reading and viewing is accelerated while the time to absorb and contemplate is displaced by the relentless flow of updates and information tidbits. The space 'outside' of media consumption shrinks as people take their devices into the public parks and streets, largely oblivious of the strangers around them, focused on their own personal window on the world unfolding before them. Of course, there are exceptions and alternatives, but the tendency is clear, and the implications for our sense of imagined community deserves a central place in any approach to the relationship between digital media and political fragmentation.

The reluctance of influential platforms such as Facebook and Twitter to view themselves as publishers, and thus responsible for the content they circulate, furthers the shift away from a notion of public – and the goal of serving it – toward that of marketing to disaggregated consumers. The imperatives of the automated information economy are shaped by the data-driven advertising models that rely primarily on 'stickiness' (the time spent on a site) and engagement (user content production and information sharing) to maximise both exposure to ads and data collection about users.[46]

One of the leading contemporary critics of the social effects of the device-based platform economy is lapsed cyber-celebrant Sherry Turkle. For Turkle, social media are fundamentally anti-social technologies insofar as they displace communion onto digital (and, we might add, commercial) networks. Her book *Alone Together* laments the deficit of sociality wreaked by hyper-connectivity:[47] the rise in playground accidents that coincides with parents and nannies focusing on phones rather than children, the college

46   Paul Lewis, '"Fiction is outperforming reality": how YouTube's algorithm distorts truth', *The Guardian* (2 February 2018) www.theguardian.com/technology/2018/feb/02/how-youtubes-algorithm-distorts-truth, accessed 30 August 2019.

47   Sherry Turkle, *Alone Together: Why We Expect More from Technology and Less from Each Other* (3rd edn, Basic Books 2017).

suitemates texting one another from room to room rather than talking, the loss of the 'raw, human part' of being with one another.[48] Turkle found that for her respondents, managing sprawling social media networks can be so time- consuming that people look for the most efficient ways to communicate: texting rather than talking by phone (which comes to be seen as too intrusive and an outdated form of 'mono-tasking'), shorthand signs of support and affirmation (likes, retweets, posts), asynchronous modes of interacting with friends and families, and so on. As Turkle puts it:

> [T]oday our machine dream is to be never alone but always in control. This can't happen when one is face-to-face with a person. But it can be accomplished with a robot, or by slipping through the portals of a digital life.[49]

One related recent development is the accelerating tendency to offload sociality onto increasingly automated platforms. A platform called Molly, for example, profiles users in order to craft automated answers to questions from other. As one press account put it:

> Eventually [...] it will provide answers that are not already in its system using machine learning. By using all the information the app can gather about you (upon creating a profile, you have the option to add social accounts from which Molly can learn), it will be able to predict an answer to a question relevant to you. Molly would confirm its formulated answer with you – to affirm yes, that's what you would say – and whoever asked the query will be sent an answer.[50]

Instead of communicating directly with an interlocutor, users interact with the bot that becomes their always-on networked presence. As the demands of constant

---

48 Catherine de Lang, 'Sherry Turkle: "We're losing the raw, human part of being with each other"' *The Guardian* (5 May 2013) www.theguardian.com/science/2013/may/05/rational-heroes-sherry-turkle-mit, accessed 30 August 2019. Some recent empirical research (Jeffrey A Hall, Michael W Kearney and Chong Xing, 'Two tests of social displacement through social media use' (2018) 22 Information, Communication & Society 1396) has pressed against the 'social displacement via social media' hypothesis, finding no support for the assumption that 'social media decreases interactions with close friends and family' (12). Although the authors cite Turkle's work as an example of the social displacement hypothesis, her findings focus not on the frequency of contact but on the rhythm and character of social interaction. Parents and children may, for example, have face-to-face contact even while their attention and focus is directed toward their devices. From the perspective of Sunstein's concerns, the question is not whether interactions with close friends and family are displaced, but whether public encounters are diminished through the privatisation of public space associated with mobile, networked devices. See more in Jeffrey A Hall et al., ibid.
49 Turkle (n 47) 157.
50 Molly McKew, 'Our Bots, Ourselves' *The Ringer* (7 March 2018) www.theringer.com/tech/2018/3/7/17089364/molly-machine-learning-social-platform-bots, accessed 30 August 2019.

connectivity pile up, automation becomes the ready response. Google is developing an AI-based automatic reply system for text messages that will allow users to eyeball its suggested response and send it off with a single tap. As the developers describe it, the system would incorporate context awareness derived from other social media apps and platforms: 'The system can apparently work out what people are saying to you and suggest one-tap answers, but Google says it will go further, taking your location, your calendar and other bits of information into account.'[51] Through the dialectical reversal enacted by automation, the acceleration of sociality culminates in its elimination via automation: the convergence of hyper-interactivity with solipsism.

VI. Neoliberal sociality

Media practices do not exist in a vacuum and the tendencies described by Turkle, Sunstein, and Pariser parallel broader claims about the resources for sociality under conditions of what Wendy Brown has described as 'statist neoliberalism'.[52] The triumph of 'consumer sovereignty', combined with technologies and practices that foster increasingly individualistic forms of media consumption and solipsistic social interaction described by Turkle, align themselves with the regulatory assault on notions of a public interest and policies that support social security and collective benefits. Brown argues that the political climate in the Trump era promotes a regulatory approach that

> literally takes apart social bonds and social welfare – not simply by promoting a libertarian notion of freedom and dismantling the welfare state, but also by reducing legitimate political claims only to those advanced by and for families and individuals, not social groups generated by social powers.[53]

The list of policy changes and proposals that fit this description continues to grow: the attempts to undermine the Affordable Care Act in the US, to dismantle environmental regulation, to de-fund public service media and publicly funded research, to cut low-cost health care for poor children and cross-subsidies for broadband access, are just a few.

What the programmes and policies under attack have in common is that they reflect a commitment to forms of mutual recognition and the sense of common, shared public interest. This commitment reflects and reproduces a crucial component of democratic culture, according to Brown: 'The saturation of the state, political culture, and the social with market rationality effectively strips

---

51   Hal 90210, 'Tired of texting? Google tests robot to chat with friends for you' *The Guardian* (14 February 2018) www.theguardian.com/technology/2018/feb/14/google-tests-robot-chat-reply-friends, accessed 30 August 2019.
52   Littler (n 5).
53   Ibid 14.

commitments to political democracy from governance concerns and political culture.'[54] Cayley Sorochan, in her related discussion of the fate of participation in the neoliberal era, observes:

> It is not simply that the political sphere has minimized its purview or become corrupted by capitalist interests, it is that the possibility of understanding the political as a distinct dimension of human life with its own logic and set of values is disappearing or made unintelligible by the ubiquity of economistic thinking.[55]

At issue in such accounts is the diminished or disappearing space for forms of political interaction that are irreducible to the economic – and thus of subject positions distinct from the individual preferences and structured competition privileged by the market.

This wide-ranging reconfiguration of the societal landscape emerges from and reproduces a suppression of the underlying forms of trust and recognition that enable the functioning of social and political life. The subject position that celebrates tax cuts paid for by the dismantling of health care for the poor refuses any conception of a common interest that foregrounds social interdependence. The emphasis on individual self-interest suppresses and misrecognises the underlying social bonds that make the market society it relies on able to function in the first place. The threat of this form of extreme misrecognition – the taxpayer screaming over the use of public money for public services that benefit others – is that we become less conscious of the underlying forms of trust that make possible even the most basic of activities in contemporary society, from vouchsafing our children to the public schools to crossing the street when the light turns red (it is certainly a symptom of contemporary social pathologies that both of these realms of trust have become highly publicised vectors of attack and vulnerability). In myriad ongoing ways, we rely on forms of trust and recognition that are all too easily ignored, overlooked, and disavowed in favour of an abstract notion of individuality that would be impossible to sustain without both these forms of sociality and their disavowal. The assault on public institutions ranging from public education to public parks and libraries to public health care provide evidence of the social amnesia upon which the forms of neoliberal governance described by Brown thrives. As the philosopher J.M. Bernstein puts it: 'The American version of these practices has, from the earliest days of the republic, made individuality autochthonous while suppressing to the point of disappearance the manifold ways that individuality is beholden to a complex and uniquely modern form of life.'[56]

54 Wendy Brown, 'American Nightmare: Neoliberalism, Neoconservatism, and De-Democratization' (2006) 34(6) Political Theory 690, 695.
55 Cayley Sorochan, *The Participatory Complex: Participation as Ideology in the Neoliberal Era* (PhD thesis, McGill University 2017) 36.
56 J M Bernstein, 'The Very Angry Tea Party' *The New York Times* (13 June 2010) http s://opinionator.blogs.nytimes.com/2010/06/13/the-very-angry-tea-party, accessed 30 August 2019.

Against this background, it comes as no surprise that the frustration of the current political moment has to do with people's inability to reach across political and ideological divides to agree upon underlying facts, evidence, and reality. The shift toward automated, customised media works in both form and content to reinforce a conception of consumerist individualism that disavows the background practices, institutions, and social relations that serve as its own conditions of possibility. Thus, the questions we should be asking of social media and the platform economy have to do not just with the diversity of content they provide, but also with the ways in which it structures and reinforces this version of solipsism. These influences are not limited to the messages we receive, but to the ways in which we encounter them.

If the underlying resources for meaningful deliberation – the ground that makes it possible for people to hear the concerns and arguments of others – are eroded, it is not clear that technical or educational fixes, as important as they might be, are sufficient. Instead, it becomes important to reconfigure the practices, platforms, and policies that reinforce an understanding of news and information as individualised, custom-tailored commodities, dismantling the sense of publicness, commonality of interest, and mutual recognition that underwrite democratic deliberation. The stakes are high because of the role deliberation plays in democratic self-governance – that is, in providing an alternative to the role of violence in resolving disagreements. As Simone Chambers put it in her work on deliberative democracy, political deliberation is predicated, in part, on 'the intuition that talking is better than fighting'.[57] If the resources available for talking dissipate, we run the danger of finding ourselves in a post-deliberative, post-diplomatic realm in which the play of force and violence is unleashed.

VII. The glut chamber

The insight resulting from such arguments is that diversity of media content and perspectives is an outmoded proxy for meaningful deliberation. Neither Sunstein[58] nor Pariser[59] celebrates diversity simply for diversity's sake: they both see the breadth of media exposure as a necessary precondition for functional public deliberation. That is, even if those who lament the rise of online echo chambers are empirically wrong about the breadth of perspectives to which people are exposed, this does not mean we no longer have to worry about the state of contemporary political deliberation. It seems increasingly possible that the most important change is not in the breadth of content, but in its efficacy. This is the paradox of the contemporary information environment: that, under certain

57 Simone Chambers, *Reasonable Democracy: Jürgen Habermas and the Politics of Discourse* (Cornell University Press 1996) 2.
58 Cass Sunstein, *#Republic: Divided Democracy in the Age of Social Media* (Princeton University Press 2017); Cass Sunstein, *Republic.com 2.0* (Princeton University Press 2007); Sunstein (n 16).
59 Pariser (n 4).

circumstances, a breath-taking expansion of the information environment might exacerbate (rather than overcome) political polarisation. Such an observation is perhaps less surprising than it might at first seem: when there are myriad conflicting accounts and perspectives, people experience greater latitude in choosing among them. In a world of proliferating media outlets, wherein even the most extreme perspectives can readily find themselves reinforced by a range of media sources and resources (as well as by a ready core of like-minded supporters), it is easier to feel that one has not only the right but the obligation to choose one's own facts. In an environment of media surfeit, one is cast adrift on a sea of narratives and counter-narratives, equipped only with the pole star of pre-existing preconceptions and pre-judices. In the digital information environment, every account can be undermined and contested, every representation deconstructed, every proof counterfeited, every theory transformed into a conspiracy and vice versa.

But perhaps glut,[60] on its own, is not enough to explain this vertiginous dis-mantling of symbolic efficiency. Isn't the whole point of evidence and reasoned argument that it can cut through the clutter of falsehood, superstition, and wrong opinion? The reality of public debate on a national scale is that it draws heavily on media representations and thus relies on some level of fundamental trust in the systems of expertise, accountability, and responsibility meant to serve as guarantors of these representations. Functional debate also relies on what might be described as good faith engagement in processes of reasoned, consistent argumentation and the ability to step outside of one's own perspective to consider that of others – that is, some degree of generalisability. The commercial platform model poses profound challenges to both of these underlying preconditions, which suggests the importance of a fundamental rethinking and reconfiguration of this model. All of which is not to say that these challenges are unique to social media, which in many ways extend the logics of hyper-commercialisation and nichification that char-acterised the development of the mass media in the late 20th century.

The truth of the 'democratising' promise of social media, then, is that it reconfigures the citizen as both consumer (and thus as an individualised target) and brand (tasked with self-marketing and self-broadcasting).[61] Simultaneously, it displaces practices of human sociality with automated sorting systems running on commercial platforms. Offloading our interactions onto bots allows us to suppress the recognition of our interdependence, our reliance on others. Hyper-con-nectivity, on this account, defaults to a form of hermetic solipsism that looks increasingly familiar in the era of the decline of symbolic efficiency.[62] The new challenge for democratic deliberation becomes not that of providing evidence and countervailing narratives and viewpoints, but of securing recognition for the

60   Mark Andrejevic, *Infoglut: How Too Much Information Is Changing the Way We Think and Know* (Routledge 2013).
61   Alison Hearn, "'Meat, Mask, Burden": Probing the contours of the branded "self"' (2008) 8(2) Journal of Consumer Culture 197.
62   Žižek (n 9).

underlying forms of interdependence that make it possible to take on the perspective and position of others – and to invite them to do the same for us.

In the automated, mass customised media environment, perhaps the real challenge to democratic deliberation is not the narrowing of content and perspectives available on social media platforms, but the combination of their indefinite proliferation with the erosion of the social preconditions for adjudicating between them. If, in the filter bubble, people are deafened to the views of others by the constant reinforcement of their preconceptions and prejudices, in a context of 'infoglut',[63] the cacophony is equally deafening. The pressing question becomes how to cultivate the resources that would calm this cacophony by facilitating the shared adjudication of mutually exclusive arguments and perspectives. If recognising the validity claims of others depends in turn on underlying forms of intersubjective recognition that are eroded by the rise of automated sociality (and the assault on practices and institutions that provide a sense of shared political and social commitment), we cannot expect the claims of whatever passes as reasoned deliberation to retain purchase on their own. We need to imagine alternatives to offloading sociality onto commercial automated networks that render hyper-communicativity ineffective for actual deliberation (listening, perspective taking, and recognition of mutuality and shared interdependency). Failing to do so would be to concede that talking no longer provides a viable alternative to fighting, relegating information to the ongoing process of weaponisation that is colonising contemporary social relations.

63 Andrejevic (n 60).

Chapter 3

Filter bubbles, democracy and conceptions of self

A brief genealogy and a Spinozist perspective

Janice Richardson

I. Background problem

Cambridge Analytica's attempt to sway voters in the 2016 United States (US) presidential election and in the United Kingdom (UK) Brexit referendum of the same year raises a number of questions about democracy, how we view ourselves as citizens, as well as adding to existing concerns about invasions of privacy. These questions arise irrespective of the genuine extent of Cambridge Analytica's success. The concerns are well known. One worry is that 'dark posts' – posts that are only visible to the intended target group – risk undermining civil society. Civil society requires a public sphere in which citizens debate common social and political problems, as illustrated by the coffee houses and salons of late 17th and 18th century[1] – albeit that these were subject to significant exclusions, for example, based on class and gender.[2] We limit both the perspective and extent of the news that we receive at the cost of broader common knowledge, which could form the basis of debate. A contemporary criticism of individuals each living in their own 'filter bubble' was detailed by Eli Pariser,[3] who has since commented on Facebook's own studies of filter bubbles, maintaining his concern that news continues to be more tailored to our own individual interests.[4]

To get a sense of what may be lost, it is worth considering an earlier work that pre-dates these online developments: Benedict Anderson's *Imagined Communities: Reflections on the Origin and Spread of Nationalism*. Anderson describes the way in which a sense of community can be evoked by thinking about simultaneity.[5] His relevant example is the daily experience of reading a newspaper. As it is likely to be read on the day it is published, the reader is aware that others are all

1   Jürgen Habermas, *The Structural Transformation of the Public Sphere: An Inquiry into a Category of Bourgeois Society* (Thomas Burger tr, Polity Press 1992).
2   Nancy Fraser, 'Rethinking the Public Sphere: A Contribution to the Critique of Actually Existing Democracy' (1990) 25–26 Social Text 56.
3   Eli Pariser, *The Filter Bubble: What the Internet Is Hiding from You* (Penguin 2011).
4   Eli Pariser, 'Did Facebook's Big Study Kill My Filter Bubble Thesis?' *WIRED* (7 May 2015) www.wired.com/2015/05/did-facebooks-big-study-kill-my-filter-bubble-thesis, accessed 3 September 2019.
5   Benedict Anderson, *Imagined Communities: Reflections on the Origin and Spread of Nationalism* (Verso 1983) 51.

reading the same news at the same time. This evokes a sense of shared language and of common interests as part of a nation. There is also a related concern that targeted advertising is not widely distributed because it provokes a narrow sense of identity based upon exclusion, by being racist, for example. Instead of evoking a widely imagined community, dark posts play upon the fears and hatreds of particular groups, reinforcing narrow group identities in ways that are socially divisive.

While the filter bubble may be new, the questions that arise about fear and other human emotions that may hamper our ability to engage actively in democracy are not. In this chapter, I examine what needed to be in place, aside from the relevant technology, in order for the perceived threats to democracy highlighted in 2016 to arise. I will start by setting the scene of neo-liberalism, the ambitions of behaviourism and the role of giant technology companies, in particular Facebook and Google. Second, I briefly trace the antecedents of neo-liberalism. In the third section, I focus in more detail on the transitional figure of John Locke and then contrast Locke's characterisation of ourselves with that of his contemporary, Spinoza. My argument is that the radical enlightenment philosopher Spinoza provides a rich resource for thinking about the political and ontological implications of communication. Finally, I demonstrate this by applying Spinoza's conceptions of ourselves to these contemporary problems raised by the electoral interference by Cambridge Analytica in 2016 and the associated problem of privacy.

It may appear odd to return to the 17th century to discuss a political and ethical problem that has only arisen because of 21st-century technology. However, it is important to note that this problem has not arisen because of technological determinism. What was required was a particularly diminished view of selfhood and of democracy, which is a crucial component of neo-liberalism. Hence my interest in asking: what beliefs and practices led to the idea that democracy is more akin to a vote in a game show than having a voice in your daily life? I trace the development of the neo-liberal image of ourselves, while recognising that the use of political philosopher's names – 'John Locke', for example – serves as shorthand for the crystallisation of particular beliefs in a society. My claim is not that individual philosophers produce wholesale changes in beliefs out of nowhere.

The reason that Spinoza is useful to consider these problems is that his *Ethics* (1677) focuses upon the importance of communication. As I will explain below, Étienne Balibar comments:

> Spinoza's philosophy is, in a strong sense of the term, a philosophy of communication – or, even better, modes of communication – in which the theory of knowledge and theory of sociability are clearly intertwined.[6]

In Spinoza's time, there were also major changes in technologies of communication. To illustrate this, Jonathan Israel describes Spinoza's Dutch Republic of the late 17th century in the following terms:

6   Étienne Balibar, *Spinoza and Politics* (Peter Snowdon tr, Verso 1998) 101.

For it was then that western and central Europe first became, in the sphere of ideas, broadly a single arena integrated by mostly newly invented channels of communication, ranging from newspapers, magazines, and the salon to the coffee-shop and a whole array of fresh cultural devices of which the erudite journals (invented in 1660s) and the 'universal' library were particularly crucial.[7]

Spinoza analysed human passions (the 'affects') and their political implications, situating human beings as part of nature and subject to natural laws (which, for Spinoza, were scientific laws). In addition, Spinoza cannot be accused of naiveté by today's neo-liberals, given that his aim was to describe human beings as they are and not as we want them to be:

> Moreover, though we've shown that reason can do much to restrain and moderate the affects (E Vp1–p10s)[8], we've also seen that the path reason teaches us to follow is very difficult (E Vp42s). So people who persuade themselves that a multitude, which may be divided over public affairs, can be induced to live only according to the prescription of reason, those people are dreaming of the golden age of the Poets. They're captive to a myth.[9]

II. Neo-liberalism, behaviourism and the giant tech companies

In his recent book, Jamie Bartlett, of the UK think tank Demos, makes a deflationary observation about the tech giants.[10] He comments that they like to portray their origin stories as part of 'hacker culture' – for example, Facebook gave itself the address of '1 Hacker Way'. In doing so, they associate themselves with a certain rebellious anti-authoritarianism and then trace their origin back to the genius figures of Ada Lovelace and Alan Turing.[11] However, as we all know, they are no longer simply 'technology companies' but are in reality now 'advertising companies', suggesting a different origin. The behaviourist psychologists John Watson[12] and later Burrhus Skinner[13] may be a more appropriate lineage for these companies today. It was the behaviourists' view of humanity as susceptible to

7   Jonathan I Israel, *Radical Enlightenment: Philosophy and the Making of Modernity 1650–1750* (Oxford University Press 2001) 4.
8   I follow the standard practice for referencing the works of Spinoza. *E* stands for the *Ethics*, I–V for its five parts, p for Proposition, d for Definition, s for Scholium, Pref for Preface; App for Appendix, Dem for Demonstration, DA for Definition of the Affects, Exp for Explanation. In this quotation from the *Political Treatise*, Curley is following this convention to cross-reference Spinoza's arguments.
9   Benedictus de Spinoza, 'Political Treatise' in Edwin M Curley (ed, tr), *The Collected Works of Spinoza: Volume 2* (Princeton University Press 2008) ch 1 §5.
10   Jamie Bartlett, *The People Vs Tech: How the internet is killing democracy (and how we save it)* (Ebury Press 2018).
11   Ibid 120.
12   John B Watson, *Behaviorism* (Norton 1924).
13   Burrhus F Skinner, *Beyond Freedom and Dignity* (Penguin 1973).

manipulation that excited companies' marketing departments of Watson's day (and onwards). Skinner even wrote a utopian novel *Walden Two* exploring how people's lives would be improved by the use of such reinforcement techniques to instil 'good behaviour',[14] not unlike the 'nudging' with which we are familiar today. Needless to say, Skinner does not have much to say about democracy.

Selling political figures and political arguments by using big data to tailor different messages to ever finely delineated categories of people is merely an extension of the usual work of advertising today. As Cathy O'Neil points out in *Weapons of Math Destruction*,[15] algorithms learn to categorise people, often focusing on their anxieties. She compares this appeal to our weaknesses to the technique used by snake oil sellers, who learned to spot their victim's anxieties in order to sell them a 'cure'. One of the most pernicious examples in the US is to identify those who are poor but want education – eligible for state funding – so that they can be sold courses in expensive for-profit universities. For example, O'Neil cites Vatterott College. A 2012 US Senate committee report on for-profit universities described their recruiting manual, which tells recruiters to target the following:

> Welfare Mom w/kids, Pregnant Ladies, Recent Divorce, Low Self-Esteem, Low Income Jobs. Experienced a Recent Death. Physically/Mentally Abused. Drug Rehabilitation. Dead-End Jobs. No-Future.[16]

O'Neil points out that they do not target anyone who would be well informed; that, in general, the middle classes would recognise that employers rank these expensive private universities lower than community colleges.[17] Like Cambridge Analytica, the marketing teams obtain the necessary data from tech giants. In this case, the for-profit universities will target people from the poorest zip codes in the US, particularly if they have clicked on an advert for payday loans. The categories of people targeted may not always be predictable. For example, Trump's team discovered that purchasers of US-made cars correlated with support for Trump. This allowed them to direct adverts to potential Trump supporters in marginal seats.[18] As the US does not have a compulsory voting system, this can make a difference by encouraging supporters to vote.

While the ambition to manipulate remains the same, there is a difference between behaviourists' attempts to apply their theories of our susceptibility to reinforcement techniques and the use of big data today. Today's advertisers, who employ big data to categorise purchaser/citizens, do not particularly care for explanations. The (in)famous comment by Chris Anderson in *Wired* refers to the

14   Burrhus F Skinner, *Walden Two* (Macmillan 1948).
15   Cathy O'Neil, *Weapons of Math Destruction: How Big Data Increases Inequality and Threatens Democracy* (Crown 2016).
16   Ibid 74.
17   Ibid.
18   Bartlett (n 10) ch 3.

'end of theory'. He states: 'Who knows why people do what they do? The point is they do it and we can track and measure it with unprecedented fidelity.'[19]

In contrast, as I will consider in the next section, neo-liberals have a clear story of why people do what they do. They treat all human abilities as if they were commodities in a market and adopt a perspective in which we treat ourselves as if we were market enterprises. Hence, parental time spent with children is viewed as an investment in the children's later earning ability, for example. As Michel Foucault explains,[20] Gary Becker[21] extends the definition of economics from the 'optimal allocation of scarce resources to alternative ends' to include irrational behaviour.[22] As a result, economics is the domain of any conduct that 'accepts reality'.[23] Commenting on Becker's neo-liberalism, Foucault, lecturing on 28 March 1979, therefore makes the link between neo-liberalism and behaviourism to conclude:

> [I]f you define the object of economic analysis as the set of systematic responses to the variables in the environment, then you can see the possibility of integrating within economics a set of techniques, those called behavioural techniques, which are currently in fashion in the United States.[24]

III. Foucault: *Homo œconomicus* and *homo juridicus*

Foucault provides a brief history of thought to situate the rise of neo-liberalism in US. These were part of a lecture series in 1979 and are even more relevant today. I will draw on these lectures to answer the question 'What beliefs about ourselves needed to be in place for the Cambridge Analytica electoral interference to have arisen?' This is an important question irrespective of whether this interference had an effect on voters. Writing for students, Foucault employs the literary device of focusing upon two different images of human beings: *homo œconomicus* (the 'subject of interest') and *homo juridicus* (the 'subject of law' – i.e. the legal subject with rights) and traces the background of their relationship to today's Western liberal democratic governments.

For Foucault, the issue that 'gets the problematic of *homo œconomicus* underway' is how this 'subject of interest' relates to the legal subject within different theoretical frameworks. Foucault starts with John Locke's *Two Treatises of Government* from 1689.[25] With Locke, Foucault argues, philosophy revealed something

19   Chris Anderson, 'The End of Theory: The Data Deluge Makes the Scientific Method Obsolete' *WIRED* (23 June 2008) www.wired.com/2008/06/pb-theory, accessed 3 September 2019.

20   Michael Senellart (ed), *Michel Foucault, The Birth of Biopolitics: Lectures at the College de France, 1978–1979* (Graham Burchell tr, Palgrave Macmillan 2008) 389.

21   Gary S Becker, 'Irrational Behavior and Economic Theory' (1962) 70(1) The Journal of Political Economy 1.

22   Foucault (n 20) 388.

23   Becker (n 21).

24   Foucault (n 20) 389.

25   Peter Laslett (ed), *Locke: Two Treatises of Government* (Cambridge University Press 1988).

new: 'the idea of a subject of interest', the idea of a human being who has specific interests (in life, liberty and property). Foucault argues that initially the image of ourselves, as *both* a subject of interest and a subject with rights, was reconciled in a period lasting from the end of the 17th century to the middle of the 18th century. He illustrates this point with an outline of the theoretical position of the jurist Blackstone who mixes the image of both *homo œconomicus* and the legal subject. Blackstone tells the social contract story such that individuals with interests (*homo œconomicus*) join the (hypothetical) social contract and agree to obey the law in order to safeguard their interests. For Blackstone, this creates the legal subject who is constituted through the social contract. To the question 'Why adhere to the social contract once you have entered into it?', Blackstone's response was that the social contract itself transforms *homo œconomicus* into a legal subject who will obey the law created by the social contract.[26] Foucault contrasts this with the argument by Hume[27] against the social contractarians (that, I note, was originally employed by Spinoza):[28] that there is no transformation through a hypothetical contract; that people obey a contract only if it is in their best interests. Hume's intervention marks a refusal to view the subject of interest as transformed into the subject of rights.

Importantly, Foucault considers the logic through which people are governed, employing these different views of ourselves. As is well known, in the 18th century economists argued that governments could not dictate what to do to *homo œconomicus*. Against state regulation of the market, *homo œconomicus* could argue that the market was too complex for any government to interfere. Instead, there would be co-ordination of interests through the mechanism of the market. This demand differs from that of the legal subject, who argues for limitations on the state's power by claiming rights.

With this background, Foucault explains a shift that occurs with contemporary neo-liberalism. Instead of arguing that the state cannot interfere with the market, *homo œconomicus* can turn around and call on the government – its departments and panoply of the state as well as all public institutions – to behave as if they were market actors and to have their performances judged accordingly. This is a very familiar idea, as academics are painfully aware, given the extent to which universities are encouraged to view themselves as market actors, adopting (and often parodying) the latest managerial and marketing slogans. It is within this context that it makes sense to reduce democracy into micromarketing because all human behaviour is viewed in market terms and so there are only private interests. It is assumed to be naïve to imagine citizens as interested in the common welfare or the creation of an 'enlarged mentality' by thinking of oneself in the position of

---

26   Sir William Blackstone, *Commentaries on the Laws of England: In Four Books* (Clarendon Press 1765).

27   David Hume, 'Of the Original Contract', in *Essays, Moral and Political* (3rd edn, A. Millar 1748) 289–294.

28   Baruch Spinoza, *Tractatus Theologico-Politicus* (Jan Rieuwertsz 1670) III/191–192.

others.[29] This view is consistent with – but more complex than – the image of citizens as merely passive consumers of political debate.

Neo-liberals therefore produce a 'truth' that rivals not only active images of citizenship but also the image of the legal subject, the subject with rights. Whereas Foucault uses the analysis of crime as an example of this way of conceptualising ourselves, it is more relevant for me to consider the example of privacy, drawing here on the work of neo-liberal Richard Posner. The legal subject can claim that the state should protect his or her rights to privacy, and we see serious efforts in this direction in the European Union. However, from the position of *homo œconomicus* in neo-liberalism, there is a market in privacy and a market in prying.[30] We relate to our privacy – not as something that is personal, relevant to 'who we are' – but as if it were merely owned by us as a commodity. It is from this market perspective that Posner can argue for the protection of companies' secrets but not recognise the importance of those held by individuals. Within this framework, Posner reduces the argument for privacy of personal information as merely a demand that individuals should be allowed to deceive their potential 'market' of friends.

To explore how anyone came to view themselves in such terms, I now turn back to an analysis of Locke in more detail. Locke is important in setting the scene because of the way in which he produces a 'private' image of selfhood ontologically and the political fiction of property in the person, in which we treat our abilities and parts of ourselves as if they were commodities. My argument is that this view of ourselves needed to be in place in order to view elections in terms of personal rather than public interests; as well as producing a weak form of democracy.

IV. Locke: Property in the person and the 'private' individual

Carole Pateman argues that, with the transition from feudal relations to a capitalist mode of production, there is a corresponding change in the way in which relationships characterised by subordination – employer/employee, husband/wife, sovereign/subject – are transformed.[31] In modernity, she argues, subordination is managed through the device of contracts that exchange 'property in the person' for wages or financial support. Hence, the exchange is merely a political or legal fiction – as envisaged by Locke in Part V of Part II *Two Treatises on Government*. For example, the treatment of human capacities as if they were commodities makes the employment contract appear to be an equal exchange of our ability to

29   Hannah Arendt, *Between Past and Future: Six Exercises in Political Thought* (Faber & Faber 1961), 234–235.

30   Richard A Posner, 'An Economic Theory of Privacy', in Ferdinand D Schoeman (ed), *Philosophical Dimensions of Privacy: An Anthology* (Cambridge University Press 1984) 333–345.

31   Carole Pateman, *The Sexual Contract* (Polity Press 1988); Carole Pateman, 'Self-Ownership and Property in the Person: Democratization and a Tale of Two Concepts' (2002) 10(1) The Journal of Political Philosophy 20.

work for a wage.[32] In fact, it means that employees expect to be given orders in the workplace rather than having a voice in decision-making. Pateman adds to this analysis by considering the position of women in the traditional marriage contract, in which they also exchanged property in the person (this time, *consortium* – i.e. sex and housework) for material support.[33] Pateman analyses the impact of both these contracts – marriage and employment – on democracy itself.

In short, she asks how there can be democracy in the *polis* when there is no democracy in the everyday life of the workplace and, historically in the West, in the home. Pateman's work is important because it puts into perspective the idea that democracy is threatened by the potential manipulation of voters. If we imagine democracy as a continuum – depending upon the extent to which people actually have a say in decisions that affect their everyday lives – then it is clear that attacks on democracy become easier when it was already weak. Democracy can be viewed as a continuum because there are degrees of participation possible. For example, the European Works Council Directive envisages worker participation; decent basic income makes workers and those subject to domestic violence less desperate to stay in their work or home. For Pateman, for whom it is axiomatic that democracy and political freedom cannot exist unless people have a say in their everyday lives, democracy must be participative. Despite Rousseau's misogyny, Pateman draws from Rousseau for one important argument: that actively taking part in decision-making *changes* people into citizens.[34] It allows them to develop the skills, confidence and expectation that are required to have their voices heard, as well as extending their understanding of their position within a greater whole.

Turning to conceptions of self rather than the political fiction of property in the person, Janet Coleman's 'Pre-modern Property and Self-Ownership Before and After Locke: Or, When Did Common Decency Become a Private Rather than a Public Virtue?'[35] is useful in underlining the extent to which Locke was a transitional figure. Unusually, Coleman employs both Locke's *The Two Treatises of Government*[36] and the *Essay Concerning Human Understanding*[37] to give a rich analysis of his conception of self and its role in creating our contemporary view, which she describes as:

> [An] impoverished, definition of what it means to be a person, not least in collapsing 'person' into private, self-conscious, self-identity of self-owners.[38]

32   Karl Marx, *Capital: Volume 1: A Critique of Political Economy* (Ben Fowkes tr, Penguin Classics 1976) 280.
33   Pateman, *The Sexual Contract* (n 31).
34   Pateman, 'Self-Ownership and Property in the Person' (n 31).
35   Janet Coleman, 'Pre-Modern Property and Self-Ownership Before and After Locke: Or, When Did Common Decency Become a Private Rather than a Public Virtue?' (2005) 4(2) European Journal of Political Theory 125.
36   Laslett (n 25).
37   Roger S Woolhouse (ed), *John Locke: An Essay Concerning Human Understanding* (Penguin 1997).
38   Coleman (n 35) 128; see also Janice Richardson, *Law and the Philosophy of Privacy* (Routledge 2015) 88–93 regarding the implications of Coleman's analysis for privacy.

One illustration is useful to distinguish Locke from neo-liberalism while also recognising how his position marks a transition towards it. For neo-liberals, we can treat all aspects of ourselves as if they were commodities that we own. A corollary of this is that we could sell ourselves into slavery through contractual exchange (but not if violence were involved).[39] However, for Locke,[40] selling oneself into slavery would be morally wrong because it would be akin to suicide. He rejects the moral acceptability of suicide on the basis that only God as our creator can make the decision as to when we die.

Just as Foucault describes Locke as being the first to think of ourselves as subjects with interests, Coleman identifies Locke as starting to think of ourselves as having an 'internal' self-identity. For Locke, we fulfil our duty to God to continue living by working. Just as we work to appropriate food (*Second Treatise*), we also (in the *Essay Concerning Human Understanding*) appropriate ideas and internalise them, having worked upon them. It is through our internal memories that we maintain our identity. With this move, it is possible to recognise the predecessor of an image of a self that then works on itself to gain human capital, the contemporary 'private, self-conscious, self-identity of self-owners' whose concern is not with a shared history and public sphere but with private interests. As Coleman puts it:

> In asserting in the *Second Treatise* that man already has a property in his own person to which nobody has any right but himself, Locke seems to be arguing that to remain a person into the future, to stay alive and be a person in one's own eyes, self-consciously, *in foro interno*, one is obliged through the activity of appropriation, mental and physical, to extend one's own independent personality into the world in present and future time and then bring it back in, as it were, through consciousness 'owning' its own acts.[41]

This 'internal' image of selfhood can be contrasted with that of Locke's contemporary, Spinoza. In his *Ethics*, Spinoza also analyses what happens when we encounter something else, such as food or ideas. For Spinoza, we do not appropriate them into ourselves through work. Instead, Spinoza gives a more complex analysis that draws out the importance of our ability to understand our encounters, for which communication with others is of central importance. I will explain Spinoza's analysis of the passions in order to consider the political implications of the use of filter bubbles. This also includes an analysis of an imagined community divided by areas of subordination. I will explore this imagined community along with implications of how we think about privacy.

---

39   Robert Nozick, *Anarchy, State, and Utopia* (Basic Books 1974), ch 9 is willing to agree to this point.
40   'Second Treatise' in Laslett (n 25) 284.
41   Coleman (n 35) 135–136.

V. Spinoza, the passions and their political implications

In the *Ethics*, Spinoza describes us as *changing* when we encounter things in the world and as naturally acting in concert with others (without the aid of contracts). He also analyses the mechanisms by which we may come to hate or love others, along with the political implications of passions such as pride. Ultimately, other human beings are important because Spinoza makes an *ontological* claim about ourselves: that, with greater understanding of our interactions with the world, we are able to live richer lives and that we are also able to form 'singular things' with other human beings and other things (*E* 2d7). It is worth considering how this comes about and the relationship between self/other in detail.

In the *Ethics*, Spinoza explains what happens when we encounter another thing whether it is a body or an idea. We initially feel joy or sadness as we register that the other thing has increased or decreased our powers of acting. We do not experience emotions if our ability to thrive remains unaffected. At this stage of understanding, we only have partial and 'mutilated' knowledge (*E* 2p40s2), which constitute the passions and the imagination and which Spinoza refers to as 'inadequate knowledge' (*E* 2p40s2). With only inadequate knowledge of an encounter, Spinoza explains how we can often be subject to superstition. For example, if we experience sad passions, then we often think of the other person or thing as bad (or 'evil'). We then explain our sadness as occurring simply because of an encounter with something or someone who is inherently bad. This makes us passive. Instead, we need to recognise that we do not understand our own bodies and cannot introspect into our minds. We gain insights about ourselves from our reactions to other things. We therefore start to understand (ourselves and the other thing) when we try to explain our initial passionate reaction. For example, if it gives us pleasure, then the other thing must have helped us to thrive in some way (e.g. as food, or by my experiencing your medical or cultural insights) or undermined it (e.g. poison or being subject to hate speech).

Everything finite that exists tries to survive and thrive and its essence is defined by what it does to further this basic aim (its *conatus E* 3p7). We do so by trying to increase our understanding, which defines the richness of the life we can lead, and our power, by which Spinoza also means our freedom and virtue (*E* 4d8). To increase our understanding is therefore our most important achievement. With greater understanding, we are able not only to associate with things that are good for us, avoiding the bad, but also to relate differently to each other. This occurs when we *reflect upon our own abilities* and recognise the importance of our ability to understand and the role others play in helping us to improve our understanding. We do not fight over adequate knowledge as if it were a scarce or positional good. Your understanding of the world helps me; for example, your cure is often my cure. So far, this sounds individualistic, with a sense that we trade ideas that we have appropriated, which would fit with Locke's analysis. However, Spinoza defines singular things in the following way:

> By singular things I understand things that are finite and have a determinate existence. And if a number of individuals so concur in one action that

together they are all the cause of one effect, I consider them all, to that extent, as one singular thing (*E* 2d7).

For Spinoza, all things, including individual human beings, are comprised of parts of parts – mitochondria, for example – and themselves comprise larger entitles, such as societies. We can act as an individual but are also able to join with other human beings (and other things) to form singular things at any given time, providing we 'are all the cause of one effect'. For example, we can pull together on a rope or think together to solve a problem. While doing so, Spinoza thinks of us as one singular thing. We can also be viewed as parts of a whole society with a history. Unlike communitarians, Spinoza does not view our place within society as dictated by our traditional role but by the ways in which we act with others to increase our powers through understanding. This action allows us to develop different areas of culture including arts as well as sciences in ways we cannot predict. With inadequate knowledge, we may view information as a commodity but, with greater understanding, we want everyone to share greater insights.

I will now apply my brief sketch of one aspect of Spinoza's *Ethics* to the political problems that I highlighted in the first paragraph which have arisen as a result of Cambridge Analytica's attempt to alter elections through the use of big data. While we get important information from our passionate immediate response (e.g. reacting to pain can save our lives) it is only partial and – as explained – can block our ability to gain an adequate understanding of an encounter if it is mistaken for a full explanation. For example, if I feel sadness or anger when subject to casual sexism, I may assume this pain arises because I have encountered a bad ('evil') person. A shift to adequate knowledge would involve a greater analysis of the history of misogyny in society and the mechanisms that perpetuate it. A white male Trump voter may be afraid of immigration or women's increased role in the work place. With only inadequate knowledge, he may react by hating or fearing immigrants and women. With a greater understanding of the society, he may be able to move beyond that inadequate knowledge to consider the causes of his fear, such as his precarious financial position within a neo-liberal society, his low status within the workplace or even the fact that his girlfriend left him (an example from Spinoza *E* 5p11). While Spinoza rejects the idea of evil in favour of a view of ignorance, this does not mean that he assumes that with reason we will simply ignore hatred. Our central concern is to thrive and survive – like all other finite things. However, we are aided by properly attributing causes and, I would add, this requires a social analysis. I will therefore apply Spinoza's framework to feminist and critical race concerns, which he did not share, by employing Spinoza's central claim that we increase our powers of acting and enrich our lives by increasing our understanding. Hence, anything that undermines our ability to communicate adequate knowledge is pernicious.

Subordination undermines such communication. 'Epistemological injustice' occurs when an audience does not judge a speaker as credible because, for example, she is female or belongs to a particular race.[42] Sometimes someone may not be viewed as credible because the audience does not realise her expertise in a particular situation. This last example differs from epistemological injustice, which tracks a person throughout her life because she belongs to a group that historically has been subject to subordination. This has come to light as women share the experience of having their arguments ignored at work and of negative descriptions of female witnesses in court.[43] Epistemological injustice is particularly pernicious from a Spinozist perspective because it does not simply undermine the individual speaker and may cause her to doubt her judgements. It also undermines the social body because it hampers the spread of adequate knowledge.

In addition, epistemological injustice or other ways in which subordination is perpetuated can encourage some to be proud and others humble. For Spinoza, pride and humility are problematic because they entail 'great ignorance of oneself' (E 4p55). Again, they therefore block our ability to understand many of our encounters, which always requires the ability to acquire knowledge of ourselves. Relations of domination therefore undermine both the individual but also society, ultimately including those who otherwise profit from it. Following this logic also provides an argument about privacy as well as those filter bubbles that perpetuate subordination by appealing to sexist and racist stereotypes, for example.

Turning briefly to privacy, Spinoza's analysis of the passions gives us a useful way of thinking about this issue. There is no easy line to be drawn between information that should and should not be disseminated. In making this decision, it is not possible 'to err on the side of caution' as both privacy and free speech are important. Some information *should* be circulated and some *should not*. Spinoza himself argued for free speech at a time when it was dangerous to do so. The *Ethics* was not published until after his death in 1677.[44] Drawing from the framework of the *Ethics*, I argue that information that would perpetuate subordination (and hence undermine our ability to join with others in order to further our understanding of the world) should be kept private.[45] Most of the most painful ways in which there have been violations of privacy have drawn from a history of subordination in which the female body has been associated with shame; homosexuality has been viewed as immoral or a sickness; the black body has been depicted as debased. Image-based sexual abuse, outing of gay activity online and racist material are examples of such privacy breaches today. Given that subordination in a society leads to epistemological injustice, it also undermines communication of adequate knowledge to the detriment of everyone, as discussed above. The effect is broader in that subordination maintains fear and other sad passions,

42 Miranda Fricker, *Epistemic Injustice: Power and the Ethics of Knowing* (Oxford University Press 2007).
43 Helena Kennedy, *Eve Was Framed: Women and British Justice* (Chatto & Windus 1992).
44 Benedictus de Spinoza, 'Theological-Political Treatise' in Edwin M Curley (ed, tr), *The Collected Works of Spinoza: Volume 2* (Princeton University Press 2008) ch 20.
45 Richardson (n 38).

along with pride and humility, all of which undermine an individual's and society's abilities to increase their understanding. As explained above, this is not simply an epistemological problem but an ontological one because for Spinoza 'who we are' – the richness of the lives we can lead – depends upon our powers of acting and hence our understanding.[46]

In conclusion, I started by considering the problem of the use of big data to micro-target individuals in the 2016 election of Trump and the Brexit referendum. My argument is that this situation did not simply arise as a result of technological determinism. It required a weak democracy (as outlined by Pateman)[47] and a particular framework of practices and beliefs about humanity, both of which are integral to neo-liberalism. I employed Foucault's outline of the rise of neo-liberalism: (1) the demands that *homo œconomicus* (a self with interests) can make of the state; (2) that individuals view themselves as if they were market actors; and (3) that individuals are treated as if their abilities (and privacy) were merely commodities. I traced a genealogy of the rise of a 'private' self, starting from Locke, drawing on Coleman's[48] analysis of Locke as a transitional figure who takes the first step of envisaging a 'private' self who appropriates things into an 'interior self' by working on both the material world and ideas. In opposition to a neo-liberal ideal, I suggest that Locke's contemporary, the more radical Spinoza, provides a more useful image of ourselves and provides an ethics in which the importance of the communication of adequate knowledge is central to our ability to thrive.

46   Janice Richardson, 'Spinoza, Feminism and Privacy: Exploring an Immanent Ethics of Privacy' (2014) 22(3) Feminist Legal Studies 225.
47   Pateman, 'Self-Ownership and Property in the Person' (n 31).
48   Coleman (n 35).

Chapter 4

Voting public

Leveraging personal information to construct voter preference

Jacquelyn Burkell and Priscilla M. Regan

In 1995, Paul Slovic, a well-known researcher in behavioural decision-making, wrote a paper entitled 'The Construction of Preference'.[1] The point of the paper is deceptively simple: Slovic argues that preferences, rather than being reflected in the results of a decision-making process, are in fact constructed in that same process. Thus, expressed preferences in the form of choices are in significant part a consequence of the environment – including the information environment – in which those choices are made. The data that Slovic assembles in his article, as well as a wide range of empirical results produced since that time, demonstrate that choices can be influenced by arguably irrelevant factors such as the order in which alternatives are encountered, emphasis on selected aspects of alternatives (e.g., positive rather than negative characteristics), or an implicit suggestion about the preferences of others like ourselves. In other words, choices can be manipulated.

Voting is the cornerstone of the democratic process; voting is also a clear instance of expressed – and thus constructed – preference. Traditional political advertising is an obvious and very public tactic to manipulate voter preferences. Recently, however, new and potentially more subtle techniques are being used to shape the information environment, and thus preferences, of voters. In particular, micro-targeting relies on personal profiling to segment the voting public according to characteristics relevant to political opinions and preferences, allowing sophisticated political communicators to use this information to create and deliver 'winning' messages constructed specifically for, and delivered specifically to, selected subsets of the voting public.

Privacy has always been recognised as critical to voter autonomy: hence the secret ballot. Micro-targeting on the basis of a vast array of personal information presents a new privacy-related threat to independent voter choice – a threat that leverages personal information to influence choice. This chapter explores the consequences of the individualised, highly selective, and manipulated information environment on voter preferences, examining the ways in which personal profiling can be used to manipulate voter preferences and thus undermine voter autonomy and processes critical to democratic government.

1 Paul Slovic, 'The Construction of Preference' (1995) 50 American Psychologist 364.

I. Traditional political science theories about political behaviour

The question of why people vote as they do and what motivates their political behaviour has been of endless interest to political scientists throughout the democratic world. Traditional political science theories hold that the key factors that empirical evidence indicates voters attend to in making political choices are political party affiliation, issues of particular interest to them, and individual candidate appeal. In terms of traditional democratic theory, political parties provide an overarching vision for the priorities the government should attune to and the ways the levers of government power should be used. When parties actually operate to achieve these two goals, parties are referred to as 'responsible parties'.[2] Generally speaking, parties in parliamentary systems are better organised than are parties in presidential systems to achieve these goals and are able to take 'ideological' stances to organise their policy goals and to appeal to voters. In presidential systems, especially the US system which is based on a 'winner take all' voting system, parties are less able to achieve these goals and developed more as loose, 'catch-all' umbrella affiliations of candidates and voters with party platforms that are less focused.[3] Because of voting rules, parliamentary forms of government tend to develop multi-party systems and presidential forms of government tend to develop two-party systems.[4] Regardless, traditional political science has highlighted the role of parties in organising the body politic and as mechanisms for bringing relevant information to members and voters. Once a voter identifies with a political party, which is most often the result of parents' party affiliation and socio-economic status, a voter is likely to remain loyal to that party. However, partisan identification appears to be weakening as influences on political socialisation increase and voters are exposed to more political information.[5]

Voters are also attuned to issues that are important to them personally or that they see as of national importance. Increasingly, single issues rather than multi-issue party platforms have become of more central concern to voters, giving rise to what has been termed 'one-issue voting', often associated in the US with social issues such as gun control and the right to choose/right to life.[6] Multiple reasons have been offered for why voters have gravitated to issues more than parties including the lack of clarity about party platforms, the emotional appeal of issues, the financial support issue campaigns have amassed, and media attention. Finally, voters pay attention to the candidate as a person – the candidate's character, personality, professional experience, personal attributes, and views on issues.[7]

2   Austin Ranney, *The Doctrine of Responsible Party Government: Its Origins and Present State* (University of Illinois Press 1954).
3   Clinton Rossiter, *Parties and Politics in America* (Cornell University Press 1960).
4   Lawrence Dodd, *Coalitions in Parliamentary Government* (Princeton University Press 1976).
5   Paul Allen Beck and M Kent Jennings, 'Family Traditions, Political Periods, and the Development of Partisan Orientations' (1991) 53(3) The Journal of Politics 742.
6   Pamela Johnson Conover, Virginia Gray, and Steven Combs, 'Single-Issue Voting: Elite-Mass Linkages' (1982) 4(4) Political Behavior 309.
7   Shawn W Rosenberg et al., 'The Image and the Vote: The Effect of Candidate Presentation on Voter Preference' (1986) 30(1) American Journal of Political Science 108.

Also of interest to political scientists is when voters make up their minds and whether they actually are motivated to vote. Voters' attention span and interest in politics vary tremendously.[8] The question of why voters choose to turn out and vote has been of overriding importance in countries where voting is not compulsory. Theories to explain turnout focus on a range of factors, such as socio-demographic characteristics, political attitudes, and environmental influences,[9] but also recognise the importance of voter mobilisation, or get out the vote, efforts, including motivating citizens to register if required.[10] At the risk of over-simplification, traditional party-line voters tend to vote regularly and regard it as part of their civic duty. Issue-oriented voters are less predictable in their behaviour, depending on how salient their issue is in an election. Candidate-inspired voters will vote if the person is one whom they like or with whom they identify.

Regardless of whether voters are motivated by party, issue, or candidate and regardless of whether they are politically motivated or not, political scientists have long recognised the important role that information plays in voters' motivations, views, and behaviours. Theories about voters' information acquisition and processing tend to begin with some form of the 'rational voter'. In a seminal book on this subject, Anthony Downs identifies the main steps of rationally deciding how to vote and then voting as follows:

- Gathering information relevant to each issue upon which important political decisions have been (or will be) made.
- For each issue, selecting from all the information gathered that which will be used in the voting decision.
- For each issue, analysing the facts selected to arrive at specific factual conclusions about possible alternative policies and their consequences.
- For each issue, appraising the consequences of every likely policy in light of relevant goals. This is a value appraisal, not a strictly factual one.
- Coordinating the appraisals of each issue into a net evaluation of each party running in the election. This is also a value judgement personally tailored to the goals of the voter himself.
- Making the voting decision by comparing the net evaluations of each party and weighing them for future contingencies.
- Actually voting or abstaining.[11]

8   Anthony Downs, 'Up and Down with Ecology: the "Issue Attention Cycle"' (1972) 28 The Public Interest 38.
9   Angus Campbell et al., *The American Voter* (Oxford University Press 1960); Sidney Verba and Norman Nie, *Participation in America: Political Democracy and Social Equality* (Harper and Row 1972).
10   Steven J Rosenstone and John Mark Hansen, *Mobilization, Participation and Democracy in America* (Macmillan 1993); Jonathan Nagler, 'The Effect of Registration Laws and Education on US Voter Turnout' (1991) 85(4) American Political Science Review 1393.
11   Anthony Downs, *An Economic Theory of Democracy* (Harper and Row 1957) 209.

Downs recognises in his model and in the real world that rational voters are limited by the amount of information the human mind can process and by the time a voter can devote to such choices.[12] Therefore, voters have to decide which information to select and which information to reject. To a large extent, rational voters delegate their information gathering and analysis to sources that they have learned to trust. Downs points out that there is a certain amount of 'free information' available to voters from a number of sources including the government, political parties, professional publishers, interest groups, private citizens, and entertainment sources, but that not all citizens receive the same amount of 'free information' or have the same amount of time to process it. Moreover, how well they are able to evaluate information also varies; Downs postulates that it is rational, but difficult, to delegate evaluative decisions because one is not always certain that the agents to whom one delegates have goals similar to one's own.

II. Insights on voter behaviour from psychology

The construction of voting as a fully rational process provides a great deal of insight into the decisions of voters. At the same time, however, there are many aspects of voting behaviour that cannot be accounted for under a model of full rationality. Herbert Simon argued, in 1985, for a 'dialogue of psychology with political science' in order to better understand political affairs. Simon concludes that 'the principle of rationality, unless accompanied by extensive empirical research to identify the core auxiliary assumptions, has little power to make valid predictions about political phenomena'.[13] In other words, Simon believes that the 'rational voter' model put forward by Downs does not fully describe the decision-making processes of voters – and decades of empirical research support this conclusion.

One of the areas of research that provides additional insight into voter behaviour is that of behavioural decision-making, and particularly the study of the heuristics and biases that people use to make real-world judgements and decisions.[14] Many researchers in the area of political psychology have recognised that cognitive heuristics affect political decision-making.[15] Kuklinski and Quirk[16] note that citizens 'use heuristics – mental shortcuts that require hardly any

12   Ibid 211.
13   Herbert A Simon, 'Human Nature in Politics: The Dialogue of Psychology with Political Science' (1985) 79(2) American Political Science Review 293.
14   See e.g. Amos Tversky and Daniel Kahneman, 'Judgement Under Certainty: Heuristics and Biases' (1974) 185(4157) Science 1124.
15   Richard R Lau and David P Redlawsk, 'Advantages and Disadvantages of Cognitive Heuristics in Political Decision Making' (2001) 45(4) American Journal of Political Science 951.
16   James H Kuklinski and Paul J Quirk, 'Reconsidering the Rational Public: Cognition, Heuristics, and Mass Opinion' in Arthur Lupia, Mathew D McCubbins, and Samuel L Popkin (eds), Elements of Reason: Cognition, Choice, and the Bounds of Rationality (Cambridge University Press 2000) 153.

information – to make fairly reliable political judgments'. As many have argued, cognitive heuristics allow decision-makers to operate more efficiently in challenging decision-making environments.[17] At the same time, these heuristics introduce bias and 'irrationality' into decisions, effects that are particularly strong under conditions of information overload,[18] lack of information[19], low levels of knowledge,[20] and relatively low levels of engagement in the issue or decision at hand.[21] Heuristic decision-making is often influenced by what has been called the 'choice architecture', including the information available during the decision process.[22] Subjective estimates of the likelihood of an event (e.g., of succumbing to a disease), for example, are influenced by how easy it is to remember specific instances, which is in turn determined in part by the frequency with which instances are covered in the media. As a result of this type of reasoning, many incorrectly estimate the likelihood of dying in an accident (which is likely to be reported in the news) as being higher than the probability of dying of a more prosaic cause such as disease.[23] Many political decisions, and particularly those made under the conditions noted above, are therefore subject to influence by factors that are, arguably, irrelevant to the decision – including the information environment in which the decision is made. Those decisions are therefore also subject to influence by those who design and deliver the messages that constitute the information environment; in other words, political choices can be engineered.

Edward Bernays first raised the idea of the 'engineering of consent' in a 1947 article of that same name. In that article, he advocated the use of the vast communications network of the time, a system in which 'a single whisper is magnified thousands of times' in the service of 'socially constructive action'.[24] He recognised the power of communications networks as a 'potent force for social good or

17   Herbert A Simon, 'Theories of Bounded Rationality' (1972) 1(1) Decision and Organization 161.
18   Robert P Abelson and Ariel S Levi, 'Decision Making and Decision Theory' in Gardner Lindzey and Elliot Aronson (eds), *The Handbook of Social Psychology Vol 1* (Random House 1985); Naresh K Malhotra, 'Information Load and Consumer Decision Making' (1982) 8(4) Journal of Consumer Research 419.
19   Susan A Banducci et al., 'Ballot Photographs as Cues in Low-Information Elections' (2008) 29(6) Political Psychology 903.
20   Lau and Redlawsk (n 14); Timothy D Wilson et al., 'A New Look at Anchoring Effects: Basic Anchoring and its Antecedents' (1996) 125(4) Journal of Experimental Psychology: General 387.
21   Scott A Hawkins and Stephen J Hoch, 'Low-Involvement Learning: Memory Without Evaluation' (1992) 19(2) Journal of Consumer Research 212; Richard E Petty et al., 'Personal Involvement as a Determinant of Argument-Based Persuasion' (1981) 41(5) Journal of Personality and Social Psychology 847.
22   Richard H Thaler and Cass R Sunstein, *Nudge: The Gentle Power of Choice Architecture* (Yale University Press 2008).
23   Barbara Combs and Paul Slovic, 'Newspaper coverage of causes of death' (1979) 56 (4) Journalism Quarterly 837.
24   Edward L Bernays, 'The Engineering of Consent' (1947) 250(1) The Annals of the American Academy of Political and Social Science 113.

possible evil' and exhorted political leaders, with the aid of technicians in the field of communications, to utilise these communications channels 'for sound social ends':[25] essentially, to lead the public to the 'right' conclusion. The perspective is profoundly patronising, suggesting that political leaders can and should direct public opinion through carefully designed persuasive communication.

Over 60 years later, Thaler and Sunstein[26] brought to prominence the notion of the decision-making 'nudge' – creating 'choice architectures' that 'steer people in particular directions, but that also allow them to go their own way'.[27] Sunstein focuses on the potential positive impact of nudges, asserting that 'desirable nudges undermine neither autonomy nor welfare [...] they can promote both values; indeed, they might be indispensable for them'.[28] Others, however, are not so sanguine about the 'gentle' and at times undetectable shaping of choices by unidentified and unaccountable actors. Tapson,[29] for example, prefers to call what some term the 'social paternalism'[30] of nudging by another name: 'soft totalitarianism'. Kerr and colleagues[31] raised concerns that this type of shaping could be undermining the notion of consent in the context of information privacy; Regan and Jesse[32] worry about the use of nudging in the educational context. Yeung[33] argues that big data analytics of behavioural data contribute to increasingly sophisticated – and individualised – design of the informational context for decisions. She uses the term 'hypernudge' to describe nudges based on this type of analytics, and argues that 'Big Data analytic nudges are extremely powerful and potent due to their networked, continuously updated, dynamic and pervasive nature'.[34]

The potential impact of 'nudges', or 'choice architectures', or individualised persuasive messaging is as great in the realm of political expression as it is in any other area of decision-making. Political psychologists recognise that candidate preferences are formed 'online', updated as new information becomes available, rather than being

25   Ibid.
26   Thaler and Sunstein (n 21).
27   Cass R Sunstein, 'Nudges, Agency, and Abstraction: A Reply to Critics' (2015) 6(3) Review of Philosophy and Psychology 511.
28   Ibid 514
29   Mark Tapson, 'The Soft Totalitarianism of Nudging: The Left's New Social Engineering Tool to Steer Americans Toward Making the "Correct" Choices', *Frontpage Mag* (13 August 2013) www.frontpagemag.com/fpm/200533/soft-totalitarianism-nudging-mark-tapson, accessed 30 September 2018.
30   David Brooks, 'The Nudge Debate' *The New York Times* (9 August 2013) A19.
31   Ian Kerr et al., 'Soft Surveillance, Hard Consent: The Law and Psychology of Engineering Consent' (2009) in Ian Kerr, Valerie Steeves, and Carole Lucock (eds), *Lessons From the Identity Trail: Anonymity, Privacy and Identity in a Networked Society* (Oxford University Press 2009) 5.
32   Priscilla M Regan and Jolene Jesse, 'Ethical challenges of edtech, big data and personalized learning: twenty-first century student sorting and tracking' (2019) 21 (3) Ethics and Information Technology 167. (https://doi.org/10.1007/s10676-018-9492-2).
33   K Yeung, '"Hypernudge": Big Data as a mode of regulation by design' (2017) 20(1) Information, Communication & Society 118.
34   Ibid.

based on a holistic evaluation of available information at voting time,[35] thus rendering the process open to shaping by the information environment. Indeed, although partisanship has traditionally been held to be a stable characteristic, recent data suggest that party preferences are malleable, potentially shaped by information delivered during election campaigns,[36] particularly personal canvassing.[37] There is also good evidence that voting preferences can be shaped in part by the media environment: not only do Fox News viewers tend to be more politically conservative,[38] but also Republican support *increases* in communities when Fox News is introduced,[39] suggesting that the partisan news coverage both reflects and shapes preferences. The notion that political behaviour is being shaped by leveraging psychological research has been raised in the popular press.[40] Indeed, John and colleagues[41] wrote an entire book examining the use of nudges to shape civic behaviour. It is precisely this concern that is raised by Jonathan Zittrain in his article entitled 'Engineering an Election',[42] and Tufecki raises similar issues under the rubric of 'computational politics' and 'engineering the public'.[43] At the root of all of these concerns lies the basic truth articulated by Slovic: preferences are *constructed* in the process of political decision-making – and political decision-makers can therefore be influenced by the information they encounter in the process of making a decision.

Psychological research also tells us that different messages are persuasive to different people: in other words, neither all messages nor all audiences are created equal. A famous theory in the area of persuasive communication – the Elaboration Likelihood Model[44] – for example, suggests that highly engaged individuals focus more on the *content* of arguments, while those less engaged in an issue attend

35 Jon A Krosnick, Penny S Visser, and Joshua Harder, 'The Psychological Underpinnings of Political Behaviour' in Susan T Fiske, Daniel T Gilbert, and Gardner Lindzey, *Handbook of Social Psychology Vol. 2* (5th edn, Wiley 2010) 1288.
36 Rüdiger Schmitt-Beck, Stephan Weick, and Bernhard Christoph, 'Shaky Attachments: Individual-Level Stability and Change of Partisanship Among West German Voters, 1984–2001' (2006) 45(4) European Journal of Political Research 581.
37 David Johann et al., 'Intra-campaign changes in voting preferences: The impact of media and party communication' (2018) 35(2) Political Communication 261.
38 Jonathan S Morris, 'Slanted Objectivity? Perceived Media Bias, Cable News Exposure, and Political Attitudes' (2007) 88(3) Social Science Quarterly 707.
39 Stefano DellaVigna and Ethan Kaplan, 'The Fox News Effect: Media Bias and Voting' (2007) 122(3) The Quarterly Journal of Economics 1187; James N Druckman and Michael Parkin, 'The Impact of Media Bias: How Editorial Slant Affects Voters' (2005) 67(4) The Journal of Politics 1030.
40 Sasha Issenberg, 'Nudge the Vote' *The New York Times Magazine* (29 October 2010) www.nytimes.com/2010/10/31/magazine/31politics-html, accessed 28 September 2018.
41 Peter John et al., *Nudge, Nudge, Think, Think: Experimenting with Ways to Change Civic Behaviour* (Bloomsbury 2013).
42 Jonathan Zittrain, 'Engineering an Election' (2013) 127 Harvard Law Review 335.
43 Zeynep Tufekci, 'Engineering the Public: Big Data, Surveillance and Computational Politics' (2014) 19(7) First Monday.
44 Richard E Petty and John T Cacioppo, 'The Elaboration Likelihood Model of Persuasion' (1986) Communication and Persuasion 1.

more to the *source* of those arguments: celebrity endorsers, therefore, will be more persuasive for those less engaged in the issue. Persuasive messages that rely on social norms as a tactic (i.e., 'do this because your peers are doing it' or 'do this because your peers think you should do it') have been demonstrated to influence behaviour.[45] In at least some cases where the social norms that are conveyed in the message condone anti-social behaviours, women are less responsive to social norm pressure than are men.[46] These and other empirical results emphasise that the most effective political messaging – messaging that will shape preferences and choices – leverages general psychological principles as well as detailed information about the intended audience. In other words, the most effective messages will be *targeted* to specific subsets of the population, and *tailored* to be particularly effective in changing the attitudes and behaviour of the selected audience.

III. Constructing political choice

What forms of targeting and tailoring work to increase message effectiveness? An exhaustive survey of the ways in which information presentation can influence decision-making in the political context is well beyond the scope of this chapter; we will instead present some examples that demonstrate the potential of message design, especially design based on knowledge of specific characteristics of the recipient.

Appearances matter – in politics as much as anywhere else. The mere *appearance* of a political candidate can influence impressions and thereby voting behaviour, particularly for less-informed citizens,[47] or in elections where the electorate knows relatively little about the candidates.[48] First impressions based on appearance drive inferences about the personalities and capabilities of candidates, and these impressions are 'sticky': difficult to overcome, retaining their influence even as new information about the candidate is provided.[49] One of the more interesting demonstrations of the impact of information shaping on political preferences involves the subtle manipulation of candidate images presented to potential voters.

45 Robert B Cialdini, Carl A Kallgren, and Raymond R Reno, 'A focus theory of normative conduct: A theoretical refinement and reevaluation of the role of norms in human behavior' (1991) 24 Advances in Experimental Social Psychology 201.
46 Toke R Fosgaard, Lars Hansen, and Marco Piovesan, 'Separating Will from Grace: An Experiment on Conformity and Awareness in Cheating' (2013) 93 Journal of Economic Behaviour and Organization 279; Tian Lan and Ying Yi Hong, 'Norm, Gender, and Bribe-Giving: Insights from a Behavioural Game' (2017) 12(12) PLOS One e0189995.
47 Gabriel S Lenz and Chappell Lawson, 'Looking the Part: Television Leads Less Informed Citizens to Vote Based on Candidates' Appearance' (2011) 55(3) American Journal of Political Science 574.
48 Banducci et al. (n 18).
49 Christopher Y Olivola and Alexander Todorov, 'Elected in 100 Milliseconds: Appearance-Based Trait Interferences and Voting' (2010) 34(2) Journal of Nonverbal Behavior 83.

New digital technologies allow the 'morphing' of two or more faces into a single image; these techniques also allow the manipulation of the contribution of each original face to the final version. Bailenson and colleagues used digital morphing techniques to create new and individualised versions of candidate faces, subtly altering the candidate images to look more (but only *slightly* more) like the individual to whom the images were presented.[50] Consistent with psychological theory that predicts increased liking of those who are similar to ourselves, viewers who received candidate images morphed with photographs of themselves expressed greater support for the candidates than did those who received candidate images morphed with photos of other people – even though the viewers were *unaware* that the images had been altered. This type of information tailoring would be unacceptable to the public,[51] not to mention manifestly unethical, yet it is also effective and difficult to detect.

Many researchers have documented a 'bandwagon' or 'rally around the winner' effect, in which decision-makers tend to support the side they believe to be 'winning' – for example, by exposure to the results of opinion polls or to online discussions favouring one side.[52] Selective communication of positive poll results in political messages could give recipients the impression that one side is winning, thus increasing support. Although the overall effect is relatively weak, and indeed has been contested in the literature, some personal characteristics seem to increase the effect. In particular, the bandwagon effect has been demonstrated to be stronger for women, and stronger for those who demonstrate specific psychological characteristics: namely, high arousability and low dominance.[53] The effect also appears to have the greatest impact among voters demonstrating relatively weak partisanship when the bandwagon effect induces them to change party alliance, among strong partisans when the bandwagon effect reinforces existing party alliance, and among those with relatively poor political awareness.[54] These results

50 Jeremy N Bailenson et al., 'Facial Similarity Between Voters and Candidates Causes Influence' (2008) 72(5) Public Opinion Quarterly 935.

51 On the acceptability of tailored political messaging, see Joseph Turow et al., 'Americans Roundly Reject Tailored Political Advertising', Annenberg School for Communication, University of Pennsylvania (July 2012) https://repository.upenn.edu/a sc_papers/398, accessed 4 October 2018.

52 Kyu S Hahn et al., 'The Influence of "Social Viewing" on Televised Debate Viewers' Political Judgment' (2018) 35(2) Political Communication 287; Albert Mehrabian, 'Effects of Poll Reports on Voter Preferences' (1998) 28(23) Journal of Applied Social Psychology 2119; Rüdiger Schmitt-Beck, 'Bandwagon Effect' in Gianpietro Mazzoleni (ed), *The International Encyclopedia of Political Communication 1–5* (Wiley 2015).

53 Mehrabian (ibid).

54 Todd Donovan and Shaun Bowler, 'Experiments on the Effects of Opinion Polls and Implications for Laws Banning Pre-Election Polling' in André Blais, Jean-François Laslier, and Karine Van der Straeten (eds), *Voting Experiments* (Springer 2016) 149; Michael Ragozzino and Todd Hartman, 'The Influence of Public Opinion Polls on Issue Preferences', SSRN (30 November 2014) https://ssrn.com/abstract=2532324, accessed 23 May 2019; Schmitt-Beck (n 51).

could be leveraged to target 'bandwagon' messages to those most likely to respond to those messages.

Empirical research in psychology has demonstrated that personality characteristics determine in part the types of messages that individuals find persuasive. Personality is typically measured in terms of the 'big five' personality dimensions: openness to experience, conscientiousness, extraversion, agreeableness, and neuroticism. Authoritarianism has also been identified as a stable personality characteristic.[55] Extraverts have been demonstrated to respond more positively to messages that are extraverted in tone (brighter colours, showing more people, text emphasising extraverted activities), while introverts prefer messages that are more measured (muted, colours, fewer people, text emphasising individual activities).[56] Authoritarianism has been demonstrated to affect receptiveness to different types of 'get out the vote' messages. High-authoritarian individuals respond better to 'fear' appeals that emphasise the negative consequences of *not* voting, while low-authoritarian individuals are more responsive to 'reward' messages that emphasise the benefits of voting.[57] Another important and relevant difference between individuals is their propensity to 'self-monitor',[58] reflected in the desire to 'fit in' to social situations. In one research study, high self-monitors evaluated more positively and responded more strongly to a socially oriented message encouraging voting that emphasised the impact of voting on personal popularity, attractiveness, and status, and also indicated that the majority of their peers were planning to vote. Low self-monitors, by contrast, were more persuaded by a values-oriented message that emphasised voting as a way for the public to express support for important values such as freedom and liberty, and an opportunity to put attitudes and beliefs into action.[59] These and other individual differences have clear implications for receptivity to different types of political messaging, and thus for the design of messages that will be most persuasive for different people.

This is only a small sample of the subtle ways in which political messages can be targeted and tailored for persuasive effect. The impact of such manipulations

55   Steven G Ludeke and Robert F Krueger, 'Authoritarianism as a Personality Trait: Evidence from a Longitudinal Behavior Genetic Study' (2013) 55(5) Personality and Individual Differences 480.

56   Sandra C Matz et al., 'Psychological Targeting as an Effective Approach to Digital Mass Persuasion' (2017) 114(48) Proceedings of the National Academy of Sciences 12714; for other demonstrations of personality differences in response to advertising, see e.g. Jacob B Hirsh, Sonia K Kang, and Galen V Bodenhausen, 'Personalized Persuasion: Tailoring Persuasive Appeals to Recipients' Personality Traits' (2012) 23(6) Psychological Science 578.

57   Howard Lavine et al., 'Threat, Authoritarianism, and Voting: An Investigation of Personality and Persuasion' (1999) 25(3) Personality and Social Psychology Bulletin 337.

58   Mark Snyder, 'The Self-Monitoring of Expressive Behavior' (1974) 30(4) Journal of Personality and Social Psychology 526.

59   Howard Lavine and Mark Snyder, 'Cognitive Processing and the Functional Matching Effect in Persuasion: The Mediating Role of Subjective Perceptions of Message Quality' (1996) 32(6) Journal of Experimental Social Psychology 580.

may – indeed, is likely to – be only a small shift in preferences for a small proportion of decision-makers. In the context of voting, however, small shifts can make a big difference. In Canada, for example, the second Quebec independence referendum in 1995 failed by just over 1% (50.58% of voters against secession vs. 49.42% in favour of the motion). A shift of 0.6% of votes cast would have removed Quebec from confederation. The 2000 US presidential election was decided by a margin of 0.008% (537 votes) in Florida: those 537 votes put George Bush rather than Al Gore in the White House, and changed the future of the United States. Elections to the Virginia House of Delegates have twice (in 1971 and 2017) been determined by random selection after a tied vote.[60] Incremental changes in voting patterns can introduce categorical – and highly meaningful – changes in outcomes.

Moreover, parties engaged in the manipulation of political preferences through message shaping and micro-targeting are unlikely to rely on only one technique. Instead, campaigns interested in nudging voters would employ a number of different approaches to achieve the same end: 'get out the vote' initiatives, for example, that target different sub-groups of voters with different messages designed to be effective for each particular group. This multi-faceted approach is certainly recommended in the area of health communication, where the tailoring of messages to achieve desired behavioural outcomes has had widespread application.[61]

Finally, there is good reason to believe that developing preferences are self-reinforcing, through mechanisms such as confirmation bias, in which decision-makers selectively attend to information supportive of their emerging preferences.[62] 'First impressions' can be powerful and 'sticky' determinants of attitudes, including political candidate evaluation.[63] Carefully structured and targeted persuasive messages might do little to change the opinions of those who have strong pre-existing preferences, but a small but effective 'nudge' to an undecided voter could set in motion a decision-making cascade that could ultimately determine voting behaviour. 'Swing' voters are both relatively common[64] and critically important in

60   Fenit Nirappil, 'Virginia Will Decide Tied Race by Pulling a Name from a Bowl. How Would You Break a Tie?', *The Washington Post* (21 December 2017) www.washing tonpost.com/news/local/wp/2017/12/21/virginia-might-decide-a-tied-race-by-p ulling-a-name-from-a-bowl-how-would-you-break-a-tie, accessed 17 October 2018.
61   Barbara K Rimer and Matthew W Kreuter, 'Advancing Tailored Health Communication: A Persuasion and Message Effects Perspective' (2006) 56(S1) Journal of Communication S184.
62   Eva Jonas et al., 'Confirmation Bias in Sequential Information Search After Preliminary Decisions: An Expansion of Dissonance Theoretical Research on Selective Exposure to Information' (2001) 80(4) Journal of Personality and Social Psychology 557.
63   Milton Lodge, Kathleen M McGraw, and Patrick Stroh, 'An Impression-Driven Model of Candidate Evaluation' (1989) 83(2) American Political Science Review 399; Olivola and Todorov (n 48).
64   Patrick Butler and Neil Collins, 'Political Marketing: Structure and Process' (1994) 28 (1) European Journal of Marketing 19; Stuart Oskamp, *Attitudes and Opinions* (2nd edn, Prentice-Hall 1991).

determining election outcomes.[65] They also make their voting decisions late in the campaign,[66] leaving plenty of time, and room, for persuasive messages to exert their effect.

IV. Micro-targeting: Targeting to and tailoring for individual voters

Effective political communicators are in the business of persuasive messaging. 'Get out the vote' initiatives, for example, are a feature of almost every election in jurisdictions where voting is not compulsory, and messages intended to influence the direction of votes are a normal and universal part of political campaigning. These broadcast messages are designed to encourage voters to cast their ballot, or to vote in a particular way, and the most effective are based on well-established persuasive communication techniques. Research suggests, for example, that voters are motivated to get out and vote by messages that affirm voting as an admirable aspect of character, rather than an action that an individual should take: thus, a message that encourages recipients to 'be a voter' will be in general more effective than one that exhorts individuals to 'get out the vote'.[67] Such persuasive messages, including those that are specifically designed to motivate behaviour based on psychological and sociological research, are a well-accepted part of the political landscape.

Broadcast political messaging delivers the same message to the entire audience. Different audience members could, and no doubt will, respond differently to the presented messages: most obviously, potential voters will be more positively disposed toward messages consistent with their own political positions and views. Given these differences in response to political messaging, it is evident that the persuasive effect of political messages can be increased through *targeting* and *tailoring* of messages.[68]

Targeted messages are delivered to a specific subset of the audience (an associated technique, identified by Turow,[69] is *signalling* to some people that they *should* be part of the audience, and to others that they should *not*). One way to target messages is to communicate a message that is persuasive to most audience members selectively to those who support (or do not support) your political position. In this way, the impact of the message is restricted to a specific subset of

65   William H Flanigan, *Political Behaviour of the American Electorate* (2nd edn, Allyn and Bacon 1972).
66   Karen S Johnson-Cartee and Gary A Copeland, *Inside Political Campaigns: Theory and Practice* (Praeger 1997); Dan Schill and Rita Kirk, 'Courting the Swing Voter: "Real Time" Insights into the 2008 and 2012 US Presidential Debates' (2014) 58(4) American Behavioral Scientist 536.
67   Marguerite Rigioglioso, 'Research-Backed Ways to Get Out the Vote' *Insights by Stanford Business* (17 April 2012) www.gsb.stanford.edu/insights/research-backed-ways-get-out-vote, accessed 30 September 2018.
68   Joseph Turow, 'Segmenting, Signaling and Tailoring, Probing the Dark Side of Target Marketing' in R Andersen and K Strate (eds), *Critical Studies in Media Commercialism* (Oxford University Press 2000).
69   Ibid.

the population. An effective 'get out the vote' message delivered selectively to the supporters of one candidate in an election, for example, could be a winning strategy.[70] Another way to target is to deliver a (generally) persuasive message specifically to those who you have reason to believe will be *most* affected by that message. This verges on *tailoring* (see below), but differs in emphasis: in this case it is the *audience* that is manipulated rather than the *message*. Targeting requires knowledge of the intended recipient of the message: in order to deliver messages specifically to your political supporters, you must be able to identify those supporters; in order to deliver a message that is most persuasive to disinterested voters, you need to identify those disinterested voters.

Tailoring (for which *targeting* is a necessary precursor) delivers to specifically identified individuals a specifically designed message – a message that is designed to be persuasive for those individuals based on information that is known about them. The most obvious form of tailoring is the personal address: contrast a general 'vote for candidate Smith' message with a message that exhorts 'Mrs Jones, vote for candidate Smith'. Personalisation of messages is certainly effective. Personalised 'calls to action' are demonstrably more effective than more general messages with the same thrust.[71] Personalisation is also manifestly evident. If you receive a personalised message, you *know* that the communication is tailored to you.

Other forms of tailoring are much more subtle. Messages can be tailored to appeal to individuals based on demographic characteristics such as age and gender. Tailoring on the basis of political affiliation or beliefs, or on the basis of core values, is also an effective way to improve message effectiveness. Messages can also be designed to appeal to individuals with particular personality characteristics or information-processing styles. Tailoring on the basis of these characteristics will not necessarily be evident to the recipient – and thus the targets of these tailored messages might not be aware that they are subject to communications designed specifically for them in order to influence their decisions and/or attitudes.

One of the important things to recognise about targeting and tailoring is that generally these strategies are revealed only by contrast – that is, in order to know that a message has been targeted and (potentially) tailored, one must know also what (if any) messages have been delivered to *other* people. This does not change the impact of the targeting or tailoring, but it does make detection, and thus regulation, of these practices that much more difficult.

'*Micro-targeting*', as practised in recent elections and discussed in the literature,[72] generally incorporates *both* targeting and tailoring of messages. Both are

70   Zittrain (n 41).
71   Henry Sauermann and Michael Roach, 'Increasing Web Survey Response Rates in Innovation Research: An Experimental Study of Static and Dynamic Contact Design Features' (2013) 42(1) Research Policy 273.
72   Jeff Chester and Kathryn C Montgomery, 'The Role of Digital Marketing in Political Campaigns' (2017) 6(4) Internet Policy Review; Balázs Bodó et al., 'Political Micro-Targeting: A Manchurian Candidate or Just a Dark Horse?' (2017) 6(4) Internet Policy Review.

achieved through the development of information-rich 'enhanced voter files' that integrate information from a wide range of sources to create detailed profiles of individual voters.[73] These profiles combine information about voters from multiple sources: information that is required (e.g., registration information), voluntarily provided (e.g., responses to questionnaires), and passively recorded (e.g., browsing behaviour),[74] enhanced with details that can be inferred on the basis of 'big data' analytics.[75] The resulting profiles allow political communicators to reach particular voters with messages designed specifically to influence them, through traditional means (e.g., telephone calls) or through new media channels (e.g., targeted advertising on social media sites).

The practice of assembling voter profiles and using these to direct political communication (e.g., door-to-door campaigning) is long-standing – and this might lead us to discount the importance of this new era of micro-targeting. Why would this new form of persuasive communication raise particular privacy concerns? The answer can be found in the impact of online behavioural tracking and big data analytics, which together allow for the assembly of far more detailed and revealing voter profiles, which in turn allows for the development and targeted delivery of more effective personalised persuasive messaging, often in ways that are not evident to the recipient.

In his 2014 article on 'Engineering an Election',[76] Jonathan Zittrain examines an important hypothetical scenario that highlights the game-changing reality of social media data mining for political communication. He invites us to consider the possibility that social media data could be mined to reveal political views and political affiliation. These data-based conclusions could be used to target 'get out the vote' initiatives to a specific subset of users: those thought to support the position or candidate that the advertiser (in the hypothetical scenario, Facebook) wishes to promote. What makes this scenario particularly – and *realistically* – concerning is that the manipulation is *not* based on the 'enhanced voter files' addressed in most discussions of micro-targeting. The manipulation Zittrain describes requires no identifying information, and does not even require direct revelation of political views by the targeted users:[77] instead, the hypothetical

73 Colin J Bennett, 'Voter Databases, Micro-targeting, and Data Protection Law: Can Political Parties Campaign in Europe as They Do in North America' (2016) 6(4) International Data Privacy Law 261.

74 Pew Research Center, 'Commercial Voter Files and the Study of U.S. Politics' (2018) www.pewresearch.org/methods/2018/02/15/commercial-voter-files-and-the-stu dy-of-u-s-politics, accessed 23 May 2019.

75 Michal Kosinski, David Stillwell, and Thore Graepel, 'Private Traits and Attributes Are Predictable from Digital Records of Human Behaviour' (2013) 110(15) Proceedings of the National Academy of Sciences 5802; Michal Kosinski and Yilun Wang, 'Deep Neural Networks Are More Accurate Than Humans at Detecting Sexual Orientation from Facial Images' (2018) 114(2) Journal of Personality and Social Psychology 246.

76 Zittrain (n 41).

77 Kosinski, Stillwell, and Graepel (n 74).

targeting is based on very *real* demonstrations of the power of data analytics applied to social media information.

Kosinski, Stillwell, and Graepel caused a stir when they demonstrated, in 2013,[78] that 'private traits and attributes are predictable from digital records of human behavior'. They used data from over 58,000 Facebook volunteers to demonstrate that Facebook 'likes' could be used to reliably predict a range of private characteristics not directly revealed in those data. Their results indicate that Facebook 'likes' reliably predict gender (male vs. female, with 93% accuracy), sexual orientation (heterosexual vs. homosexual, with 88% accuracy for men and 75% accuracy for women), race (discriminating with 95% accuracy between African Americans and Caucasian Americans), religious affiliation (82% accuracy distinguishing between Christian and Islamic affiliation), and political party support (85% accurate in distinguishing Democrat and Republican supporters). Moreover, accurate prediction extends beyond this type of (relatively simple) *category assignment*. The same information was demonstrated to reliably predict age (correlation of 0.75), social network density (correlation of 0.52), social network size (correlation of 0.47) and, perhaps most concerning, the psychological trait of openness with almost the same degree of accuracy as the standard multi-item questionnaire used to assess the characteristic. In order to *identify* these reliable relationships, they required volunteer participants to reveal the personal characteristics that were being predicted (e.g., to accurately identify gender and age, and to complete standardised personality assessments that measured psychological traits). Critically, however, the *application* of algorithms based on the revealed relationships to *new* Facebook users (not in the original sample) does not require that this information be disclosed.

Subsequent research has demonstrated that social media and online behavioural tracking information can be used to predict personality characteristics, with particular success in the case of extraversion and life satisfaction.[79] Moreover, when the judgements based on social media data and judgements made by friends and family are compared with actual measures of these qualities (collected from the individuals themselves), the social-media-based predictions prove *more accurate*.[80] The words, phrases, and topics that appear in social media postings are highly indicative of age and gender, and show (with appropriate analysis) strong relationships to the 'big five' personality traits of extraversion, agreeableness, onscientiousness, neuroticism, and openness.[81]

78   Ibid.
79   Michal Kosinski et al., 'Manifestations of User Personality in Website Choice and Behaviour on Online Social Networks' (2014) 95(3) Machine Learning 357.
80   Wu Youyou, Michal Kosinski, and David Stillwell, 'Computer-Based Personality Judgments Are More Accurate Than Those Made by Humans' (2015) 112(4) Proceedings of the National Academy of Sciences 1036.
81   Gregory Park et al., 'Automatic Personality Assessment Through Social Media Language' (2015) 108(6) Journal of Personality and Social Psychology 934; H Andrew Schwartz et al., 'Personality, Gender, and Age in the Language of Social Media: The Open Vocabulary Approach' (2013) 8 PLOS One e73791.

Other researchers have leveraged photos and photo-related activities to successfully predict personality traits.[82]

These same types of data can be used to predict other private characteristics. Kosinski and Wang,[83] for example, demonstrated that sexual orientation can be accurately inferred from social media profile pictures. Zhong and colleagues[84] used location check-ins to infer a variety of demographic characteristics including gender, age, educational background, and marital status. Religion, relationship status, language, countries of interest, and parental status can be determined reliably from another ready source of information: the apps installed on a mobile device.[85] Twitter data has been used to accurately predict Democratic vs. Republican political affiliation among US users,[86] and such predictions are even more accurate if user information is integrated with information derived from online social ties.[87] Search query histories have been demonstrated to be reliably associated to age, gender, and political and religious views.[88]

This is not, and does not intend to be, an exhaustive list – indeed, such a goal is unattainable, since the list is a moving target. Researchers are constantly harnessing new data sources to predict different individual characteristics – and if there is a message to be gleaned, it is that *no prediction* is out of the realm of possibility, given enough data and enough computing power. Moreover, although any individual prediction of a characteristic (say, for example, political affiliation) is good but *imperfect*, there is no reason why different predictive models could not be used together to more accurately identify the characteristic in question and target the individual with information tailored to their personal characteristics.

The end result is, and should be, disturbing. Political communicators can purchase voter files that include an incredible amount of highly personal information about individual voters, including traditionally protected personally identifiable

82   Azar Eftekhar, Chris Fullwood, and Neil Morris, 'Capturing Personality from Facebook Photos and Photo-Related Activities: How Much Exposure Do You Need?' (2014) 37 Computers in Human Behaviour 162.
83   Kosinski and Wang (n 74).
84   Yuan Zhong et al., 'You Are Where You Go: Inferring Demographic Attributes from Location Checkin-Ins' (2015) Proceedings of the Eighth ACM International Conference on Web Search and Data Mining 295.
85   Suranga Seneviratne et al., 'Predicting User Traits from a Snapshot of Apps Installed on a Smartphone' (2014) 18(2) ACM SIGMOBILE Mobile Computing and Communications Review 1.
86   Michael D Conover et al., 'Predicting the Political Alignment of Twitter Users' (2011) Privacy, Security, Risk and Trust (PASSAT) and 2011 IEEE Third International Conference on Social Computing (SocialCom), 2011 IEEE Third International Conference 192.
87   Faiyaz Al Zamal, Wendy F Liu, and Derek Ruths, 'Homophily and Latent Attribute Inference: Inferring Latent Attributes of Twitter Users from Neighbors' (2012) 270 ICWSM.
88   Bin Bi et al., 'Inferring the Demographics of Search Users: Social Data Meets Search Queries' (2013) Proceedings of the 22nd International Conference on the World Wide Web 131.

information that is integrated with behavioural tracking records and augmented by otherwise invisible characteristics inferred on the basis of big data analytics.[89] That information can be used to develop and target particularly effective political messaging – messaging that has the effect of influencing choice, through 'nudging' and the creation of 'choice architectures' that favour particular opinions or outcomes. The hyper-individualised nature of online communication – the fact that every internet user can and indeed does interact in an information environment structured particularly for them – means that message manipulations are difficult to detect. As a result, voters may be unaware that they are being subjected to invisible persuasion by unidentified actors. The situation is one where intrusions on privacy, represented by the collection and use of personal information for the purposes of targeted political communication, have clear implications for autonomy, which in turn has clear implications for democratic principles and practices – and as such we must carefully consider appropriate regulation.

V. Implications for democracy

One can view democratic theory, particularly liberal democratic theory, as being built on three reinforcing pillars (in italics): the '*self*' or autonomous individual whose 'free will' leads her to choose to participate as a member of a *civil society or body politic* in which she and others in that civil society have the *ability to influence political actors and actions* in ways that are consistent with their preferences. As we analyse the implications of targeting, tailoring, and micro-targeting of political messages, we need to be conscious of each of these pillars, the processes associated with each, and, of most interest in this analysis, the importance of privacy in achieving each.

If the autonomous individual, the 'self', is the basic unit in a democratic system, the question is: how does such an individual develop? Early political philosophers, such as Enlightenment thinkers, to some extent idealised the notion of the self as a somewhat self-evident rational being who was able to know her preferences (self-interest) and make (rational) choices. In early thinking on privacy, Warren and Brandeis[90] referred to the protection of one's 'inviolate personality', a form of this autonomous self. Ruth Gavison underscored the importance of privacy 'in a democratic government because it fosters and encourages the moral autonomy of the citizen, a central requirement of democracy'.[91] Modern political philosophers recognise a more complicated, less fully formed self, affected by the times, individuals, and society around them – a socially constructed self. Julie Cohen identifies a 'dynamic theory of individual autonomy' where the individual is valued 'as an agent of self-determination and community-building' and where 'productive

---

89   Pew Research Center (n 73).
90   Samuel Warren and Louis Brandeis, 'The Right to Privacy' (1890) Harvard Law Review 193.
91   Ruth Gavison, 'Privacy and the Limits of the Law' (1980) 89(3) Yale Law Journal 455.

expression and development [...] have room to flourish'.[92] Without the space privacy protects to engage in the 'conscious construction of the self',[93] individuals' beliefs and desires are more likely to track with the mainstream and expected, rather than with what the self might become if unencumbered with the clutter of constant stimuli and messages. As Cohen elaborates in her 2012 book, the modern individual is widely recognised as a socially constructed, 'situated, embodied being',[94] and privacy plays an important role in allowing individuality and creativity to flourish, and protecting against the tyranny of the majority.[95] Similarly, Beate Rössler argues that 'the true realization of freedom, that is a life led autonomously, is only possible in conditions where privacy is protected'.[96]

Within democratic systems, a number of principles and practices are considered fundamental to the development of an autonomous self. Freedom of conscience, ensuring that individuals can develop their own beliefs and values, represents the importance of such autonomy.

Freedom of speech, the ability to hear others and to engage in discussions with others, is essential to the development of a 'marketplace of ideas'[97] which enables individuals to arrive at their values and preferences. Core to this is the notion that individuals can reflect on what is occurring around them using their 'free will' – that despite the noise, there is an autonomous individual who is independently thinking, perhaps (indeed most assuredly) not rationally, but thinking as she wants to process the incoming information. That, as Slovic points out, her ideas are formed in the process of thinking about what she is learning and hearing around her. The key point is that *she* is the one processing and deciding: there is no 'invisible hand' guiding her thoughts, no outside force 'nudging' her to a particular conclusion.

Assuming for the moment that the development of autonomous individuals has been accomplished, then how is the development of a 'body politic' or 'civil society' achieved and what role does autonomy play? Paul Schwartz[98] anchors a public value of privacy in civic republicanism and the importance of democratic deliberation and of individual self-determination:

> The need is to insulate an individual's reflective facilities from certain forms of manipulation and coercion. Privacy rules for cyberspace must set aside areas of

92   Julie E Cohen, 'Examined Lives: Informational Privacy and the Subject as Object' (2000) 52 Stanford Law Review 1377.
93   Ibid 1424.
94   Julie E Cohen, *Configuring the Networked Self: Law, Code and the Play of Everyday Practice* (Yale University Press 2012) 6.
95   Ibid 110–111.
96   Beate Rössler, *The Value of Privacy* (Polity Press 2005) 72.
97   Alexander Meiklejohn, *Free Speech and Its Relation to Self-Government* (Harper & Brothers 1948).
98   Paul M Schwartz, 'Privacy and Democracy in Cyberspace' (1999) 52 Vanderbilt Law Review 1607.

limited access to personal data in order to allow individuals, alone and in association with others, to deliberate about how to live their lives.[99]

Schwartz notes the importance of protecting privacy in order to generate 'the kind of public, quasi-public, and private spaces necessary to promote democratic self-rule'.[100]

Regan argues that privacy is independently important to the democratic process as the development of commonality, essential to the construction of a 'public' or Arendt's 'community of one's peers', requires privacy.[101] Arendt highlights the political importance of the capacity to think representationally by placing oneself in the position of others, what Kant referred to as 'enlarged mentality', which gives individuals the ability to judge impartially and disinterestedly.[102] Without privacy, it would be difficult for autonomous individuals to come together as relative equals in order to recognise their common interests. This is similar to Rawls' 'veil of ignorance' which is designed to shield particular, differentiated interests and force people to see the interests of all.[103] However, as Beate Rössler notes, the 'public realm is turned into an "Arendtian nightmare" in which boundaries between public and private are blurred, rendering it difficult to formulate or identify a civic commitment to public welfare, or indeed with any notion of "public"'.[104] Culnan and Regan raise this concretely with respect to the campaign mailing lists of the 1990s:

> [T]he creation of campaign mailing lists treats the individual as an assemblage of parts rather than as a citizen sharing interests with others – that is, as a consumer to be appealed to on the basis of certain characteristics rather than as an intelligent, thinking member of the body politic.[105]

Although targeted campaign messages may give individual voters information relevant to them and thus increase their participation, that participation will be geared to protecting or promoting their individualised interests rather than their interests as a member of a political community.

---

99   Ibid 1653.
100   Ibid 1660.
101   Priscilla M Regan, *Legislating Privacy: Technology, Social Values, and Public Policy* (University of North Carolina Press 1995) 226.
102   Maurizio Passerin d'Entreves, 'Hannah Arendt' in Edward N Zalta (ed) *The Stanford Encyclopedia of Philosophy* (Spring 2019 Edition) https://plato.stanford.edu/a rchives/spr2019/entries/arendt, accessed 23 May 2019.
103   John Rawls, *A Theory of Justice* (Harvard University Press 1971). In this work, Rawls talked about (male) heads of household as being in the original position. He later accepted Susan Moller Okin's criticism that this assumption imports an empirical position into the thought experiment. See further Susan Moller Okin, 'Reason and Feeling in Thinking About Ethics' (1989) 99 Ethics 229; Susan Moller Okin, *Justice, Gender and the Family* (Basic Books 1989).
104   Rössler (n 95) 170.
105   Mary J Culnan and Priscilla M Regan, 'Privacy Issues and the Creation of Campaign Mailing Lists' (1995) 11(2) The Information Society 86.

A number of principles and policies reflect long-standing concerns about protecting the formation and health of the 'body politic'. First Amendment 'freedom of association' is designed to protect spaces where autonomous individuals can meet to realise their common values and goals without government interference, and free from surveillance of discussions or reporting of members. However, with more group activities taking place in online spaces, it has become far easier to identify formal or informal members, to document their contributions to group decision-making, and to analyse membership interactions in order to target political messages. This can be viewed as not only as a fragmentation of the body politic but also as a result of a panoptic sorting,[106] discriminating among voters allocating options and messages on the basis of selected characteristics. Such infringements on freedom of association appear to have taken on new proportions as demonstrated by the Facebook/Cambridge Analytica revelations of Russian hackers and by the actions of social bots. Hackers created competing political events, drawing those sympathetic to each cause into likely confrontations during the 2016 US election.[107] During the election, social media bots participated in online discussions, a practice that Bessi and Ferrara found 'can indeed negatively affect democratic political discussion rather than improving it, which in turn can potentially alter public opinion and endanger the integrity of the Presidential election'.[108] This is not unique to the US, as Russian Twitter 'bots' actively denigrated Conservative candidates and promoted Labour candidates in the 2017 UK elections.[109] These seemingly successfully attempts to participate in and influence elections not only raise questions about foreign influence but also underscore how vulnerable freedom of association has become as a result of access to social media data and increased capabilities of manipulating messages.

In terms of developing a 'body politic', theorists and policymakers have also recognised the importance of having the 'marketplace of ideas' operate as a competitive, open, and unbiased market. To that end, for example, the Radio Act of 1927 (US) regulated broadcasters, who were using the public airwaves to transmit their messages, to operate in the 'public interest, convenience, and necessity'.[110] The Act characterised

106 Oscar Gandy, *The Panoptic Sort: A Political Economy of Personal Information* (Westview Press 1993).

107 Matthew Rosenberg, Nicholas Confessore, and Carole Cadwalladr, 'How Trump Consultants Exploited the Facebook Data of Millions' *The New York Times* (17 March 2018) www.nytimes.com/2018/03/17/us/politics/cambridge-analytica-trump-campaign.html, accessed 20 September 2018.

108 Alessandro Bessi and Emilio Ferrara, 'Social Bots Distort the 2016 U.S. Presidential Election Online Discussion' (2016) 21(11) First Monday, https://doi.org/10.5210/fm.v21i11.7090, accessed 23 May 2019.

109 Camilla Turner, 'Russian Twitter "bots" Attempted to Influence Election by Supporting Jeremy Corbyn, Investigation Finds' *The Telegraph* (28 April 2018) www.telegraph.co.uk/news/2018/04/28/russian-twitter-bots-attempted-in fluence-election-supporting, accessed 10 October 2018.

110 Glen O Robinson, 'The Federal Communications Act: An Essay on Origins and Regulatory Purpose' in Max D Paglin (ed), *A Legislative History of the Communications Act of 1934* (Oxford University Press 1989) 3.

broadcasters as '"public trustees" who were "privileged" to use a scarce public resource' – the public airwaves and the broadcast spectrum.[111] The Act emphasised the 'social responsibilities' of broadcasters and the goal to ensure that 'the interest, the convenience, and the necessity of the listening public', and not that of the 'individual broadcaster or the advertiser', was 'first and foremost'.[112] In the 1970s and 1980s, the increase in the number of broadcasting stations and other communications providers obviated an argument based on scarcity and regulations, and as a result the 'fairness doctrine' and 'equal time' requirements were lifted. At the same time, ownership regulations on newspapers, designed to ensure that readers had access to multiple viewpoints, were also lifted. The prevailing view was that there was a significant number of ways that the *public* could get information and that the free 'marketplace of ideas' would function well absent regulation. Targeting of one set of ideas to certain groups and another set of ideas to others, however, undermines such a free market of unconstrained information and ideas, and undercuts the possibility of the emergence of a 'body politic' with some shared understandings of the world around them. The current 'war on truth' provides a profound and telling example of the result of this.

The final pillar of democratic theory is the ability of individuals to influence political actors and actions in ways that are consistent with their preferences. This assumes that people have developed their own preferences, that these have emerged as a result of their autonomous thinking as members within a common 'body politic', and that they can act on these preferences without interference or pressure. The sacredness accorded to the secret ballot attests to the importance of this, as do various laws protecting workers' political activities from management influence and laws protecting anonymous and pseudonymous expression. However, this is the last step in the process, and if citizens have not developed their views not only as individual decision-makers but also as members of a 'body politic', then a focus on this last step is actually meaningless – it is simply too late. Protecting the privacy of the voter as she casts her ballot does not protect her autonomy if it has been compromised at the earlier stages.

VI. Conclusion

The problems and trends that we have identified in this chapter are not new. Indeed, privacy scholars, democratic theorists, and political psychologists have been writing about them since the late 1980s when it became clear that political consultants, parties, interest groups, and candidates all realised that the databases of personal information that had been amassed for voting purposes and for commercial purposes presented a treasure trove of valuable information for targeting voters. These problems have not gone unnoticed but have been reported on and analysed at each stage as the technology became more

111 Erwin G Krasnow and Jack N Goodman, 'The "Public Interest" Standard: The Search for the Holy Grail' (1998) 50(3) Federal Communications Law Journal 605, 609.
112 Ibid 610.

sophisticated and powerful at reaching individual voters – slicing and dicing the body politic. Analysts have raised concerns that voters will be discriminated against, that voters will refrain from participating in politics, that partisanship will be exacerbated, and that single-issue voting will dominate choices.[113] And there has by no means been a lack of proposals and recommendations for addressing these problems – in the United States, for example, usually entailing more effective or expanded information privacy regulation such as expanding the Federal Trade Commision's authority, providing protections for state voter databases, and creating a right to 'reasonable inferences'.[114]

However, none of these recommendations has received serious legislative attention, while voter information has increased exponentially and targeting techniques have become increasingly sophisticated. What was a cottage industry consisting of a few political consulting firms has grown into a vast, global, well-funded network of commercial, social media, and political orga-nisations sharing (or at least making available) reams of personal data on minute characteristics and activities of individuals – data that has now taken on the proportions of 'big data' as it is merged, refined, and processed with sophisticated artificial intelligence/machine learning techniques to create yet more data about individual voters. There is no one point of intervention in this network of data flows that would specifically address the problems posed by targeting, tailoring, and micro-targeting in the political arena. However, as pointed out above, the problems for democratic government are profound and have arguably reached something of a crisis as democratic systems deal with polarised, angry, and fragmented citizens who increasingly only see messages and news with which they are likely to agree. Dealing effectively with these problems will entail dealing effectively with what has become the infrastructure of the online information economy as a whole.

---

113 Daniel Kreiss, 'Yes We Can (Profile You): A Brief Primer on Campaigns and Political Data' (2012) 64 Stanford Law Review Online 70; Daniel Kreiss and Philip Howard, 'New Challenges to Political Privacy: Lessons From the First US Presidential Race in the Web 2.0 Era' (2010) 4 International Journal of Communication 1032; Solon Barocas, 'The Price of Precision: Voter Microtargeting and its Potential Harms to the Democratic Process' (2012) Proceedings of the First Edition Workshop on Politics, Elections, and Data 31.

114 Ira S Rubinstein, 'Voter Privacy in the Age of Big Data' (2014) 5 Wisconsin Law Review 861; Bennett (n 72); Kwame N Akosah, 'Cracking the One-Way Mirror: How Computational Politics Harms Voter Privacy, and Proposed Regulatory Solu-tions' (2015) 251(3/4) Fordham Intellectual Property, Media, and Entertainment Law Journal 1007; Sandra Wachter and Brent D Mittelstadt, 'A Right to Reasonable Interferences: Re-Thinking Data Protection Law in the Age of Big Data and AI' (2019) Columbia Business Law Review (forthcoming).

Part II

Public international and European law

International law and new challenges to democracy in the digital age

Big data, privacy and interferences with the political process

Dominik Steiger[1]

While for some time now the threats to human rights in the digital age have taken centre stage in popular and academic debate, the threats to democracy are gradually starting to receive attention, too. *The Telegraph*, for instance, recently explained to its readers 'Why big data is killing western democracy'.[2] In an academic, sober and thus less alarmist way, the invitation to our workshop referred to concerns 'that big data may jeopardise the future of the democratic process more broadly'. This chapter aims to analyse whether and how democracy is actually threatened by big-data-based operations and what role international law can play to respond to this possible threat.

I. Introduction: Big-data-based threats to democracy

One of the first big-data-based operation that led to a world-wide outcry was the mass surveillance programme revealed by Edward Snowden in 2013.[3] Using software like PRISM or X-KEYSCORE, the United States' (US) National Security Agency (NSA) scans, stores and evaluates not only mass communication but also individual communication on the internet. The contribution of European intelligence services has also been the subject of manifold enquiries.[4] While primarily viewed as a diplomatic affront and a human rights interference, these operations

---

1 The author thanks Fanni Andristyak, Anna Kampfmann and Robert Tonndorf for their valuable help. Unless otherwise stated, all websites were last accessed on 12 March 2019.

2 Peter Foster, 'Why big data is killing western democracy – and giving authoritarian states a new lease of life' *The Telegraph* (24 April 2018) www.telegraph.co.uk/news/2018/04/24/big-data-killing-western-democracy-giving-authoritarian-states.

3 Cf. Russell A Miller (ed), *Privacy and Power: A Transatlantic Dialogue in the Shadow of the NSA Affair* (Cambridge University Press 2017); Jennifer S Granick, *American Spies: Modern Surveillance, Why You Should Care, and What to Do About It* (Cambridge University Press 2017).

4 See e.g. European Parliament, 'Resolution on the US NSA surveillance programme, surveillance bodies in various Member States and their impact on EU citizens' fundamental rights and on transatlantic cooperation in Justice and Home Affairs' (12 March 2014) 2013/2188(INI).

may also be understood as a challenge to democracy.[5] While China is not a democracy, the Chinese Social Credit System,[6] ingeniously portrayed in the latest season of the BBC/Netflix series *Black Mirror*,[7] is a highly informative example of how big-data-based operations work. The basic idea of this system, which will be implemented all over China in 2020[8] and which is already in use in certain areas, is to rate the behaviour of all Chinese citizens. This includes public behaviour, such as paying one's taxes or obeying traffic laws, and private behaviour, such as playing video games or buying diapers.[9] Social media activity is supposedly not yet being monitored, but the algorithm is, of course, secret, so there is no way of knowing for sure.[10] Not only does one's behaviour affect one's personal rating, but also the behaviour and ratings of friends and family.[11] This rating has repercussions in the real world, as certain services and privileges are only offered to people with a certain rating. In 2018 alone, people were barred from travelling via plane or train in China 23 million times.[12] Face recognition, which was *inter alia* tested in the author's main train station, Berlin Südkreuz,[13] is another big-data-based form of state action which might interfere with the political process – for instance, in the event that it is used by the police to surveil demonstrations against the government, which is already done, for example, in the US.[14]

5   Editorial, 'Surveillance: A Threat to Democracy' *The New York Times* (11 June 2013) www.nytimes.com/2013/06/12/opinion/surveillance-a-threat-to-democracy.html. Annenberg School of Communication, 'Mass Surveillance: Why democracy is at stake, and how you can defend it: A MARC and Penn for Privacy Event with Shahid Buttar' (27 March 2017) www.asc.upenn.edu/news-events/events/shahid-buttar-surveillance.

6   Josh Chin and Gillian Wong, 'China's New Tool for Social Control: A Credit Rating for Everything' *The Wall Street Journal* (28 November 2016) www.wsj.com/articles/china s-new-tool-for-social-control-a-credit-rating-for-everything-1480351590; Maya Wang, 'China's Chilling "Social Credit" Blacklist' *The Wall Street Journal* (11 December 2017) www.wsj.com/articles/chinas-chilling-social-credit-blacklist-1513036054.

7   Gabrielle Bruney, 'A "Black Mirror" Episode is Coming to Life in China' *Esquire* (17 March 2018) www.esquire.com/news-politics/a19467976/black-mirror-social-cred it-china; Sadaf Ahsan, 'Black Mirror's chilling social credit score is a reality in China' *National Post* (20 March 2018) http://nationalpost.com/entertainment/television/ black-mirrors-chilling-social-credit-score-is-a-reality-in-china.

8   Rachel Botsman, 'Big data meets Big Brother as China moves to rate its citizens' *Wired* (21 October 2017) www.wired.co.uk/article/chinese-government-social-credit-score-p rivacy-invasion.

9   Nicole Kobie, 'The complicated truth about China's social credit system' *Wired* (21 January 2019) www.wired.co.uk/article/china-social-credit-system-explained.

10 Botsman (n 8).

11 Ibid.

12 Joe McDonald, 'China bars millions from travel for "social credit" offenses' *The Washington Times* (22 February 2019) www.washingtontimes.com/news/2019/feb/ 22/china-blocks-travel-for-social-credit-offenses.

13 Maximiliane Koschyk, 'Big brother in Berlin: Face recognition technology gets tested' *DW* (31 July 2017) www.dw.com/en/big-brother-in-berlin-face-recognition-techno logy-gets-tested/a-39912905.

14 Matt Cagle, 'Amazon Teams Up with Law Enforcement to Deploy Dangerous New Face Recognition Technology' *ACLU NorCal* (22 May 2018) www.aclunc.org/blog/ama zon-teams-law-enforcement-deploy-dangerous-new-face-recognition-technology.

But the state is not the only actor in this field. Non-state actors – companies like Google's mother company, Alphabet, as well as Facebook and Amazon – are collecting, using and selling the data we leave behind while surfing the internet. Aggregating and mining this data – that is, big data analytics – can then be used to produce nuanced profiles of users, thereby making it easier to predict and influence their behaviour.[15] This concerns individuals either as consumers or – more importantly from our perspective – as *citoyens*, and thus poses a challenge to democracy. The best-known example of a private company's power in the democratic arena through big data analytics is offered by Cambridge Analytica. The company employed 1.5 billion so-called 'Facebook dark posts' in the 2016 US election on behalf of Donald Trump's presidential campaign. These posts were advertisements specifically tailored to the psychological profile of Facebook users and could only be seen by the addressee of the post. It has been argued that this technique was highly important for Donald Trump in winning the 2016 US presidential election.[16]

Finally, an example of the combination of state and non-state actors is how Russia has tried to covertly influence voters in the 2016 US presidential election by maintaining large troll farms and entertaining fake Facebook and Twitter profiles that appeared to belong to ordinary US citizens. In reaction, US Special Counsel Robert Mueller indicted 13 Russians, *inter alia* for conspiracy to commit an offence against the United States.[17]

15 See generally Julia Lane et al. (eds), *Privacy, Big Data, and the Public Good: Frameworks for Engagement* (Cambridge University Press 2014); see Facebook's Elections designated page: Facebook, 'Find your voters on Facebook' https://politics.fb.com/en-gb; Kenneth Cukier and Viktor Mayer-Schoenberger, 'The Rise of Big Data: How It's Changing the Way We Think About the World' (2013) 92 Foreign Affairs 28; Kenneth Cukier and Viktor Mayer-Schönberger, *Big Data: A Revolution That Will Transform How We Live, Work and Think* (Eamon Dolan/Mariner Books 2013).

16 Carole Cadwalladr, 'Robert Mercer: the big data billionaire waging war on mainstream media' *The Guardian* (26 February 2017) www.theguardian.com/politics/2017/feb/26/robert-mercer-breitbart-war-on-media-steve-bannon-donald-trump-nigel-farage.
    While prior to Trump, Barack Obama was also using big data in his 2012 election campaign, this has supposedly not amounted to the same degree of manipulation, *inter alia* because the posts disclosed its author. Sasha Issenberg, 'How Obama used Big Data to Rally Voters, Part 1' *MIT Technology Review* (16 December 2012) www.technologyreview.com/s/508836/how-obama-used-big-data-to-rally-voters-part-1.

17 *United States of America v Internet Research Agency LLC A/K/A Mediasintez LLC A/K/A Glavset LLC A/K/A Mixinfo LLC A/K/A Azimut LLC A/K/A Novinfo LLC* Case 1;18-cr-00032-DLF (United States District Court for the District of Columbia, 16 February 2018) www.justice.gov/file/1035477/download, [32]; Bob Abeshouse, 'Troll factories, bots and fake news: Inside the Wild West of social media' *Al Jazeera* (8 February 2018) www.aljazeera.com/blogs/americas/2018/02/troll-factories-bots-fake-news-wild-west-social-media-180207061815575.html accessed 19 February 2019; Scott Shane, 'The Fake Americans Russia Created to Influence the Election' *The New York Times* (7 September 2017) www.nytimes.com/2017/09/07/us/politics/russia-facebook-twitter-election.html; Graham Starr, 'Did You Like or Follow Facebook Pages From a Russian Troll Farm?' *Wired* (12 December 2017) www.wired.com/story/did-you-like-or-follow-facebook-pages-from-a-russian-troll-farm; Nancy Scola, 'How

These are only a few examples evidencing how digitalisation has changed the landscape that international law is meant to regulate. The emergence of the digital age means that international and domestic affairs may now be interfered with in ways not previously foreseen. This chapter sheds light on how big-data-based operations (Part II) challenge democracy and how international law can help in defending it. In order to do so, the chapter will focus on the following two theses: first, both state and non-state actors may undermine democracy through big data operations (Part III); second, although democracy as such is a rather underdeveloped concept in international law – which is often more concerned with effectivity than legitimacy[18] – international law protects against these challenges via a democracy-based approach rooted in international human rights law on the one hand, and the principle of non-intervention on the other hand (Part IV).

II. The power of big-data-based cyber operations: NSA surveillance, Russian troll farms and Cambridge Analytica

There is no single definition of big data. Elements that are constitutive are the collection, storage and use of data on a massive scale with the aim of being able to predict and thus influence the future.[19] This exercise takes place in cyberspace. While many different challenges to democracy through big data operations exist – as the introduction has already shown – this chapter will concentrate on three recent and prominent examples of challenges to democracy through big-data-based operations only. While the NSA mass surveillance system and the Russian troll factories are state-led and authorised operations, Cambridge Analytica was a non-state actor manipulating voters. It adds further complexity that the Russian as well as Cambridge Analytica's operations were taking place in privately owned environments – Facebook and Twitter. How these operations are big-data-based will be explored in the following.

In the summer of 2013, the world realised that almost all global internet traffic is scanned, stored and evaluated by the US government.[20] As this is well

   chatbots are colonizing politics' *Politico* (10 November 2016) www.politico.com/story/
   2016/10/chatbots-are-invading-politics-229598; Jordan Robertson, Michael Riley and
   Andrew Willis, 'How to Hack an Election' *Bloomberg Businessweek* (31 March 2016)
   www.bloomberg.com/features/2016-how-to-hack-an-election.
18   Cf. Niels Petersen, 'The Principle of Democratic Teleology in International Law'
   (2008) 34 Brooklyn Journal of International Law 33: "[F]or a long time, democracy
   was a non-issue in international law." Thomas Franck, 'Legitimacy in the International System' (1988) 82 American Journal of International Law 705.
19   Cukier and Mayer-Schoenberger (n 15) 29, 39; Gloria Gonzáles Fuster and Amandine Scherrer, 'Big data and smart devices and their impact on privacy' (Directorate-General for Internal Policies of the Union, study 2015) 10f, www.europarl.europa.
   eu/RegData/etudes/STUD/2015/536455/IPOL_STU(2015)536455_EN.pdf.
20   Miller (n 3); Granick (n 3); Anne Peters, 'Privacy, Rechtsstaatlichkeit, and the Legal
   Limits on Extraterritorial Surveillance' in Miller (n 3) 145; see also Ian Bron and
   Douwe Korff, 'Foreign Surveillance: Law and Practice in a Global Digital Environment' (2014) 3 European Human Rights Law Review 243.

known and has been the subject of extensive and painful discussions,[21] it suffices to point to the famous dictum by NSA director General Keith Alexander, who said that in order to find a needle in the haystack one needs a haystack.[22] This dictum highlights the crucial role of big data in the context of mass surveillance.

In 2016, the US presidential election was meddled with in different ways. The Russian hacks into the servers of the US Democratic National Committee in 2016 and the subsequent release of e-mails[23] which influenced the US election can be regarded as cyber-interventions, which are measures short of the use of force.[24] While their goal might have been to gain large amounts of data, these operations were not based on big data. Rather, they were specifically tailored to well-known targets. This is different to the Russian Project Lakhta, which was led by Yevgeniy Viktorovich Prigozhin, a Putin ally.[25] According to the indictment by US Special Counsel Mueller, Russian trolls who pretended to be US American citizens , inter alia through stealing online personae of US citizens,[26] posted offensive and often divisive comments aimed at sowing discord and division among the American people, dissuaded voters to vote for Hillary Clinton and organised support for

21   See e.g. Richard A Clarke, *The NSA Report. Liberty and Security in a Changing World* (Princeton University Press 2014).
22   J D Tuccille 'Why Spy on Everybody? Because "You Need the Haystack to Find the Needle," Says NSA Chief' *Reason* (19 July 2013) http://reason.com/blog/2013/07/19/why-spy-on-everybody-because-you-need-th.
23   Thomas Rid, 'How Russia Pulled Off the Biggest Election Hack in U.S. History' *Esquire* (20 October 2016) www.esquire.com/news-politics/a49791/russian-dnc-emails-hacked; Shane (n 17); Eric Lipton, David E Sanger and Scott Shane, 'The Perfect Weapon: How Russian Cyberpower Invaded the U.S.' *The New York Times* (13 December 2016) www.nytimes.com/2016/12/13/us/politics/russia-hack-election-dnc.html.
24   Thorsten Benner and Mirko Hohmann, 'Europe in Russia's Digital Cross Hairs' *Foreign Affairs* (16 December 2016) www.foreignaffairs.com/articles/france/2016-12-16/europe-russias-digital-cross-hairs.
25   Marwa Eltagouri, 'The rise of "Putin's chef," the Russian oligarch accused of manipulating the U.S. election' *The Washington Post* (Washington, 17 February 2018) www.washingtonpost.com/news/worldviews/wp/2018/02/16/the-rise-of-putins-chef-yevgeniy-prigozhin-the-russian-accused-of-manipulating-the-u-s-election; Neil MacFarquhar, 'Yevgeny Prigozhin, Russian Oligarch Indicted by U.S., Is Known as "Putin's Cook"' *The New York Times* (16 February 2018) www.nytimes.com/2018/02/16/world/europe/prigozhin-russia-indictment-mueller.html.
26   Shane (n 17); *United States of America v Internet Research Agency* (n 17) Indictment [4]; Barrie Sander, 'Democracy Under the Influence: Paradigms of State Responsibility for Cyber Influence Operations on Elections' (2019) 18 Chinese Journal of International Law 22; Samantha Bradshaw and Philip N Howard, 'Troops, Trolls and Troublemakers: A Global Inventory of Organized Social Media Manipulation' (2017) Computational Propaganda Research Project Working Paper 12/2017, 11 with further references, https://comprop.oii.ox.ac.uk/wp-content/uploads/sites/89/2017/07/Troops-Trolls-and-Troublemakers.pdf.

Donald Trump.[27] Their work was supported by social bots – that is, automated software programmes that perform tasks within social networks and pretend to be human beings. These bots can behave like trolls, programmed to post controversial comments on websites or on Facebook, or use fake Twitter accounts and other means to magnify the comments of the trolls and make their work more effective.[28] These operations only function on the basis of big data.[29] The trolls created hundreds of social media accounts and many different thematic groups on diverse issues such as the Black Lives Matter movement and immigration control while making users believe them to be Americans.[30] Some of these groups had hundreds of thousands of people following them.[31] One Instagram account which seemingly belonged to the Black Lives Matter movement posted: '[A] particular hype and hatred for Trump is misleading the people and forcing Blacks to vote Killary. We cannot resort to the lesser of two devils. Then we'd surely be better off without voting AT ALL.'[32] Besides these publicly viewable posts, individualised messages were used.[33] Lastly, advertisements on social media platforms were bought – which function and target audiences on the basis of algorithms and are thus based on big data. Russia was very active in Florida and organised a so-called 'Florida Goes Trump' rally. Advertisements for this rally reached an audience of more than 59,000 Facebook users in Florida alone. More than 8,300 Facebook users clicked on these advertisements and were led to a fake Facebook page called 'Being Patriotic'.[34] According to Facebook, between January 2015 and August 2017, fake accounts associated with the Internet Research Agency, a Russian troll farm, bought more than 3,000 advertisements that promoted around 120 Facebook pages, including more than 80,000 posts which were then received by up to 126 million users.[35] These users

27   Jens David Ohlin, 'Election Interference: The Real Harm and The Only Solution' (2018) Cornell Legal Studies Research Paper 18, 1; *United States of America v Internet Research Agency* (n 17) Indictment [32].

28   Neil MacFarquhar, 'Inside the Russian Troll Factory: Zombies and a Breakneck Pace' *The New York Times* (18 February 2018) www.nytimes.com/2018/02/18/world/europe/russia-troll-factory.html: 'Once a blog post was created, the troll exclaimed, "Then the magic began!" The computers were designed to forward the post to the agency's countless fake accounts, opening and closing the post to create huge numbers of fake page views.'

29   Ricardo Murer, 'Big Data and the rise of bots in social media' (2017) www.academia.edu/34799775/Big_Data_and_the_rise_of_bots_in_social_media.

30   Ohlin (n 27) 1, 12; *United States of America v Internet Research Agency* (n 17) Indictment [32].

31   *United States of America v Internet Research Agency* (n 17) Indictment [34].

32   Ibid [46] with further examples.

33   Ibid [54].

34   Ibid [71] with many further examples on Russian involvement in Florida. For further examples of Russian cyber-meddling with foreign elections, see Michael N Schmitt, '"Virtual Disenfranchisement": Cyber Election Meddling in the Grey Zones of International Law' (2019) 19 Chicago Journal of International Law 30, 36f. For examples of US meddling with foreign elections see ibid 38.

35   Sander (n 26) [25] with further references.

were chosen on the basis of big data because of their Facebook profiles and interests.[36]

Turning to the last example, the private analysis company Cambridge Analytica claimed to have won the US presidential election for Donald Trump.[37] It is not a new insight that the private sector collects data.[38] Usually, the main aim is to better predict customers' behaviour in order to make profits more efficiently.[39] But the data can also be used to manipulate voters. How does that work? First, by amassing as much personal data as possible – in the case at hand of nearly all US Americans eligible to vote: 220 million people. This data was collected from various publicly accessible sources, including Facebook.[40] Second, a so-called Ocean Score was extracted from this data which divides people into five basic types.[41] It is said that the algorithm already knows you better than a friend by taking into account only 70 Facebook likes.[42] With 150 likes, it knows you better than your parents and with 300 likes it knows you better than your partner.[43] Third, the results were used for the purpose of direct marketing. For example, if the Ocean Score identified someone as a rather fearful person and in addition that person had liked the National Rifle Association's (NRA) Facebook page, a Trump advertisement with an image of men breaking into a house was displayed on that person's Facebook newsfeed. If the Ocean Score showed that somebody is a rather extroverted person, a parent and had also liked the NRA's Facebook page, a Trump advertisement with an image of a happy family hunting ducks was displayed. Such ads are called Facebook dark posts – dark post because it can be seen only by the target person and will often not even be disclosed as an ad.[44] Four thousand different dark posts reaching between 1.4 and 1.5 billion of viewers were apparently used in the 2016 election campaign of Senator Ted Cruz.[45] On the day of the

36   Renee DiResta et al, 'The Tactics & Tropes of the Internet' (2018) Research Agency 34 https://cdn2.hubspot.net/hubfs/4326998/ira-report-rebrand_FinalJ14.pdf.
37   Cadwalladr (n 16).
38   Issenberg (n 16).
39   Cf. Tal Yellin, Dominic Aratari and Jose Pagliery, 'What is a bitcoin?' *CNN Money* (December 2013) http://money.cnn.com/infographic/technology/what-is-bitcoin.
40   See generally Fuster and Scherrer (n 19) 10ff.
41   See generally Oliver P John, Laura P Naumann and Christopher J Soto, 'Paradigm Shift to the Integrative Big Five Trait Taxonomy' in Oliver P John, Richard W Robins and Lawrence A Pervin (eds), *Handbook of Personality: Theory and Research* (3rd edn, Guilford Press 2008) 114, 114–117.
42   Douglas Quenqua, 'Facebook Knows You Better Than Anyone Else' *The New York Times* (19 January 2015) www.nytimes.com/2015/01/20/science/facebook-knows-you-better-than-anyone-else.html.
43   Ibid.
44   Cf. Hannes Grassegger and Mikael Krogerus, 'Cambridge Analytica/Big data and the Future of Democracy: The Matrix world behind the Brexit and the US Elections', *Diplomat Magazine* (5 March 2017) www.diplomatmagazine.nl/2018/03/22/cambridge-analytica-big-data-and-the-future-of-democracy-the-matrix-world-behind-the-brexit-and-the-us-elections.
45   Cadwalladr (n 16); Nathaniel Persily, 'Can Democracy Survive the Internet?' (2017) 28 Journal of Democracy 63, 65.

third television debate between Trump and Clinton, 175,000 different variations of dark posts were tested.[46] A comparison to ordinary commercial dark posts shows the effectiveness of this tool: click rates increase by 60% compared with non-personalised advertising.[47] The conversion rate, which indicates the percentage of those who click and those who actually become buyers, rises by an extraordinary 1,400%.[48]

Without the use of big data, none of these operations would have been possible. Only big data allows for such a targeted and thus intrusive approach into a person's mind – the effect of which is not yet fully understood but whose ramifications are very well known.

III. How is democracy being challenged? Seven elements of democracy

In the public and academic debate, the NSA system of mass surveillance, Facebook in general and the Cambridge Analytica case in particular are mainly framed as privacy issues.[49] While this is certainly not wrong,[50] the current chapter seeks to expand this view and to understand whether and how democracy is at stake.[51] This does not seem an obvious connection to make. Take, for example, the decisions of the Court of Justice of the European Union (ECJ) in the Schrems case that brought down the safe harbour agreement between the US and the European Union (EU),[52] the Google Spain case[53] or the data retention case of Digital Rights Ireland.[54] In all these cases, the ECJ did not even think about framing

---

46   Grassegger and Krogerus (n 44).
47   Ibid.
48   Ibid.
49   See e.g. Craig Terence and Mary E Ludloff, *Privacy and Big Data* (O'Reilly 2011); Manon Oostveen, *Protecting Individuals Against the Negative Impact of Big Data* (Wolters Kluwer 2018); Nils Gruschka et al., 'Privacy Issues and Data Protection in Big Data: A Case Study Analysis under GDPR' (2018) Working Paper, https://arxiv.org/pdf/1811.08531.pdf; Jim Isaak and Mina J Hanna, 'User Data Privacy: Facebook, Cambridge Analytica, and Privacy Protection' (2018) 51 Computer 65.
50   See below Part IV. B. 2.
51   See, most recently, Graham Cluley, 'New ESET research uncovers Gazer, the stealthy backdoor that spies on embassies', *We Live Security* (30 August 2017) www.welivesecurity.com/2017/08/30/eset-research-cyberespionage-gazer; Amos N Guiora, *Cybersecurity: Geopolitics, Law, and Policy* (CRC Press 2017); see further David P Filder, 'Cyberspace, Terrorism and International Law' (2016) 21 Journal of Conflict and Security Law 475; Emma L Briant, *Propaganda and Counter-Terrorism* (Manchester University Press 2016); Mark Weinstein, 'Encryption Is Not the Problem', *Huffington Post* (23 November 2015) www.huffingtonpost.com/mark-weinstein/encryption-is-not-the-pro_b_8626416.html.
52   Case C-362/14 *Maximillian Schrems v Data Protection Commissioner* ECLI:EU:C:2015:650.
53   Case C-131/12 *Google Spain SL, Google Inc. v Agencia Espanola de Proteccion de Datos, Mario Costeja Gonzalez* ECLI:EU:C:2014:317.
54   Case C-293/12 and C-594/12 *Digital Rights Ireland Ltd v Minister for Communications, Marine and Natural Resources* ECLI:EU:C:2014:238.

violations of privacy as challenges to democracy. The same is true for the German Federal Constitutional Court (GFCC) in its recent cases on digital surveillance.[55]

In particular, the reluctance of the GFCC is rather surprising, given that the Court drew a link between privacy and democracy as early as 1983. In its still-leading case on human rights protection in times of mass surveillance capabilities, the Census Judgment, it pointed out that state-run monitoring measures 'affect not only [...] the individual [...] but also the common good because self-determination is an elementary functional condition of a free democratic community based on its citizens' capacity to act and participate'.[56] This jurisprudence has been picked up by the European Court of Human Rights (ECtHR). The ECtHR repeatedly points to the link between democracy and human rights in surveillance cases and emphasises:

> In view of the risk that a system of secret surveillance for the protection of national security may undermine or even destroy democracy under the cloak of defending it, the Court must be satisfied that there exist adequate and effective guarantees against abuse.[57]

However, no further arguments as to why democracy is threatened are submitted by either court. The same holds true for the Australian Privacy Charter which was prepared by private experts. While an explicit connection between the notions of democracy and privacy is made – the preamble states that a 'free and democratic society requires respect for the autonomy of individuals, and limits on the power of both state and private organisations to intrude on that autonomy'[58] – the Charter does not elaborate on why this is the case.

One of the reasons for this deficit may be that democracy is a contested notion in itself.[59] This rings even more true in the inter- and transnational realm.[60] There are many different ways in which democracy can be understood. In general, democracy means collective self-determination,[61] allowing a people (*demos*, δῆμος) to govern (*kratos*, κράτος) itself. In a representative democracy, this is achieved through regular elections.[62] Another necessary element of democracy is majority

---

55   BVerfG, 2 BvR 1454/13, 6 July 2016; BVerfG, 1 BvQ 42/15, 8 June 2016; BVerfGE 141, 220; BVerfGE 133, 277; BVerfGE 125, 260; BVerfGE 120, 274.
56   BVerfGE 65, 1 [125].
57   See e.g. *Klass v Germany* (1978) Series A no 28 (ECtHR, 6 September 1978).
58   Australian Privacy Charter Council, 'Australian Privacy Charter' (6 December 1994) www.privacy.org.au/apcc/Charter.html.
59   See David Held, *Models of Democracy* (3rd edn, Stanford University Press 2006) 6.
60   Ibid 305.
61   See Dominik Steiger, 'A Constitutional Theory of Imperative Participation – Delegated Rulemaking, Citizens' Participation and the Separation of Powers Doctrine' (2016) 79 Albany Law Review 101.
62   See e.g. Article 3 of the First Protocol to the European Convention on Human Rights.

rule.[63] Other authors highlight the importance of deliberative and participatory notions in order to allow for collective self-determination by the people.[64] At least according to German constitutional understanding, participation in decision making by concerned individuals might be in contradiction to majority rule.[65] While, of course, German constitutional disputes are not decisive on an international level, they nevertheless show the difficulties of defining democracy. In order to avoid theoretical disputes on the exact meaning of democracy and to understand the complex challenges digitalisation poses for the functioning of democracy, this chapter takes a different path: it focuses on seven elements which all form part of democracy. These seven elements are based on the jurisprudence of different courts such as the ECtHR and the GFCC, the views of different UN bodies such as the UN Human Rights Committee (HRC) as well as on democracy scholarship: first, anonymity;[66] second, the electorate's freedom of forming a political will;[67] third, the openness of the discourse;[68] fourth, democratic control

63   James W Prothro and Charles M Grigg, 'Fundamental Principles of Democracy: Bases of Agreement and Disagreement' (1960) 2 The Journal of Politics 276, 282f, 291.

64   Cf. Jürgen Habermas, *Faktizität und Geltung* (Suhrkamp 1994) 151ff, 349ff; Hubert Heinelt, *Governing Modern Societies. Towards Participatory Governance* (Routledge 2010) 8; Jon Elster (ed), *Deliberative Democracy* (Cambridge University Press 1998); James Fishkin, *When the People Speak: Deliberative Democracy and Public Consultation* (Oxford University Press 2009).

65   Cf. Alfred Rinken, 'Demokratie und Hierarchie: Zum Demokratieverständnis des Zweiten Senats des Bundesverfassungsgerichts' (1996) 79 Kritische Vierteljahreshefte 282, 304ff; Thomas Blanke, 'Funktionale Selbstverwaltung und Demokratieprinzip: Anmerkungen zu dem Vorlagebeschluss des Bundesverwaltungsgerichts v. 17.12.1997' in Kritische Justiz (ed), *Demokratie und Grundgesetz: Eine Auseinandersetzung mit der verfassungsgerichtlichen Rechtsprechung* (Nomos 2000), 32–58, 54.

66   Mauno Pihelgas, 'Back-Tracing and Anonymity in Cyberspace' in Katharina Ziolkowski (ed), *Peacetime Regime for State Activities in Cyberspace* (NATO CCD COE 2013) 31–60; Duncan B Hollis, 'An e-SOS for Cyberspace' (2011) 52 Harvard International Law Journal 373; BVerfGE 123, 267 [247f]; BVerfGE 107, 59 [167f]; cf *Delfi AS v Estonia* App no 64569/09 [2013] ECHR 1218 [148].

67   Gregory H Fox, 'Democracy, Right to, International Protection' in Rüdiger Wolfrum (ed), *The Max Planck Encyclopedia of Public International Law*, vol 3 (OPIL 2012) [9]; Christoph Grabenwarter and Katharina Pabel, *Europäische Menschenrechtskonvention* (C.H. Beck 2016) [108], [114]; HRC, 'General Comment No 25: The Right to Participate in Public Affairs, Voting Rights and the Right to Equal Access to Public Service' (1996) UN Doc CCPR/C/21/Rev.1/Add.7 para 1; BVerfGE 123, 267 [219f]; BVerfGE 144, 20 [542], [760]; European Commission for Democracy Through Law (Venice Commission), 'Code of Good Practice in Electoral Matters: Guidelines and Explanatory Report' (2002) CDL-AD(2002)023rev para 26; cf. *Namat Aliyev v Azerbaijan* App no 18705/06, [2010] ECHR 489 [77].

68   Björnstjern Baade, *Der Europäische Gerichtshof für Menschenrechte als Diskurswächter* (Springer 2017) 307, 327; Habermas (n 64) 349ff; Joseph E Stiglitz, 'On Liberty, the Right to Know, and Public Discourse: The Role of Transparency in Public Life' (Oxford Amnesty Lecture, 27 January 1999); BVerfGE 123, 267 [249f]; *Sik v Turkey* App no 53413/11, [2014] ECHR 725 [104].

and accountability;[69] fifth, the acceptance of a majority's decision;[70] sixth, plural-ism;[71] and, seventh, transparency.[72]

Voter anonymity is one of the pillars of election rules in order to guarantee a fair vote.[73] Another reason why anonymity is of particular importance is that it fosters freedom and an open society.[74] While big data as such does not necessarily require that the anonymity of individuals is lifted, Cambridge Analytica and the mass surveillance activities by the NSA aim at nullifying anonymity because their goal is to know as much as possible about their targets. Conversely, the Russian trolls do not care to lift the anonymity of their targets. However, the trolls them-selves need to stay anonymous in order to be effective: if the US voters had known that their tweets and Facebook posts came from Russia and not from 'ordinary Americans', the posts would not have had the same influence as they did.[75]

69 See e.g. United Nations Commission on Human Rights, 'Promotion of the right to democracy' (199) UN Doc E/CN.4/RES/1999/57 para 2(f); BVerfGE 123, 267 [36f]; HRC, 'General Comment No 25' (n 67) para 7; *Sik v Turkey* App no 53413/11, [2014] ECtHR 725 [103].

70 Prothro and Grigg (n 63) 276; BVerfGE 123, 267 [319]; Theodor Schilling, '"Gesetz" und Demokratieprinzip: Eine Inkohärenz in der Rechtsprechung des EGMR?' (2006) 19 Archiv des Völkerrechts 57, 61; *Refah Partisi (The Welfare Party) v Turkey* App no 41340/98, [2001] ECtHR 495 [43]; with more differentia-tion: *Christian Democratic People's Party v Moldova* App no 28793/02, [2006] ECHR 132[64].

71 See e.g. Conference on Security and Cooperation in Europe (CSCE), 'Moscow Docu-ment' (10 September to 4 October 1991), para 6 preamble; *The United Communist Party of Turkey v Turkey* App no 19392/92 [1998] ECHR 1 [57]; *Socialist Party v Turkey* App no 21237/93, [1998] ECHR 45, [41], [45], [47]; *Freedom and Democracy Party (ÖZDEP) v Turkey* App no 23885/94, [1999] ECHR 139 [37]; *Yazar v Turkey* App nos 22723/93, 22724/93, 22725/93, [2002] ECHR 408 [46]; *Refah Partisi* (n 70) [88]; *Konrad v Germany* App no 35504/03, ECHR 2006-XIII; *Manole v Moldova* App no 13936/02, [2010] ECHR 1112 [95]; *Centro Europa 7 S.R.L. and Di Stefano v Italy* App no 38433/09 [2012] ECHR 974 [129]; Aernout Nieuwenhuis, 'The Con-cept of Pluralism in the Case-Law of the European Court of Human Rights' (2007) 3 European Constitutional Law Review 367, 384: '(P)luralism forms an essential part of the concept of democracy.'

72 E.g. United Nations Commission on Human Rights (n 69); Charles F Bahmueller, *Elements of Democracy: The Fundamental Principles, Concepts, Social Foundations, and Process for Democracy* (Center for Civic Education 2007) 106; BVerfGE 123, 267 [357f]; *Yumak and Sadak v Turkey* App no 10226/03 [2007] ECHR 89 [147].

73 The other fundamental rules are that the vote has to be general, free and that all votes need to count equally, cf. International Covenant on Civil and Political Rights, art. 25(b); Niels Petersen, 'Elections, Right to Participate in, International Protection', *The Max Planck Encyclopedia of Public International Law* (October 2012) paras 3ff, http://opil.ouplaw.com/view/10.1093/law:epil/9780199231690/law-9780199231690-e785; for Europe see European Commission for Democracy Through Law (Venice Commission), 'Code of Good Practice in Electoral Matters: Guidelines and Explanatory Report' (2002) CDL-AD (2002)023rev2-cor 5ff.

74 Christopher Slobogin, *Privacy at Risk: The New Government Surveillance and the Fourth Amendment* (University of Chicago Press 2008) 159.

75 Ohlin (n 27) 14.

The electorate's freedom of forming a political will does not necessarily seem to be challenged by big data operations, even if these are aimed at predicting future conduct.[76] However, Cambridge Analytica and the Russian trolls – using techniques different to those of the NSA[77] – tried to do just that: by (micro-)targeting voters with their 'information', they aimed at influencing voters' behaviour. But why is that problematic? Political marketing has always sought to influence voters. In some European states, political advertisements are even privileged during election times and television stations are obliged to air them.[78] However, TV advertising works differently compared to social media ads on Facebook or Twitter. Broadcasters, unlike internet service providers, bear special responsibilities. The posts by the Russians and by Cambridge Analytica were embedded in entirely different environments. In the words of a German constitutional judge: 'One of the most important tasks of television and radio in a democratic state is to enable the citizens to form their own views through the most diverse, deep and balanced information possible.'[79] While this is an ideal that even public broadcasting cannot always attain, it is clear that neither Facebook nor Twitter come close to achieving it, as the ubiquity of fake news shows.[80] Fake news certainly impairs the process of forming a democratic will and taints the discourse. However, not all tweets or posts by the Russians or by Cambridge Analytica can be said to have been lies. Some seemed to be 'only' tendentious and oversimplified matters and were thus comparable to typical advertisements. Furthermore, pluralism, acceptance of a majority's decision and democratic control did not seem affected by the actions of Russian trolls and Cambridge Analytica. Is everything all right, then? No. Let us take a step back and take a closer look at the environment in which the speech acts take place. This is of crucial importance: both Twitter and Facebook's environments are characterised by echo chambers and filter bubbles,[81] and are thus in themselves anti-pluralistic. Both Twitter and Facebook lack transparency, which has

---

76   For the limits of the predictive analytics of big data operations, see generally Fuster and Scherrer (n 19) 11 with further references.

77   While the Chinese social rating system tries to influence behaviour – in fact, this is its raison d'etre – it is not about voting behaviour.

78   E.g. in Poland, cf. 1992 Broadcasting Act, art. 24; 2011 Election Code Act, arts 117–122; Beata Klimkiewicz, 'PL – Poland' in Maja Cappello (ed), *Media Coverage of Elections: The Legal Framework in Europe* (IRIS Special, European Audiovisual Observatory 2017) 89, 91f.

79   BVerfGE 136, 9 [126] (separate opinion of Justice Paulus).

80   CORDIS, 'Media Accountability and Transparency in Europe' (1 February 2010) https://cordis.europa.eu/project/rcn/94354/reporting/en. See also Hunt Allcott and Matthew Gentzkow, 'Social Media and Fake News in the 2016 Election' (2017) 31 Journal of Economic Perspectives 211; Björnstern Baade, 'Fake News and International Law' (2018) European Journal of International Law 2018 1357, 1362.

81   Eli Pariser, *The Filter Bubble: What the Internet is Hiding from You* (Penguin 2011); and already Cass R Sunstein, *Echo Chambers: Bush v. Gore. Impeachment, and Beyond* (Princeton University Press 2001). But see Elizabeth Dubois and Grant Blank, 'The Echo Chamber is Overstated: The Moderating Effect of Political Interest and Diverse Media' (2018) 21 Information, Communication & Society 729.

made it possible for the Russians to work with fake accounts. Both Twitter and Facebook allow for one-on-one communication that cannot be viewed by outsiders and thus cannot be democratically challenged or controlled, be it by the media or by an electoral commission whose task it is to ensure fair and free elections.[82] In contrast, TV spots are by their very nature visible to all and open to public challenge and control. In addition, the entire process of who is targeted and who is shown a post is steered by algorithms. Algorithms are a black box and currently not subject to external control, which poses an additional accountability problem.[83] Moreover, the individual does not know that a Twitter or Facebook account is fake and may not even know that certain posts they see have been paid for: Contrary to Article 6 of the EU Directive on Electronic Commerce,[84] Facebook's terms and conditions expressly stated that Facebook does not always characterise paid services and communications as such. This was only changed in April 2019.[85] Lastly, because of this lack of transparency, individuals might not even realise that they are in a filter bubble. Thus, individualised advertising lacks a public resonance space in which the ads can be discussed and questioned. It is not by chance that the advertising is called dark post. This fragmentation negatively affects the public discourse. Pluralism is also jeopardised by these mechanisms, since awareness of other views is the minimum prerequisite for pluralism. Differing opinions do not exist in filter bubbles. Through this, the environments of Facebook and Twitter lead to a decline in the acceptance of majority decisions and the democratic system as a whole.

While these findings cannot be transferred to the system of mass surveillance, mass surveillance is also problematic from a democratic point of view, as held by the above-mentioned cases of the GFCC and the ECtHR.[86] Here, the chilling effect of mass surveillance on individual behaviour is viewed critically[87] as it upsets anonymity, curbs the electorate's freedom of forming a political will and

---

82   But see the new regulations by Facebook which provide that after 7 May 2018, all ads will be posted in the Ad Archive, together with other information such as amount spent, the number of ads, demographic information such as location, gender and age of the audience, and the name of the client, www.facebook.com/help/1991443604424859. However, it still needs to be made sure that this includes all 'political ads', cf. Herb Lin, 'Developing Responses to Cyber-Enabled Information Warfare and Influence Operations' *Lawfare Blog* (6 September 2018) www.lawfareblog.com/developing-responses-cyber-enabled-information-warfare-and-influence-operation.

83   Cf. e.g. Anton Vedder and Laurens Naudts, 'Accountability for the Use of Algorithms in a Big Data Environment' (2017) 31 International Review of Law, Computers & Technology 206.

84   Council Directive 2000/31/EC on certain legal aspects of information society services, in particular electronic commerce, in the Internal Market [2000] OJ L178/1 (Directive on electronic commerce).

85   www.facebook.com/legal/terms/previous; www.law.kuleuven.be/citip/en/news/item/facebooks-revised-policies-and-terms-v1-2.pdf, p. 44 f.

86   See n 56–57.

87   Cf. David M Howard, 'Can Democracy Withstand the Cyber Age? 1984 in the 21st Century' (2018) 69 Hastings Law Journal 1355, 1368f with further references.

jeopardises the openness of discourse:[88] '[T]he evidence is mounting: Americans are staying away from the political process, censoring what they say, write, and research, limiting who they talk to, and avoiding cultural or religious communities because of surveillance.'[89] Furthermore, dissent and thus pluralism are threatened.[90] Lastly, democratic control, oversight and accountability of secret services is lacking.[91]

While not all elements of democracy may be challenged by the three big-data-based threats to democracy outlined in this chapter, all of them challenge certain elements of democracy and thus democracy in general, albeit with varying intensity. In the next step, it shall be analysed how public international law may protect against these challenges to democracy.

IV. The ability of international law to protect democracy

In order for international law to protect democracy in the digital age it must be applicable in cyberspace (below A) and provide substantive norms that are able to protect democracy. Both human rights norms (below B) and the principle of non-intervention (below C) play an important role in this regard and help to safeguard democracy.

A. Big data and the application of public international law to cyberspace

For public international law, the territory of a state is the traditional space of concern. But this territory has supposedly been transcended in the digital age. While, in reality, territory is still of utmost importance, as proven *inter alia* by the refugee crisis and the election of a US president who wants to build a 'beautiful wall'[92] to keep out foreigners, it is indeed true that a new space has come into being. This understanding can, for example, be found in the new Chinese National Military

---

88 PEN America, 'Chilling Effects: NSA Surveillance Drives U.S. Writers to Self-Censor' (12 November 2013) www.pen.org/sites/default/files/Chilling%20Effects_PEN%20American.pdf.

89 Brynne O'Neal, 'What Americans Actually Do When the Government Is Watching' *Brennan Center for Justice* (20 July 2015) www.brennancenter.org/blog/what-americans-actually-do-when-government-watching.

90 See e.g. Elizabeth Stoycheff, 'Under Surveillance: Examining Facebook's Spiral of Silence Effects in the Wake of NSA Internet Monitoring' (2016) 93 Journalism and Mass Communication Quarterly 296.

91 Hans Born and Ian Leigh, 'Democratic Accountability of Intelligence Services' (2007) Geneva Centre for the Democratic Control of Armed Forces, Policy Paper No 19, www.dcaf.ch/sites/default/files/publications/documents/PP19_Born_Leigh.pdf; Jan-Hendrik Dietrich et al. (eds), *Nachrichtendienste im demokratischen Rechtsstaat* (Mohr Siebeck 2018).

92 See e.g. Glenn Kessler, 'Fact Checker Analysis: President Trump says his "beautiful wall" is being built. Nope' *The Washington Post* (Washington, 5 April 2018) www.washingtonpost.com/news/fact-checker/wp/2018/04/05/president-trump-says-his-beautiful-wall-is-being-built-nope.

Strategy. It states that the military must defend Chinese territory, air, territorial waters, space – and now also cyberspace.[93] While the first four spaces are governed by states, the governance of cyberspace is in many respects still unclear.[94] In the beginning of the internet, it was declared to be free from the rule of states.[95] Today, instead of 'code is law'[96] – implying that cyberspace is not governed by law but by technology and thus in an anarchist way – rather 'law is law' applies to cyberspace, with international law playing an important role in governing it.[97] This has been aptly recognised by now.[98] The current norms of international law apply not only outside but also inside the digitalised world.[99]

B. Human rights and the protection of democracy

The threats to democracy identified above can be contained by existing human rights norms, which in turn are strengthened and reinforced by following a democracy approach.

I. Preliminary questions of application

Before turning to the substantive human rights norms, two preliminary questions must be addressed. The first pertains to the application *ratione loci*, the other to the application to private actors.

93 M Taylor Fravel, 'China's Changing Approach to Military Strategy: The Science of Military Strategy from 2001 and 2013' in Joe McReynolds (ed), *China's Evolving Military Strategy* (Jamestown Foundation 2017), 40, 54; John Costello and Peter Mattis, 'Electronic Warfare and the Renaissance of Chinese Information Operations' in McReynolds (n 93), 173, 185; Academy of Military Science, *The Science of Military Strategy* (2013), for a copy in Chinese: https://fas.org/nuke/guide/china/sms-2013.pdf.

94 The German Chancellor Angela Merkel in 2013 even called it: 'Neuland': Carsten Knop, 'Angela Merkel im #Neuland der Häme', *Frankfurter Allgemeine Zeitung* (19 June 2013) www.faz.net/aktuell/wirtschaft/wirtschaftspolitik/obama-besuch-in-berlin-angela-merkel-im-neuland-der-haeme-12237056.html.

95 See e.g. Barbara M Ryga, 'Cyberporn: Contemplating the First Amendment in Cyberspace' (1995) 6 Seton Hall Constitutional Law Journal 221.

96 Lawrence Lessig, *Code: And Other Laws of Cyberspace* (Basic Books 1999) 6; Lawrence Lessig, *Code: And Other Laws of Cyberspace, Version 2.0* (2nd edn, Basic Books 2006) 1; Uta Kohl, 'Jurisdiction in Cyberspace' in Nicholas Tsagourias and Russell Buchan (eds), *Research Handbook on International Law and Cyberspace* (Edward Elgar 2015) 30ff.

97 Brian J Egan, 'International Law and Stability in Cyberspace' (2017) 35 Berkeley Journal of International Law 169, 171; Harold Koh, 'International Law in Cyberspace' (2012) 54 Harvard International Law Journal 1, 3.

98 Stefanie Schmahl, 'Regulierung des Cyberspace' (2018) 73 Zeitschrift für öffentliches Recht 3, 5.

99 Cf. Jack Goldsmith and Tim Wu, *Who Controls the Internet? Illusions of a Borderless World* (Oxford University Press 2006); Anders Henriksen, 'Politics and the development of legal norms in cyber space' in Karsten Friis and Jens Ringsmose (eds), *Conflict in Cyber Space: Theoretical, Strategic and Legal Perspectives* (Routledge 2016) 151–164.

The threat to privacy and communication in the digital age is – different from earlier times – not based on the locality of either the user or the violator.[100] Both can be anywhere. So, do human rights apply *ratione loci*? Generally, human rights only apply to public officials acting on the territory of their home state. If the act is carried out outside a state's territory, the question of extra-territorial application of human rights arises. But cyberspace is not detached from territory:[101] human rights intrusions are necessarily carried out physically by an actual person (or an algorithm that has been programmed by an actual person) which is located on the territory of a state.[102] As long as state officials act on the territory of their home state, they will be bound by human rights norms, no matter where the target person is situated.[103] This is also the view of the HRC[104] as well as of the ECtHR.[105] Thus, human right norms will generally apply in cyberspace on a territorial basis.

The second preliminary observation concerns the application of human rights to private companies. It is undisputed that *de facto* private companies can also infringe upon human rights. However, it is far from clear whether and how human rights *de jure* bind private individuals. Indirectly, human rights are applied to

100 Cf. Martha Finnemore and Duncan B Hollis, 'Constructing Norms for Global Security' (2016) 110 American Journal of International Law 1; Jordan J Paust, 'Can you hear me now? Private Communication, National Security, and the Human Rights Disconnect' (2015) 15 Chicago Journal of International Law 612; Marko Milanovic, 'Human Rights Treaties and Foreign Surveillance: Privacy in the Digital Age' (2015) 56 Harvard International Law Journal 81.

101 Mark A Lemley, 'Place and Cyberspace' (2003) 91 California Law Review 521; Pieter J Slot and Mielle Bulterman, *Globalisation and Jurisdiction* (Kluwer Law International 2004) 113ff; Joel Trachtmann, 'Cyberspace, Sovereignty, Jurisdiction and Modernism' (1998) 5 Indiana Journal of Global Legal Studies 561, 577.

102 Russell Buchan and Nicholas Tsagourias, 'Non-State Actors and Responsibility in Cyberspace: State Responsibility, Individual Criminal Responsibility and Issues of Evidence' (2016) 21 Journal of Conflict and Security Law 377, 379f; Jason Healey, 'Beyond Attribution: Seeking National Responsibility for Cyber Attacks' (Atlantic Council, Issue Brief 2011) 6, www.atlanticcouncil.org/images/files/publication_p dfs/403/022212_ACUS_NatlResponsibilityCyber.PDF, 9; see in general David Gray and Stephen E Henderson (eds), *The Cambridge Handbook of Surveillance Law* (Cambridge University Press 2017); Kriangsak Kittichaisaree, *Public International Law of Cyberspace* (Springer 2017); Constantine Antonopoulos, 'State responsibility in cyberspace' in Nicholas Tsagourias and Russell Buchan (eds), *Research Handbook on International Law and Cyberspace* (Edward Elgar 2015) 55.

103 Schmahl (n 98) 13; Martin Weiler, 'The Right to Privacy in the Digital Age: the Commitment to Human Rights Online' (2014) 58 German Yearbook of International Law 654.

104 See HRC, 'Concluding observations on the fourth periodic report of the United States of America' (23 April 2014) CCPR/C/USA/CO/4 paras 4, 22; Ben Quinn, 'United Nations Human Rights Committee Resolves to Protect Privacy' *The Guardian* (26 November 2014) www.theguardian.com/law/2014/nov/26/united-na tions-human-rights-privacy-security.

105 *Liberty v UK* App no 58243/00, [2011] ECHR 1273 [64ff].

private individuals via a state's 'duty to protect'.[106] According to this duty, a state must, under certain circumstances, protect individuals from *de facto* human rights violations by other private actors.[107] What is striking here is that the state will usually protect the former by interfering with the human rights of the latter. The duty to protect is recognised by the HRC[108] and the ECtHR[109], among others. In its Google Spain decision,[110] in which the ECJ developed the right to be forgotten, the Court did not directly engage with this question. However, the ECJ found that Google is required to delete certain search results and stated:

> [T]he activity of a search engine [...] affect[s] significantly [...] the fundamental rights to privacy and to the protection of personal data. [T]he operator of the search engine [...] must ensure [...] that effective and complete protection of data subjects, in particular of their right to privacy may actually be achieved.[111]

This decision is not based on fundamental rights as such, but on the European Data Protection Directive,[112] which was an emanation of the duty to protect by enforcing the right to privacy within third-party relationships. This shows that at least in the European context the right to privacy, mediated formerly through the European Data Protection Directive and now the General Data Protection Regulation (GDPR),[113] is binding upon companies as well.

2. Substantive human rights norms: The right to democratic participation and the right to privacy

An obvious connection between human rights and democracy is made by Article 25 of the International Covenant on Civil and Political Rights (CCPR) and Article

106 Cf. Eckart Klein, 'The Duty to Protect and to Ensure Human Rights Under the International Covenant on Civil and Political Rights' in Eckart Klein (ed), *The Duty to Protect and to Ensure Human Rights* (Berliner Wissenschaftsverlag 2000) 295–318.
107 Frédéric Mégret, 'Nature of Obligations' in Daniel Moeckli, Sangeeta Shah and Sandesh Sivakumaran (eds), *International Human Rights Law* (3rd edn, Oxford University Press 2018) 86, 97f; Olivier De Schutter, *International Human Rights Law* (Cambridge University Press 2010) 379ff.
108 See e.g. HRC, 'General Comment No 36: Right to Life' (2018) CCPR/C/GC/36 paras 18ff.
109 See e.g. *X and Y v Netherlands*, Series A no 91 (ECtHR, 26 March 1985) [23]; *Plattform 'Ärzte für das Leben' v Austria*, Series A no 139 (ECtHR, 21 June 1988) [23]; *Ouranio Toxo v Greece* App no 74989/01, ECHR 2005-X [37]; *Khurshid Mustafa & Tarzibachi v Sweden* App no 23883/06, [2011] ECHR 1277 [32].
110 *Google Spain* (n 53).
111 Ibid [38].
112 Directive 95/46/EC of the European Parliament and of the Council on the protection of individuals with regard to the processing of personal data and on the free movement of such data (Data Protection Directive) [1995] OJ L 281/31.
113 Regulation (EU) 2016/679 of the European Parliament and of the Council on the protection of natural persons with regard to the processing of personal data and on the free movement of such data, and repealing Directive 95/46/EC (General Data Protection Regulation) [2016] OJ L 119/1.

3(1) of the First Optional Protocol to the European Convention on Human Rights (ECHR). Both articles guarantee that, in essence, representatives must be 'freely chosen'. According to the HRC, this presupposes that 'the free expression of the will of electors' needs to be ensured,[114] 'without undue influence or coercion of any kind which may distort or inhibit the free expression of the elector's will. Voters should be able to form opinions independently, free of violence or threat of violence, compulsion, inducement or manipulative interference of any kind.'[115] While both norms do not directly bind individuals or states interfering with a foreign election,[116] it is recognised that the freedom to vote can also indirectly be infringed upon by individuals.[117] This shows that states are generally under a duty to protect their own elections against inside or outside interference and thus against manipulations as they were undertaken by Cambridge Analytica and Project Lakhta.

Turning to the right to privacy, all international human rights documents as well as the constitutions of most democratic states provide for a right to private life,[118] which also protects personal data.[119] In addition, specific digital rights exist. The EU Charter of Fundamental Rights provides for an explicit right to the protection of personal data in Article 8. A pioneer in this regard is the Council of Europe, which as early as 1981 adopted the Convention on the Protection of Individuals in the Automatic Processing of Personal Data.[120]

114 HRC, 'General Comment No 25' (n 67) para 9.
115 Ibid para 19.
116 See generally Sarah Joseph and Sam Dipnall, 'Scope of Application' in Moeckli, Shah and Sivakumaran (n 107) 110, 111.
117 *Communist Party of Russia v Russia* App no 29400/05, [2012] ECHR 1050, [124]; European Commission for Democracy Through Law (Venice Commission), 'Code of Good Practice in Electoral Matters: Guidelines and Explanatory Report' (2002) CDL-AD(2002)023rev, para 26.
118 See e.g. International Covenant on Civil and Political Rights, arts 17 and 23(1); European Convention on Human Rights, art. 8; Charter of Fundamental Rights of the European Union, art. 7.
119 If more than one person is involved, the freedom of correspondence and communication may be applicable, see e.g. International Covenant on Civil and Political Rights, art. 19; European Convention on Human Rights, art. 10; Charter of Fundamental Rights of the European Union, art. 11. Although the freedom of correspondence stems from a time where e-mail and WhatsApp were yet unknown, it can also be applied in the digital age. *Kennedy v UK* App no 26839/05, [2008] ECHR 1575, [118]; *Copeland v UK* App no 62617/00, [2007] ECHR 253, [41]; critically assessing the adequacy of that protection: Paust (n 100); Carly Nyst and Tomaso Falchetta, 'The Right to Privacy in the Digital Age' (2017) 9 Journal of Human Rights Practice 104; Jacopo Coccoli, 'The Challenges of New Technologies in the Implementation of Human Rights: an Analysis of Some Critical Issues in the Digital Era' (2017) 1 Peace Human Rights Governance 223.
120 Council of Europe Convention for the Protection of Individuals with regard to Automatic Processing of Personal Data [1981] ETS 108.

Big data operations may interfere with the right to protection of personal data and the right to privacy. This is undisputed for mass surveillance operations.[121] But is this also the case for the Cambridge Analytica and the Russian troll operations? Different from the mass surveillance cases, they only took place within social networks. The collection and storage of personal data by private companies may interfere with the right to privacy.[122] However, Facebook users have agreed to the collection and use of their data by Facebook.[123] So why would the right to privacy be interfered with? It is important to understand that the use and disclosure of data can generate new data. This would concern the compilation of an Ocean Score by Cambridge Analytica, which is of a new and different quality to the original data and therefore amplifies the implications of data collection with regard to potential interferences.[124] While the General Data Protection Regulation does not directly apply *ratione temporis* to the Cambridge Analytica situation, it regulates such kind of situations since 25 May 2018. According to its recital 32, consent should be given by a clear affirmative act establishing a freely given, specific, informed and unambiguous indication of the data subject's agreement to the processing of personal data relating to him or her. Since consent was given 'in general terms, buried in Facebook's terms of service', it may be argued that Facebook – and with it anybody relying on these violations – breached the right to privacy.[125] Applying another norm of the GDPR, Article 25 which provides for 'privacy by design', leads to the same result, as Facebook by design allows third parties to access personal data.[126] In applying the Data Protection Act 1998 (UK),

121 See e.g. Peter Schaar, *Privacy as a Human Right: Edward Snowden and the Control of Power* (Blätter für Internationale Politik 2015); Miller (n 3); Granick (n 3); Milanovic (n 100).
122 Cf. Johann Čas, 'Social and Economic Costs of Surveillance' in David Wright and Reinhard Kreissl (eds), *Surveillance in Europe* (Routledge 2015) 211, 215; BVerfG, 1 BvR 2368/06, 23 February 2007 [38], [50]–[52]; BVerfGE 65, 1 [154]; BVerfGE 69, 315 [71]; BVerfGE 139, 378 [9], [11].
123 Facebook (n 85); cf. also statement by the *Bundeskartellamt* expressing its doubt concerning the admissibility of Facebook's conditions of use, 'Bundeskartellamt initiates proceeding against Facebook on suspicion of having abused its market power by infringing data protection rules' (Press Release, 2 March 2016): 'In order to access the social network, users must first agree to the company's collection and use of their data by accepting the terms of service. It is difficult for users to understand and assess the scope of the agreement accepted by them. There is considerable doubt as to the admissibility of this procedure, in particular under applicable national data protection law.' www.bundeskartellamt.de/SharedDocs/Meldung/EN/Pressemitteilungen/2016/02_03_ 2016_Facebook.html.
124 It appears that Project Lakhta did not employ similar micro-targeting techniques.
125 Cambridge Analytica, 'Facebook & the Privacy Problem' *Lawyer Monthly* (12 March 2018) www.lawyer-monthly.com/2018/03/your-thoughts-cambridge-analytica-facebook-the-privacy-problem.
126 Ira S Rubinstein and Nathaniel Good, 'Privacy by Design: A Counterfactual Analysis of Google and Facebook Privacy Incidents' (2013) 28 Berkeley Technology Law Journal 1333; Gordon Hull, Heather Richter Lipfold and Celine Latulipe, 'Contextual gaps: privacy issues on Facebook' (2011) 13 Ethics and Information Technology 289, 297f.

which is based on the 1995 European Data Protection Directive, the UK Information Commissioner's Office found a privacy breach and fined Facebook the maximum penalty of £500,000 as it did not protect its users' data and was not transparent about the use of the data.[127] Furthermore, the unwarranted display of posts on one's Facebook newsfeed based on data which has been accumulated via a privacy breach is arguably also an interference with one's right to privacy, as it perpetuates the first interference.[128]

3. Limitation clauses: Which role to play for democracy?

While, at least indirectly, the right to democratic participation has been interfered with by Project Lakhta and Cambridge Analytica and the right to privacy by Cambridge Analytica and the NSA mass surveillance programme, it is only with regard to the right to democratic participation that the nexus to democracy is obvious. Whether other human rights, especially the right to privacy, help in safeguarding democracy depends on the human rights limitation clauses. In a first step, the situation in which a state interferes with a human right will be scrutinised (a.); in a second step this chapter will turn to interferences through private actors (b.).

A. PROTECTION OF DEMOCRACY AS A LIMIT TO INTERFERENCES WITH HUMAN RIGHTS

Generally, the exercise of human rights may be limited in order to achieve a legitimate aim as long as the interference is proportionate. Mass surveillance operations aim at protecting the state, society and individuals from terrorist attacks and other harm.[129] The decisive question is whether these mass surveillance operations are in accordance with the proportionality principle. In that case, the right to privacy will not be violated. The proportionality test limits the power of the state to interfere with human rights and requires balancing the

---

127 Alex Hern and David Pegg, 'Facebook fined for data breaches in Cambridge Analytica scandal' *The Guardian* (11 July 2018) www.theguardian.com/technology/2018/jul/11/facebook-fined-for-data-breaches-in-cambridge-analytica-scandal.

128 In Germany, the sending of unwarranted advertisements to one's mailbox is regarded as an interference with the right to informational self-determination, which in essence protects the right to privacy: LG Lüneburg, 4 S 44/11, 4 November 2011. See also UN Special Rapporteur on Counter Terrorism and Human Rights, 'Report of the UN Special Rapporteur on the Promotion and Protection of Human Rights and Fundamental Freedoms While Countering Terrorism' (2014) UN Doc. A/69/397 para 28, who argues that 'individuals should have an area of personal autonomous development, interaction and liberty free from State intervention and excessive unsolicited intrusion by other uninvited individuals'.

129 Daniel Fenwick, 'Terrorism, CCTV and the Freedom Bill 2011: Achieving Compatibility with Article 8 ECHR' (2011) 24 International Review of Law, Computers and Technology 183; Margaret Hu, 'From the National Surveillance State to the Cyber-surveillance State' (2017) 13 Annual Review of Law and Social Sciences 161.

competing interests.[130] Here, 'protection of democracy' comes into play as one aspect in the balancing act in order to strengthen the protection of the right to privacy against state interferences. For the European context, such an understanding follows from the wording of the ECHR, which requires that the needs of a 'democratic society' be fulfilled.[131] Similarly, Article 52 of the EU Charter of Fundamental Rights requires that democracy, which is a foundational value of the EU as recognised in Article 2 of the Treaty on the European Union, be adhered to. Furthermore, on a universal level, states are restrained by democratic considerations in case they interfere with human rights. While this is only explicitly stated in Articles 21 and 22 of the CCPR which guarantees the freedom of assembly and association respectively, Article 17 of the CCPR explicitly states that 'unlawful' or 'arbitrary' interferences with the right to privacy are prohibited. Interferences that collide with democratic principles are difficult to reconcile with these conditions, which demand that any interference has to be 'reasonable' and in conformity with 'the provisions, aims and objectives of the Covenant'.[132] This is especially true in light of Article 25 of the CCPR.

The theoretical and practical repercussions of such a democracy-based approach are immense as they might tip the scale in favour of finding an interference. Even if one assumes that mass surveillance operations pursue the legitimate aim of protecting society and individuals against terrorist attacks and that their interference with the right to privacy is outweighed by the need for protection against terrorist attacks,[133] a consideration of the damages done to democracy[134] should provide for a different result of the balancing act and lead to the illegality of mass surveillance operations. Thus, such a democracy-based approach strengthens the human rights approach.

B. NON-STATE ACTORS AND DEMOCRACY AS A LEGITIMATE AIM

Turning to non-state actors, it first needs to be acknowledged that this situation is not only different to but also more complicated than the case of state actors and therefore needs to be unravelled cautiously. If non-state actors are involved, the

---

130 *Weber and Saravia v Germany* App no 54934/00, [2006] ECHR 1173, [106].
131 Ibid.
132 HRC, 'General Comment No 16: Article 17, The Right to Respect of Privacy, Family, Home and Correspondence, and Protection of Honour and Reputation' (1988) HRI/GEN/1/Rev.9 vol 1 paras 3, 4.
133 See e.g. Kevin D Haggerty, 'What's Wrong with Privacy Protections? Provocations from a Fifth Columnist' in Austin Sarat (ed), *A World Without Privacy. What Law Can and Should Do?* (Cambridge University Press 2015) 190; Kirsty Hughes, 'The social value of privacy, the value of privacy to society and human rights discourse' in Beate Roessler and Dorota Mokrosinska (eds), *Social Dimensions of Privacy, Interdisciplinary Perspectives* (Cambridge University Press 2015) 225.
134 See above Part III.

typical two-actor operation[135] turns into a three-actor operation[136] or even a four-actor operation if these acts take place within social networks.[137]

All non-state actors involved may claim human rights themselves, be it the right to privacy, the right to freedom of expression or the right to property.[138] In this situation, the state – which is bound to protect the right of privacy of individuals due to its duty to protect – must take into consideration not only the human rights of the non-state actors that interfere with the right to privacy on the one hand, but also those of the non-state actors providing the social network on the other hand. Thus, since a non-state actor is at least indirectly bound to human rights in this duty-to-protect situation, the rights of others – for example, the right to privacy of a second non-state actor – may serve as a legitimate aim to interfere with the human rights of the first non-state actor – for example, the right to freedom of expression. In addition, democracy may serve as a legitimate aim to justify an interference with the human rights of the first non-state actor. How can that be done?

None of the documents provide that democracy is a specific aim that allows for the interference with human rights. However, the limitation clause of Article 19 of the CCPR, which protects freedom of opinion and expression, uses the formulation 'such as'. By this it shows that it is open to other, non-enumerated aims. The limitation clauses of Articles 21 and 22 of the CCPR do not provide for specific aims and are thus equally open to different aims. That democracy can be such an aim is underlined by Article 25 of the CCPR. While the reference to a 'democratic society' in the ECHR limitation clauses is not primarily concerned with the legitimate aim but with the standard of proportionality, it also indirectly shows that the protection of democracy is able to justify interferences with human rights. This holds especially true as democracy is the only form of government foreseen by the Convention.[139] Lastly, according to Article 52 of the EU Charter of Fundamental Rights, limitations of human rights are in principle possible if they genuinely meet objectives of general interest recognised by the Union. Democracy as a foundational value of the EU as recognised in Article 2 of the Treaty on the European Union is one of these objectives. Thus, in principle, the state is allowed – and may be, because of its duty to protect, even obliged – to interfere with private actions in the privately owned space of Facebook and Twitter in order to safeguard not only privacy but also democracy. This concerns not only the rights of Cambridge Analytica but also of Facebook and Twitter.

135 The state interferes with human rights of (at least) one individual as in the mass surveillance operations.
136 The state protects the right to privacy of one individual against intrusions by another individual (here: Cambridge Analytica).
137 The state protects the right to privacy of one individual against intrusions by another individual (here: Cambridge Analytica), within a virtual environment maintained by another individual (here: Facebook or Twitter).
138 Cf. José E Alvarez, 'The Human Right of Property' (2018) 72 University of Miami Law Review 580.
139 *Refah Partisi* (n 70) [86].

C. CONCLUSION: HUMAN RIGHT TO FREE ELECTIONS, DEMOCRACY AS A LEGITIMATE AIM AND PART OF THE PROPORTIONALITY TEST

In essence, democracy plays a role thrice in evaluating big-data-based operations. First, democracy is protected via the right to democratic participation which needs to be safeguarded by states. Second, democracy plays a role in the proportionality analysis and thus limit states' authority to interfere with human rights. Third, on the level of the legitimate aim, the protection of democracy might justify an interference with a human right of private actors. Thus, democracy may serve as a basis to limit human rights, but it may also serve as a reason to find a human rights interference disproportionate. To conclude, the big-data-based cases at hand must be evaluated differently by taking democracy into account: mass surveillance operations, if not already understood as illegal on pure human rights grounds, become illegal and operations such as those of Cambridge Analytica and Project Lakhta must be fought against in a manner that protects the right to democratic participation and to privacy.

C. The principle of non-intervention as a means to protect democracy

Democracy can be protected not only by individual human rights law but also by norms of international law which focus on the collective. The principle of non-intervention,[140] the principle of sovereignty,[141] the right to self-determination,[142] the no-harm principle and the due diligence principle[143] have all been identified by different authors to live up to that task.

The present chapter will restrict itself to the principle of non-intervention as all other principles suffer from deficiencies that seem highly improbable to overcome: There is no general norm prohibiting the violation of a state's sovereignty[144] but only specific rules that substantiate the general principle of

---

140 Steven J Barela, 'Cross-Border Cyber Ops to Erode Legitimacy: An Act of Coercion' *Just Security* (12 January 2017) www.justsecurity.org/36212/cross-border-cyber-op s-erode-legitimacy-act-coercion; Steven J Barela, 'Zero Shades of Grey: Russian-Ops Violate International Law' *Just Security* (29 March 2018) www.justsecurity.org/ 54340/shades-grey-russian-ops-violate-international-law.

141 Schmitt, 'Virtual Disenfranchisement' (n 34) 39ff.

142 Ohlin (n 27) passim. The right to self-determination is understood as a human right, *inter alia* because it can be found in Article 1 of the CCPR but serves not primarily the individual but the collective.

143 Schmitt, 'Virtual Disenfranchisement' (n 34) 53ff; Martin Ney and Andreas Zimmermann, 'Cyber-Security Beyond the Military Perspective: International Law, "Cyberspace", and the Concept of Due Diligence' (2015) 58 German Yearbook of International Law 51; Michael N Schmitt (ed), *Tallinn Manual 2.0 on the International Law Applicable to Cyber Operations* (2nd edn, Cambridge University Press 2017) 30–50.

144 UK Attorney General Jeremy Wright QC MP, 'Cyber and International Law in the 21st Century' (London, 23 May 2018) www.gov.uk/government/speeches/cyber-and-in ternational-law-in-the-21st-century; Brian J Egan, 'International Law and Stability in

sovereignty, such as the norms on sovereign immunity or the prohibition of intervention, which is 'the corollary of every State's right to sovereignty'.[145] The right to self-determination, which is directed against a government that exercises a certain amount of control vis-à-vis a people, like the central government of a state to which the people belong or a colonised territory under the rule of a foreign state, is not applicable to the situation at hand.[146] While the no-harm principle could indeed serve as a rule of international law which protects against election interferences,[147] there is no need to rely on it where the principle of non-intervention is violated as the principle of non-intervention prohibits certain acts while the no-harm principle only prohibits certain effects of acts which are *per se* legal.[148] Furthermore, the no-harm principle is often confused with the due diligence principle,[149] which in itself is not a rule but an annex norm to another norm.[150]

Hence, we need to turn to the principle of non-intervention which follows from the principle of sovereign equality and is affirmed *inter alia* in Article 2 (1) of the United Nations Charter.[151] It protects states against coercive outside interference with their internal affairs by other states and thus might protect against the interferences of Project Lakhta. Two elements are of specific importance and need further clarification: the domaine réservé and the coercion element.

Cyberspace' (2017) 35 Berkeley Journal of International Law 169, 174 (at that time US State Department Legal Adviser).

145 Robert Jennings and Arthur Watts (eds), *Oppenheim's International Law*, vol 1 (9th edn, Oxford University Press 2008) 418; similarly, *Military and Paramilitary Activities in and against Nicaragua (Nicaragua v United States of America)* (Merits) [1986] ICJ Rep 14 [202].

146 See Schmitt, '"Virtual" Disenfranchisement' (n 34) 55; but see Sander (n 26) para 77 with further reference to Antonio Cassese, *Self-Determination of Peoples: A Legal Reappraisal* (Cambridge University Press 1995) 67–140.

147 See e.g. Andreas von Arnauld, 'Freiheit und Regulierung in der Cyberwelt: Transnationaler Schutz der Privatsphäre aus Sicht des Völkerrechts' in Nina Dethloff, Georg Nolte and August Reinisch (eds), *Freiheit und Regulierung in der Cyberwelt. Rechtsidentifikation zwischen Quelle und Gericht* (Berichte der Deutschen Gesellschaft für Internationales Recht 2016) 1, 19. For a general overview on the no-harm principle see Jelena Bäumler, 'Rise and Shine: The No Harm Principle's Increasing Relevance for the Global Community' (2017) Global Community Yearbook of International Law 149.

148 Jelena Bäumler, 'Implementing the No Harm Principle in International Economic Law: A Comparison Between Measure-Based Rules and Effect-Based Rules' (2017) 20 Journal of International Economic Law 807.

149 See e.g. Sander (n 26) para 46; Schmitt, *Tallinn Manual 2.0* (n 143) 30.

150 Cf. Beatrice A Walton, 'Duties Owed: Low-Intensity Cyber Attacks and Liability for Transboundary Torts in International Law' (2017) 126 Yale Law Journal 1496.

151 For further sources see Terry D Gill, 'Non-Intervention in the Cyber Context' in Ziolkowski (n 66) 217, 220.

I. The object of protection: The will of the states to decide and act freely

The principle of non-intervention protects states' ability to decide and act according to their own will against outside interference in matters falling into the domaine réservé. The choice of the political system belongs to that domaine réservé;[152] elections and preparations for elections go to the heart of the matter as they are decisive in forming the will of a state and are the basis of all decisions and acts of a state.[153] Regime change is regarded as a 'clear violation'[154] of the principle of non-violation. Furthermore, the free will of states is impaired when, in order to safeguard the legitimacy of their liberal democratic system, they have to react to foreign undertakings aimed at undermining democracy.

2. Prohibited means of intervention: Coercion

Far more problematic is the second prerequisite, coercion. An exact definition of coercion is lacking.[155] On the one hand, it is clear that while military force is coercive, the threshold of coercion in the context of intervention must be lower, as the prohibition of military force is found in a separate norm, Article 2(4) of the UN Charter. On the other hand, the coercion threshold requires that a state does more than mere spying: although espionage is a criminal offence in national law, it is regarded as neutral by international law – that is, espionage is neither unlawful nor lawful.[156] Thus, the principle of non-intervention cannot provide any protection against mass surveillance operations. But can it protect against covert operations by foreign states that aim at influencing the voting behaviour of individuals, such as Project Lakhta?

Coercion is about protecting the sovereign will of states against certain forms of pressure which do not include mere speech acts, verbal criticism, moral support or

152 *Military and Paramilitary Activities in and against Nicaragua* (n 145) para 205; United Nations General Assembly, 'Declaration Principles of International Law concerning Friendly Relations and Co-operation among States in accordance with the Charter of the United Nations' (26 October 1970) A/RES/2625 (XXV).

153 See the many examples in Marco Athen, *Der Tatbestand des völkerrechtlichen Interventionsverbots* (Nomos 2017) 220ff.

154 Maziar Jamnejad and Michael Wood, 'The Principle of Non-Intervention' (2009) 22 Leiden Journal of International Law 345, 368.

155 Ibid 345; Hitoshi Nasu, 'Revisiting the Principle of Non-Intervention: A Structural Principle of International Law or a Political Obstacle to Regional Security in Asia?' (2013) 25 Asian Journal of International Law 25, 46; Philip Kunig, *Das völkerrechtliche Nichteinmischungsprinzip* (Nomos 1981) 25–28.

156 A John Radsan, 'The Unresolved Equation of Espionage and International Law' (2007) 28 Michigan Journal of International Law 596, 601ff; Dieter Fleck, 'Individual and State Responsibility for Intelligence Gathering' (2007) 28 Michigan Journal of International Law 687; Simon Chesterman, 'The Spy Who Came in from the Cold War: Intelligence and International Law' (2006) 27 Michigan Journal of International Law 1071, 1077; Gill (n 152) 224; Katharina Ziolkowski 'Peacetime Cyber Espionage – New Tendencies in Public International Law' in Ziolkowski (n 66) 425, 431ff.

deceit.[157] According to Oppenheim, 'the interference must be forcible or dictatorial, or otherwise coercive, in effect depriving the state intervened against of control over the matter in question'.[158] The International Court of Justice (ICJ) also speaks of 'methods of coercion'[159] and thus appears to exclude a reading which focuses on the effects and not the methods. Since deceit through aggressive manipulations and clandestine changes of voters' perception of reality is at the core of the Russian method, the prohibition of intervention does not appear to be applicable.

Nevertheless, the case law of the ICJ has also considered methods which in themselves are not coercive but only have an indirect coercive effect. The ICJ understands financial support for subversive groups as coercive.[160] Furthermore, it is recognised that 'incitement or support for attempts to overthrow or undermine or subvert a State's government or its electoral process'[161] may already constitute a form of prohibited intervention. Here, the method of influencing a state's behaviour is in itself non-coercive, yet it is legally regarded as coercive since the intended effect on the target state act is coercive. Thus, it is not the method which needs to be coercive but the effect of the action.[162]

A typical example of a coercive effect would be the application of physical pressure against an organ of that state.[163] Another sort of physical pressure – and even a 'quintessential example'[164] of the non-intervention principle – is any physical act through which votes recorded in an election are altered, thereby affecting the election results.[165] It is determinative in this case that votes are affected and altered, thus undermining the political process. Would it make a difference whether this is done physically or virtually? If the answer were yes, the principle of non-intervention could not apply in cyberspace. However, as the principle applies in cyberspace, virtual pressure needs to be understood as coercion as well.[166] But does virtual pressure only include tampering with data or also tampering with people's minds? It seems that manipulating the voters and deceiving them is something quite different from virtual or physical pressure.

157 Gill (n 152) 223.
158 Jennings and Watts (n 145) 418.
159 *Military and Paramilitary Activities in and against Nicaragua* (n 145) para 205.
160 Ibid para 242.
161 Gill (n 152) 223.
162 For a specific consequentialist view, see Myres S McDougal and Florentino P Feliciano, 'International Coercion and World Public Order: The General Principles of the Law of War' (1958) Yale Law Journal 771.
163 For relevant cases of prohibited means of intervention see e.g. Andreas von Arnauld, *Völkerrecht* (3rd edn, C.F. Müller 2016) 153ff.
164 Gary P Corn and Robert Taylor, 'Sovereignty in the Age of Cyber' (2017) 111 American Journal of International Law Unbound 207, 208.
165 Ibid; Brian J Egan, 'International Law and Stability in Cyberspace' (2017) 35 Berkeley Journal of International Law 169, 175 (at that time State Department Legal Adviser); Ohlin (n 27) 7 agrees, but subsumes it under 'usurpation' and not 'coercion'.
166 Schmitt, *Tallinn Manual 2.0* (n 143) 318.

The coercive element of voters' manipulation surfaces by focusing on the effect of the Russian acts: by manipulating voters – no physical pressure is involved here in the same way as there is no physical pressure involved in financing rebel groups – these voters affect the election results, force a different result upon the state and coerce the state to either accept the result or call new elections. Whereas 'force' or coercion is not the word one would usually use for the effect election results have on the composition of a new government, this is exactly what is happening in essence: the results of the election compel the loser of the election to accept defeat and the winner to take office according to the constitutional rules of the target state. The voters decide with legal force and their decision is binding and coerces all state organs to act accordingly.

There is, of course, a difference between a physical manipulation of voting machines and a psychological manipulation of voters, as the votes themselves are not altered and may thus not be 'wrong' in the ordinary sense of the word. However, democracy fundamentally relies on free elections. If this precondition is tampered with against or without the will of the state, the democratic state is coerced into a situation of contested legitimacy.[167] Articles 25 of the CCPR and 3 of the First Protocol to the ECHR show that representatives must be 'freely chosen'. If the voter is heavily manipulated, such as in cases in which she or he does not even know that manipulation is taking place, the free election, which as a matter of international law has to be guaranteed by the home state, has been interfered with.[168] Such a reading of coercion is further supported by the International Law Commission (ILC). In its draft commentary to what later became Article 41 of the Vienna Convention on the Law of Diplomatic Relations, the ILC explicitly stated that it follows from the principle of non-interference that diplomats 'must not take part in political campaigns'.[169]

One could, however, argue that it makes a difference whether the election result has actually been altered or not. In the case of Project Lakhta, this cannot be proven,[170] even if the 'absence of evidence is not evidence of absence'.[171] However, the flawed process as such damages the legitimacy of the results, the legitimacy of the future government and of its decisions.[172] The methods applied pose an asymmetric threat to democracies,[173] as the very functioning of states depends

167 Cf. Barela, 'Cross-Border Cyber Ops to Erode Legitimacy' (n 140); Barela, 'Zero Shades of Grey' (n 140).
168 Ohlin (n 27) 13.
169 United Nations, *Yearbook of the International Law Commission*, vol 2 (United Nations 1958) 104.
170 Highly sceptical that fake news changed the outcome: Allcott and Gentzkow (n 80).
171 Ohlin (n 27) 13.
172 Cf. examples of possible scenarios given by Gill (n 152) 234.
173 Such tools are also employed by democratic states with sufficient capabilities. See e.g. Glenn Greenwald, 'Hacking Online Polls and Other Ways British Spies Seek to Control the Internet' *The Intercept* (14 July 2014) https://theintercept.com/2014/07/14/manipulating-online-polls-ways-british-spies-seek-control-internet.

on what their citizens think or even feel about their realities. The fundament of the democratic state is seriously impaired through the manipulation: instead of collective self-determination, 'other-determination' takes place.[174] Accordingly, the main goal of Project Lakhta has been to damage the legitimacy of and to harm the liberal democratic state. While the means and methods of this undertaking are rooted in deceit, the intended effect is coercive: through deceiving the people, the democratic state is forced to either accept the tainted result or deal with a situation of contested legitimacy.

Thus, different to conventional propaganda which in general does not pass the threshold of coercion, Project Lakhta and any similar acts do. The prohibition of intervention therefore serves as a normative foundation for protecting democracy through international law.

V. Conclusion: International law protects against violations of democracy from the inside and outside

The NSA affair, the Russian troll farms and the Cambridge Analytica operation are only a few, albeit highly important, examples that show that democracy is indeed challenged by big-data-based operations. This poses an existential threat not only to human rights law, especially the right to privacy, but also to the democratic state. At the same time, however, international law governs the internet and, with it, big-data-based operations. As we have seen, the substantive norms of international law can deal with these interferences with the political process and allow – and might even demand – the regulation of and protection against state and private actors alike. Human rights law allows for a democracy-based approach which strengthens privacy and democracy. Furthermore, the principle of non-intervention helps in protecting democracy against outside interference with the political process by state actors. Thus, although democracy does not play a major role in international law, international law nevertheless is able to protect democracy against challenges from the inside as well as outside.

174 Ohlin (n 27) 13.

Chapter 6

Social media in election campaigns

Free speech or a danger for democracy?

Udo Fink

I. Introduction

Theory seems to be clear. Free speech is essential for democracy. Information about relevant political topics and a pluralistic market of ideas enable citizens to make reasonable decisions in elections or in a referendum.[1] Law should make sure that the process of disseminating facts and opinions is self-determined and not state-controlled. As a former judge of the German Federal Constitutional Court, Ernst-Wolfgang Böckenförde, once stated:

> Every liberal, secularised state lives from preconditions which it cannot guarantee itself. A liberal state can [...] only succeed if the freedom which it grants its citizens is self-regulated from within, as a result of the moral substance of each individual and the homogeneity of its society.[2]

Does this mean that any interference with the free flow of information is dangerous for democracy and unjustified? Should all individuals be free to decide for themselves which information and opinion is relevant for them or should the use of free speech in itself be limited by public interests such as democracy, transparency and personal honour of third persons? Or, conversely, are states under a duty to protect these public and private interests?

Traditionally, free speech depends vitally on mass media such as newspapers, books, radio and television. These mass media spread facts, encourage public accountability and multiply opinions. The European Court of Human Rights

---

1   Oliver Wendell Holmes wrote in his dissenting opinion to *Abrams v United States*, 250 US 616 (1919): 'But when men have realized that time has upset many fighting faiths, they may come to believe even more than they believe the very foundations of their own conduct that the ultimate good desired is better reached by free trade in ideas – that the best test of truth is the power of the thought to get itself accepted in the competition of the market, and that truth is the only ground upon which their wishes safely can be carried out.'

2   Ernst-Wolfgang Böckenförde, *Staat, Gesellschaft, Freiheit: Studien zur Staatstheorie und zum Verfassungsrecht* (Suhrkamp 1976) 60.

names these functions as the 'vital public-watchdog role of the press'.[3] But the press and other traditional mass media are no longer the only watchdogs. More recently, the Court has accepted that social platforms operating on the internet can have a similar role;[4] they have since been described as 'social watchdog(s)'.

An important characteristic that distinguished traditional media from social network platforms is that they have a bottleneck and function as a gatekeeper.[5] The editor of a newspaper decides which information or opinion will be published. Newspapers usually have a political leaning. A conservative newspaper will not usually publish socialist ideas and vice versa. Radio and television stations often work differently. Public broadcasters who follow the model of the British Broadcasting Corporation try to inform in a balanced way, avoiding one-sided political opinions. Of course, there are also others like state-controlled broadcasters or private broadcasters such as Fox News in the United States (US) which push a political agenda.[6]

Ideally, traditional media also work as a guarantor for valuable information. Quality press and serious broadcasters only publish news gathered by professional journalists. Professional journalism follows certain core principles such as truthfulness, accuracy, objectivity, impartiality, fairness and public accountability.[7]

The internet has enabled more voices to reach a broad audience. This seems to make the communication landscape more pluralistic, maybe even more democratic. The classic gatekeepers are no longer necessary to disseminate facts and opinions. Everybody can use social media, chat rooms or blogs to share their own ideas with others and, in principle, everybody else can access these ideas.[8] This means that our worldwide market of ideas is far more colourful and functions to a certain point as a safeguard against a one-sided information policy of governments that are not founded on democratic legitimation and do not allow free press and

3   *Goodwin v United Kingdom* App no 17488/90, [1996] ECHR 16.
4   *Magyar Helsinki Bizottság v Hungary* App no 18030/11, [2016] ECHR 975, [166]: 'The Court has also acknowledged that the function of creating various platforms for public debate is not limited to the press but may also be exercised by, among others, non-governmental organisations, whose activities are an essential element of informed public debate. The Court has accepted that when an NGO draws attention to matters of public interest, it is exercising a public watchdog role of similar importance to that of the press (see *Animal Defenders International v the United Kingdom* [GC], no. 48876/08, § 103) and may be characterised as a social "watchdog" warranting similar protection under the Convention as that afforded to the press.'
5   Gabrielle Tutheridge, 'What is the role of gatekeeping journalist's in today's media environment?' *Medium* (18 May 2017) https://medium.com/@gabrielletutheridge/what-is-the-role-of-gatekeeping-journalists-in-today-s-media-environment-2034a30ba850.
6   Media bias/Fact check, *Fox News*, https://mediabiasfactcheck.com/fox-news.
7   International Federation of Journalists, 'Declaration of Principles on the Conduct of Journalists' (1954, amended 1986) www.ifj.org/who/rules-and-policy/principles-on-conduct-of-journalism.html.
8   Anand Giridharadas, 'The New Gatekeepers of Media' *The New York Times* (8 April 2011) www.nytimes.com/2011/04/09/us/09iht-currents09.html.

broadcasting. As *Louis Brandeis* wrote in his concurring opinion in the case *Whitney v California*: 'The remedy to be applied (to falsehood and fallacy) is more speech, not enforced silence.'[9]

II. Old-fashioned media versus the internet

However, for some time now we have been able to observe that completely unregulated internet speech can also be a real danger for democracy and specifically for free elections and referenda.[10] Of course, the old world of gatekeepers has also never been free of one-sided or even fake news. But at least the public generally knows or can find out who is responsible for the reported facts and ideas.[11] Newspapers have reputations for being right- or left-wing, or for being serious or sensationalist. Since, traditionally, there is good and bad journalism, people are able to categorise specific commentaries and have developed standards to evaluate the truth of specific information.[12]

The same happens with radio and TV. For example, in Germany public broadcasting has a reputation for not being one-sided and for professional journalism, while private broadcasting is definitely not on the same level. Private broadcasters are generally run to pursue market-driven objectives, which leads to programmes that are attractive to a mass audience but do not represent the whole range of information, experiences and values existing in our society. This is the main reason for the German Federal Constitutional Court acknowledging that public broadcasting has an indispensable role in securing media plurality in a democratic society[13] and accepting the constitutional validity of a system of public financing through a compulsory charge on every household.[14]

In contrast, where news is published by non-traditional media on the internet, the reliability of the information and its sources is often hard to evaluate.[15] News on the internet can be published by private individuals or groups who lack the means or even the goodwill to check their information. In other cases, the information

9   274 US 357 (1927).
10   Simon Wilson, 'Is the internet a danger to democracy?' *Money Week* (21 April 2018) https://moneyweek.com/486794/is-the-internet-a-danger-to-democracy.
11   Under German law each newspaper is obliged to publish an 'impressum', which contains information about the publisher, all journalists of the newspaper and the person responsible for a specific article. Under US law there is no such obligation, but responsible media usually disclose the authorship of articles.
12   Fran Yeoman, 'The value of professional journalism' *The Independent* (4 December 2013) www.independent.co.uk/voices/comment/the-value-of-professional-journalism -8982792.html.
13   BVerfGE 136, 9 [36].
14   This charge currently gives public broadcasters access to about 8 billion Euro per year: Kommission zur Ermittlung des Finanzbedarfs der Rundfunkanstalten, *21. Bericht* (KEF 2018) https://kef-online.de/fileadmin/KEF/Dateien/Berichte/21._Bericht.pdf.
15   Zeynep Tufekci, 'It's the (democracy-poisoning) golden age of free speech' *WIRED* (16 January 2018) www.wired.com/story/free-speech-issue-tech-turmoil-new-censorship.

published originates from foreign states or agencies who have a range of agendas and intentions, with fake news becoming an issue of increasing concern.[16]

III. The Cambridge Analytica scandal

The recent activities of the now-defunct British consulting company Cambridge Analytica[17] provide striking illustrations of the current challenges that arise from political communications on social media. According to the testimony of a former Cambridge Analytica employee, Christopher Wylie, given to the European Parliament in an official hearing, Cambridge Analytica sought to heavily influence public opinion during the Brexit campaign and was also involved in the last US presidential elections in 2016.[18] Cambridge Analytica was assisted in this process by obtaining access to the personal profiles of millions of users of the social media platform Facebook, when they or their friends chose to share their personal data with the app 'thisisyourdigitallife'. Giving this app permission to access information of the users' friends resulted in the revelation of the personal data of millions of Facebook users. Cambridge Analytica was able to use the data profiles generated to send targeted information or disinformation to try to influence voters in these two campaigns.[19]

IV. Social bots

One of the major tools that companies such as Cambridge Anlaytica use are bots (software applications that run automated tasks over the internet). Bots can be used to create fake online identities (known as sockpuppets). For example, they can be used to operate social media accounts which automatically generate or disseminate content to other users of social platforms and otherwise interact with their accounts. Networks of such bots are called 'botnets', describing a collection of connected computers with programs that communicate across multiple devices.[20]

16   Nick Anstead and Ben O'Loughlin, 'Social Media Analysis and Public Opinion: The 2010 UK General Election' (2015) 20 Journal of Computer-Mediated Communication 204.
17   Cambridge Analytica ceased operations and filed for bankruptcy in 2018. It previously provided consumer research, targeted advertising and other data-related services to political and corporate clients: see David Ingram, 'Factbox: Who is Cambridge Analytica and what did it do?' *Reuters* (20 March 2018) www.reuters.com/article/us-fa cebook-cambridge-analytica-factbox/factbox-who-is-cambridge-analytica-and-wha t-did-it-do-idUSKBN1GW07F.
18   In his testimony to the European Parliament's Committee on Civil Liberties, Justice and Home Affairs on 4 June 2018, Wylie said: 'I don't believe Brexit would have happened were it not for the data targeting technology and network of actors set up by Cambridge Analytica.'
19   Kevin Granville, 'Facebook and Cambridge Analytica: What You Need to Know as Fallout Widens?' *The New York Times* (19 March 2018) www.nytimes.com/2018/ 03/19/technology/facebook-cambridge-analytica-explained.html.
20   Samuel Woolley and Marina Gorbis, 'Social media bots threaten democracy. But we are not helpless' *The Guardian* (17 October 2017) www.theguardian.com/comm entisfree/2017/oct/16/bots-social-media-threaten-democracy-technology.

Bots can work automatically, but very often they are guided by human beings who may start the conversation about certain topics, develop specific ideas and thereby drive discussion in online communities.[21] The ideas are then multiplied by so-called 'amplifier bots'. By liking, retweeting or replying to specific content, bots create the impression that a whole community supports specific ideas and thus give the content more credibility. Bots can also be used to attack ideas and even to harass people who hold different opinions, using 'shit storms' to poison public discussion and discourage or drown out critical voices.

Social bots are particularly active on Twitter, but they are also found on the many other social media platforms that increasingly form part of the system of political communication in many countries. Some scholars have argued that 66% of all tweets on popular news and current event websites are made by suspected bots. These bot profiles can be identified by the fact that they lack basic account information such as screen names or profile pictures.[22]

A Russian so-called 'troll farm', with close ties to the Russian Government, the St Petersburg–based 'Internet Research Agency', has become notorious for making widespread use of bots in its attempts to manipulate public opinion. It employs dozens of specialists to spread its preferred views on Facebook, YouTube and elsewhere.[23] In China, the so-called '50 Cent Army' uses a massive number of personal accounts to flood the internet with comments.[24]

Human users have difficulty differentiating between a social bot and a human user. In a study evaluating the 2016 US presidential election, the authors presented internet users with comments genuinely generated by humans as well as automatically generated comments. In 50% of cases, users were unable to identify whether a comment came from another user or was generated automatically.[25] According to a study by Howard and Kollanyi, the two single most active accounts from each side of the Brexit debate were bots. These accounts followed a similar algorithm. Neither generated new content; they merely mechanically retweeted messages from their side of the debate.[26]

21   Brad Stone and Matt Richtelju, 'The Hand That Controls the Sock Puppet Could Get Slapped' *The New York Times* (16 July 2007) www.nytimes.com/2007/07/16/technology/16blog.html.

22   Stefan Wojcik et al., 'Bots in the Twittersphere', *Pew Research Centre* (9 April 2018) www.pewinternet.org/2018/04/09/bots-in-the-twittersphere.

23   Dan Mangan and Mike Calia, 'Special counsel Mueller: Russians conducted "information warfare" against US during election to help Donald Trump win' *CNBC* (16 February 2018) www.cnbc.com/2018/02/16/russians-indicted-in-special-counsel-robert-muellers-probe.html.

24   Michael Bristow, 'China's internet "spin doctors"' *BBC News* (16 December 2008) http://news.bbc.co.uk/2/hi/asia-pacific/7783640.stm.

25   Onur Varol et al., 'Online Human-Bot Interactions: Detection, Estimation, and Characterization', Proceedings of the Eleventh International AAAI Conference on Web and Social Media (ICWSM 2017), 280 passim.

26   Philip N Howard and Bence Kollanyi, 'Bots, #Strongerin, and #Brexit: Computational Propaganda During the UK-EU Referendum', Working Paper 2016.1, Project on Computational Propaganda (20 June 2016) http://dx.doi.org/10.2139/ssrn.2798311.

V. The EU Commission campaign

In 2018, the EU Commission started a campaign called 'Tackling online disinformation', giving the following for the rationale for its initiative:

> While technologies offer new and easy ways, notably through social media, to disseminate information on a large scale and with speed and precision, they can also be used as powerful echo chambers for disinformation campaigns. Disinformation erodes trust in institutions and in digital and traditional media and harms our democracies by hampering the ability of citizens to take informed decisions. It can polarise debates, create or deepen tensions in society and undermine electoral systems, and thus have a wider impact on European security.[27]

It even erodes free speech by manipulating people's views and covertly influencing their decisions.[28]

The Commission expressed the view that public authorities have a duty to make citizens aware of and protect them against such activities. It proposed as remedies an EU-wide Code of Practice on Disinformation, support for an independent network of fact-checkers, and tools to stimulate quality journalism.[29]

VI. Free speech and the right to vote under the European Convention of Human Rights

In Europe, the European Convention on Human Rights and the EU Charter of Fundamental Rights define the fundamental rules for free speech and democratic voting. While the European Convention is binding on all Member States of the Council of Europe, the Charter contains the human rights obligations for the European Union (EU) and its Member States. Both instruments are closely linked, the European Convention defining the minimum standard, which under Art. 53 of the Charter is legally binding also for the EU. Both Treaties protect freedom of speech, the Charter in its Art. 11, the Convention in its Art. 10.

---

27   European Commission, 'Tackling online disinformation', Fact Sheet (26 April 2018), MEMO/18/3371 http://europa.eu/rapid/press-release_MEMO-18-3371_en.htm.
28   High Level Expert Group on Fake News and Online Disinformation, 'A multi-dimensional approach to disinformation', Report (Office of the European Union, 2018) https://ec.europa.eu/digital-single-market/en/news/final-report-high-level-expert-group-fake-news-and-online-disinformation.
29   European Commission, 'Action Plan against Disinformation', Joint Communication to the European Parliament, the European Council, the Council, the European Economic and Social Committee and the Committee of the Regions (5 December 2018), JOIN(2018) 36 final, https://eeas.europa.eu/sites/eeas/files/action_plan_against_disinformation.pdf.

Importantly, the Convention contains a provision that is not contained in the EU Charter and is of particular note for election campaigns. Article 3 of Additional Protocol No. 1 to the Convention states:

> The High Contracting Parties undertake to hold free elections at reasonable intervals by secret ballot, under conditions which will ensure the free expression of the opinion of the people in the choice of the legislature.[30]

The field of application of this provision is limited to parliamentary elections and elections of other state organs that perform legislative functions, such as presidents in several states. It was not directly applicable to the Brexit referendum. Apart from Member States, it also applies to the EU and the elections for the European Parliament. The European Parliament performs a role similar to national parliaments because it is one of the main actors in EU law-making and EU law can be directly applicable in all Member States. As the European Court of Human Rights stated in *Matthews v UK*:

> The Court thus finds that the European Parliament is sufficiently involved in the specific legislative processes leading to the passage of legislation under Articles 189b and 189c of the EC Treaty, and is sufficiently involved in the general democratic supervision of the activities of the European Community, to constitute part of the 'legislature' of Gibraltar for the purposes of Article 3 of Protocol No. 1.[31]

Art. 3 of Protocol No. 1 would be applicable whenever actions similar to the activities of Cambridge Analytica occur during parliamentary elections of any Member State or of the EU Parliament would be affected by such distortions. The main purpose of Art. 3 of Protocol No. 1 is to guarantee democratic participation in all Member States. As the European Court of Human Rights stated in *Ždanoka v Latvia*:[32]

> Democracy constitutes a fundamental element of the 'European public order'. That is apparent, firstly, from the Preamble to the Convention, which establishes a very clear connection between the Convention and democracy by stating that the maintenance and further realisation of human rights and fundamental freedoms are best ensured on the one hand by an effective political democracy and on the other by a common understanding and observance of human rights. The Preamble goes on to affirm that European countries have a common heritage of political traditions, ideals, freedom and the rule of law.

---

30 Council of Europe, *Protocol to the European Convention on Human Rights*, ETS No. 009.
31 *Matthews v United Kingdom* App no 24833/94, [2011] ECHR 1895, [54].
32 *Ždanoka v Latvia* App no 58278/00, [2004] ECHR 268.

This common heritage consists in the underlying values of the Convention; thus, the Court has pointed out on many occasions that the Convention was in fact designed to maintain and promote the ideals and values of a democratic society. In other words, democracy is the only political model contemplated by the Convention and, accordingly, the only one compatible with it.[33]

The Court regards the rights guaranteed under Art. 3 of Protocol No. 1 as crucial to establishing and maintaining the foundations of an effective and meaningful democracy governed by the rule of law. Despite it being worded with reference to the obligations of Member States to 'undertake to hold free elections', Art. 3 of Protocol No. 1 guarantees individual rights, including the right to vote and to stand for election.[34] As the Court in its landmark decision *Mathieu-Mohin and Clerfayt v Belgium* stated:

> The [reasons for] inter-State colouring of the wording of Article 3 [P1–3] [...] seem to lie [...] in the desire to give greater solemnity to the commitment undertaken and in the fact that the primary obligation in the field concerned is not one of abstention or non-interference, as with the majority of the civil and political rights, but one of adoption by the State of positive measures to 'hold' democratic elections [...][35]

The Court adopts a fairly pragmatic approach to the rights and obligations arising under the Convention. In its interpretation of the Convention, the Court gives Member States a margin of appreciation in implementing such rights. Yet it requires that the rights and obligations be effective and that all measures concerned be proportionate. In the case of *Aliyev v Azerbaijan,* [36] the Court stated:

> The rights bestowed by Article 3 of Protocol No. 1 are not absolute. There is room for 'implied limitations' and Contracting States have a wide margin of appreciation in the sphere of elections. It is, however, for the Court to determine in the last resort whether the requirements of Article 3 of Protocol No. 1 have been complied with. In particular, it has to satisfy itself, among other things, that the conditions in which individual rights are exercised in the course of the electoral process do not curtail the rights in question to such an extent as to impair their very essence and deprive them of their effectiveness

---

33 See, among many other examples, *United Communist Party of Turkey v Turkey* App no 19392/92, [1998] ECHR 1, [45]; *Refah Partisi (the Welfare Party) v Turkey* App no 41340/98, 41342/98, 41343/98, 41344/98, [2001] ECHR 495 [86]; *Gorzelik v Poland* App no 44158/98, [2001] ECHR 878 [89].

34 See *Mathieu-Mohin and Clerfayt v Belgium* App no 9267/81, (1987) Series A no 113 [46]–[51].

35 Ibid.

36 *Aliyev v Azerbaijan* App no 18705/06, [2010] ECHR 489.

[…] Such conditions must not thwart the free expression of the people in the choice of the legislature – in other words, they must reflect, or not run counter to, the concern to maintain the integrity and effectiveness of an electoral procedure aimed at identifying the will of the people through universal suffrage.[37]

In summary, the guarantee of 'democratic elections' means much more than that Member States must allow their citizens to vote in, or to stand for, elections. There is a close link between democratic elections and all human rights under the Convention which guarantee a free flow of information.[38] Art. 3 Protocol No. 1 requires that Member States have to make sure that during election campaigns the people can exercise their rights to express an opinion, to get information about politically relevant facts, to assemble and to found and run political parties or other civil associations.

VII. Freedom of the press

Traditionally, there is a specific focus on the freedom of the press guaranteed by Art. 10 ECtHR. The Court has for decades made clear that the traditional press plays a crucial role in imparting information and ideas on matters of public concern. In this context, the most careful scrutiny on the part of the Court is called for when the measures taken by a national authority are capable of discouraging the participation of the press, one of society's 'watchdogs', in the public debate on matters of legitimate public interest.[39]

But this function has its limits depending on the topic being reported and the way information is gathered. In the decision *von Hannover v Germany (No. 1)* the Court stated:

> The Court considers that a fundamental distinction needs to be made between reporting facts – even controversial ones – capable of contributing to a debate in a democratic society relating to politicians in the exercise of their functions, for example, and reporting details of the private life of an individual who, moreover, as in this case, does not exercise official functions.

---

37 *Mathieu-Mohin* (n 34) [52]; *Matthews* (n 31) [63]; *Labita v Italy* App no 26772/95, [2000] ECHR 161 [201].

38 In *Bowman v United Kingdom* App no 24839/94, [1998] ECHR 4, the Court stated at [42]: 'Free elections and freedom of expression, particularly freedom of political debate, together form the bedrock of any democratic system. The two rights are interrelated and operate to reinforce each other: for example, freedom of expression is one of the conditions necessary to ensure the free expression of the opinion of the people in the choice of the legislation.'

39 See *Observer and Guardian v United Kingdom* App no 13585/88, (1991) Series A no 216 [59]; *Thorgeir Thorgeirson v Iceland* App no 13778/88, (1992) Series A no 239.

In this case, the publication of photographs in the yellow press depicting scenes of the daily life of prominent people did not serve any public interest.[40] While in the case of politically relevant information the press exercises its vital role of 'watchdog' in a democratic society by contributing to imparting information and ideas on matters of public interest, it does not do so in the latter case.[41] In its later decision *von Hannover v Germany (No. 2)*, the Grand Chamber of the Court added that the rumoured marital difficulties of the president of a country or the financial difficulties of a famous singer did not qualify for protection as matters of general interest.[42]

Further on in its decision, the Court stated:

> Lastly, the Court has already held that the context and circumstances in which the published photos were taken cannot be disregarded. In that connection regard must be had to whether the person photographed gave their consent to the taking of the photos and their publication or whether this was done without their knowledge or by subterfuge or other illicit means.[43]

If the protection of true facts differs in intensity under the Convention depending on their contribution to a debate on matters of public concern, the dissemination of fake news cannot enjoy any protection at all. In *Lingens v Austria*, the Court made clear that 'a careful distinction needs to be made between facts and value-judgments. The existence of facts can be demonstrated, whereas the truth of value-judgments is not susceptible of proof.'[44]

In the case of *Pentikäinen v Finland*,[45] the Grand Chamber of the Court stated that the 'protection afforded by Article 10 of the Convention to journalists is subject to the provision that they act in good faith in order to provide accurate and reliable information in accordance with the tenets of responsible journalism'.[46] While the Court's case law makes clear that the concept of responsible journalism is focused mainly on issues relating to the contents of a publication,[47] it also

---

40 *Von Hannover v Germany (No 1)* App no 59320/00, [2004] ECHR 294 [65]: '[T]he Court considers that the publication of the photos and articles in question, the sole purpose of which was to satisfy the curiosity of a particular readership regarding the details of the applicant's private life, cannot be deemed to contribute to any debate of general interest.'

41 Ibid 63.

42 Ibid 110.

43 Ibid 113.

44 *Lingens v Austria* App no 9815/82, (1986) Series A 103 [46].

45 *Pentikäinen v Finland* App no 11882/10, [2014] ECHR 283.

46 Ibid § 90. See also *Bladet Tromsø and Stensaas v Norway* App no 21980/93, [1999] ECHR 29 [65]; *Fressoz and Roire v France* App no 29183/95, [1997] ECHR 194 [54]; *Kasabova v Bulgaria* App no 22385/03, [2011] ECHR 701 [61], [63]–[68]; *Times Newspapers Ltd v United Kingdom No 1 and 2* App no 3002/03 and 23676/03, [2009] ECHR 451 [42].

47 *Bladet Tromsø* (n 46) [65]–[67]; *Fressoz and Roire* (n 46) [52]–[55]; *Krone Verlag GmbH v Austria* App no 27306/07, [2012] ECHR 1246 [46]–[47]; *Novaya Gazeta and Borodyanskiy v Russia* App no 14087/08, [2013] ECHR 251 [37]; *Perna v Italy*

means that journalists who exercise their freedom of expression are not absolved from other duties and responsibilities. For example, 'notwithstanding the vital role played by the media in a democratic society, journalists cannot, in principle, be released from their duty to obey the ordinary criminal law'.[48] In *Pentikäinen v Finland*, the applicant's failure to obey a police order to leave the scene of a demonstration that had turned into a riot was a relevant, if not decisive, consideration when determining whether he or she had acted responsibly.

Adherence to the rules of responsible journalism is especially crucial during election campaigns. As the example of the Italian elections in 1994 shows, the influence of manipulated mass media during the campaign can heavily change the outcome of the result of the elections. At that time, Silvio Berlusconi was not only the head of the newly founded political party Forza Italia and candidate for the office of prime minister, but also controlled nearly the whole market of private television in Italy. Apart from engaging in political attacks on other parties, Berlusconi spread fake news about prominent competitors such as Romano Prodi and Piero Fassino. Forza Italia ended up winning the elections, and Berlusconi went on to become four-time prime minister.[49]

VIII. Bloggers and private postings

With some variation, these principles are also applicable to non-professional media such as bloggers or private postings. In a case originating in 2005,[50] the applicant before the Court was a non-governmental organisation whose declared aim was to promote fundamental rights, as well as to strengthen civil society and the rule of law in Hungary. The Court stated:

> The function of the press includes the creation of forums for public debate. However, the realisation of this function is not limited to the media or professional journalists. In the present case, the preparation of the forum of public debate was conducted by a non-governmental organisation. The purpose of the applicant's activities can therefore be said to have been an essential element of informed public debate. The Court has repeatedly recognised civil society's important contribution to the discussion of public affairs. [...] In these circumstances, the Court is satisfied that its activities warrant similar Convention protection to that afforded to the press.[51]

App no 48898/99, [2003] ECHR 230, [47]; *Times Newspapers Ltd* (n 46) § 45; *Ungváry and Irodalom Kft v Hungary* App no 64520/10, [2013] ECHR 1229 [42]; *Yordanova and Toshev v Bulgaria* App no 5126/05, [2012] ECHR 1768 [53], [55].
48 *Pentikäinen v Finland* App no 11882/10, [2015] ECHR 926 [91].
49 Bruno Mastroianni, 'Fake news, free speech and democracy: A (bad) lesson from Italy?' (2019) 25(1) Southwestern Journal of International Law 42.
50 *Társaság a Szabadságjogokért v Hungary* App no 37374/05, [2009] ECHR 618.
51 Ibid § 27.

The cases show that freedom of the press and all other forms of (electronic) media depends on their ability and willingness to inform people about socially relevant topics. The yardstick to evaluate the relevance of their publications is their level of journalistic professionalism. Only information derived from trustful sources and double-checked according to professional standards can lead to a well-informed society being able to perform its democratic functions.

In the case of *Pihl v Sweden*, [52] the Court attributed protection under Art. 10 of the Convention also to the blog of a small non-profit association. In assessing its obligations towards protecting the private life of a person who was falsely accused by a comment on a blog post, it took into account its small circulation, as well as how it responded to the offending comment once it had been alerted to it.

In contrast, where a news portal is professionally run and due to its size has a greater significance for public opinion, the Court took a different view. In *Delfi AS v Estonia*, [53] the Grand Chamber of the Court stated:

> Moreover, the Court has previously held that in the light of its accessibility and its capacity to store and communicate vast amounts of information, the Internet plays an important role in enhancing the public's access to news and facilitating the dissemination of information in general. At the same time, the risk of harm posed by content and communications on the Internet to the exercise and enjoyment of human rights and freedoms, particularly the right to respect for private life, is certainly higher than that posed by the press.[54]

Based on the circumstances of the case, the Court held that imposing liability on the news site did not impose a disproportionate burden on the applicant's freedom of expression.[55]

52   *Pihl v Sweden* App no 74742/14 (ECtHR, 9 March 2017).
53   *Delfi AS v Estonia* App no 64569/09 [2015] ECHR 586 [48]; *Times Newspapers Ltd* (n 46) [27].
54   *Delfi AS v Estonia* (n 53) [133].
55   Ibid [162]: 'Based on the concrete assessment of the above aspects, taking into account the reasoning of the Supreme Court in the present case, in particular the extreme nature of the comments in question, the fact that the comments were posted in reaction to an article published by the applicant company on its professionally managed news portal run on a commercial basis, the insufficiency of the measures taken by the applicant company to remove without delay after publication comments amounting to hate speech and speech inciting violence and to ensure a realistic prospect of the authors of such comments being held liable, and the moderate sanction imposed on the applicant company, the Court finds that the domestic courts' imposition of liability on the applicant company was based on relevant and sufficient grounds, having regard to the margin of appreciation afforded to the respondent State. Therefore, the measure did not constitute a disproportionate restriction on the applicant company's right to freedom of expression.'

IX. Obligations of Member States under the Convention

The intentional dissemination of wrong facts, hiding one's own identity or the deceptive use of bots in public discourse are incompatible with the precepts of professional journalism. They also pose serious challenges to the concept of freedom of expression under Art. 10 of the Convention. The duty on Member States to grant conditions under which democratic processes run in conformity with the Conventions and the duty to enable a free flow of information makes it imperative for Member States to create legal and factual conditions that minimise the occurrence of this type of undemocratic influence.

But, of course, there is a high degree of uncertainty about the suitable concepts to reach this goal. The Study Group set up by the European Union Commission to tackle online disinformation identified five difficult topics of paramount relevance.[56] These are:

- To enhance transparency of online news, involving an adequate and privacy-compliant sharing of data about the systems that enable their circulation online;
- To promote media and information literacy to counter disinformation and help users navigate the digital media environment;
- To develop tools for empowering users and journalists to tackle disinformation and foster a positive engagement with fast-evolving information technologies;
- To safeguard the diversity and sustainability of the European news media ecosystem;
- To promote continued research on the impact of disinformation in Europe to evaluate the measures taken by different actors and constantly adjust the necessary responses.

Social media companies including Google, Facebook and Twitter signed up voluntarily to a Code of Conduct, which contained a range of commitments against disinformation and for greater transparency of political advertising.[57] Self-regulation may be a useful way to tackle the problem, but when confronted with fundamental legal problems, lawyers usually think about regulations.

In France, Parliament passed new legislation in November 2018 that enables emergency legal action by authorities to remove specific content or even block the website during times of elections. These regulations also include more transparency about sponsored content. Websites are obliged to make clear who is financing them, and the amount of money for sponsored content can be capped.[58]

---

56 High Level Expert Group on Fake News and Online Disinformation (n 28).
57 European Commission, 'Code of practice against disinformation: Commission takes note of the progress made by online platforms and urges them to step up their efforts', STATEMENT/19/1757 (20 March 2019) http://europa.eu/rapid/p ress-release_STATEMENT-19-1757_en.htm.
58 Loi relative à la lutte contre la manipulation de l'information, Loi no° 2018–1202, 22 December 2018 (JO n° 0297 of 23 December 2018).

In Germany, a Network Enforcement Act came into force in October 2017.[59] The new law defines binding standards for effective and transparent complaints management for social media content that contains insults, malicious gossip, defamation, public incitement to crime or incitement to hatred, or disseminates portrayals of violence and threatens the commission of a felony. The operators of social networks will be subject to the following obligations:

- They must offer users an easily recognisable, directly accessible and permanently available procedure for reporting criminally punishable content.
- They must immediately take notice of content reported to them by users and examine whether that content might violate criminal law.
- They must take down or block access to manifestly unlawful content within 24 hours of receiving a complaint.
- Other criminal content must generally be taken down or blocked within seven days of receiving a complaint. Alternatively, social networks may refer the content concerned to a 'recognised institution of regulated self-governance' on the understanding that they will accept the decision of that institution. The institution must then also make its decision on whether the content is unlawful within seven days.
- They must inform users of all decisions taken in response to their complaints and provide justification.

This law remains highly contentious because of its potential effects on free speech on the internet. Critics argue that the short timeframes combined with the threat of significant fines will lead social networks to be overly cautious and delete huge amounts of content even it is protected by free speech.[60] However, it is worth noting that the new Act does not itself prohibit content, but makes reference only to already existing free speech regulations in the German Criminal Code, which have been judicially assessed over many years for their compatibility with free speech. The innovation is that the complaints management has been strengthened to provide enhanced and faster protection against unlawful speech on the internet.

X. Conclusion

Recent developments and revelations have highlighted new risks for democracy, privacy and even free speech on the internet. Without question, there remains an urgent need for a profound discussion about possible solutions that promote the

---

59   Gesetz zur Verbesserung der Rechtsdurchsetzung in sozialen Netzwerken (Netzwerkdurchsetzungsgesetz – NetzDG), 1 September 2017 (BGBl. I S. 3352).
60   See Markus Reuter, 'Anhörung zum NetzDG: Mehrheit der Experten hält Gesetzentwurf für verfassungswidrig' *Netzpolitik* (19 June 2017) https://netzpolitik.org/2017/anhoerung-zum-netzdg-mehrheit-der-experten-haelt-gesetzentwurf-fuer-verfassungswidrig.

competing interests as far as possible. These interests include the free flow of information, transparent and trustworthy news-reporting on the basis of accepted rules of professional journalism and the protection of privacy and democratic decision-making. It will be not easy to balance these principles in a fair and effective way, and the rapid change of our electronic world will soon give us new challenges. It is more important than ever to agree on the basics, so that we can find the proper answers.

Chapter 7

Freedom of processing of personal data for the purpose of electoral activities after the GDPR

Maeve McDonagh

I. Introduction

Concern has been expressed over recent years with respect to the processing of personal data in connection with electoral activities,[1] and revelations relating to the interactions between Facebook and Cambridge Analytica have further highlighted the problems arising from such processing. Many of these concerns relate to practices such as the use of personal data obtained from social media sites, data brokers and publicly available information sources to build profiles of personality and voting behaviour, and the use of the resultant profiles to micro-target individual voters with messages in keeping with their particular interests and values. Such practices, which are often undertaken on a covert basis, may be directed at manipulating voters and ultimately subverting the electoral process.[2] They may be carried out not only by established political parties and candidates for election but also by entities and individuals not directly involved in party politics but with a particular political leaning or

---

1   UK Information Commissioner's Office, 'Democracy Disrupted? Personal information and political influence', Report (11 July 2018) https://ico.org.uk/media/2259369/democracy-disrupted-110718.pdf; Colin J Bennett, 'Trends in Voter Surveillance in Western Societies: Privacy Intrusions and Democratic Implications' (2015) 13(3/4) Surveillance and Society 370; Colin J Bennett, 'Voter databases, micro-targeting, and data protection law: Can political parties campaign in Europe as they do in North America?' (2016) 6(4) International Data Privacy Law 261 ('Voter databases'); Ira Rubinstein, 'Voter Privacy in the Age of Big Data' (2014) 5 Wisconsin Law Review 861.

2   European Data Protection Supervisor, 'Opinion 3/2018 EDPS Opinion on online manipulation and personal data' (19 March 2018) https://edps.europa.eu/sites/edp/files/publication/18-03-19_online_manipulation_en.pdf, 11–12; Frederik J Zuiderveen Borgesius et al., 'Online Political Microtargeting: Promises and Threats for Democracy' (2018) 14(1) Utrecht Law Review 83; Demos, 'The Future of Political Campaigning', Report commissioned by the UK Information Commissioner's Office (July 2018) www.demos.co.uk/project/the-future-of-political-campaigning.

interest (including extra-territorial individuals or entities[3] and even foreign governments[4]), social media platforms, data brokers and data analytics companies.

This chapter will examine the regulation of the processing of personal data for the purpose of electoral activities in the EU. The strength of the protections available under the GDPR will be evaluated along with the extent to which they mandate the adoption of a uniform approach across the Member States.

II. Regulation of the processing of personal data for electoral activities in Europe

The main source for the regulation of personal data in the context of electoral activities in Europe is the General Data Protection Regulation[5] (GDPR), which succeeded the Data Protection Directive[6] in May 2018. Account must be taken in the interpretation of the GDPR of the fundamental rights protected by the Charter of Fundamental Rights of the EU (CFEU) including the right to respect for private life,[7] right to protection of personal data[8] and the right to freedom of expression, including political expression.[9]

The GDPR includes specific provisions relating to the processing by political parties of personal data revealing political opinions.[10] However, in an era when profiling techniques have made it possible to identify an individual's political leanings and influence their voting behaviour through the processing of data that appears to bear no relationship to their political ideology,[11] it is important to note that many types of personal data may be processed for the purpose of electoral

---

3   For example, the Irish Standards in Public Office Commission noted with concern in the context of several impending referenda in 2017 that 'individuals and organisations based outside of Ireland may fund political advertising or launch digital campaigns financed outside the State': Standards in Public Office Commission, 'Annual Report' (2017) www.sipo.ie/en/Reports/Annual-Reports/2017-Annual-Report/2017-Annua l-Report.html, 6.

4   Office of the US Director of National Intelligence, 'Assessing Russian Activities and Intentions in recent US Elections' (6 January 2017) www.dni.gov/files/documents/ ICA_2017_01.pdf.

5   Regulation (EU) 2016/679 of the European Parliament and of the Council of 27 April 2016 on the protection of natural persons with regard to the processing of personal data and on the free movement of such data, and repealing Directive 95/46/ EC (General Data Protection Regulation) [2016] OJ L 119, 1.

6   Directive 95/46/EC of the European Parliament and of the Council of 24 October 1995 on the protection of individuals with regard to the processing of personal data and on the free movement of such data: [1995] OJ L 281, 31.

7   CFEU, art. 7.

8   Ibid art. 8.

9   Ibid art. 11.

10   Ibid art. 9(2)(d).

11   For example, it has been suggested that the strength of a person's reaction to repulsive images is an accurate forecaster of political ideology: Woo-Young Ahn et al., 'Nonpolitical Images Evoke Neural Predictors of Political Ideology' (2014) 24(22) Current Biology 2693.

activities. Such data include not only data revealing a person's political opinions, but also data as diverse as information concerning their family and relationship status, their ethnicity, their cultural and sporting interests – in sum any personal data relating to them. This chapter will therefore consider the application of the GDPR in relation to the processing for the purpose of electoral activities of all types of personal data.

The discussion is confined to electoral activities specifically rather than to political communication generally, on the grounds that communications that take place during the lead-up to an election have the greatest capacity to impact on the democratic process. This was recognised by the European Court of Human Rights in *Animal Defenders v UK* when the Grand Chamber of the Court expressed the view that 'the risk to pluralist public debates, elections and the democratic process would evidently be more acute during an electoral period'.[12] The term 'electoral activities' is not defined in the GDPR and it is encountered only once in the text.[13] For the purposes of this chapter, electoral activities shall be broadly construed to include activities concerning the process of campaigning, getting elected and remaining in office, but to exclude political communications not concerned with any particular election.

The processing of personal data for electoral purposes may be undertaken directly by data controllers[14] or it may be carried out on their behalf by third parties known as 'data processors'.[15] The European Commission has emphasised that 'the role as data controller or data processor has to be assessed in each individual case' with political parties, individual candidates and political foundations being, in most instances, data controllers, while platforms and data analytics companies can be controllers (or joint controllers) or processors for a given processing depending on the degree of control they have over the processing concerned.[16] The European Data Protection Supervisor has pointed out that '[t]he greater the freedom that company has to decide what data to collect and how to apply its analytics techniques, the more possible the company will be considered a joint controller'.[17] Data controllers are obliged only to use data processors that provide sufficient guarantees that processing will meet the requirements of the GDPR[18] and this obligation is supported by the requirement that

12   App no. 48876/08, [2013] ECHR 362 [111].
13   In GDPR rec. 56, which is associated with art. 9(2)(g) concerning the processing of personal data in the public interest. See III.A.3.
14   Defined in GDPR art. 4(7) as 'means the natural or legal person, public authority, agency or other body which, alone or jointly with others, determines the purposes and means of the processing of personal data'.
15   Defined in GDPR art. 4(8) as 'natural or legal person, public authority, agency or other body which processes personal data on behalf of the controller'.
16   European Commission, 'Free and Fair elections: Commission guidance on the application of Union data protection law in the electoral context', Guidance Document COM(2018) 638 final (12 September 2018) https://ec.europa.eu/commission/sites/beta-political/files/soteu2018-data-protection-law-electoral-guidance-638_en.pdf, 4.
17   European Data Protection Supervisor (n 2) 15.
18   GDPR art. 28(1).

a data controller enter into contractual arrangements with any data processor it engages,[19] the minimum requirements of which are spelt out in art. 28 of the GDPR.

III. The GDPR and the processing of personal data for electoral activities

The processing of data in connection with electoral activities was not raised in debates leading up to the adoption of the GDPR. The provisions of the GDPR of most relevance to the processing of personal data for such purposes (apart from the general data protection principles provided for in art. 5) are the following: the rules governing the lawful processing of personal data (art. 6) and the processing of special categories of data (art. 9); and the following rights conferred on the data subject by Chapter 2 of the GDPR: the transparency requirements provided for in arts 13 and 14; the right to object and the right to object to direct marketing found in art. 21; and the profiling restrictions in art. 22.

A. Lawful processing provisions and the processing of special categories of data: arts 6 and 9

The types of personal data that can be used to divine a person's political leanings and influence their voting behaviour are not confined to data revealing their political opinions but can encompass all kinds of personal data about them. Consideration of the legitimacy, from a GDPR perspective, of the processing of all categories of personal data for electoral purposes is therefore necessary.

The GDPR requires that the processing of personal data be performed on the basis of a lawful processing condition identified in art. 6. Where the data in question belongs to a 'special category' of personal data,[20] the processing of such data is prohibited unless one of the exceptions provided for in art. 9 applies. The Article 29 Working Party on Data Protection (A29WP) has underlined that in the case of special categories of data, meeting the requirements of art. 9 is not necessarily sufficient to ensure lawfulness under art. 6: analysis has to be undertaken on a case-by-case basis as to whether art. 9 'in itself provides for stricter and sufficient conditions, or whether a cumulative application of both Article [6] and [9] is required to ensure full protection of data subjects'.[21] The

---

19 GDPR art. 28(3).
20 The special categories of personal data are: personal data revealing racial or ethnic origin, political opinions, religious or philosophical beliefs, or trade union membership, genetic data, biometric data processed for the purpose of uniquely identifying a natural person and data concerning health or data concerning a natural person's sex life or sexual orientation: art. 9(1).
21 A29WP Opinion 06/2014 on the notion of legitimate interests of the data controller under Article 7 of Directive 95/46/EC, European Commission, 9 April 2014, 15 ('A29WP Opinion 06/2014'). The articles referenced in Opinion 06/2014 are arts 7 and 8 of the former Data Protection Directive (Directive 95/46/EC of the European Parliament and of the Council of 24 October 1995 on the Protection of Individuals with Regard to the Processing of Personal Data and on the Free Movement of Such

A29WP expressly references in its discussion of this issue, the processing of personal data by a political party, noting that while such processing may be permitted in some situations by the exception provided for in art. 9(2)(d),[22] this does not mean that any processing within the scope of that provision is necessarily lawful under art. 6: the legitimacy of the processing under art. 6 will have to be assessed separately and the controller may have to demonstrate, for instance, that 'the data processing is necessary for the performance of a contract [...] or that its legitimate interest [...] prevails'.[23]

I. Consent

In the case of both arts 6 and 9, obtaining the consent of the data subject to the processing of the data will meet the requirements of the GDPR, though in the case of art. 9, the consent must be explicit.[24]

The GDPR defines consent as 'any freely given, specific, informed and unambiguous indication of the data subject's wishes by which he or she, by statement or by a clear affirmative action, signifies agreement to the processing of personal data relating to him or her'.[25] This means that, as described by the A29WP Guidelines on Consent (A29WP Consent Guidelines),[26] 'if the data subject has no real choice, feels compelled to consent or will endure negative consequences if they do not consent, then consent will not be valid'.[27] A component of this is that the data subject must also have the right to withdraw consent to processing at any time and it must be as easy to withdraw as to give consent.[28]

The procedural conditions for consent to data processing are set out in art. 7 of the GDPR. This article places the obligation to demonstrate consent on the data controller.[29] It also requires that where the consent is given in a written declaration that concerns other matters, the request for consent must be presented in a way that is clearly distinguishable from the other matters and

Data, [1995] OJ L 281, the DPD), which are the counterparts of GDPR arts 6 and 9 respectively. The Article 29 Working Party on Data Protection was established under DPD art. 29 to play an advisory role in respect of the protection of individuals with regard to the processing of personal data. Since the coming into force of the GDPR (on 25 May 2018), it has been replaced by the European Data Protection Board.

22   See discussion below at III.A.3.

23   A29WP Opinion 06/2014 (n 21). The articles referenced in Opinion 06/2014 are arts 7 and 8 of the Data Protection Directive which are the counterparts of arts 6 and 9 respectively of the GDPR.

24   GDPR art. 6(1)(a) and art. 9(2)(a). Article 7 sets out the conditions for consent.

25   GDPR art. 4(11). In assessing whether consent is freely given, 'utmost account' must be taken of whether the performance of a contract is made conditional on consent to data processing.

26   A29WP Guidelines on Consent under Regulation 2016/679, adopted on 28 November 2017, rev'd and adopted 10 April 2018, WP257 rev.01 ('A29WP Consent Guidelines').

27   Ibid 5.

28   GDPR art. 7(3).

29   GDPR art. 7(1).

in an intelligible and clearly accessible form, using plain and clear language.[30] Data subjects must be informed of their right to withdraw consent prior to giving the consent.[31] They must also be informed as to how to exercise the withdrawal right.[32]

For data revealing political opinion, there is the additional requirement that the consent be 'explicit'.[33] The A29WP Consent Guidelines state that the term 'explicit' refers to the way consent is expressed by the data subject and requires that the data subject has given an express statement of consent.[34]

Questions have been raised with respect to the use of consent as the basis for the processing of personal data in general, especially in an era of big data analytics.[35] In the first place, it is difficult to expect individuals to provide consent at the time of collection because they may not know what they are consenting to, while bodies handling information may not know what to seek consent for.[36] The complexity of data processing also renders reliance on consent problematic. Cate and Mayer-Schönberger point out that the processing of data has become very 'complicated as datasets are combined and data processors and users change',[37] rendering it difficult for data controllers to provide sufficient information to data subjects so as to obtain informed consent. Consent notices can also be overly complex.[38] The issue of consent is further complicated by the imbalance of power that can exist between the data subject and the data controller. Such imbalances are readily observed in 'the business terms and privacy policies of online providers [which] are normally drafted in favour of those providers and are not negotiable'.[39] Another problem is that it may be said that there is no real choice when it comes to consenting to the use of

---

30   GDPR art. 7(2).
31   GDPR art. 7(3).
32   A29WP Consent Guidelines (n 26) 22 (drawing on GDPR, rec. 39).
33   GDPR art. 9(2)(a). This enhanced requirement also applies to other special categories of data: data revealing racial or ethnic origin, political opinions, religious or philosophical beliefs, or trade union membership, as well as genetic and biometric data for the purpose of uniquely identifying a natural person and data concerning a natural person's sex life and sexual orientation.
34   A29WP Consent Guidelines (n 26) 18.
35   Moira Paterson and Maeve McDonagh, 'Data Protection in an Era of Big Data: The Challenges Posed by Big Personal Data' (2018) 44(1) Monash University Law Review 1.
36   Daniel J Solove, 'Introduction: Privacy Self-Management and the Consent Dilemma' (2013) 126(7) Harvard Law Review 1880, 1902; Alessandro Mantelero, 'The Future of Consumer Data Protection in the EU: Re-Thinking the "Notice and Consent" Paradigm in the New Era of Predictive Analytics' (2014) 30(6) Computer Law & Security Review 643, 645.
37   Fred H Cate and Viktor Mayer-Schönberger, 'Notice and Consent in a World of Big Data' (2013) 3(2) International Data Privacy Law 67, 67–8.
38   Fred H Cate, 'The Limits of Notice and Choice' (2010) 8(2) IEEE Security & Privacy 59, 60 suggests that in the US in particular notices tend to be overly complex.
39   Judith Rauhofer, 'One Step Forward, Two Steps Back? Critical Observations on the Proposed Reform of the EU Data Protection Framework' (2013) 6(1) Journal of Law & Economic Regulation 57, 76.

one's data: this phenomenon is referred to by Mantelero as 'social lock-in'.[40] The only choice the user is offered most of the time is to 'take-it-or-leave-it'.[41]

The problems associated with consent in the context of political micro-targeting were highlighted by the UK Information Commissioner when she undertook a formal investigation of the use of data analytics for political purposes in connection with alleged micro-targeting of political adverts involving Cambridge Analytica and Facebook during the UK EU Referendum and the 2016 US Presidential election. The Commissioner regarded the consent given by users of an app to allow access to their Facebook data and that of their friends as not being sufficiently informed and stated that it was not made sufficiently clear how and where the data could be sold on to a third-party organisation, and how it would be processed or used in the ways described.[42]

In the absence of consent which meets the requirements of the GDPR, a range of other legal bases for the processing of personal data in compliance with both art. 6 and art. 9 are also provided for and those most relevant to the processing of personal data in the electoral context will now be examined.

2. Article 6

In the case of art. 6, the following two legal bases for the processing of personal data for the purpose of electoral activities may apply: art. 6(1)(e): processing of personal data necessary for the performance of a task carried out in the public interest or in the exercise of official authority vested in the controller;[43] and art. 6 (1)(f): processing necessary for the purposes of the legitimate interests pursued by the controller or by a third party. In both cases, processing is lawful to the extent that one of the grounds for processing applies. The requirement that processing be 'necessary' for the performance of a task carried out in the public interest means that it must be genuinely necessary for the performance of the task as opposed to being unilaterally imposed on the data subject by the controller.[44]

---

40   Mantelero (n 36) 645.
41   Rauhofer (n 39) 76.
42   UK Information Commissioner's Office, 'Investigation into the Use of Analytics in Political Campaigns: Investigation – Update' (11 July 2018) https://ico.org.uk/m edia/action-weve-taken/2259371/investigation-into-data-analytics-for-political-purp oses-update.pdf, 21.
43   Of the two bases for legitimate processing provided for in art. 6(1)(e), the discussion will focus on the processing of personal data necessary for the performance of a task carried out in the public interest rather than on the processing of personal data in the exercise of official authority vested in the controller. This is because the discussion is concerned with processing of personal data for electoral purposes by entities such as political parties, social media platforms and data analytics companies who would not be processing such data in the exercise of official authority.
44   See the discussion of 'necessary' in A29WP Opinion 06/2014 (n 21) 16.

ART. 6(1)(E): PROCESSING OF PERSONAL DATA NECESSARY FOR THE PERFORMANCE OF A TASK
CARRIED OUT IN THE PUBLIC INTEREST

An important threshold requirement for the invocation of art. 6(1)(e) for the
lawful processing of personal data is that the basis for the processing of such data
in the public interest must be laid down by Union or Member State law to which
the controller is subject.[45] The purpose of the processing must be 'necessary for
the performance of a task carried out in the public interest' and the legal basis may
contain specific provisions 'to adapt the application of rules'[46] of the GDPR,
including general conditions governing the lawfulness of processing by the controller; the types of data which are subject to the processing; the data subjects
concerned; the entities to, and the purposes for which, the personal data may be
disclosed; the purpose limitation; storage periods, and processing operations and
processing procedures, including measures to ensure lawful and fair processing.
The law must also meet an objective of public interest and be proportionate to the
legitimate aim pursued.[47]

One question that must be considered is whether the application of art. 6(1)(e)
is confined to the processing of personal data by public authorities or whether it
can apply to processing by all of the players engaged in the processing of personal
data for the purpose of electoral activities such as political parties, elected representatives and candidates for office, social media platforms, data brokers and data
analytics companies. While the text of art. 6(1)(e) does not address this question,
rec. 45 states that it should be for Union or Member State law to determine
whether a controller performing a task carried out in the public interest should be
a public authority or another natural or legal person governed by public law or
'where it is in the public interest to do so, including for health purposes such as
public health and social protection and the management of health care services, by
private law, such as a professional association'. Thus rec. 45 suggests that a
Member State may introduce a law that permits entities other than public authorities to process personal data in the public interest on the basis of art. 6(1)(e).

Political parties and candidates for election are governed by public law (i.e.
electoral legislation) and the processing of personal data by political parties and
candidates in the electoral context could be viewed as being necessary for the
performance of a task carried out in the public interest. The application of art. 6
(1)(e) to the processing of personal data by political parties and candidates is
supported by the European Commission which, in a report on the application of
EU data protection law in the electoral context, stated that '[p]olitical parties and
foundations can also process data on the grounds of public interest if so provided
by national law'.[48]

---

45   GDPR art. 6(3).
46   Ibid.
47   Ibid.
48   European Commission (n 16) 5.

Since art. 6(1)(e) allows processing only to the extent necessary for the performance of a task carried out in the public interest, political parties are limited in terms of the nature of the processing they may engage in. It is clear that the processing must be in the public interest as opposed to the interest of the political party engaging it. The UK Information Commissioner provided an example of the form of processing permitted when she acknowledged that the processing of personal data for the purpose of 'activities such as those covered by electoral law, for example sending mail outs allowed to each voter' could come within the scope of art. 6(1)(e).[49]

The processing of personal data by entities such as social media platforms, data brokers and data analytics companies is less likely to come within the scope of art. 6(1)(e). It would be difficult to argue that the processing of personal data in the electoral context by players such as platforms, data brokers and analytics companies is in the public interest, especially in light of the Cambridge Analytica revelations, and it is noteworthy that the European Commission[50] has indicated that the most appropriate art. 6 bases for the processing of personal data by data brokers and data analytics companies as data controllers in the electoral context are consent (art. 6(1)(a)) or legitimate interests (art. 6(1)(f)). Where data brokers and analytics companies act as data processors on behalf of political parties, it would, as previously explained, be necessary to establish that the processing by the political party is in the public interest and not just in the interest of the political party concerned.

ART. 6(1)(F): PROCESSING OF PERSONAL DATA NECESSARY FOR THE PURPOSES OF THE LEGITIMATE INTERESTS PURSUED BY THE CONTROLLER OR BY A THIRD PARTY

Assuming consent to processing is not obtained, art. 6(1)(f) is most likely to be invoked as the basis for the processing of personal data for the purpose of electoral activities. Article 6(1)(f) permits the processing of personal data to the extent necessary for the purposes of the legitimate interests pursued by the controller or by a third party. It includes the important proviso that processing on the basis of this condition may not be undertaken where 'such interests are overridden by the interests or fundamental rights and freedoms of the data subject'. Recital 47 states that the existence of a legitimate interest needs careful assessment, including whether a data subject can reasonably expect, at the time and in the context of the collection of the personal data, that processing for that purpose may take place.

The A29WP has taken the view that application of the legitimate interests condition (as provided for in art. 6(1)(f) of the GDPR) calls for a balancing test in which the

---

49   UK Information Commissioner's Office, 'Data Protection Bill, House of Commons Public Bill Committee – Information Commissioner's further written evidence' (19 March 2018) https://ico.org.uk/media/about-the-ico/documents/2258463/data-protection-bill-public-bill-committee-ico-evidence.pdf [9].

50   European Commission (n 16) 10.

legitimate interests of the controller (or third parties) must be balanced against the interests or fundamental rights and freedoms of the data subject.[51] The A29WP states that account must be taken in carrying out the balancing test of the following two elements: the nature and source of the legitimate interests and the impact on the data subjects. Factors relevant to assessing the nature and source of the legitimate interests are said to include: whether the exercise of any fundamental rights are at stake; the public interest or the interest of the wider community; whether any other legitimate interests are at stake; and the extent of legal and cultural/societal recognition of the legitimacy of the interests. In terms of the impact on the data subject, the relevant factors are: the range of both positive and negative consequences of the processing; the nature of the data;[52] the way the data are being processed; the reasonable expectations of the data subject; and the status of the data controller and data subject.

The fundamental rights of which account must be taken are those provided for in the CFEU, and the A29WP specifically references the need to balance the rights to privacy and to the protection of personal data against other rights including the right to freedom of expression and information.[53] Balancing the controller's legitimate interests against the interests and fundamental rights of data subjects requires careful assessment which must take into account the circumstances of the specific case. It also requires the undertaking of a proportionality analysis.[54] While freedom of political expression may support the processing of personal data for electoral purposes,[55] this must be weighed against the rights to privacy and data protection in a manner which takes account of the circumstances of the case. The A29WP cites as an example of the exercise of the right to freedom of expression which renders the processing of personal data legitimate under art. 6(1)(f), the use by a candidate in a local election of the electoral register to send to each potential voter in her election district an introduction letter promoting her campaign for the upcoming elections.[56] The use of the local electoral register for such a purpose is viewed by the A29WP as coming within the reasonable expectation of individuals, provided that it takes place in the pre-election period. In such circumstances, the interest of the controller is said to be clear and legitimate. The 'limited and focused use of the information' is viewed by the A29WP as tipping the balance in favour of the legitimate interest of the controller.

It can be argued that activities such as the use by any of the players in the electoral process of personal data obtained from social media sites, data brokers and publicly available information sources to build profiles of personality and voting behaviour, and the use of the resultant profiles to micro-target individual voters with messages in keeping with their particular interests and values would be

---

51 A29WP Opinion 06/2014 (n 21) 23.
52 The more sensitive the data, the more it will weigh the balance in favour of the data subject's interests: A29WP Opinion 06/2014 (n 21) 39.
53 Ibid 34.
54 CFEU art. 52(1).
55 Zuiderveen Borgesius et al. (n 2). The right to freedom of expression is protected by CFEU art. 11.
56 A29WP Opinion 06/2014 (n 21) 60.

unlikely to qualify as the exercise of the right to freedom of expression so as to render such processing legitimate under art. 6(1)(f). Such activities would be unlikely to be viewed as involving limited and focused use of information since the range of personal data used for profiling purposes is intentionally open-ended.

In the case of other factors identified by the A29WP as relevant to the operation of the balancing test – namely, the public interest, the interest of the wider community; whether any other legitimate interests are at stake; the extent of legal and cultural/societal recognition of the legitimacy of the interests, the positive and negative consequences of the processing; the nature of the data; the way the data are being processed; the reasonable expectations of the data subject; and the status of the data controller and data subject – arguments can be made on both sides and their strength will vary depending on the circumstances of each case. For example, there is clearly a public interest in having a well-informed electorate, but where personal data is used to target voters in a manner that is designed to manipulate voting patterns, the public interest would clearly weigh against such practices. Questions would also arise as to whether data subjects could be said to reasonably expect that their personal data would be used in this manner. Another of the factors identified by the A29WP as being relevant to determining the legitimacy of the processing of personal data is the way in which the data is being processed. Where data is being processed to communicate a political message to a prospective voter in a transparent manner, it is suggested that it would be likely to meet the requirements of art. 6, but where it is done on a covert basis with a view to manipulating voters, it could fall short. To summarise, the application of the balancing test will be crucial in determining whether the processing of personal data comes within the scope of art. 6(1)(f) and it is likely that certain forms of processing of personal data in the electoral context will not pass muster.

3. Article 9

In the case of special categories of data, the GDPR requires that the explicit consent of the data subject is obtained for data processing.[57] A range of other legal bases for the processing of special categories of data (i.e. exceptions to the prohibition on processing of such data provided for in art. 9(1)) are provided for in art. 9(2). The exceptions most likely to be applicable include exceptions in art. 9(2)(g) and 9(2)(d).

EXCEPTION 9(2)(G)

Exception 9(2)(g), which applies where 'processing is necessary for reasons of substantial public interest on the basis of Union or Member State law',[58] is, like its

---

57   GDPR art. 9(2)(a). See the discussion of the difficulties around consent at III.A.1.
58   And provided that certain conditions are met, namely that the law is proportionate to the aim pursued, respects the essence of the right to data protection and provides for suitable and specific measures to safeguard the fundamental rights and the interests of the data subject.

counterpart in art. 6, reliant on EU or national law to provide the basis for the processing of data on this ground. The law must be proportionate to the aim pursued, it must respect the essence of the right to data protection, and it must provide for suitable and specific measures to safeguard the fundamental rights and the interests of the data subject. Recital 56 provides an example of when processing of special categories of data may be permitted by political parties under exception 9(2)(g). It states:

> Where in the course of electoral activities, the operation of the democratic system in a Member State requires that political parties compile personal data on people's political opinions, the processing of such data may be permitted for reasons of public interest, provided that appropriate safeguards are established.

Similar questions to those raised in the discussion of art. 6(1)(e) arise with respect to the availability of exception art. 9(2)(g) when sensitive personal data are processed for electoral purposes. However, the requirement that the public interest be 'substantial' clearly sets a higher threshold for the application of exception 9(2)(g) than is required by art. 6(1)(e), making it more difficult to use this provision as a basis for the processing of personal data for electoral purposes. The European Commission has nonetheless indicated that political parties and foundations can process special categories of data on the basis of Union or Member State law if there is substantial public interest and provided that appropriate safeguards are in place.[59] The reference to 'appropriate safeguards' derives from rec. 56. There is no definition of this term, which means that standards may vary between the various Member States. While rec. 56 supports the processing of special categories of personal data by political parties, but only where 'the operation of the democratic system in a Member State requires that political parties compile personal data on people's political opinions', it appears that the processing of such data by other players such as data brokers and data analytics companies would be difficult to justify on the grounds of substantial public interest.

EXCEPTION 9(2)(D)

Finally, we come to exception 9(2)(d) which applies where the processing of special categories of data is carried out –

> in the course of its legitimate activities with appropriate safeguards by a foundation, association or any other not-for-profit body with a political, philosophical, religious or trade union aim and on condition that the processing relates solely to the members or to former members of the body or to persons who have regular contact with it in connection with its purposes and that the

59   European Commission (n 16) 5.

personal data are not disclosed outside that body without the consent of the data subjects.

This provision can be summarised as permitting the processing of special categories of data subject to the following conditions:

1   that the processing be undertaken in the course of its legitimate activities with appropriate safeguards by a foundation, association or any other not-for-profit body with a political, philosophical, religious or trade union aim;
2   that the processing relates solely to the members or to former members of the body or to persons who have regular contact with it in connection with its purposes;
3   that the personal data may not be disclosed outside the political party without the consent of the data subjects.

The scope of this exception is potentially wide. Article 9(2)(d) is not limited to the processing by bodies with a political aim of personal data revealing political opinions but rather it applies to the processing by any of the bodies referred to of any of the special categories of data. Thus, provided that the conditions referred to in exception 9(2)(d) are fulfilled, it could be used as the basis for processing by a political party of data relating to an individual's racial origin, for example. Likewise it could be used as the basis for the processing by a body with philosophical, religious or trade union aims of personal data revealing a person's political opinions. Exception 9(2)(d) cannot be directly invoked by platforms, data brokers or analytics companies as data controllers to enable them to process special categories of data, but where such entities are acting in the capacity of data processors who are processing such data on behalf of a body with a political aim (who is the data controller), they may process such data provided that they do so in a manner that meets the requirements of the GDPR and is the subject of contractual arrangements with the data controller that meet the specific requirements of art. 28.[60]

The level of 'appropriate safeguards' required to invoke exception 9(2)(d) is not specified. This could result in the rules on processing of special categories of data by such entities varying in different Member States.[61] It is clear that the more sensitive the personal data is, the higher the standard of 'appropriate safeguards' that would be required. This is in keeping with the A29WP approach to the application of the legitimate interests balancing test, which is that the more sensitive the data, the more it will weigh the balance in favour of the data subject's interests.[62]

60   See II.
61   European Digital Rights (EDRi), 'Proceed with Caution: Flexibilities in the General Data Protection Regulation' (5 July 2016) https://edri.org/files/GDPR_analysis/EDRi_analysis_gdpr_flexibilities.pdf, 10.
62   A29WP Opinion 06/2014 (n 21) 39.

The requirement that the personal data relate to 'members or former members' of a body appears straightforward. It cannot, for example, be used by a political party to process data of prospective members or voters.[63] The scope of the term 'persons who have regular contact with' a political foundation or party in connection with its purposes is less clear. If a person were to enter into correspondence with a political party in order to question its policies, for example, it is not clear whether it would come within the scope of exception 9(2)(d). The French data protection supervisory authority, the Commission Nationale de l'Informatique et Libertés (CNIL), has drawn a distinction between regular contact and casual contact in this context. It has defined regular contacts as those who 'engage with a political party in a positive way in order to maintain regular exchanges in relation to the party's political action'. CNIL views the following as coming within the scope of regular contacts for the purposes of art. 9(2)(d): those who follow someone on Twitter or become 'friends' on Facebook and, more generally, people who, through social networks, have clearly manifested their willingness to maintain regular contact with the party policy or candidate. On the other hand, according to CNIL, those who merely 'like', comment, share or 'retweet' content posted on social networks must be considered to be casual rather than regular contacts.[64]

The only restriction mandated by exception 9(2)(d) in terms of the nature of the processing is that it must be undertaken in the course of the processor's 'legitimate activities', a term which is not defined. Nor is any guidance provided in the GDPR with respect to the phrase 'legitimate activities'.

It is important to note that bodies which invoke art. 9(2)(d) in order to process special categories of data are not allowed to disclose this data to third parties; it can only be disclosed within the political party or foundation.[65]

B. Transparency: arts 13 and 14

The UK Information Commissioner has identified the characteristics that distinguish new techniques in digital campaigning from traditional forms of campaigning as follows:

[T]hese techniques are – by their nature – more opaque. Messages are often received in an 'echo chamber' online, where voters may not hear the other side of the argument. Voters may not understand why they are receiving particular messages, or the provenance of the messages.[66]

---

63   European Commission (n 16) 6.
64   Commission Nationale de l'Informatique et Libertés (CNIL), 'Campagnes électorales: tout savoir sur les règles CSA et CNIL' www.cnil.fr/sites/default/files/atoms/files/guide_cnil_et_csa.pdf, 18; see also Colin Bennett, 'Political Opinions, Political Affiliations, Political Behavior and Political Inferences: The Protection of Privacy in the Data-Driven Election' (2013) 8(5) First Monday, https://firstmonday.org/ojs/index.php/fm/article/view/4789/3730; see also Bennett, 'Voter databases' (n 1).
65   European Commission (n 16) 5.
66   UK Information Commissioner's Office (n 1) 10.

The European Commission has noted that the 'Cambridge Analytica case has shown the importance of fighting opacity and properly informing the individuals concerned'[67] and the A29WP has cited the importance of transparency in the context of profiling on the grounds that '[t]he process of profiling is often invisible to the data subject'. Arts 13 and 14 of the GDPR impose obligations with respect to transparency of the processing of personal data. These transparency requirements apply in all circumstances in which personal data (including special categories of data) is processed, regardless of the basis of such processing.

Article 13, which applies where the data has been collected from the data subject, requires that data subjects be informed *inter alia* of the identity of the data controller, the purposes of the processing and its legal basis, where processing is based on the controller's 'legitimate interests' what those interests are, the recipients of the personal data and of any intention on the part of the controller to transfer the data outside of the EEA.[68] Article 13(2) further requires that the data subject be furnished with information concerning the data subject's right in respect of that data, such as the rights of access, rectification and erasure. Article 13 also requires that where the controller intends to further process the personal data for a different purpose, the data subject must be informed of that purpose and must be furnished with the information referred to in art. 13(2).

Article 14 sets out the transparency requirements applicable where the data has been obtained from a source other than the data subject. These are similar to the requirements of art. 13 but they also include that information be made available regarding the source from which the personal data originated. A range of exceptions to the transparency requirements of art. 14 are provided for in art. 14(5).

Article 14(5)(b) states that these obligations do not apply, in so far as 'the provision of such information proves impossible or would involve a disproportionate effort, in particular for processing for archiving purposes in the public interest, scientific or historical research purposes or statistical purposes'[69] or in so far as the obligation to inform the data subject 'is likely to render impossible or seriously impair the achievement of the objectives of that processing'.[70] In each of these cases, the controller must take 'appropriate measures to protect the data subject's rights and freedoms and legitimate interests, including making the information publicly available'.[71] This exception would appear to be available outside the context of archiving and scientific or historical research: this is supported by the exhortation of the A29WP that 'this exception should not be routinely relied upon where personal data is not being processed for the purposes of archiving in the public interest, for scientific or historical research purposes or

---

67 European Commission (n 16) 6.
68 GDPR art. 13(1).
69 GDPR art. 14(5)(b).
70 Ibid.
71 Ibid.

statistical purposes',[72] which implicitly acknowledges that the exception may be invoked on a non-routine basis outside of the these settings.

The manner in which the data subjects' rights, freedoms and legitimate interests are to be protected is not detailed, but the A29WP has suggested that where reliance is placed on this exception, the data controller should carry out a balancing exercise to assess the effort involved in providing the information against the impact and effects on the data subject if he or she were not provided with the information.[73] The appropriate measures to be taken are not spelt out in art. 14 (5)(b) but they include making the information publicly available. The A29WP notes that this can be done in a number of ways – for instance, by putting the information on the data controller's website, or by proactively advertising the information in a newspaper or on posters on its premises. Other appropriate measures are said to depend on the circumstances of the processing, but may include: undertaking a data protection impact assessment; applying pseudonymisation techniques to the data; minimising the data collected and the storage period; and implementing technical and organisational measures to ensure a high level of security.[74]

A further exception is provided for in art. 14(5)(c), which applies where the obtaining or disclosure of personal data is expressly laid down by Union or Member State law that provides 'appropriate measures to protect the data subject's legitimate interests'.[75] The A29WP takes the view that the data controller should make it clear to data subjects that it is obtaining or disclosing personal data in accordance with the law in question, unless there is a legal prohibition preventing the data controller from so doing.[76]

C. The right to object: art. 21

Article 21 confers on data subjects two rights to object: a general right to object under art. 21(1) and a right to object to direct marketing under art. 21(2).

4. The general right to object: art. 21(1)

Article 21(1) gives data subjects a right to object at any time to processing of their data, but only where the processing of the personal data was based on the performance of a task carried out in the public interest (art. 6(1)(e)) or on the legitimate interests of the data controller (art. 6(1)(f)), and it includes a right to object to profiling based on either of those provisions. Where personal data has been processed for electoral purposes on either of these grounds, it will be open to the

---

72   A29WP Guidelines on transparency under Regulation 2016/679, WP260 rev.01, Revised version adopted 11 April 2018, [61] ('A29WP Transparency Guidelines').
73   Ibid.
74   Ibid [64].
75   GDPR art. 14(5)(c).
76   A29WP Transparency Guidelines (n 72) [66].

data subject to object. Where a data subject objects to the processing of his or her data, the controller must no longer process the data 'unless the controller demonstrates compelling legitimate grounds for the processing which override the interests, rights and freedoms of the data subject'.[77] The data subject is required to object 'on grounds relating to his or her particular situation', and thus it will not be open to him or her to submit a generalised objection. The burden of proof with respect to establishing 'compelling legitimate grounds' that override the objection is on the data controller and the use of the word 'compelling' suggests that the threshold is high.[78]

The A29WP explained the relationship between art. 6(1)(f) and the right to object as follows:

> [W]here the processing is allowed [under art. 6(1)(f)] further to a reasonable and objective assessment of the different rights and interests at stake, the data subject still has an additional possibility to object on grounds relating to his/ her particular situation. This will then have to lead to a new assessment taking into account the particular arguments submitted by the data subject.[79]

There is no definition in the GDPR of 'compelling legitimate grounds'.[80] The A29WP suggests that in determining whether 'compelling legitimate grounds' exist that override the interests of the data subject in the context of the right to object to profiling, the controller should carry out a balancing exercise and it should consider the importance of the profiling to their particular objective as well as the impact of the profiling on the data subject's interest, rights and freedoms (which should be limited to the minimum necessary to meet the objective).[81] Where an objection is made to the processing of personal data for electoral purposes including profiling, the rights of the data subject to privacy and data protection would have to be weighed against the importance of profiling to the objectives of the entity carrying it out, which would include the exercise of the right to freedom of political expression.

5. The right to object to direct marketing: art. 21(2)

Article 21(2) provides data subjects with a right to object at any time to the processing of their data for direct marketing purposes, 'which includes profiling to the extent that it is related to such direct marketing'.[82] This is an absolute right of the

---

77   GDPR art. 21(1).
78   A29WP Guidelines on Automated individual decision-making and Profiling for the purposes of Regulation 2016/679. European Commission, WP251rev.01, 19 ('A29WP Guidelines on Automated individual-decision making').
79   Ibid 45.
80   Nor is guidance on the meaning of this term provided in GDPR rec. 69 with which art. 21 is associated.
81   A29WP Guidelines on Automated individual decision-making (n 78) 18–19.
82   GDPR art. 21(2).

data subject. The invocation of this right in the context of electoral activities depends on whether the activities in question can be construed as amounting to direct marketing for the purposes of art. 21.

Direct marketing is not defined in the GDPR and the recitals do not shed any light on its possible application in the context of political campaigning. The term 'marketing' seems to indicate a degree of commercial engagement, so it is not immediately clear whether it encompasses electoral activities. There is a link between the GDPR and the ePrivacy Directive[83] in terms of the regulation of direct marketing in so far as art. 13 of the ePrivacy Directive prohibits the sending of unsolicited electronic mail and text messages for direct marketing purposes without prior consent. In common with the GDPR, the ePrivacy Directive does not define direct marketing and nor does it make any reference to communica tions associated with electoral activities, but the A29WP has expressed the view that it covers 'any form of sales promotion, including direct marketing by charities and political organisations (e.g. fund raising, etc.)'.[84] The inclusion of fund raising by political parties by the A29WP as an example of direct marketing is not surprising in so far as it is in keeping with the commercial aspect of direct marketing. The UK Information Commissioner has, however, gone further in delineating the scope of direct marketing in the context of electoral activities:[85]

> Direct marketing is not limited to the offer for sale of goods or services only, but also includes the promotion of the aims and ideals of any organisation including political campaigns. This would include appeals for funds or support for a campaign, encouraging individuals to take some form of direct action or vote for a particular political party or candidate.[86]

The scope of this interpretation can be questioned. In particular, it is not clear that encouraging people to vote in a particular way amounts to direct marketing for the purposes of the GDPR.

Article 13 of the ePrivacy Directive provides for an exception to the prohibition on the sending of unsolicited electronic mail and text messages for direct

---

83 Directive 2002/58/EC, [2002] OJ L 201, 37.
84 A29WP Opinion 5/2004 on unsolicited communications for marketing purposes under Article 13 of Directive 2002/58/EC, adopted on 27 February 2004, WP 90, 7. In arriving at this conclusion, the A29WP relied on rec. 30 of the Data Protection Directive 95/46/EC, which stated that 'Member States may similarly specify the conditions under which personal data may be disclosed to a third party for the purposes of marketing whether carried out commercially or by a charitable organisation or by any other association or foundation, of a political nature for example, subject to the provisions allowing a data subject to object to the processing of data regarding him, at no cost and without having to state his reasons'.
85 The ePrivacy Directive was transposed into UK law by the Privacy & Electronic Communications (EC Directive) (Amendment) Regulations 2011, SI 1208/2011.
86 UK Information Commissioner's Office, 'Direct marketing', Guidance (3 March 2018) https://ico.org.uk/media/1555/direct-marketing-guidance.pdf.

marketing purposes without prior consent. It permits an entity to use the contact details of a customer for the purpose of sending him or her a message for the direct marketing of the entity's own similar products or services provided that the contact details were obtained by the entity in the context of the sale of a product or a service to the customer.[87] It appears that this exception is not available to political parties since it is confined to the collection of customer contact details obtained in the context of the sale of a product or a service.

The ePrivacy Directive will shortly be replaced by the ePrivacy Regulation.[88] The ePrivacy Regulation continues the prohibition on the sending of unsolicited direct marketing communications in similar terms to the ePrivacy Directive. In contrast to its predecessor, the most recent draft of the ePrivacy Regulation provides a definition of direct marketing. It is expressed in the following terms: 'any form of advertising, whether written or oral, sent to one or more identified or identifiable end-users of electronic communications services'.[89] This definition does not explicitly refer to communications made for electoral purposes; however, the reference to 'any form of advertising' would suggest that its scope is quite broad and could extend beyond the purely commercial environment. Moreover, rec. 32 of the draft ePrivacy Regulation states:

> In addition to the offering of products and services for commercial purposes, Member States may decide that direct marketing communications may include messages sent by political parties that contact natural persons via electronic communications services in order to promote their parties.[90]

Thus it appears to be open to Member States to decide to include such messages in the scope of the protection against receipt of unsolicited direct marketing messages afforded by the ePrivacy Regulation.

Where Member States do not take up this opportunity, it appears that the default position will be that the prohibition on the sending of direct marketing

---

87 This exception applies subject to the proviso that customers are clearly and distinctly given the opportunity to object, free of charge and in an easy manner, to such use of electronic contact details when they are collected and on the occasion of each message.

88 Proposal for a Regulation concerning the respect for private life and the protection of personal data in electronic communications and repealing Directive 2002/58/EC (Regulation on Privacy and Electronic Communications), COM/2017/010 final, 2017/03. On the relationship between the GDPR and the draft ePrivacy Directive, see European Data Protection Board, 'Opinion 5/2019 on the interplay between the ePrivacy Directive and the GDPR, in particular regarding the competence, tasks and powers of data protection authorities' (12 March 2019).

89 GDPR art. 4(3)(f).

90 Proposal for a Regulation of the European Parliament and of the Council concerning the respect for private life and the protection of personal data in electronic communications and repealing Directive 2002/58/EC (Regulation on Privacy and Electronic Communications) Interinstitutional File: 2017/0003 (COD), 6467/19 (19 February 2019).

communications will not apply to messages sent by political parties to natural persons in order to promote their parties. Where Member States take up the option of deciding that direct marketing communications include messages sent by political parties to promote their parties or where political parties engage in direct marketing involving activities other than the sending of messages to promote a party, consent will be required. In the case of direct marketing for electoral purposes carried out by persons or entities other than political parties, consent will similarly be required.

The A29WP has criticised the scope of the definition of direct marketing communications in the draft ePrivacy Regulation as being too narrow. The use of the word 'sent' in the definition was objected to by the A29WP on the basis that it implies the use of technological means of communication

> that necessarily involve the conveyance of a communication, whereas most advertising on the web (through social media platforms or on websites) would not involve 'sending' advertisements in the strict sense.[91]

It was suggested by the A29WP that the proposal be amended to include all advertising 'sent, directed or presented to one or more identified or identifiable end-users'.[92] The A29WP also suggested that behavioural advertisements (based on the profiles of end-users) should be considered to be direct marketing communications directed at one or more identified or identifiable end-users on the grounds that such advertisements are targeted to specific, identifiable users.[93]

D. Restrictions on automated decision making and profiling: art. 22

Article 22 states that a data subject shall have the right not to be subject to a decision based solely on automated processing, including profiling, which produces legal effects concerning him or her or similarly significantly affects him or her. Article 22 therefore applies in respect of two activities, automated decision making and profiling. There is no definition in the GDPR of 'automated decision making' but rec. 71 provides some guidance on its scope: it refers to automatic refusal of an online credit application or e-recruiting practices without any human intervention as examples of decisions based solely on automated processing.

The restriction on profiling is of particular relevance in the context of the processing of personal data for electoral purposes. Profiling is defined in art. 4 as

> any form of automated processing of personal data consisting of the use of personal data to evaluate certain personal aspects relating to a natural person,

---

91   A29WP Opinion 01/2017 on the Proposed Regulation for the ePrivacy Regulation (2002/58/EC), WP 247 (4 April 2017) 20.
92   Ibid 21.
93   Ibid.

in particular to analyse or predict aspects concerning that natural person's performance at work, economic situation, health, personal preferences, interests, reliability, behaviour, location or movements.

The definition of profiling covers both analysing and predicting. It is clear from this definition that profiling does not need to result in the making of an automated decision and that the practice of analysing individuals' characteristics without engaging in prediction of their behaviour constitutes profiling for the purposes of art. 22.[94] The definition requires that personal data be used to evaluate aspects of a natural person. The aspect most likely to apply in the context of electoral activities is that of the personal preferences and behaviour of the person concerned. It can be argued that voting intentions constitutes an aspect of their behaviour and therefore that the profiling of personal data to analyse how a person might vote would qualify as profiling under art. 22.

Article 22 applies to decisions 'based solely on automated processing, including profiling' but the definition of profiling in art. 4 does not include the word 'solely'. This suggests that profiling involving an element of human intervention might come within the scope of art. 22. The A29WP has taken the view that profiling has to involve some form of automated processing but that 'human involvement does not necessarily take the activity out of the definition'.[95]

Article 22 only applies where the profiling in question produces legal effects concerning a data subject or similarly significantly affects him or her. On the question whether profiling in connection with electoral activities has legal effects for the purposes of art. 22, the A29WP has taken the view that a legal effect requires 'that the decision, which is based on solely automated processing, affects someone's legal rights, such as the freedom to associate with others, vote in an election'.[96] It could be argued that where profiling (and the targeted advertising which it facilitates) results in a person exercising their right to vote in a particular way, it affects the exercise of their right to vote.

In order for data processing to significantly affect someone, according to the A29WP, the effects of the processing must be

> sufficiently great or important to be worthy of attention. In other words, the decision must have the potential to: significantly affect the circumstances, behaviour or choices of the individuals concerned; have a prolonged or permanent impact on the data subject; or at its most extreme, lead to the exclusion or discrimination of individuals.[97]

The A29WP has stated that targeted advertising based on profiling may qualify as having a significant effect on an individual depending on the particular

94   A29WP Guidelines on Automated individual decision-making (n 78) 7.
95   Ibid.
96   Ibid 21.
97   Ibid.

characteristics of the case, such as the intrusiveness of the profiling process, the expectations and wishes of the individuals concerned, the way the advert is delivered, or the use of knowledge of the vulnerabilities of the targeted data subjects.[98]

There is a case for arguing that art. 22 applies to profiling carried on in connection with electoral activities, in particular on the grounds that such profiling could have a significant effect on the individual. For example, the profiling of individuals for electoral purposes could result in voters being 'inundated with a constant stream of skewed, politically interested messaging' designed to influence them to vote for a party or candidate that they would not otherwise have supported, thus interfering with their voter autonomy.[99] This interpretation is supported by the UK Information Commissioner, who has expressed the view that '[m]icro-targeting by political parties and campaigns may be a type of automated decision making that does have sufficiently significant effects on individuals to bring this under Article 22'.[100]

Three exceptions are provided for in art. 22. The right does not apply if the decision:

1   is necessary for entering into, or performance of, a contract between the data subject and a data controller [the contractual exception];
2   is authorised by Union or Member State law to which the controller is subject and which also lays down suitable measures to safeguard the data subject's rights and freedoms and legitimate interests [the authorised-by-law exception]; or
3   is based on the data subject's explicit consent [the consent exception].

The application of these exceptions is subject to two sets of safeguards: in the case of the contractual and consent exceptions, art. 22(3) requires the data controller to implement suitable measures to safeguard the data subject's rights and freedoms and legitimate interests, at least the right to obtain human intervention on the part of the controller, to express his or her point of view, and to contest the decision. The safeguarding of the data subject's rights and freedoms and legitimate interests is also built into the authorised-by-law exception although it does not specifically reference the right to human intervention.[101]

IV. Derogations under GDPR

While the GDPR is a directly applicable Regulation,[102] it permits Member States to derogate from its requirements in certain circumstances. Article 23 allows Members

98   A29WP Guidelines on Automated individual decision making (n 78) 22.
99   Damian Tambini, 'Social Media Power and Election Legitimacy' in Damian Tambini and Martin Moore (eds), *Digital Dominance: The Power of Google, Amazon, Facebook, and Apple* (Oxford University Press 2018) 265, 270.
100   UK Information Commissioner's Office (n 1) 16.
101   GDPR art. 22(2)(b).
102   GDPR art. 99.

States to introduce national measures that restrict the rights provided for in arts 12–22. Derogations made under art. 23 must respect 'the essence of [...] fundamental rights and freedoms' and be 'necessary and proportionate [...] in a democratic society'. They must be aimed at safeguarding one of a range of interests including national security, defence, public security, the prevention, investigation, detection or prosecution of criminal offences, other important objectives of general public interest, in particular an important economic or financial interest of the Union or of a Member State. It is not clear that any of these grounds for derogating from the rights protected by arts 12–22 of the GDPR apply to the processing of personal data for electoral purposes.

Article 85(1) requires Member States, by law, to reconcile data protection with the right to freedom of expression and information, including processing for journalistic purposes and the purposes of academic, artistic or literary expression. More specifically, art. 85(2) requires, among other things, that Member States provide for appropriate exemptions or derogations from many of the most important provisions of the GDPR[103] for processing carried out for journalistic, academic, artistic or literary expression purposes, if they are necessary to reconcile the two rights. Although the processing of personal data for electoral purposes is unlikely to qualify as processing for journalistic purposes or for the purposes of academic, artistic or literary expression, it could be viewed as giving rise to issues concerning the reconciliation of data protection with the right to freedom of expression, thus potentially bringing it within the scope of art. 85, but there is a lack of clarity on this question.

V. Conclusion

The GDPR provides significant scope for the processing of personal data for the purpose of electoral activities. The processing of such data may be undertaken on the basis of the consent (or, in the case of special categories of personal data, the explicit consent) of the data subject even though, as we have seen, the use of consent as the basis for the processing of personal data can be highly problematic, in particular in an era when data that can be analysed to predict voting preferences may be collected from social media platforms ostensibly with the consent of the data subject. In the absence of consent, art. 6 may, depending on the circumstances, permit processing of such data based on the public interest (art. 6(1)(e)) or on the legitimate interests of the data controller (art. 6(1)(f)), while art. 9 contains exceptions which may permit the processing of special categories of data for electoral purposes, in particular under art. 9(2)(d) for the processing in the course of legitimate activities by a body with a political aim; and under art. 9(2)(g): processing necessary for reasons of substantial public interest.[104] In the absence of consent, the scope for processing of personal data for electoral purposes is clearly much greater in the case of political parties and candidates than in the

103 Including all of those considered in this chapter viz GDPR arts 6, 9, 13, 14, 21 and 22.
104 Such processing may only be undertaken in the course of their legitimate activities and it is subject to certain conditions and to safeguards being put in place.

case of social media platforms, data brokers and data analytics companies but that is not to say definitively that the latter will be unable to engage in the lawful processing of personal data for such purposes.

The application of the rights conferred on data subjects by Chapter 2 of the GDPR is subject to a range of limitations that may impact on the processing of personal data for electoral purposes. The art. 14 transparency requirements,[105] which are imposed where personal data is obtained from a source other than the data subject, are subject to a range of exceptions. In particular, the disproportionate effort exception[106] may apply to the processing of personal data for electoral purposes. Furthermore, it is open to Member States to create an exception from the art. 14 transparency requirements by introducing legislation providing expressly for the obtaining or disclosure of the personal data in question.[107] More generally, the practical consequences of transparency obligations provided for in art. 14 are problematic in the context of the use of personal data for the purposes of profiling of voters since profiling operates 'by creating derived or inferred data about individuals – "new" personal data that has not been provided directly by the data subjects themselves'.[108]

While the general right to object provided for in art. 21(1) appears to apply to the processing of personal data for the purposes of electoral activities, it can be overridden by the compelling legitimate interests of the processor. Such interests could be viewed as including the interest in freedom of political expression,[109] thus permitting the overriding of the data subject's right to object. While political parties and candidates may be able to rely on freedom of political expression, this may be more difficult in the case of the other players in the electoral process.

The usefulness of the right to object to direct marketing contained in art. 21(2) in the context of the processing of personal data for electoral purposes is questionable given the lack of a definition of direct marketing in the GDPR. While it is likely that the application of art. 21(2) will be informed by the definition of direct marketing contained in the ePrivacy Regulation, there is uncertainty as to the application of the draft Regulation to direct marketing for political purposes, with Member States being given the option to decide whether or not to include within the scope of direct marketing, messages sent by political parties to promote their parties. It is also unclear whether the definition of direct marketing in the draft Regulation includes commonly utilised online political campaigning techniques such as advertising on the web, through social media platforms or on websites, or behavioural advertising.

In terms of the right under art. 22 not to be subject to a decision based solely on automated processing, including profiling, there is uncertainty as to whether

---

105 Which apply in respect of data not obtained from the data subject.
106 GDPR art. 14(5)(b).
107 GDPR art. 14(5)(c).
108 A29WP Guidelines on Automated individual decision-making (n 78) 9.
109 Zuiderveen Borgesius et al. (n 2) 93.

profiling for electoral purposes can be said to produce legal effects concerning a data subject or similarly significantly affect him or her. In any case, it is open to Member States to introduce a legislative exception authorising the use of profiling for electoral purposes.

Overall, while the GDPR imposes limitations on the processing of personal data for the purpose of electoral activities, there are significant gaps in the protection afforded to the processing of personal data in this context. An overarching difficulty which derives from the potential for the transparency requirements provided for in art. 14 to be bypassed in the electoral context in the manner already described is that it may result in the data subject being unaware that his or her data has been processed for such purposes and, in particular, being unaware of the nature of that processing, including whether it has been used to identify him or her for receipt of targeted advertising. This lack of awareness could result in the data subject failing to exercise any rights he or she may have under Chapter 2 of the GDPR.

It is unclear to what extent, if at all, measures limiting the operation of the GDPR in order to protect freedom of political expression come within the scope of art. 85, but the fact that the GDPR allows for significant variation in the application by Member States of the provisions relevant to the processing of personal data for electoral purposes can be viewed as problematic. As we have seen, it appears to be open to Member States to introduce legislation permitting personal data to be processed for electoral purposes on public interest grounds under both art. 6(1)(e) and art. 9(2)(g). Moreover the level of 'appropriate safeguards' that must be put in place by Member States in order for exception 9(2)(d) to be invoked as the basis for the processing by political parties of special categories of data is not specified. These aspects of the regime for the processing of personal data provide scope for variations in approach across the Member States. The provision made in art. 14 for Member States to legislate for an exception to the transparency requirements also provides scope for inconsistencies to arise between Member States in this respect. The fact that the draft ePrivacy Regulation leaves it open to Member States to decide whether or not to include within the scope of direct marketing, messages sent by political parties to promote their parties enables further differences in approach across the Member States to arise. Finally, the inclusion in the protection afforded by art. 22 against profiling and automated decision making of an exception that permits such practices to be authorised by Member State law adds a further layer of uncertainty and scope for inconsistent approaches to be adopted. To conclude, the regulation of the processing of personal data for the purpose of electoral activities in the EU following the entry into force of the GDPR is not only compromised in terms of its overall strength, but also has the potential to vary significantly from one jurisdiction to another, thus impeding the harmonisation of the data protection laws of the Member States, one of the primary goals of the GDPR.[110]

---

110 GDPR rec. 10. While differences in the electoral systems of the Member States could render the lack of harmony less problematic, it could have significant implications for the conduct of elections to the European parliament.

Part III

Domestic laws in Canada, Australia, the United States and the United Kingdom

From the doorstep to the database

Political parties, campaigns, and personal privacy protection in Canada

Colin J. Bennett and Michael McDonald

I. Introduction

In most democracies, the opportunities to capture and use personally identifiable data to identify and target voters are severely constrained by comprehensive data protection laws that define information on 'political opinions' as highly sensitive, and which typically require express consent for processing. This is not the case in Canada. Political parties in Canada, as in the US but not in Europe, are generally viewed as outside the scope of federal or provincial information privacy laws. Therefore, the extent to which candidates and parties abide by commonly agreed principles of information privacy protection has largely been a matter of choice, rather than compulsion. For the most part, individuals have no legal rights to learn what information is contained in party databases, to access and correct those data, to remove themselves from the systems, or to restrict the collection, use, and disclosure of their personal data. Parties typically have no legal obligations to keep that information secure, to only retain it for as long as necessary, and to control who has access to it. Canada's privacy protection regime depends on an uneasy distinction between the commercial and governmental processing of personal data. Political parties are a hybrid; and they tend to fall between the cracks. This gap in our law has increasingly come to the attention of parliamentary committees, the federal and provincial privacy commissioners, civil liberties organizations, electoral regulatory bodies, and the media.[1]

These shortcomings have permitted Canadian elections to be influenced by trends in voter analytics from south of the border: the widespread use of voter relationship management (VRM) platforms; the increasing use of mobile applications for household canvassing; contracts with voter analytics companies and

---

1   Colin J Bennett and Robin Bayley, 'Canadian Federal Political Parties and Personal Privacy Protection: A Comparative Analysis' (March 2012) Office of the Privacy Commissioner of Canada, www.priv.gc.ca/en/opc-actions-and-decisions/research/ explore-privacy-research/2012/pp_201203, accessed 1 March 2019; Colin J Bennett, 'Data-Driven Elections and Political Parties in Canada: Privacy Implications, Privacy Policies and Privacy Obligations' (2018) 16(2) Canadian Journal of Law and Technology 195.

consultants; and the increasing use of social media to analyse issue trends and reach out to precise segments of the electorate through 'micro-targeting'.[2] We contend therefore that the Canadian experience offers some international lessons of the various risks to privacy, and wider civil liberties, when US-style campaigning techniques are imported into a country with a very different party system, electoral process, financing rules, and political culture.

This chapter begins with a brief overview of the broader political and constitutional contexts which have encouraged the development of 'data-driven' elections in Canada. We then examine the Canadian trends in voter analytics, followed by the various statutory and constitutional rules that govern the processing of personal data by political parties and candidates: the protection of electoral communications under the Charter of Rights and Freedoms; the privacy and security provisions within the Canada Elections Act (CEA), and its provincial equivalents; the application of telemarketing rules; the coverage of the new Canada Anti-Spam legislation (CASL); and the application of the only provincial law that covers parties, British Columbia's Personal Information Protection Act (PIPA).

The final purpose of the chapter is to outline the various privacy risks that attend the processing of personal data on political opinions. The recent publicity about Cambridge Analytica, Facebook, and the Canadian company Aggregate IQ has tended to focus on the most dramatic and controversial practices, and particularly those that involve foreign interference in domestic elections. Our review provides a more comprehensive survey of the broader array of other privacy risks. We contend that the Canadian experience offers some unique insights into these risks, and important lessons for data-driven elections in other parliamentary democracies.

II. The Canadian political arena

The larger context of privacy regulation needs to be understood according to the unique attributes of Canadian federalism. The *Constitution Act 1867* (previously entitled the *British North America Act 1867*) divided jurisdictional powers between the federal government and provincial governments. Under s. 91, the federal government was granted twenty-nine powers to make laws related to such areas as federal taxation, national defence, banking and currency, naturalization, and criminal law.[3] Conversely, s. 92 granted provincial legislatures control over sixteen areas including provincial taxation, municipalities, property, the administration of justice, and healthcare.[4] This jurisdictional division of powers has had enormous implications for the development of Canadian public policy, regularly

---

2   Colin J Bennett, 'Trends in Voter Surveillance in Western Societies: Privacy Intrusions and Democratic Implications' (2015) 13(3–4) Surveillance and Society 370, https://doi.org/10.24908/ss.v13i3/4.5373, accessed 1 March 2019.
3   The Constitution Act, 1867 (UK), 30 & 31 Victoria, c 3, s 91.
4   Ibid s 92.

pitting federal and provincial governments against one another as 'each [sought] to maximize its autonomy, jurisdiction, and standing with voters'.[5] As a result, it is quite common for there to be significant legislative and regulatory differences between provincial and federal public policy.

Privacy protection is such an example of a legal regime that has emerged pragmatically at both federal and provincial levels. Federal public sector agencies are governed by the *Privacy Act*,[6] and there are separate laws that regulate the processing of personal data by provincial public bodies, most of which also offer access to information rights, such as those in Ontario and British Columbia (BC).[7] Federally regulated private sector industries (banking, transportation, and communications), as well as companies that transmit personal data across international and interprovincial borders for commercial purposes, are governed by the *Personal Information Protection and Electronic Documents Act (PIPEDA)*.[8] Similarly, there are a handful of provincial laws (in Quebec, BC, and Alberta) that govern the private sector in those provinces, including the *BC Personal Information Protection Act (PIPA)*, discussed below.[9] The Office of the Privacy Commissioner of Canada oversees compliance with the *Privacy Act* and *PIPEDA*,[10] and similar offices exist in each province to oversee compliance with relevant provincial legislation. The vast majority of personal data captured by public and private organizations is covered by privacy law at some level. Yet the patchwork is complicated, not entirely comprehensive, and often mired in inter-jurisdictional confusion.

All jurisdictions employ a single-member-plurality (SMP) or first-past-the-post (FPTP) electoral system. At the federal level, 338 Members of Parliament (MPs) are elected from geographically bound electoral districts or ridings.[11] Whichever candidate receives a plurality of votes in a given riding, receives a seat in the House of Commons; the party that wins the most seats typically forms government.[12] Election campaigns are required to last at least 36 days[13] and elections now occur on a fixed date every four years,[14] though they could occur earlier in a minority parliament.

5   Herman Bakvis and Grace Skogstad, 'Canadian Federalism: Performance, Effectiveness, and Legitimacy' in Herman Bakvis and Grace Skogstad (eds), *Canadian Federalism* (3rd edn, Oxford University Press 2012) 6.
6   Privacy Act, RSC 1985, c P-21.
7   Freedom of Information and Protection of Privacy Act, RSBC 1985, c 165; Freedom of Information and Protection of Privacy Act, RSO 1990, c F.31.
8   Personal Information Protection and Electronic Documents Act, SC 2000, c 5.
9   Personal Information Protection Act, SBC 2003, c 63.
10 Office of the Privacy Commissioner of Canada, 'About the OPC' www.priv.gc.ca/en/about-the-opc, accessed 1 March 2019.
11 Elections Canada, 'The Electoral System of Canada' www.elections.ca/content.aspx?dir=ces&document=part1&lang=e&section=res, accessed 1 March 2019.
12 Ibid.
13 Elections Canada, 'Elections in Canada: An Overview' www.elections.ca/content.aspx?section=vot&dir=bkg&document=ec90556&lang=e, accessed 1 March 2019.
14 Canada Elections Act, SC 2000, c 9, ss 56.1(2).

The Canadian party system varies across jurisdictions, so the choices faced by the electorate are not the same across the country. This militates against strong and enduring feelings of partisan attachment. At the federal level, Canada's political system has been dominated by the centrist Liberal Party of Canada (LPC) – which governed for 80 of 110 years between 1896 to 2006 – and a centre-right Conservative Party of Canada (CPC), which is the only other party to form government.[15] A third party in the Cooperative Commonwealth Federation (CCF) emerged in 1932, later becoming the New Democratic Party (NDP) in 1961; it espouses a social democratic, centre-left ideology.[16] There have also been periodic instances of so-called 'insurgent parties' winning seats, such as in the 1993 election when regional parties – such as the right-wing Reform Party and the separatist Bloc Québécois – managed to collectively secure over one-third of the popular vote.[17]

Canada's multi-party system tends to confound Duverger's Law, which suggests that SMP electoral systems will produce two-party systems.[18] Today in Ottawa, the LPC, CPC, and NDP predominate, with the Bloc and the Green Party of Canada (GPC) holding a small number of seats. Furthermore, the dominance of a centrist party – the LPC – is unusual as most centrist parties in other national contexts move left or right, vacating the middle ground.[19] Rather, the LPC have historically subscribed to brokerage politics,[20] which involves 'a commitment to the broadest possible support base', attained through 'electoral pragmatism' and ideological elasticity.[21]

Canadian politics has also been characterized by declining voter turnout and membership in political parties. The highest voter turnout occurred in the 1958 federal election with 79.4% of electors voting.[22] Turnout remained above 69% through the 1993 federal election, but then began to decline hitting a record low of 58.8% in 2008.[23] While the 2015 election bucked the trend with a 68.3%

15   Richard Johnston, *The Canadian Party System: An Analytic History* (University of British Columbia Press 2017) 14–19 and 43–45.
16   Ibid 22 and 43–45.
17   Ibid 19.
18   Maurice Duverger, *Political Parties: Their Organization and Activity in the Modern State* (Barbara North and Robert North trs, John Wiley & Sons 1963); Johnston (n 15) 3.
19   Johnston (n 15) 45–46.
20   Alex Marland and Thierry Giasson, 'From Brokerage to Boutique Politics: Political Marketing and the Changing Nature of Party Politics in Canada' in Alain-G Gagnon and A Brian Tanguay (eds), *Canadian Parties in Transition* (4th edn, University of Toronto Press 2017) 344.
21   Kenneth Carty and William Cross, 'Political Parties and the Practice of Brokerage Politics' in John C Courtney and David E Smith (eds), *The Oxford Handbook of Canadian Politics* (Oxford University Press 2010) 193–194.
22   Elections Canada, 'Voter Turnout at Federal Elections and Referendums' www.elections.ca/content.aspx?dir=turn&document=index&lang=e&section=ele, accessed 1 March 2019.
23   Ibid.

turnout,[24] it is too early to know whether higher turnouts will continue in the 2019 election and beyond. Further, only a small portion of higher-income Canadians belong to a political party; 7% of the population with annual incomes of Can $80,000 or more belong to a political party or group, as opposed to just 3% of people with incomes below Can$40,000.[25] This suggests that the partisan dealignment occurring in most Western democracies[26] is also apparent in Canada. With fewer partisans, there are theoretically more electors for parties to persuade with fine-tuned messaging. Simultaneously, Canada appears to be experiencing increased polarization, with higher levels of 'partisan sorting' on the left and the right.[27]

It is also necessary to provide a brief overview of the regulation of elections and election financing laws. Canadian federal elections are overseen by an independent, non-partisan agency of Parliament known as Elections Canada and must be conducted in accordance with the CEA.[28] Provincial elections are similarly overseen by their respective non-partisan provincial bodies in accordance with provincial legislation.

The CEA also regulates financial contributions to federal campaigns. Reforms occurred in 2003 when the Jean Chrétien Liberal government banned corporate and union donations and set a cap of Can$5000 on individual contributions to parties or candidates.[29] It also created a government per-vote subsidy, paid quarterly to any political party that received either 2% of the national vote or 5% in the electoral districts where it ran candidates.[30] These changes altered the financing of Canadian elections, prioritizing individual contributions and state funding, while reducing the influence of corporations and unions. After winning government in 2006, Stephen Harper's Conservative government moved to lower the cap on individual contributions to Can$1,000 (indexed to inflation) and, after securing a majority in 2011, they succeeded in phasing out the per-vote subsidy.[31] In 2019, individuals may donate Can$1,600 to each registered party and an additional Can

---

24 Ibid.
25 Martin Turcotte, 'Civic engagement and political participation in Canada' in *Spotlight on Canadians: Results from the General Social Survey* (Catalogue No 89-652-X2015006, Statistics Canada 14 September 2015) www150.statcan.gc.ca/n1/pub/89-652-x/89-652-x2015006-eng.htm#a6.
26 Russell J Dalton and Martin P Wattenberg, *Parties without Partisans: Political Change in Advanced Industrial Democracies* (Oxford University Press 2012).
27 Anthony Kevins and Stuart N Soroka, 'Growing Apart? Partisan Sorting in Canada, 1992–2015' (2018) 51(1) Canadian Journal of Political Science 103. http://doi.org.ezproxy.library.uvic.ca/10.1017/S0008423917000713.
28 Elections Canada, 'The Role and Structure of Elections Canada' www.elections.ca/content.aspx?section=abo&dir=role&document=index&lang=e, accessed 13 September 2019.
29 Lisa Young, 'Money, Politics, and the Canadian Party System' in Alain-G Gagnon and A Brian Tanguay (eds), *Canadian Parties in Transition* (4th edn, University of Toronto Press 2017) 35.
30 Ibid.
31 Ibid 36–38.

$1,600 to all registered associations, nomination contestants, and candidates of each registered party.[32]

In summary, the volatile party system, a declining engagement with political parties, a culture of electoral pragmatism, and strict limitations on campaign financing all increase the importance of gathering and deploying data on actual and potential voters. Parties are incentivized to use data to both affirm existing partisan support, to encourage donors, and persuade those who do not have a strong partisan preference. In addition, the relative weakness of privacy protection rules has made Canada a suitable environment for the importation of a range of voter analytics practices pioneered in the US. As a result, elections in Canada are now to a large extent, and perhaps irreversibly, 'data-driven'.

III. Data-driven elections in Canada

Each major political party has devoted considerable resources to the development of VRM systems, often partnering with American consultants and companies. These databases track engagement with voters and, more specifically, party supporters, donors, and volunteers. The Constituent Information Management System (CIMS), developed in 2004 by the Conservative Party, was the first VRM system in Canada.[33] The database mirrors 'the Voter Vault software that has powered Republican Party systems', which allows CIMS to generate lists for door knocking, phone calling, distributing lawn signs, and emailing supporters.[34] While the CPC attempted to replace CIMS with a new customized C-Vote database in 2013, the replacement was scrapped at a cost to the party of Can$7–9 million.[35]

Since the 2013 debacle, the party has turned its focus to upgrading and maintaining its current system. In preparation for the 2019 campaign, the CPC has launched Medallion, a platform supported by Nationbuilder that is designed to interact with CIMS and enhance its functionality. Specifically, Medallion provides for phone, email, and text message outreach, mapping and turf cutting, list segmentation, donation and event management, and the easy creation of petitions.[36] Medallion also allows for the automatic CIMS importation of donor information, as well as improved social media integration. Such efforts are attempts to enhance the CIMS database in light of the 2015 election loss to the Liberal Party.

32   Elections Canada, 'Limits on Contributions' www.elections.ca/content.aspx?sec tion=pol&document=index&dir=lim&lang=e, accessed 1 March 2019.

33   Tom Flanagan, *Harper's Team: Behind the Scenes in the Conservative Rise to Power* (2nd edn, McGill-Queen's University Press 2014) 85–87.

34   Colin J Bennett and Robin M Bayley, 'Data Analytics in Canadian Elections: Our Data, Ourselves' (June 2018) *Tactical Tech* 12, https://ourdataourselves.tacticaltech. org/media/ttc-influence-industry-canada.pdf, accessed 1 March 2019.

35   Laura Payton, 'Conservative campaign database fiasco costs party millions' *CBC News* (23 October 2019) www.cbc.ca/news/politics/conservative-campaign-database-fia sco-costs-party-millions-1.2187603, accessed 1 March 2019.

36   Conservative Party of Canada, 'Medallion', http://medallion.conservative.ca, accessed 1 March 2019.

Medallion is representative of the feedback loop between competing parties that has come to dominate data-driven elections in Canada. One party falls behind in VRM software, and so it seeks to innovate and improve its efforts for the next campaign.

For its part, the Liberal Party purchased the services of NGP VAN to develop its own VRM system called Liberalist in 2011. NGP VAN is a US company with a decidedly progressive political persuasion, providing software to most Democratic Party campaigns.[37] They are responsible for VoteBuilder, which powered the 2008 and 2012 Obama campaigns' 'voter contact, volunteer, fundraising, and compliance operations in all 50 states'.[38] Modelled after VoteBuilder, Liberalist was re-packaged following the LPC's 2011 election loss, becoming a powerful tool in time for the 2015 federal election. Indeed, the Liberal Party saw its electoral fortunes collapse in 2011, falling to third place in seat count and popular vote for the first time in history.[39] The Liberal Party recognized that it was 'out-campaigned' by the Conservative Party, and the party president declared that 'LPC is flying half-blind and well behind when it comes to election technology and digital know-how'.[40] This belief incentivized the party elite to fully invest in a data-driven campaign that could match and exceed that of the Conservatives.

Liberalist played a significant role in the LPC's landslide 2015 victory. The user guide highlights some of its key functionalities.[41] The system allows for the easy creation of lists of supporters, donors, and volunteers so that campaigns can effectively manage their resources. It provides a turf-cutting tool for the simple creation of door-knocking lists, and allows campaigns to set up a 'Virtual Phone Bank' to engage supporters and identify voters' political affiliations. Campaigns with at least ten volunteers at any given time can use a predictive dialer to sift through voicemails and unanswered calls, so that volunteers are presented with live callers only. Candidates can easily send 'blast emails' to anyone who has provided an email address to the party, and an event management tool allows for easy scheduling of events and the tracking of participants. Such data are particularly valuable when trying to build a volunteer base; someone who attended a party event is far more likely to make phone calls or open up their cheque book. Liberalist serves as the mechanism to facilitate engagement, track supporter information, maximize volunteer time, and run an effective get-out-the-vote campaign.

The NDP's Populus is the third and current iteration of its VRM software since 2011, and, given its relative newness, some have reported that it was not ready for

37   NGP VAN, 'About Us' www.ngpvan.com/about, accessed 1 March 2019.
38   Ibid.
39   Elections Canada, 'Official Voting Results: Forty-First General Election 2011' www. elections.ca/scripts/ovr2011/default.html> accessed 1 March 2019.
40   Bennett and Bayley, 'Data Analytics in Canadian Elections' (n 34) 14; Susan Delacourt, *Shopping for Votes: How Politicians Choose Us and We Choose Them* (2nd edn, Douglas and McIntyre 2016) 288.
41   Liberal Party of Canada, 'User Guide' https://liberalist.liberal.ca/user-guide-new, accessed 1 March 2019.

the 2015 campaign.[42] In the lead-up to the campaign, the NDP relied heavily on Obama's former national field coordinator Jeremy Bird of 270 Strategies.[43] While he is said to have stressed the importance of building strong local organizations to cultivate national success, the central NDP campaign appears to have missed that message.[44] In fact, the party neglected the grassroots organization, leaving local campaigns to act independently, all the while putting the party behind in volunteer recruitment and mobilization.[45] The NDP's 2015 return to third-party status – after their brief tenure as Official Opposition – has prompted renewed debates on whether the party should continue to invest in data analytics, or whether it should return to more traditional forms of voter mobilization.

Canadian parties have also relied on data brokerage firms to assist in voter analytics and 'micro-targeting'. One such company is Environics whose proprietary software, the PRIZM5 segmentation system, contains '68 lifestyle classifications based on demographics, marketplace preferences, and psychographic social values'.[46] The Conservative Party and the NDP are both reported to have used Environics data in their campaigns.[47] This demographic information can be collated with existing VRM information to provide a fuller picture of neighbourhoods in particular electoral districts.[48] The Conservatives also employ Politrain Consulting who partner with Spectrum electoral demographics to overlay election outcomes with demographic mapping.[49] It has also been reported that the current campaign manager for the Conservatives' 2019 campaign is enamoured with the kinds of psychographic profiling of voters for which Cambridge Analytica became notorious.[50] In the case of the Liberal Party, its 2015 campaign was heavily dependent on the services of Data Sciences Inc., run by Tom Pitfield, a friend of Prime Minister Justin Trudeau and the spouse of the past-president of the Liberal

42   Geoffrey Rafe Hall, 'How the New Democrats defeated themselves' *iPolitics* (20 November 2015) https://ipolitics.ca/2015/11/20/how-the-new-democrats-defeated-themselves , accessed 1 March 2019.

43   Thierry Giasson and Tamara A Small, 'Online, All the Time: The Strategic Objectives of Canadian Opposition Parties' in Alex Marland, Thierry Giasson and Anna Lennox Esselment (eds), *Permanent Campaigning in Canada* (University of British Columbia Press 2017) 119.

44   Hall (n 42).

45   Ibid.

46   Bennett and Bayley, 'Data Analytics in Canadian Elections' (n 34) 11.

47   Joe Friesen, 'Micro-targeting lets parties conquer ridings, one tiny group at a time' *Globe and Mail* (22 April 2011) www.theglobeandmail.com/news/politics/micro-targeting-lets-parties-conquer-ridings-one-tiny-group-at-a-time/article4359559 , accessed 1 March 2019; Delacourt (n 40) 274.

48   Bennett and Bayley, 'Data Analytics in Canadian Elections' (n 34) 11.

49   Ibid; 'Spectrum Electoral Demographics' http://pollmaps.ca/Demographics.aspx, accessed 1 March 2019.

50   Guest, 'Andrew Scheer's Campaign Manager says he builds creepy psychological profiles of voters too' *Georgia Straight* (23 March 2018) www.straight.com/news/1048791/press-progress-andrew-scheers-campaign-manager-says-he-builds-creepy-psychological, accessed 15 March 2019.

Party.[51] To create a pertinent message, parties also rely on the services of consulting firms. Particularly, the Liberals have employed the Gandalf Group, and the Conservatives, the Responsive Marketing Group.[52] Such firms avail themselves of a variety of methodological techniques, 'including focus groups, interviews, online discussion groups', and other techniques.[53]

In order to reduce the volunteer hours spent on data entry, many parties are rapidly turning to mobile applications that can be used to enter data on the doorstep. The Liberal Party uses the MiniVAN app, designed by NGP VAN, which seamlessly interfaces with Liberalist. Volunteers can download canvass lists, which provide the names of voters by household, and enter voter responses directly on their mobile devices. Munroe and Munroe report that in addition to recording a voter's political affiliation, volunteers are also encouraged to collect information ranging from ethnicity to the approximate ages of children in the household.[54] Volunteers are encouraged to fully engage in conversations on the doorstep, but only to enter the responses as they walk to the next house.[55] Such efforts are presumably undertaken because the party recognizes voters would be uncomfortable with the recording of their personal information.[56] The Conservative Party uses a similar app called CIMS to Go or 'C2G', which also allows volunteers to input data remotely.[57] Volunteers use C2G to select a happy face, neutral face, or sad face to measure a voter's support.[58]

Political parties increasingly use social media to connect with supporters and to target their messages. Facebook is seen as the most dominant platform, given that it has 23 million Canadian users and that it allows parties 'to find a highly segmented and representative audience across the entirety of the Canadian population'.[59] Parties can create customized audiences through the upload of 'hashed' phone and email lists, and can then monitor the efficacy of their advertising efforts.[60] During the 2015 campaign, the Liberal Party was the most successful at using Facebook to adapt and evolve its message.[61] Parties are also active on other

51 Bennett and Bayley, 'Data Analytics in Canadian Elections' (n 34) 14; Anne Kingston, 'Inside the progressive think tank that really runs Canada' *Macleans* (12 Oct 2017) www.macleans.ca/politics/ottawa/inside-the-progressive-think-tank-that-really-runs-canada, accessed 15 March 2019.
52 Bennett and Bayley, 'Data Analytics in Canadian Elections' (n 34) 11.
53 Ibid.
54 Kaija Belfry Munroe and H D Munroe, 'Constituency Campaigning in the Age of Data' (2018) 51(1) Canadian Journal of Political Science 135, 143, doi:10.1017/S0008423917001135.
55 http://liberalist.liberal.ca/using-minivan, accessed 13 September 2019.
56 Bennett and Bayley, 'Data Analytics in Canadian Elections' (n 34) 21.
57 Haydn Watters, 'Conservative app puts voter identification in campaign workers' hands' *CBC News* (12 June 2015) www.cbc.ca/news/politics/conservative-app-puts-voter-identification-in-campaign-workers-hands-1.3104470, accessed 15 March 2019.
58 Munroe and Munroe (n 54) 143.
59 Bennett and Bayley, 'Data Analytics in Canadian Elections' (n 34) 10.
60 Ibid.
61 Delacourt (n 40) 306.

platforms such as Twitter and Instagram, and these efforts are focused on harnessing this technology to advertise, retool messaging, and connect with supporters.[62] Social media platforms are not, then, simply used as broadcast mechanisms. They can also be employed to network, interact, and engage with more precisely defined segments of the electorate.

These various trends are not nearly as extensive as in the United States. However, they have all taken a foothold to the extent that they now accentuate the inherently competitive instincts of political parties. Whether or not they are effective is less important than the fact that they are widely believed to be. These trends therefore raise a host of privacy questions about the capture and processing of personal data. The remainder of this chapter is devoted to analyzing the current rules in place for the processing of personal data in the electoral context, and to reviewing the different privacy risks.

IV. The Rules and the Protections

The various legal provisions that apply to the processing of personal data in the electoral context come in a number of categories: first the broader constitutional framework under the Canadian Charter, which protects electoral communication; second, the various statutory provisions within Canadian election law; third, assorted standards about electoral communication; and, finally, the only relevant Canadian privacy protection statute in BC.

The constitutional protections for political parties

The Canadian Charter of Rights and Freedoms sets out a comprehensive rights framework for Canadian citizens, inclusive of democratic rights. Specifically, s. 3 of the Charter guarantees the following: 'Every citizen of Canada has the right to vote in an election of members of the House of Commons or of a legislative assembly and to be qualified for membership therein.'[63] While this provision may be construed only as a protection of the right to vote, the judiciary has acknowledged that the purpose of s. 3 extends beyond the act of voting alone. In *Reference re Provincial Electoral Boundaries (Sask.)* (1991), Justice McLachlin affirmed that the purpose of s. 3 is 'the right to "effective representation"'.[64] As such, in determining whether s. 3 democratic rights are violated, the judiciary should consider a variety of factors.

The Supreme Court of Canada considered the applicability of s. 3 in reference to political parties in *Figueroa v Canada* (2003).[65] The appellant, Miguel

---

62 Tamara Small, 'Canadian Politics in 144 Characters: Party Politics in the Twitterverse' (2010) 33(2) Canadian Parliamentary Review 39.
63 Canadian Charter of Rights and Freedoms, Part I of the Constitution Act, 1982, being Schedule B to the Canada Act 1982 (UK), 1982, c 11, s 3.
64 *Reference re Prov. Electoral Boundaries (Sask.)*, [1991] 2 SCR 158, 183 (McLachlin J).
65 *Figueroa v Canada (Attorney General)*, 2003 SCC 37, [2003] 1 SCR 912.

Figueroa, asked the Court to consider whether Elections Canada provisions that required a party to nominate candidates in 50 or more electoral districts, in order to qualify as a registered political party, violated s. 3 of the Charter.[66] Unregistered political parties were unable to issue tax receipts for contributions received outside of an election period, candidates were not permitted 'to transfer unspent election funds to the party', and, perhaps most significantly, candidates could not 'list their party affiliation on the ballot'.[67] The Court determined that the principle of effective representation in s. 3 encompasses 'the right of each citizen to play a meaningful role in the electoral process', and consequently found that 'political parties act as both a vehicle and outlet for the meaningful participation of individual citizens in the electoral process'.[68] Moreover, parties are important to citizens regardless of whether they nominate candidates in more or fewer than 50 electoral districts.[69] Given this, the Court found that Elections Canada party registration requirements violated s. 3 of the Charter and that the infringement was not 'reasonable and demonstrably justified' under s. 1 of the Charter.[70]

The precedent established in *Figueroa* provides citizens the right to engage in democratic discourse through political parties, and subsequently ensures that political parties are free from unreasonable restrictions on their interactions with citizens. This sentiment is echoed in the CEA, which defines a political party as 'an organization one of whose fundamental purposes is to participate in public affairs by endorsing one or more of its members as candidates and supporting their election'.[71] Therefore, in considering the application of existing privacy legislation to political parties, governments must assess whether such an application would violate s. 3 of the Charter. However, it is unlikely that requiring political parties to adhere to the same privacy legislation that regulates either private or public entities, respectively, would constitute a violation of s. 3 rights. Indeed, BC currently regulates parties under PIPA, which applies to private sector organizations, and no such concerns have arisen. Even if the judiciary somehow found an infringement of s. 3 rights, it is probable that such an infringement would be permitted under s. 1 of the Charter,[72] which provides for 'reasonable limits' on Charter rights.

Election law, voters lists and personal privacy protection

Section 44 of the CEA provides: 'The Chief Electoral Officer [CEO] shall maintain a register of Canadians who are qualified as electors, to be known as the Register of Electors.' The Register contains the surname and given name of each elector included in it, their sex, date of birth, and civic and mailing addresses. Each

66 Ibid para 3 (Iacobucci J).
67 Ibid para 4.
68 Ibid para 37, 39.
69 Ibid para 46.
70 Ibid para 58, 94.
71 Canada Elections Act (n 14) ss 2(1).
72 Charter of Rights and Freedoms (n 63) s 1.

elector is assigned a unique identifier, randomly created by Elections Canada. The *raison d'être* of the National Register of Electors is the production of lists of electors, both for the purposes of elections and the distribution on an annual basis to Members of Parliament and, on request, to registered political parties.

During an election, returning officers (the election officials responsible for the running of the election in each of Canada's 338 electoral ridings) produce lists of the electors, disaggregated by each poll, for their electoral district or riding, using the data contained in the National Register of Electors. The preliminary lists of electors are produced as soon as possible after the issue of the writ for the election. Pursuant to s. 93(2) of the CEA, they contain only the name and address of each elector as well as their unique identifier – so no phone numbers. The returning officer distributes a paper copy and an electronic copy of the lists to each candidate in the electoral district who requests them.[73] Following revision of these lists by the returning officer and his or her staff, candidates who request it may obtain an electronic copy of the updated preliminary lists of electors.[74] Following Election Day, a printed and electronic copy of the final lists of electors for a given electoral district is provided to each political party that ran candidates in the district.[75] Thus, major parties that run candidates nationwide, in all 338 electoral districts, are given access to the lists of electors in their entirety.

The voter lists provided to registered political parties are subject to reasonably strict rules concerning security, retention, unauthorized access, and so on. The CEA specifies that parties, candidates, and MPs are expressly authorized to use the lists for communicating with electors, including using them for soliciting contributions and recruiting members.[76] However, the CEA also provides that no person may knowingly use personal information that is recorded in a list of electors for a purpose other than the one specified above or to administer the CEA or Referendum Act; there are penalties for failing to comply in Part 19 of the CEA.[77] In addition, the CEA states that '[a]t the written request of an elector, the [CEO] shall send the elector all the information in the [CEO's] possession relating to him or her'.[78]

Some provincial election authorities have begun to insist that parties follow certain basic privacy practices if they wish to continue to receive these voter lists. In BC, for instance, following a revision to BC's Election Act in 2015, all candidates, political parties, and other individuals who wish to access personal information available under the Election Act are required to first file an acceptable privacy policy with the CEO.[79] The Office of the CEO has published a template against

73 Canada Elections Act (n 14) s 94.
74 Ibid s 104.1.
75 Ibid s 109(2).
76 Ibid s 110, s 111.
77 Ibid s 275.
78 Ibid s 54.
79 Election Act, RSBC 1996, c 106, s 275; Elections BC, 'Privacy policy template for political parties' https://elections.bc.ca/docs/privacy/00157.pdf, accessed 15 March 2019.

which privacy policies are reviewed. Privacy policies may be reviewed on request, but there is no obligation to publish them, and the CEO has no authority to force them to be published. In June 2017, Elections Ontario published *Guidelines for the Use of Electoral Products Ontario*. Ontario's Election Act also requires any registered political party to file a privacy policy with Elections Ontario, which has also offered a sample policy covering restrictions on use, tracking of distribution, loss and theft of personal information, and the responsibilities of candidates and Members of the Provincial Parliament.[80] Again, however, there is no responsibility to publish the privacy policy, nor do the privacy requirements cover any information beyond that provided by Elections Ontario in the Permanent Register of Electors (PREO).

Following these provincial precedents, the government of Canada has introduced, as part of the Elections Modernization Act (Bill C-76), some modest provisions requiring registered political parties to have a publicly available, easily understandable policy describing the collection, protection, and sale of personal information, procedures for staff training, and the identity of a designated person to whom privacy concerns can be addressed. The submission of this policy is part of their application for registration with Elections Canada.[81] These provisions have been met with almost universal criticism for their incompleteness, vagueness, and lack of any real enforcement mechanism.[82] In consultation with Elections Canada, the Privacy Commissioner has recommended amendments, and in particular a specification that the privacy policies must be consistent with the principles within the Model Code for the Protection of Personal Information, found in Schedule 1 of PIPEDA, and that the Privacy Commissioner's Office should be responsible for oversight.[83]

On Election Day, all parties focus on getting their supporters to the polls. To do this, they rely on so-called 'bingo sheets', provided by each polling station, that indicate which electors have voted. The CEA requires poll clerks to produce these

80 Election Act, RSO 1990, c E.6; Elections Ontario, 'Guidelines for the Use of Electoral Products' (June 2017) www.elections.on.ca/content/dam/NGW/sitecontent/2017/resources/policies/Guidelines%20For%20the%20Use%20of%20Electoral%20Products.pdf, accessed 15 March 2019.
81 Bill C-76, Elections Modernization Act: An Act to amend the Canada Elections Act and consequential amendments, 1st Sess, 42nd Parl, 2018.
82 Colin J Bennett, 'Election bill does little more than reinforce the status quo' *iPolitics* (7 May 2018) https://ipolitics.ca/2018/05/07/election-bill-does-little-more-than-reinforce-the-status-quo, accessed 15 March 2019; Teresa Scassa, 'A federal bill to impose privacy obligations on political parties in Canada falls (way) short of the mark' (2 May 2018) www.teresascassa.ca/index.php?option=com_k2&view=item&id=276:a-federal-bill-to-impose-privacy-obligations-on-political-parties-in-canada-falls-way-short-of-the-mark&Itemid=80, accessed 15 March 2019.
83 Daniel Therrien, 'Appearance before Standing Committee on Procedure and House Affairs on the study about Bill C-76, Elections Modernization Act' (5 June 2018) Office of the Privacy Commissioner of Canada, www.priv.gc.ca/en/opc-actions-and-decisions/advice-to parliament/2018/parl_20180605/#amendments, accessed 15 March 2019.

sheets at the end of each day of advance voting and in 30-minute intervals on Election Day.[84] Parties typically send volunteers to collect these sheets and enter them into their VRMs as quickly as possible. This allows a party to overlay its list of supporters with an updated list of electors who have voted; parties can then dispatch door and phone canvassers to contact supporters who have yet to vote. In the past, parties needed to collect and enter all bingo sheets to ensure they had an accurate record of who voted. These efforts were cumbersome and time consuming, so it likely came as a great relief to parties that the 2015 federal election was the first one in which each party was given a list of all electors who voted.[85] With a more complete picture of who voted in the last election, parties are better able to target voters in future campaigns.

The various rules about the protection of personal information in the CEA do not, however, address the broader problem explained above. For the most part, elections law and elections administration can only cover the personal information circulated through the National Register of Electors. These rules do not apply to the range of other personal data parties might collect, on the doorstep, over the phone, from petitions, from third-party providers, or from social media. So they do not affect the vast majority of data contained in the respective VRMs. There is a regulatory gap, and a growing sense that something needs to be done about it.

Rules for unsolicited communications

The rules about unsolicited communications over phone or email also tend to treat political parties and political communication somewhat differently from other forms of marketing. Political parties are expected to follow the basic telecommunications rules for unsolicited communications, stipulated by the Canadian Radio Telecommunications Commission (CRTC). When making unsolicited calls, they are expected to identify the person on whose behalf the call is made, provide contact information, and display the originating phone number. Political parties and other political entities are, however, exempted from the National 'Do not Call List' (DNCL) procedures implemented through the CRTC. As provided for in the Telecommunications Act, the National DNCL Rules do not apply in respect of a telecommunication made by a registered party, a party candidate, or a nomination or leadership contestant.[86] They must maintain an internal 'do not call list', but are not obliged to disclose that they do so to callers.[87]

There are also specific rules in place for the use of Automatic Dialing-Announcing Devices (ADAD), better known as 'robocalls'. In the 2011 election, robocalls

---

84   Canada Elections Act (n 14) ss 162(i.1–i.2).

85   Robin Levinson King, 'What Canada's political parties know about you' *The Star* (23 September 2015) www.thestar.com/news/canada/2015/09/23/what-canadas-poli tical-parties-know-about-you.html, accessed 18 March 2019.

86   Telecommunications Act, SC 1993, c 38 s 41.7.

87   CRTC, 'Rules for Unsolicited Telecommunications made on behalf of Political entities' https://crtc.gc.ca/eng/phone/telemarketing/politi.htm, accessed 18 March 2019.

claiming to be from Elections Canada were used to give voters incorrect polling information in Guelph, Ontario. A Conservative staffer was later convicted of attempting to prevent electors from voting.[88] Such blatant efforts to interfere in a federal election have resulted in strict rules governing the use of robocalls. A robocall must begin by identifying the person or organization making the call, give the purpose of the call, and provide contact information for the group making the call.[89] Calls can only be made between 9 a.m. and 9.30 p.m. on weekdays and 10 a.m. and 6 p.m. on weekends, and they may not be used to solicit donations.[90]

Parties are also exempt from CASL if the primary purpose of the message is to solicit a monetary or non-monetary contribution, although, as discussed below, some parties say that they comply voluntarily, by including an unsubscribe option at the end of each message. If parties use email for purposes other than soliciting contributions, they must obtain consent, include identifying information, and ensure an unsubscribe option is present.[91] In general, parties are relatively unconstrained in contacting voters by email or text.

The application of Canadian privacy law to political parties

As noted above, unlike in many other countries that have passed comprehensive information privacy – or data protection – legislation in one package, Canada's experience was incremental, thus leaving some categories of organization unregulated.[92] Political parties stand as the principal example of those agencies that 'fell through the cracks' of a privacy regime that regulates either public bodies or organizations involved in explicitly commercial activity.

Whether or not the government expressly intended to exempt parties from PIPEDA, parties have certainly behaved as if the legislation does not regulate them, and the federal Privacy Commissioner has generally accepted that position as well. It is also, of course, likely that any attempt over the last 30 years to include political parties within public or private sector privacy legislation would have been met with stiff resistance from all political quarters. Canadian parties are highly competitive, but they are also entrenched and prone to collectively defend their interests against regulators. Indeed, there is some literature that suggests that they operate as a form of 'cartel' in relation to other regulations concerning ballot

---

88 'Key facts in Canada's robocalls controversy' *CBC News* (14 August 2014) www.cbc.ca/news/politics/key-facts-in-canada-s-robocalls-controversy-1.2736659, accessed 18 March 2019.

89 CRTC (n 87).

90 Ibid.

91 Ibid.

92 See Office of the Privacy Commissioner of Canada, 'Summary of privacy laws in Canada' www.priv.gc.ca/en/privacy-topics/privacy-laws-in-canada/02_05_d_15, accessed 18 March 2019.

access or campaign financing.[93] In the case of privacy protection, however, there was no observable debate or conflict concerning the regulation of political parties under either federal or provincial privacy laws. The issue was simply not on the agenda when either federal or provincial privacy legislation has been passed over the last 30 years.

That said, as described above, political parties do engage in a variety of activity that is very similar to that of commercial marketing companies. They develop lists. They hire consultants. They sometimes purchase data from data brokers. They engage in similar outreach practices – by mail, email, phone, and social media. The distinctions, therefore, are not as clear as has been assumed, and there is an increasing number of voices that have argued that the basic principles underlying PIPEDA can apply without difficulty to the parties' activities. For example, the House of Commons Standing Committee on Access to Information, Privacy, and Ethics (ETHI), after a series of hearings into the vulnerabilities of Canada's democratic system, arising from the breach of personal data involving Cambridge Analytica and Facebook, recommended 'that the Government of Canada take measures to ensure that privacy legislation applies to political activities in Canada, either by amending existing legislation or enacting new legislation'.[94]

The gap in privacy regulation for federal political parties is even harder to justify when one considers BC's PIPA, which does cover 'organizations' (other than public bodies) regardless of whether or not they are engaged in commercial activity. The Office of the Information and Privacy Commissioner of BC (OPICBC) therefore has jurisdiction over political parties, and has already conducted three investigations. One involving the BC New Democratic Party (BC NDP) and the other involving the BC Liberals served to establish that the OIPCBC did indeed have jurisdiction in this area.[95] Those precedents led to a broader analysis of compliance with PIPA by all major political parties in BC, published in 2019.[96]

The report concluded that BC political parties needed to be more transparent about how they collect data on voters; too much was being gathered without the

---

93   Heather MacIvor, 'Do Canadian Political Parties Form a Cartel?' (1996) 29(2) Canadian Journal of Political Science 317; Anika Gauja, 'Building Competition and Breaking Cartels? The Legislative and Judicial Regulation of Political Parties in Common Law Democracies?' (2014) 35(3) International Political Science Review 338.

94   House of Commons, Standing Committee on Access to Information, Privacy and Ethics, 'Addressing Digital Privacy Vulnerabilities and Potential Threats to Canada's Democratic Electoral Process: Report of the Standing Committee on Access to Information, Privacy and Ethics' (June 2018), Report (Chair: Bob Zimmer) 35.

95   Office of the Information and Privacy Commissioner of BC, 'Summary of the Office of the Information and Privacy Commissioner's Investigation of the BC NDP's use of social media and passwords to evaluate candidates' www.oipc.bc.ca/mediation-summaries/1399, accessed 20 March 2019; Office of the Information and Privacy Commissioner of BC, 'Sharing of Personal Information as Part of the Draft Multicultural Strategic Outreach Plan: Government of British Columbia and BC Liberal Party' (1 August 2013) Investigation Report F13-04, www.oipc.bc.ca/investigation-reports/1559, accessed 20 March 2019.

96   Office of the Information and Privacy Commissioner of BC, 'Full Disclosure: Political Parties, Campaign Data and Voter Consent' (6 February 2019) Investigation Report P19-01, www.oipc.bc.ca/investigation-reports/2278, accessed 6 February 2019.

individual's consent. There are a number of recommendations, and parties are now expected to revise their privacy policies and reform their practices in consultation with the OIPCBC and the CEO. The next question is whether or not the BC PIPA applies to the riding associations of federal political parties when they capture personal data in BC. In August 2019, the Commissioner answered the question in the affirmative, raising the issue of whether the federal parties will have to implement one set of privacy rules for BC and another for the rest of the country. It is likely that the courts will ultimately have to decide this question.[97]

The major value of this report is its portrayal of the range of data captured by Canadian political parties, and of various practices that have gradually crept into the political culture. A similar picture is provided by a report on Quebec elections by Élections Québec. As elsewhere, Quebec parties leverage the data from the electoral lists to build databases to determine their various persuasion strategies and to personalize the messages delivered to voters. Volunteers have easy access to these databases through smartphone- and tablet-based software. The parties use various algorithms to segment the electorate and develop voter profiles. And there is also an extensive use of social media for broadcasting messages, and for advertising through Facebook. Political parties are not covered by Quebec's privacy legislation.[98] Élections Québec has therefore recommended that both provincial and municipal political parties should be brought within the general legal framework for the protection of personal information.[99]

We are therefore beginning to get a more precise indication of the kinds of privacy questions that have been, and will continue to be, raised in Canada. These reports from regulators in BC and Quebec, the accumulation of stories in the media, parliamentary inquiries, and academic research all indicate the kinds of risks associated with the processing of huge amounts of personal data within the electoral context. The concluding section outlines those various risks.

V. Personal data and political parties: The privacy risks

The first, and perhaps most familiar, set of questions relate to *inappropriate communication* during campaigns. Some people find electoral communications intrusive – especially from parties and candidates they do not support. Some data protection authorities (DPAs) have issued guidance on inappropriate telemarketing,

97 Office of the Information and Privacy Commissioner of BC, 'Courtenay-Alberni Riding Association of the New Democratic Party of Canada' (28 August 2019) Order P19-02, www.oipc.bc.ca/orders/2331, accessed 23 September 2019.
98 Act respecting the protection of personal information in the private sector, CQLR c P-39.1.
99 Élections Québec, 'Partis politiques et protection des renseignements personnels: exposé de la situation québécoise, perspectives comparées et recommandations' (2019) www.pes.electionsquebec.qc.ca/services/set0005.extranet.formulaire.gestion/ouvrir_fichier.php?d=2002, accessed 20 March 2019.

especially through 'robo-calling' or ADADs.[100] At the conclusion of the highly controversial and public robo-calling scandal during the 2011 general election, a question lingered. All calls went to the homes of opposition supporters, something that could only have been known by someone with access to the CIMS database. The scandal contributed to the heightened publicity about privacy and security protections for the parties' VRMs, and led to a series of (unheeded) recommendations by Elections Canada to apply basic privacy principles to Canadian political parties.[101]

A set of larger questions concerns whether political marketing should be considered equivalent to commercial marketing. As noted above, the Canadian approach has been to treat them quite differently, with respect to both telephone and email communications. As mentioned, political parties are not obliged to match their lists against the National DNCL administered by the CRTC and they are exempt from CASL. It is likely that these exemptions will be reconsidered in the years ahead. Clearly, Canadian laws have not kept up with the realities of modern communications.

A second set of issues, canvassed at some length in the 2019 BC report, relates to the capture of personal data *without appropriate notice and consent*. An increasing amount of data are captured at the doorstep during canvassing, and may include identifiers such as email addresses or phone numbers, and information on the issues the voter thinks are important. Some parties may also collect information on gender, ethnicity, or religion.[102] In the heat of an election campaign, canvassers are under extraordinary pressure to knock on as many doors as possible, and often do not have the time to collect information beyond whether the person is going to vote and, if so, for whom. On the other hand, evidence suggests that additional information may be recorded and inferred about the household, and will be entered into party databases.[103] Similar issues arise when parties also collect personal information through telephone canvassing. The BC Commissioner ruled that the canvasser cannot fish for information about other people in the household, beyond the person on the line.[104] Parties also capture data through petitions, which is legal as long as the data collected is used for the purpose of furthering the objectives of that petition. If it is going to be used for other purposes, then the parties need to get consent.[105]

A related set of issues concerns the inappropriate use of lists from other sources for the purposes of political communication. These questions often involve elected members of the legislature who have access to personal data in that capacity, and

100 UK Information Commissioner's Office, 'Guidance on Political Campaigning' http s://ico.org.uk/media/for-organisations/documents/1589/promotion_of_a_politica l_party.pdf, accessed 21 March 2019.
101 Elections Canada, 'Preventing deceptive communications with electors: Recommendations from the Chief Electoral Officer of Canada following the 41st General Election' (2013) www.elections.ca/res/rep/off/comm/comm_e.pdf, accessed 21 March 2019.
102 Office of the Information and Privacy Commissioner of BC, 'Full Disclosure' (n 96) 15.
103 Ibid 16.
104 Ibid 18.
105 Ibid 19.

who then use that information, deliberately or unwittingly, for electoral advantage. There are several Canadian examples. In 2006, Conservative Party MP Cheryl Gallant sent birthday cards to her constituents using data from passport applications, an incident later investigated by the Office of the Ethics Commissioner under the Conflict of Interest Code for Members of the House of Commons. In October 2007, Rosh Hashanah cards were sent by the Prime Minister's Office to supporters with 'Jewish-sounding' names, many of who were unsettled and left wondering how such a list could be compiled. In 2011, about 10,000 people signed a petition addressed to Jason Kenney and his ministry, Citizenship and Immigration Canada, demanding that a young Nicaraguan gay artist facing deportation be allowed to stay in Canada. Kenney later sent out an email message to those who had signed the petition, extolling what the government of Canada had been doing to promote 'gay and lesbian refugee protection', startling many in the LGBTQ+ community that a federal minister had their contact information at his disposal.[106] Obviously, personal data on constituents should not be used for political purposes, and there should be a strong firewall between those two roles and the data captured under those roles.

A third set of issues relate to *the use of social media*. Parties in Canada, as elsewhere, are becoming increasingly adept at using social media to target messages, to recruit volunteers and donors, and to track issue engagement. Social media can also provide a far cheaper way to communicate to a larger audience than more traditional broadcast methods. But can political parties capture personal data from social media under the impression that it is already 'out there' and fair game? The BC report tackled this question. If an individual is already communicating with a political party through social media, then it is implied that the party can collect that information through those same channels. What BC law does not permit is the 'scraping' of personal data from social media sites, or linking email addresses with social media profiles, a practice that is common for those candidates that use the popular platform, Nationbuilder, and which has in fact been ruled illegal in some European countries.[107]

Parties in Canada increasingly use Facebook to target relevant audiences. Furthermore, parties may hand over lists of supporters (which may include donor information, email, phone number, date of birth) to Facebook to utilize the 'Lookalike' audience tool for political advertising. According to the BC report, this is also not permitted without consent: 'disclosing supporter email addresses for data analysis and profiling by Facebook's "Lookalike" tool is also entirely different from the political parties [sic] stated or inferred reason for collecting the email address'.[108] Furthermore, 'liking' a party on Facebook displays the icon of that party on that individual's social media page, perhaps unintentionally disclosing

---

106 These cases are discussed at greater length in Bennett and Bayley, 'Federal Political Parties and Personal Privacy Protection' (n 1).
107 Office of the Information and Privacy Commissioner of BC, 'Full Disclosure' (n 96) 21.
108 Ibid 26.

that individual's political beliefs. Additionally, a user 'liking' a party, prior to implementing appropriate privacy controls, can result in the user's name and photo being listed on the parties' social media page. Thus, the practices of political parties, and the privacy rights of their members, are closely related to the privacy policies and mechanisms embedded within these social media platforms, matters of huge and continuing controversy.[109]

A fourth set of issues relates to *voter profiling*. All Canadian parties have developed personalized scoring systems to predict a voter's likely support or opposition. The Conservative Party employs a scale from –15 to +15 to rank voter support, ranging from least likely to most likely.[110] Similarly, the Liberal Party uses a tiered system, placing definite Liberals in tier 1 and their strongest opponents in tier 10.[111] According to Munroe and Munroe, the LPC uses a predictive ranking to assign a tier 1–10 score for each individual voter.[112]

These ranking systems allow parties to focus their efforts on the voters who are most likely to support them, and to improve a party's ability to recruit new volunteers and donors. At first glance, this might seem innocuous. But political profiling can be sensitive for some citizens, and most would not be aware that their political views are being measured in this way. Further, political ideology is complex, multifaceted, and not amenable to unidimensional scoring. Might voters be able to access their scores or insist on their amendment? The BC Commissioner found that most parties were calculating 'support scores', and that they would refuse access to such information on the grounds that it would reveal confidential commercial information that would harm the competitiveness of the political party. The Commissioner rejected this argument, stating explicitly that the 'inferred data and support scores that parties assign to individuals' are not commercial information, and therefore parties would be required to make it available upon request to an individual.[113]

The final issue concerns *data breaches*. Many legislatures around the world have enacted legislation mandating notice to individuals about the loss or unauthorized acquisition of personal information. The scope and standards of these laws vary, and some of them limit liability when the data are suitably encrypted. However, many organizations that suffered a breach learned that the cost of providing notice to data subjects can be great, and the damage to reputation significant. No type of organization has been immune from such losses, including political parties.[114]

---

109 A thorough analysis of the use of Facebook in the electoral arena is provided in UK Information Commissioner's Office, 'Democracy Disrupted? Personal information and political influence' (11 July 2018) https://ico.org.uk/media/2259369/democracy-disrupted-110718.pdf, accessed 22 March 2019.
110 Colin J Bennett, 'Trends in Voter Surveillance' (n 2) 375.
111 Delacourt (n 40) 308; Bennett and Bayley, 'Data Analytics in Canadian Elections' (n 34) 13.
112 Munroe and Munroe (n 54) 146.
113 Office of the Information and Privacy Commissioner of BC, 'Full Disclosure' (n 96) 5.
114 DataBreaches.net, 'Home' www.databreaches.net, accessed 22 March 2019.

Thus far, there has not been a massive breach of electoral data from political parties during an election campaign that we know of; one can only speculate on the political consequences of a major loss of personal data at such a time. There have been reports at the provincial level, however. In 2012, there was a leak of more than two million voter files from Elections Ontario. Two USB keys went missing containing names, addresses, genders, birth dates, and whether a person voted in the last election, for residents in as many as 25 ridings. An investigation by the Ontario Information and Privacy Commissioner found systemic failures in privacy management within Elections Ontario.[115] In November 2016, it was reported that the CIMS of the Progressive Conservative Party of Ontario was hacked through a ransomware virus, a fact that only came to light two months later.[116] More common are the anecdotal incidents where party workers inappropriately use party databases to find out how people they know have voted, or to satisfy their curiosity about the political affiliations of notable people who live in their riding. In the 2018 Ontario provincial election, one Conservative candidate resigned after accusations that he had illegally accessed customer data from the 407 ETR toll highway in Toronto.[117]

All databases carry serious risks of abuse; party databases are no exception. The OIPCBC recommended that all political parties needed to do a better job training their staff and volunteers in privacy and security, and destroying obsolete information.[118] Appropriate security training is particularly crucial given the publicity about cyber-attacks and the risks of hacking party databases. In response to the global publicity about foreign influence in the US presidential election, the government of Canada asked the Communications Security Establishment (CSE), Canada's national cryptologic agency, to conduct an overall security and risk assessment of cyber threats to Canada's democratic process. In its June 2017 report, the CSE identified the stealing or manipulation of party databases as one of the key vulnerabilities to hackers, cybercriminals, and cyber-espionage.[119] The CSE made its security consultants available to the main parties for advice about how to improve their security procedures and the integrity of their VRMs.[120]

115 Information and Privacy Commissioner Ontario, 'Elections Ontario's Unprecedented Privacy Breach: A Special Investigation Report' (31 July 2012) www.ipc.on.ca/wp-con tent/uploads/2012/07/2012-07-31-elections-ont_1.pdf, accessed 20 March 2019.
116 'Ontario Progressive Conservative Party Database hacked: sources' CP24 News (28 January 2018) www.cp24.com/news/ontario-progressive-conservative-party-databa se-hacked-sources-1.3779326, accessed 20 March 2019.
117 Shawn Jeffords, 'Ford says Ontario PCs looking into allegations involving candidate who resigned' Globe and Mail (17 May 2018) www.theglobeandmail.com/canada/a rticle-ford-accepted-ontario-pc-candidates-resignation-after-learning-about, accessed 22 March 2019.
118 Office of the Information and Privacy Commissioner of BC, 'Full Disclosure' (n 96) 29.
119 Communications Security Establishment, 'CyberThreats to Canada's Democratic Process' (2017) www.cse-cst.gc.ca/sites/default/files/cse-cyber-threat-assessment-e. pdf, accessed 15 March 2019.
120 Alex Boutilier, 'Despite risk of cyber attacks, political parties still handle Canadians' data with no rules in place' The Star (19 June 2017) www.thestar.com/news/cana

VI. Conclusion

There is no question that the furore over the processing of personal data in the last presidential election in the US and the EU referendum in the UK has elevated these questions to higher levels of public and media scrutiny. Cambridge Analytica has become a household name, and a symbol for corporate irresponsibility and highly intrusive data analytics practices in the electoral context. But more broadly, the inappropriate capture, use, and disclosure of personal data by political actors does not only implicate privacy but may also affect electoral outcomes and damage the credibility of democratic institutions. For the processing of personal data in the electoral context, the stakes are therefore a lot higher than in other areas.

This chapter argues, however, that there still remain a range of more traditional questions related to informational privacy and data protection, which require analysis and resolution. Historically, DPAs have been reluctant to enter this territory. With the exception of the Commission Nationale de l'Informatique et Libertés (CNIL) in France, and the Information Commissioner's Office (ICO) in the UK, one would be hard-pressed to find other investigations of political parties and candidates. The explanation is probably obvious. These agencies are typically small and under-resourced. They typically do not want to be placed in a position of investigating, and sanctioning, the politicians on whom they rely for their budgets and for a favourable reception when they wish to amend the legislation they oversee. If anything, the current publicity about the increasing role of personal data in elections will likely push other DPAs to enter this territory as a result of domestic scrutiny and pressure.[121]

It is this international context that makes the Canadian case so interesting. As a parliamentary and federal system influenced by US practices, we are engaged in a debate about why, rather than how, political parties should be regulated by privacy protection law. This debate is raising important issues about the appropriate balance between the rights to privacy and the legitimate needs of political parties and candidates to engage the electorate. The debate is also requiring Canadians to consider whether political parties should indeed be treated any differently from commercial entities. Political parties have indeed a unique function in society, but should this special role actually make any difference to their data privacy obligations?

Furthermore, underlying this broader contention are a host of more nuanced questions about the application of the standard information privacy principles to the electoral context. Those questions have been raised by the recent report in BC. But this report represents just the initiation of the debate, serving to raise and

da/2017/06/19/despite-risk-of-cyber-attacks-political-parties-still-handle-canadia ns-data-with-no-rules-in-place.html, accessed 20 March 2019.
121 Colin J Bennett, 'Voter databases, micro-targeting and data protection law: Can political parties campaign in Europe as they do in North America?' (2016) 6(4) International Data Privacy Law 261.

address the important questions about notice and consent in the electoral arena, and prompting a far more nuanced analysis of the appropriate rules for privacy protection, as well as the important public interest in motivating voter mobilization, engagement, and participation.

Chapter 9

Voter privacy in an era of big data

Time to abolish the political exemption in the
Australian Privacy Act

Moira Paterson and Normann Witzleb

I. Introduction

Despite the fact that the Facebook/Cambridge Analytica scandal affected citizens around the globe, the political and regulatory responses to the revelations have differed sharply. There is little doubt that the United Kingdom (UK) House of Commons Digital, Culture, Media and Sport (DCMS) Committee and the Information Commissioner's Office engaged in the most public and most comprehensive enquiries into the uncovered malpractices. As a result, the evidence gathered and recommendations made in its two Reports[1] contain many important lessons for democracies around the globe. The DCMS Committee's recommendations on reforming the regulatory framework of political communication should be of particular interest to Australia, given that Australian political parties are likewise becoming increasingly reliant on using modern technologies to interact with potential voters, that Australian regulation imposes notoriously lax restrictions on the use of personal data by political actors, and that the information systems of the Australian Parliament and the major political parties have been subject to malicious interference by foreign actors. Similarly, it was the UK Information Commissioner's Office which took the lead from a regulatory perspective in investigating the practices and prosecuting wrongdoing. Given that the Australian Privacy Act does not apply to registered political parties[2] or to many political acts and practices,[3] the scope for regulatory action in Australia has been much reduced.

In the absence of transparency requirements, the actual data-handling practices engaged in by Australian parties remain shrouded in secrecy, but it is known that both the Labor Party and the Liberal Party have databases which build on electoral roll data obtained from the Australian Electoral Commission and log all

---

1 UK Parliament, Digital, Culture, Media and Sport Committee, *Disinformation and 'fake news': Interim Report* (HC 2017–19, 363); Digital, Culture, Media and Sport Committee, *Disinformation and 'fake news': Final Report* (HC 2017–19, 1791).
2 See ibid.
3 Ibid.

interactions a constituent has with an electorate office.[4] The user manual of the Liberal Party's software solution 'Feedback' was leaked in 2016. The manual pointed out that Feedback is a 'confidential database, which is not subject to privacy laws' and that 'it is important to remember that we do not discuss Feedback outside of this office'.[5] Discussion in the media about a website allegedly with links to an Australian politician also highlights the potential for the existence of databases created by politicians in relation to specific campaigns.[6] Most Australians are unaware that political parties are able to record and mine the personal information of voters largely without regulatory oversight. In the most recent Community Attitude Survey on Privacy, which the Australian Privacy Commissioner periodically commissions, 64% of respondents assumed wrongly that Australia's privacy laws apply also to political parties.[7] It appears unlikely that Australian voters would take well to the political parties' current practices, if they were known more widely.

In early 2018, Fairfax newspapers reported[8] that Facebook approached both parties during the last federal election campaign with an offer for 'advanced matching'. Facebook's so-called 'Custom Audience' feature enables customers to match data they hold on their databases with data collected from Facebook profiles. In the political arena, such practices allow parties not only to improve the quality of data they already hold but also to extend their database and identify voters who are most likely to be influenced by campaigning. Data matching with Facebook apparently requires data held on Australian voters to be sent overseas. The Liberal Party therefore rejected the Facebook offer out of concerns that this may put it in breach of its obligations under electoral laws and privacy laws;[9] the Labor Party confirmed

4   Paul Smith, 'How the smart use of software helped define the 2016 election campaign' *AFR* (17 July 2016) www.afr.com/technology/how-the-smart-use-of-software-helped-define-the-2016-election-campaign-20160715-gq6czc#ixzz5AFtEf9d8, accessed 19 February 2019.

5   Conor Duffy, 'Feedback: Major parties abusing voter tracking software, former Liberal MP Dennis Jensen says' *ABC News* (10 June 2016) www.abc.net.au/news/2016-06-09/voter-feedback-software-company-donated-$1million-liberal-party/7498024, accessed 19 February 2019.

6   See Andre Obeler, 'Tim Wilson's "retirement tax" website doesn't have a privacy policy. So how is he using the data?' *The Conversation* (8 February 2019) https://theconversation.com/tim-wilsons-retirement-tax-website-doesnt-have-a-privacy-policy-so-how-is-he-using-the-data-111076, accessed 22 July 2019.

7   Australian Government, Office of the Australian Information Commissioner, Australian Community Attitudes to Privacy Survey (2017) www.oaic.gov.au/resources/engage-with-us/community-attitudes/acaps-2017/acaps-2017-report.pdf, accessed 19 February 2019.

8   John McDuling and Fergus Hunter, 'Revealed: the powerful Facebook data matching tool the Liberal Party rejected over legal fears' *Sydney Morning Herald* (Sydney, 23 March 2018) www.smh.com.au/politics/federal/revealed-the-powerful-facebook-data-matching-tool-the-liberal-party-rejected-over-legal-fears-20180322-p4z5rh.html, accessed 19 February 2019.

9   Ibid.

that it used the tool, although it remains unclear to what extent and with what precautions.[10]

Australian law imposes minimal restrictions on the use of voter data by political parties. The key law which regulates information privacy in Australia is the Privacy Act 1988 (Cth) (Privacy Act). This Act regulates the handling of identifiable or potentially identifiable personal information[11] via a set of Australian Privacy Principles (APPs).[12] The Privacy Act applies to Commonwealth government agencies[13] and, since its extension to the private sector in 2000, to some private sector organisations.[14] Importantly, however, it does not apply to registered political parties[15] or to the political acts and practices of specified organisations.[16] These exemptions, which were included in the Act when it was extended to cover private sector organisations,[17] were justified on the basis of freedom of political communication.[18] The then Attorney General stated: 'Freedom of political communication is vitally important to the democratic process in Australia. This exemption is designed to encourage that freedom and enhance the operation of the electoral and political process in Australia.'

When the Australian Law Reform Commission (ALRC) conducted its review of the Privacy Act in 2008, it recommended that the political exemptions should be abolished.[19] As with many of the recommendations in the report, this recommendation has not been implemented. While a former Privacy Commissioner recently made a call for it to be reconsidered,[20] representatives of the two major political parties defended the status quo and saw no need for the laws to be changed.[21] However, it is our view that the time has come to reconsider this

10   Tyler Durden, 'Facebook Approached Australian Political Parties to Microtarget Voters' *ZeroHedge* (26 March 2018) www.zerohedge.com/news/2018-03-25/fa cebook-approached-australian-political-parties-microtarget-voters, accessed 19 February 2019.
11   See the definition of 'personal information' in the Privacy Act 1988 (Cth) s 6(1).
12   An act or practice of an APP entity (i.e. an agency or organisation) that breaches an APP constitutes an interference with the privacy of an individual: see the Privacy Act 1988 (Cth) s 13(1) and s 6(1) definition of an APP entity.
13   The expression 'agency' is defined in the Privacy Act 1988 (Cth) s 6(1).
14   See the definitions of organisation in the Privacy Act 1988 (Cth) s 6C.
15   See ibid.
16   Ibid.
17   Privacy Amendment (Private Sector) Act 2000 (Cth).
18   Australian Commonwealth House of Representatives, Parliamentary Debates (12 April 2000) 15749, 15753.
19   Australian Law Reform Commission, 'For Your Information: Australian Privacy Law and Practice' (2008) ALRC Report 108, Rec 41-1.
20   Nicole Hasham, 'Former privacy chief lambasts "incredibly secretive" political parties' *Sydney Morning Herald* (Sydney, 24 March 2018) www.smh.com.au/politics/federa l/former-privacy-chief-lambasts-incredibly-secretive-political-parties-20180324-p 4z62j.html, accessed 19 February 2019.
21   Kelsey Munro, 'Australia's major parties defend privacy exemption over Cambridge Analytica' *The Guardian* (22 March 2018) www.theguardian.com/australia-news/ 2018/mar/22/australias-political-parties-defend-privacy-exemption-in-wake-of-cam bridge-analytica, accessed 19 February 2019.

question in the light of the recent reports about misuse of data in political campaigning overseas and having regard to the newer case law concerning the implied freedom of political communication.[22]

The next part of this chapter provides an overview of the political exemptions in the Privacy Act and discusses the data protection issues raised by the current trend towards micro-targeting of Australian electors. The chapter then explores the case law on the implied freedom of political communication, including developments that have taken place since the political exemption was first debated in 1990, and considers whether and to what extent it precludes rolling back the political exemptions in the Privacy Act, having regard to the special issues that arise in the new context of big data and the micro-targeting of electors. The chapter concludes that the political exemptions in the Privacy Act should be abolished.

II. The political exemptions in the Australian Privacy Act

The Privacy Act regulates information handling by requiring compliance with a set of APPs. It provides that an act or practice of an 'APP entity' (i.e. a public sector 'agency' or a private sector 'organisation'[23]) constitutes an interference with the privacy of an individual if it breaches an APP (or relevant APP code) in relation to that individual's personal information.[24] Coverage of political activities is determined in part by the definition of 'APP entity' and in part by the scope of the exemption for certain 'acts and practices'.[25]

The Act does not require the vast majority of political parties to comply with the APPs as the definition of 'organisation' specifically excludes 'a registered political party',[26] which is defined as 'a political party registered under Part XI of the *Commonwealth Electoral Act 1918*.[27] To be eligible for registration under that Act a body must be:

a political party that:
    (a) either:
        (i) is a Parliamentary party; or
        (ii) has at least 500 members; and
    (b) is established on the basis of a written constitution (however described) that sets out the aims of the party.[28]

---

22   More recent cases include: *Brown v Tasmania* [2017] HCA 43, (2017) 261 CLR 328; *McCloy v New South Wales* [2015] HCA 34, (2015) 257 CLR 178; *Monis v The Queen* [2013] HCA 4, (2013) 249 CLR 92; *Unions NSW v New South Wales* [2013] HCA 58, (2013) 252 CLR 530.
23   An APP entity means an 'agency or organisation': Privacy Act 1988 (Cth) s 13.
24   Ibid s 13(1).
25   Ibid s 7(1)(ee).
26   Ibid s 6(1) and 6C.
27   Ibid s 6(1).
28   Commonwealth Electoral Act 1918 (Cth) s 123(1).

The consequence of this exclusion is that a body that qualifies as a 'registered political party' falls outside the scope of the Privacy Act in respect all of its activities.

In addition, section 7C of the Privacy Act contains a further exemption from the application of the APPs in respect of any act that is done or practice that is engaged in for any purpose in connection with:

(a)   an election under an electoral law; or

(b)   a referendum under a law of the Commonwealth or a law of a State or Territory; or

(c)   the participation by the political representative in another aspect of the political process.[29]

The expressions 'electoral law' and 'Parliament' are defined broadly with reference to the Commonwealth, States and Territories and, in the case of 'electoral law', to the local government authorities.[30] 'Political representatives' includes members of parliament and local government councillors. The Act also excludes specific acts and practices of contractors and sub-contractors and by volunteers for registered parties.[31]

The idea of excluding political parties from privacy obligations did not meet with universal approval even prior to the privacy-invasive practices facilitated by big data.[32] However, the government justified the enactment of the political exemptions in the Privacy Act with the significance of the freedom of political communication. It also included similar exclusions in other privacy-related legislation. The Do Not Call Register Act 2006 (Cth) contains an exception for unsolicited calls or faxes authorised by political parties, independent members of parliament, candidates and others as specified in Schedules 1 and 1A.[33] Similarly, the Spam Act 2003 (Cth) includes messages authorised to be sent by registered

29   Ibid s 7C(1).

30   Ibid s 7C(6).

31   Ibid ss 7C(2), (3) and (4).

32   The House of Representatives' Standing Committee on Legal and Constitutional Affairs proposed to draft the exemption in narrower terms: Parliament of the Commonwealth of Australia, *Advisory Report on the Privacy Amendment (Privacy Sector) Bill 2000* (2000) Recs 11–13. The Senate Legal and Constitutional Legislation Committee was divided on the appropriateness of the exemption: Parliament of the Commonwealth of Australia, *Inquiry into the Provisions of the Privacy Amendment (Private Sector) Bill 2000* (2000).

33   Do Not Call Register Act 2006 (Cth) sch 1, cl 3 and sch 1A, cl 3. These operate by including them in the definition of 'designated telemarketing call' (with the effect that they are not subject to prohibition in s 11 against making unsolicited telemarketing calls to numbers registered on the Do Not Call Register) and in the definition of 'designated marketing fax' (with the effect that they are not subject to prohibition in s 12B against sending unsolicited marketing faxes to numbers registered on the Do Not Call Register).

political parties in the definition of 'designated commercial electronic message', which are exempt from the prohibition on unsolicited messaging.[34]

III. Big data and micro-targeting

When the ALRC considered the political exemptions in the Privacy Act,[35] it noted that electoral databases might contain a range of personal information about voters, including 'policy preferences and party identification as well as such matters as the individual's occupation, membership of community organisations, and so on'.[36] It referred to

> concerns about political parties withholding from voters information they have stored; inaccurate information being stored on databases without giving voters the right to correct the record; political parties failing to inform voters that information is being compiled about them; and representatives of political parties failing to identify themselves appropriately when collecting information.[37]

The issues arising from the use of electoral databases have changed considerably with the advent of big data analytics. While there is no commonly agreed definition of big data, it is most frequently described with reference to the three Vs: volume, velocity and variety.[38] This definition is 'routed in magnitude'[39] and refers to 'the increasing size of data, the increasing rate at which it is produced and the increasing range of formats and representations employed'.[40] In addition, big data relies on the concurrent advances in analytical technologies that are now employed to mine it for useful information and insights. These include artificial intelligence (the development of computer systems able to perform tasks normally requiring human intelligence) and, in particular, machine learning (the application of artificial intelligence to allow machines to learn for themselves). Also relevant is the semantic web (an extension of the web that *inter alia* provides common formats for the interchange of data and a common language for recording how data relates to real-world objects), which facilitates increased retrievability and easier combination of data.

---

34 See Spam Act 2003 (Cth) sch 1, cl 3. This has the effect of excluding them from the prohibition in s 16 against sending unsolicited commercial electronic messages.
35 Australian Law Reform Commission (n 19) Rec 41.
36 Ibid Rec 41.13.
37 Ibid.
38 NIST Big Data Public Working Group Definitions and Taxonomies Subgroup, 'Interoperability Framework: Volume 1, Definitions' (2015) NIST Special Publication 1500–1, https://bigdatawg.nist.gov/_uploadfiles/NIST.SP.1500-1.pdf, accessed 19 February 2019, 4.
39 Jonathan Ward and Adam Barker, 'Undefined by Data: A Survey of Big Data Definitions' (2013) arXiv preprint arXiv:1309.5821.
40 Ibid, referring to Doug Laney, '3D Data Management: Controlling Data Volume, Velocity and Variety' *META Group* (6 February 2011) https://blogs.gartner.com/doug-laney/files/2012/01/ad949-3D-Data-Management-Controlling-Data-Volume-Velocity-and-Variety.pdf, accessed 19 February 2019.

Whether or not big data analytics are living up to their hype remains in dispute,[41] but they are increasingly being embraced and utilised in a wide variety of contexts, and this use has, in turn, generated concerns about their potential to cause harm. Where big data analytics involves the processing of personal information, it generates concerns about individual privacy, especially given that this processing generally takes place in the absence of informed consent. Depending on the context in which it is used, big data analytics may raise issues about the potential unfairness of decision-making, including concerns about discrimination and the absence of due process.[42] It also makes possible the development of practices that are inappropriately manipulative. This issue can arise in the consumer context, where online behavioural advertising as well as price and search discrimination are becoming areas of increasing concern.[43] However, manipulative political advertising raises broader, and arguably more urgent, issues because of its effect on our system of representative government.

IV. The issue of political micro-targeting

The use of big data analytics in political advertising has received its most detailed examination in the US (in the context of the Obama[44] and Trump[45] elections) and in the UK (in the context of the 2016 Brexit referendum).[46] However, it has

41   For example, see Cristian S Calude and Giuseppe Longo, 'The Deluge of Spurious Correlations in Big Data' (2017) 22(3) Foundations of Science 595.

42   See Scott R Peppet, 'Regulating the Internet of Things: First Steps toward Managing Discrimination, Privacy, Security and Consent' (2014) 93 Texas Law Review 85; Kate Crawford and Jason Schultz, 'Big Data and Due Process: Toward a Framework to Redress Predictive Privacy Harms (2014) 55 Boston College Law Review 93.

43   See Jakub Mikians et al., *Detecting Price and Search Discrimination on the Internet* (HotNets-XI Proceedings of the 11th ACM Workshop on Hot Topics in Networks, 2012), 79–84; Andre Oboler, Kristopher Welsh and Lito Cruz, 'The danger of big data: Social media as computational social science' (2012) 17(7) First Monday, https://uncommonculture.org/ojs/index.php/fm/article/view/3993>.

44   See e.g. Lynda Lee Kaid, Juliana Fernandes and David Painter, 'Effects of Political Advertising in the 2008 Presidential Campaign' (2011) 55(4) American Behavioral Scientist 437; Bruce Bimber, 'Digital Media in the Obama Campaigns of 2008 and 2012: Adaptation to the Personalized Political Communication Environment' (2014) 11 Journal of Information Technology & Politics 130.

45   Nathaniel Persily, 'The 2016 U.S. Election: Can Democracy Survive the Internet?' (2017) 28 Journal of Democracy 63; Samuel C Woolley and Douglas R Guilbeault, 'Computational Propaganda in the United States of America: Manufacturing Consensus Online' (2017) Working Paper No. 2017.5, http://comprop.oii.ox.ac.uk/wp-content/uploads/sites/89/2017/06/Comprop-USA.pdf, accessed 19 February 2019; Roberto J González, 'Hacking the citizenry? Personality profiling, "big data" and the election of Donald Trump' (2017) 33 Anthropology Today 9.

46   Carole Cadwalladr, 'The great British Brexit robbery: How our democracy was hijacked' *The Guardian* (7 May 2017) www.theguardian.com/technology/2017/may/07/the-great-british-brexit-robbery-hijacked-democracy, accessed 19 February 2019; Marco Bastos and Dan Mercea, 'The public accountability of social platforms: lessons from a

reportedly also affected electoral campaigns elsewhere.[47] Much of the discussion on the role of data has focused on the now defunct political consultancy firm, Cambridge Analytica, and its use of Facebook data.[48] Cambridge Analytica, which was an offshoot of SCL Group,[49] used a methodology that combined psychometric scores with individual Facebook profiles to build up demographic and psychological profiles, which could then be used for micro-targeting.[50]

Political micro-targeting refers to 'the use of data and analytics to craft and convey a tailored message to a subgroup or individual members of the electorate'.[51] While it shares some of the features of commercial advertising, it is generally subject to less stringent regulation and is potentially open to more misuse, including by foreign state actors, as demonstrated by the alleged Russian meddling in recent US elections.[52]

study on bots and trolls in the Brexit campaign' Philosophical Transactions of the Royal Society A (4 June 2018) https://royalsocietypublishing.org/doi/pdf/10.1098/rsta.2018.0003, accessed 19 February 2019.

47   See Rachel Halliburton, 'How big data helped secure Emmanuel Macron's astounding victory' Prospect Magazine (10 June 2017) www.prospectmagazine.co.uk/politics/the-data-team-behind-macrons-astounding-victory, accessed 19 February 2019; Sam Bright, 'After Trump, "big data" firm Cambridge Analytica is now working in Kenya' BBC News (3 August 2017) www.bbc.com/news/blogs-trending-40792078, accessed 19 February 2019.

48   See e.g. Hannes Grassegger and Mikael Krogerus, 'The Data That Turned the World Upside Down' Motherboard (29 January 2017) https://motherboard.vice.com/en_us/article/mg9vvn/how-our-likes-helped-trump-win, accessed 19 February 2019.

49   This has advertised that it 'extract[s] value from data, narrowing sizeable data sets to meaningful audience segments and reducing the time and money spent to reach these audiences'. See 'SCL Group – The Company Behind the Cambridge Analytica/Facebook Scandal' (18 July 2019) http://viableopposition.blogspot.com/2018/04/scl-group-company-behind-cambridge.html, accessed 13 September 2019.

50   This built on the work of academic researchers: see Michal Kosinski, David Stillwell and Thore Graepe, 'Private traits and attributes are predictable from digital records of human behavior' Proceedings of the National Academy of Sciences of the United States of America (9 April 2013) www.pnas.org/content/110/15/5802, accessed 19 February 2019; Renaud Lambiotte and Michal Kosinski, 'Tracking the Digital Footprints of Personality' Proceedings of the Institute of Electrical and Electronics Engineers (2015); Michal Kosinski et al., 'Facebook as a Social Science Research Tool: Opportunities, Challenges, Ethical Considerations and Practical Guideline' (2015) 70 American Psychologist 543.

51   Balázs Bodó, Natali Helberger and Claes H de Vreese, 'Political micro-targeting: A Manchurian candidate or just a dark horse?' (2017) 6(4) Internet Policy Review, doi: 10.14763/2017.4.776.

52   Ibid. See further Lauren Gambino, 'Senior Trump adviser says Russian election meddling "beyond dispute"' The Guardian (18 February 2018) www.theguardian.com/us-news/2018/feb/17/donald-trump-hr-mcmaster-russia-election-meddling-investigation, accessed 19 February 2019; Ben Riley-Smith, Alec Luhn and Rozina Sabur, 'Thirteen Russians charged with US election meddling as shocking detail of allegations is laid bare' The Telegraph (London, 17 February 2018) www.telegraph.co.uk/news/2018/02/16/us-investigators-charge-13-russians-election-meddling, accessed 19 February 2019.

How well micro-targeting works remains a matter of controversy.[53] Some empirical work on the 2016 US presidential election suggests that its effects may differ depending on demographic factors, with male voters, Republican supporters and less educated voters appearing to be more susceptible to political messaging on Facebook than other groups.[54] There is also debate as to whether such difference that it does make impacts negatively on the electoral process. On the one hand, there is evidence that social media can play a useful role in reaching otherwise disenfranchised groups and that it enhances participation in the democratic process in that way.[55] On the other hand, it raises issues of possible manipulation.[56] Manipulative practices – whether in the form of pork barrelling or using emotive language – are by no means new to the electoral process and have long been tolerated. What is at issue in relation to the use of these practices, such as those attributed to Cambridge Analytica, is whether they overstep a red line and, if so, how and why.

A key concern relates to manipulation in the sense of getting voters 'to hold opinions that they would not hold if aware of the best available information and analysis'[57] and the point at which manipulation should be considered illegitimate. There appears to be a strong case for arguing that micro-targeting is harmful when it is used to mislead voters or keep them ignorant about matters relevant to their

53   See e.g. Elizabeth Gibney, 'The scant science behind Cambridge Analytica's controversial marketing techniques' *Nature* (29 March 2018) www.nature.com/articles/d41586-018-03880-4, accessed 19 February 2019; Nicholas Confessore and Danny Hakim, 'Data Firm Says "Secret Sauce" Aided Trump; Many Scoff' *The New York Times* (6 March 2017) www.nytimes.com/2017/03/06/us/politics/cambridge-ana lytica.html, accessed 19 February 2019.

54   Federica Liberini et al., 'Politics in the Facebook Era: Evidence from the 2016 US Presidential Elections' (October 2018) University of Warwick, Department of Economics Centre for Competitive Advantage in the Global Economy, https://warwick.ac.uk/fac/soc/economics/staff/mredoanocoppede/politics_in_the_facebook_era__evidence_from_the_2016_us_presidential_elections__cagewp.pdf, accessed 19 February 2019.

55   See e.g. Anna Elena Maria Ferrari, 'Electorate databases: good or bad for democracy? A lesson from political marketing' *The New Federalist* (16 April 2017) www.the newfederalist.eu/electoral-databases-good-or-bad-for-democracy-a-lesson-from-poli tical, accessed 19 February 2019.

56   For example, Howard and Kreiss refer the problem of 'informational asymmetries between candidates and voters' which 'undermine the mechanisms of political representation, enabling candidates to conjure up issue publics for their agendas and tailor narrow appeals for the support of voters': see Philip N Howard and Daniel Kreiss, 'Political parties and voter privacy: Australia, Canada, the United Kingdom, and United States in comparative perspective' (2010) 15(1) First Monday, http://firstm onday.org/article/view/2975/2627.

57   Lawrence R Jacobs and Robert Y Shapiro, *Politicians Don't Pander: Political Manipulation and the Loss of Democratic Responsiveness* (University of Chicago Press 2000) xv, as quoted in Murray Goot, 'Politicians, public policy and poll following: Conceptual difficulties and empirical realities' (2005) 40(2) Australian Journal of Political Science 189, 189.

vote. This might occur where a political party describes itself as standing for different issues depending on its analysis of the individual whom it targets. For example, Borgesius and colleagues identify the risk that a 'political party could [...] misleadingly present itself as a one-issue party to each individual. A party may highlight a different issue for each voter, so each voter sees a *different* one-issue.'[58] Micro-targeting can also reduce transparency about a party's promises as '[v]oters may not even know a party's views on many topics'.[59]

A further issue relates to the deliberate dissemination of false news, including by bots, with a view to influencing election results.[60] Analysis of recent elections campaigns in the US and elsewhere indicates increasing exploitation of social media to manipulate and alter public opinion.[61] A research paper on the use of Twitter in the 2016 US election notes that bots are particularly prevalent on Twitter, although they also exist on the multitude of social media platforms 'that increasingly form part of the system of political communication in many countries'.[62] The study found that 'political bot activity reached an all-time high for the 2016 campaign' and that '[t]he use of automated accounts was deliberate and strategic throughout the election, most clearly with pro-Trump campaigners and programmers'.[63] Such activities can take place in the absence of detailed information about voters, but they have additional power when they are targeted at voters with certain personal traits that appear to make them particularly receptive to such messaging.[64]

A research study on the use of social media bots in the 2017 French election suggested 'the possible existence of a black-market for reusable political disinformation bots'.[65] In particular, it identified the 'presence of bots that existed

---

58 Frederik J Zuiderveen Borgesius et al., 'Online Political Microtargeting: Promises and Threats for Democracy' (2018) 14(1) Utrecht Law Review 82, 87.

59 Ibid.

60 For a useful discussion of the broader issue of media manipulation, see Alice Marwick and Rebecca Lewis, 'Media Manipulation and Disinformation Online' *Data & Society Research Institute* (2017) https://datasociety.net/pubs/oh/DataAndSociety_Media ManipulationAndDisinformationOnline.pdf, accessed 19 February 2019.

61 See e.g. Alessandro Bessi and Emilio Ferrara, 'Social Bots Distort the 2016 US Presidential Election Online Discussion' (2016) 21 (11) First Monday, http://firstm onday.org/article/view/7090/5653; Samuel Woolley, 'Automating power: Social bot interference in global politics' (2016) 21(4) First Monday, http://firstmonday. org/article/view/6161/5300; Sara El-Khalili, 'Social media as a government propaganda tool in post-revolutionary Egypt' (2013) 18(3) First Monday, http://firstm onday.org/article/view/4620/3423.

62 Bence Kollanyi, Philip N Howard and Samuel C Woolley, 'Bots and Automation over Twitter during the U.S. Election' (2016) Project on Computational Propaganda Data Memo 2016.4, www.politicalbots.org, accessed 19 February 2019.

63 Ibid.

64 See e.g. Aaron Weinschenk and Costas Panagopoulos, 'Personality, Negativity, and Political Participation' (2014) 2(1) Journal of Social and Political Psychology 164.

65 Emilio Ferrara, 'Disinformation and Social Bot Operations in the Run Up to the 2017 French Presidential Election' (2017) 22(8) FirstMonday, https://firstmonday.org/a rticle/view/8005/6516, accessed 22 July 2019.

during the 2016 US Presidential election campaign period to support alt-right narratives, went dark after November 8, 2016, and came back into use in the run up days to the 2017 French presidential election'.[66] Equally concerning is evidence of the use of bots by agents of foreign governments to try to influence voters, as in the case of their use by Russian agents in the Trump election.[67]

While Australia has not to date been a focus of academic commentaries on these issues, there are worrying indications that political campaigning in Australia is moving in a similar direction to that in the US and UK. This is not surprising as micro-targeting follows naturally from the trend towards increased use of electoral databases by political parties, which was noted as far back as 2004 by van Onselen and Errington.[68] As already discussed, more recent developments have included pitching by Cambridge Analytica to Australian political parties.[69]

V. Political communications and democracy

The rationale for protecting political communication is that it serves an important democratic role. As stated by Barendt, political speech has a special status 'because it is a dialogue between members of the electorate and between governors and governed'.[70] It is justified by democratic theory on the basis that it 'encourages a well-informed, politically sophisticated electorate able to confront government on more or less equal terms'.[71]

66   Ibid.
67   See Scott Shan, 'How Unwitting Americans Encountered Russian Operatives Online' *The New York Times* (New York, 18 February 2018) www.nytimes.com/2018/02/18/us/politics/russian-operatives-facebook-twitter.html, accessed 19 February 2019; Brennan Weiss, 'A Russian troll factory had a $1.25 million monthly budget to interfere in the 2016 US election' *Business Insider Australia* (17 February 2018) www.businessinsider.com.au/russian-troll-farm-spent-millions-on-election-interference-2018-2, accessed 19 February 2019.
68   Peter van Onselen and Wayne Errington, 'Electoral databases: big brother or democracy unbound?' (2004) 39 Australian Journal of Political Science 349; see also Peter van Onselen and Wayne Errington, 'Suiting Themselves: Major parties, electoral databases and privacy' (2005) 20 Australasian Parliamentary Review 21.
69   See Melanie McCartney, 'Is Cambridge Analytica the Liberal Party's 2019 Trump card?' *Independent Australia* (8 April 2017) https://independentaustralia.net/business/business-display/is-cambridge-analytica-the-liberal-partys-2019-trump-card,10187, accessed 19 February 2019; Katharine Murphy, 'Cambridge Analytica: Trump's data mining advisers to meet Australia's Liberal MPs' *The Guardian* (5 April 2017) www.theguardian.com/austral-news/2017/apr/05/donald-trumps-data-mining-advisers-to-meet-liberal-mps-in-canberra, accessed 19 February 2019; Fergus Hunter, 'Cambridge Analytica, the "psychographic" data firm behind Donald Trump, Eyes Australia' *The Sydney Morning Herald* (Sydney, 23 January 2017) www.smh.com.au/federal-politics/political-news/cambridge-analytica-the-psychographic-data-firm-behind-donald-trump-eyes-australian-move-20161212-gt926e.html, accessed 19 February 2019.
70   Eric Barendt, *Freedom of Speech* (2nd edn, Oxford University Press 2005) 155.
71   Ibid 156.

Whether political communication based on micro-targeting serves to enhance, or threaten, democracy depends not only on the effectiveness of micro-targeting (as discussed above) but also on how the electoral system operates and the role of informed decision-making in the democratic process.

Political campaigning is an important aspect of political communication, although it is open to question whether campaigning via the use of social media bots can be regarded as a communication between governors and the governed. Micro-targeting facilitates political speech to the extent that it makes it easier for political parties to communicate with electors about issues that are likely to be of interest to these electors. The extent to which this is important depends on the rules which govern elections. Where voting is not compulsory, it is important for parties not only to appeal to their potential voters but also to motivate them to get out and vote, or, conversely, to dissuade supporters of opposing parties from casting their ballot. However, voter activation or voter suppression is not a major concern in Australia where voting for all levels of government is compulsory and participation rates are very high.

The key question raised by Australian campaigning based on micro-targeting is the extent to which any manipulation or disinformation detracts from the ideal of a well-informed electorate. This requires consideration of the democratic theory which underpins our system of government.

Patmore identifies three models which are commonly used to describe Westminster-style (i.e. cabinet-based) systems of representative government: protective, participatory and elite.[72] Each of these models attaches importance to freedom of political communication, but for different reasons. *Protective* theory emphasises accountability by rulers to the ruled. Citizen participation has the narrow function of protecting their interests in good government. The 'choice of good representatives'[73] depends on voters being informed by exposure to political discussion, including among 'electors, the elected and the media'.[74] *Participatory* theory attributes to citizen participation the wider function of creating and preserving a democratic society. Freedom of political communication is relevant insofar as it contributes to political decision-making and the development of capacity in individuals for democratic decision-making. Finally, *elite* theory views democracy essentially in terms of a struggle for leadership and emphasises 'freedom to compete for leadership in free elections',[75] including a 'considerable amount of freedom of discussion for all and freedom of the press'.[76]

---

72 Glenn Patmore, 'Making Sense of Representative Democracy and the Implied Freedom of Political Communication in the High Court of Australia – Three Possible Models' (1998) 7 Griffith Law Review 97, 99–107.
73 Carole Pateman, *Participation and Democratic Theory* (Cambridge University Press 1970) 19, cited in ibid 100.
74 Patmore (n 72) 100.
75 Ibid 106.
76 Ibid, citing Joseph A Schumpeter, *Capitalism, Socialism and Democracy* (Allen & Unwin 1943) 272 and Carole Pateman, *Participation and Democratic Theory* (Cambridge University Press 1970) 4.

Manipulation and disinformation are arguably problematic regardless of which theory of representative government is applied. They are inimical to the democratic process, as understood by both the protective and participation theory, because they hinder good decision-making by the electorate. Manipulation is problematic from the perspective of protective theory to the extent that it undercuts accountability and, in the case of participation theory, more broadly to the extent that it affects the development of the individual's capacity for democratic decision-making. Manipulation and disinformation make less difference in the case of elite theory where the emphasis is on competition between political actors. However, even under this model, they are problematic because they may hinder the choice of the best political representatives.

VI. The implied freedom of political communication

When the ALRC reviewed the political exemptions in 2008, it concluded:

> [P]olitical parties and those engaging in political acts and practices should be subject to the Privacy Act – provided that the legislation can accommodate adequately the constitutional doctrines of implied freedom of political communication and parliamentary privilege.[77]

Its report accordingly included a recommendation to remove both the exemption for registered political parties and the exemption for political acts and practices.[78] It also recommended amending the Act 'to provide that [it] does not apply to the extent, if any, that it would infringe any constitutional doctrine of implied freedom of political communication or parliamentary privilege'.[79] This recommendation was based on a model provision issued by the Office of Parliamentary Counsel.[80] Provisions of this type exist in other Australian statutes[81] and are designed to ensure that the Acts can be read down to ensure their constitutional validity. The ALRC commented that this enabled the constitutional validity of specific acts and practices to be 'determined on a case-by-case basis by the relevant court or tribunal',[82] thereby allowing for a more fine-tuned approach to invalidity than a blanket exemption. However, while this approach avoids the risk that the proposed amendment to remove the political exemptions will be held to be invalid, it also creates practical uncertainty given the complexity of the implied freedom of

77   Australian Law Reform Commission (n 19) [41.16].
78   Ibid Rec 41.1.
79   Ibid Rec 41.2.
80   The current version of this model provision is contained in: Parliament of the Commonwealth of Australia, Parliamentary Counsel, *Drafting Direction, No. 3.1 Constitutional law issues* (October 2012) 6.
81   See e.g. the identical provisions in: Spam Act 2003 (Cth) s 44; Do Not Call Register Act 2006 (Cth) s 43; Telecommunications Act 1997 (Cth) s 138.
82   Australian Law Reform Commission (n 19) [41.48].

political communication. It is therefore important to consider how this doctrine has been interpreted, including in more recent cases, and to what extent (if any) it might preclude an extension of the obligations in the Privacy Act to political parties, having regard to the issues discussed above.

The implied freedom of political communication has its origins in two decisions of the Mason High Court: *Nationwide News Pty Ltd v Wills* [83] and *Australian Capital Television Pty Ltd v Commonwealth*.[84] This doctrine is more accurately described as a freedom than a right, as it 'acts to restrict the powers of the executive and legislature and is not a personal right granted to individuals'.[85] As stated by McHugh J in *Levy v The State of Victoria*:[86]

It is a freedom *from* laws that effectively prevent the members of the Australian community from communicating with each other about political and government matters relevant to the system of representative and responsible government provided for by the Constitution.[87]

The concept of an implied freedom of political communication is a unique response to the Australian context, which lacks both a constitutional Bill of Rights and any other federal human rights legislation. The majority judges in the early cases on the implied freedom of communication held that it derived from the system of representative government that underlies the Australian Constitution. This is implicit in Mason CJ's statement in *Australian Capital Television* that without the implied freedom, 'representative government would fail to achieve its purpose of government of the people through their elected representatives; government would cease to be responsive to the needs and wishes of the people, and, in that sense, to be truly representative'.[88]

Similarly, Deane J's described the implied freedom in *Theophanus v Herald & Weekly Times Ltd* as being 'critical to the working of a democratic system of representative government of the type which the Constitution incorporates'.[89]

However, in the unanimous judgment in *Lange v Australian Broadcasting Corporation*,[90] the High Court anchored the protection of the implied freedom more firmly in specific provisions in the Constitution. These include ss 7 and 24 (which require respectively that members of the Senate and the House of

83 (1992) 177 CLR 1.
84 (1992) 177 CLR 106.
85 Leanne Griffiths, 'The Implied Freedom of Political Communication: The State of the Law Post Coleman and Mulholland' (2005) 12 James Cook University Law Review 93.
86 [1997] HCA 31, (1997) 189 CLR 579.
87 Ibid 622.
88 *Australian Capital Television Pty Ltd v Commonwealth* (1992) 177 CLR 106, 139.
89 *Theophanous v Herald & Weekly Times Ltd* (1994) 182 CLR 104, 180. See also the comments of Deane and Toohey JJ in *Nationwide News v Wills* (1992) 177 CLR 1, 69–70.
90 *Lange v Australian Broadcasting Corporation* [1997] HCA 25, (1997) 189 CLR 520.

Representatives must be chosen at elections 'directly by the people') and s 128 (which provides that the Constitution cannot be altered except by a referendum).[91]

Lange was also significant because it formulated the following twofold test for determining whether the implied freedom applied:

> First, does the law effectively burden freedom of communication about government or political matters either in its terms, operation or effect? Second, if the law effectively burdens that freedom, is the law reasonably appropriate and adapted to serve a legitimate end the fulfilment of which is compatible with the maintenance of the constitutionally prescribed system of representative and responsible government and the procedure prescribed by s 128 for submitting a proposed amendment of the Constitution to the informed decision of the people […]?[92]

Subsequent courts have accepted this test, but reformulated the second limb to ask whether the law at issue has 'the effect of preventing or controlling communication upon political and governmental matters *in a manner which is inconsistent* with the system of representative government for which the Constitution provides'.[93] More recently, the second limb has been further modified by the majority decision in *McCloy v New South Wales*, as discussed below.[94]

In applying the modified *Lange* test to the removal of the political exemption – or, more precisely, to data-handling requirements under the Privacy Act that would apply to political parties and to other political actors in the absence of the current political exemption – two preliminary issues arise. The first is whether a law that imposes limits on how political parties and actors may handle personal information of voters impermissibly burdens freedom of communication about government or political matters. The second is whether it is relevant that the communications affected may be counterproductive to democracy in the sense that they may confuse or mislead, rather than inform, voters about political matters.

The decision of the High Court in *Monis v The Queen*[95] suggests that the answer to both is no. In that case, the constitutional validity of a law that made it an offence to use a postal or similar service in a way that 'reasonable persons would regard as being, in all the circumstances, menacing, harassing or offensive' was in issue.[96] In the context of the first limb of the *Lange* test, it was submitted that certain insubstantial or indirect curtailments of the freedom were not

91 Ibid 107 and 112.
92 *Lange v Australian Broadcasting Corporation* (1997) 189 CLR 520, 567–8.
93 *Levy v Victoria* (1997) 189 CLR 579 Kirby J at 646; *Coleman v Power* (2004) 220 CLR 1, 51 (para 95–96).
94 *McCloy v New South Wales* [2015] HCA 34, (2015) 257 CLR 178.
95 *Monis v The Queen* [2013] HCA 4, (2013) 249 CLR 92.
96 Criminal Code Act 1995 (Cth) s 471.12.

incompatible with it because they did not 'effectively burden' it. While differing in their approaches, the judges in *Monis* agreed to reject this submission. Hayne J considered the premise of this submission to be fundamentally flawed. In his opinion, the test of 'effectively burden' called for an assessment of whether the legislation had the effect of burdening the freedom, not whether there was more than a slight burdening. To similar effect, French CJ held that the distinction between direct and indirect effects on political communication was relevant only at the second stage of the test.[97] The plurality judgment of Crennan, Kiefel and Bell JJ accepted that legal effects which are 'so slight as to be inconsequential' might not be sufficient to create an effective burden,[98] but agreed that this was not the case with the offence provision in question.

This judgment makes it likely that legislation to remove the political exemption from the Privacy Act would likewise be held to 'effectively burden' the freedom of political communication. The Privacy Act, among other things, would then impose restrictions on how personal information of voters is collected, used and disclosed. It could be argued that, unlike the circumstances in *Monis*, privacy obligations would not prohibit the communication of a particular content but primarily restrict the process by which addressees for a particular communication are identified and targeted. However, it is doubtful whether this distinction would carry weight. As French CJ pointed out in *Monis*, whether legislation imposes a burden on the implied freedom is 'answered not only by consideration of the content of the communications it affects but also by the range of mechanisms for making such communications to which it applies'.[99] If, for example, the application of the Privacy Act would impede certain forms of micro-targeting that are currently permitted, this would limit the avenues by which parties could seek out voters with whom they wish to communicate, thereby effectively burdening the freedom of political communication.

If the first limb of the *Lange* enquiry were to be decided in the affirmative, as is likely, the enquiry moves on to the next stage, which is concerned with determining whether the legislative acts in question impose justifiable limits on the rights and freedoms granted by the Constitution. Prior to *McCloy*, the *Lange* test required that the impugned legislation was 'reasonably appropriate and adapted to serve a legitimate end in a manner which is compatible with the maintenance of the constitutionally prescribed system of representative and responsible government'. In *McCloy v New South Wales*,[100] the Court was divided over the question of whether it should continue to adhere to this approach. While the minority saw no need for change, the joint judgment of the majority favoured the adoption of a more structured proportionality framework.[101]

This modified approach splits up the second limb of the *Lange* test into two components. Under so-called 'compatibility testing', it is necessary to assess

97   *Monis v The Queen* [2013] HCA 4, (2013) 249 CLR 92, para 64.
98   Ibid para 343.
99   Ibid para 68.
100 *McCloy v New South Wales* [2015] HCA 34, (2015) 257 CLR 178.
101 Ibid 215–216, para 73–74 (French CJ, Kiefel, Bell and Keane JJ).

whether the purpose of the law is legitimate, in the sense that it is compatible with the constitutionally prescribed system of representative government.[102] Under so-called 'proportionality testing', it is necessary to address whether the law is reasonably appropriate and adapted to advance that legitimate object. The latter proportionality testing is structured by reference to three considerations that have been in use in overseas jurisdictions, notably in Europe:

- Suitability – whether the law had a rational connection to the purpose of the provision';
- Necessity – whether there was an obvious and compelling alternative, reasonably practicable means of achieving the same purpose with a less restrictive effect on the freedom;
- Adequacy in its balance – whether the extent of the restriction imposed by the impugned law was outweighed by the importance of the purpose it served.[103]

The High Court is still grappling with the consequences of adopting this new approach. However, for the purposes of this chapter, it is not necessary to fully engage with the difficult questions of whether the structured proportionality analysis applies equally in all cases and whether it is indeed preferable to the previous approach. The issue to be addressed here is limited to the question of whether a law removing the current political exemptions would be likely to be held incompatible with the implied freedom of political communication. This question can be quite confidently answered in the negative.

It is likely that subjecting political parties and political acts and practices to the data-handling principles that already apply to other organisations and to other acts and practices is compatible with the constitutionally prescribed system of representative government. The Privacy Act has the explicit objective of protecting the right to information privacy.[104] The link between privacy and democratic systems of representative government has long been recognised and explained in a number of different ways. As Regan points out, 'some commonality among individuals is necessary to unite a political community and the development of commonality requires privacy'.[105] Boehme-Neßler focuses instead on the fact that autonomy is integral to democracy and that privacy is necessary to allow people to 'develop, learn and then exercise autonomy'.[106] In similar vein, the Victorian Law Reform

---

102 This is the test as restated in *Brown v Tasmania* [2017] HCA 43, (2017) 261 CLR 328, para 104 (Kiefel CJ, Bell and Keane JJ); para 196 (Gageler J); para 271 (Nettle J).

103 Ibid para 3 (French CJ, Kiefel J, Bell J and Keane J); see also *Murphy v Electoral Commissioner* [2016] HCA 36, (2016) 261 CLR 28, para 37 (French CJ and Bell J).

104 Privacy Act 1988 (Cth) s 2A(a).

105 Priscilla M Regan, *Legislating Privacy: Technology, Social Values, and Public Policy* (University of North Carolina Press 1995) 126–127.

106 Volker Boehme-Neßler, 'Privacy: a matter of democracy. Why democracy needs privacy and data protection' (2016) 6(3) International Data Privacy Law 222, citing Beate Rössler, *Der Wert des Privaten* (Suhrkamp Verlag 2001) 331.

Commission has stated that privacy has an important democratic dimension because it 'gives people the freedom to develop, discuss and criticise society and government "anonymously [...] and without fear of community reprisal"'.[107] Based on these views, privacy protection is an indispensable aspect of allowing voters to identify their preferred representatives and to come together to exercise their political choices. It follows that protecting voters from undue surveillance or interference with their personal information by political parties or other political actors, would clearly serve a legitimate end. It is not incompatible with the constitutional system of representative government, and would in fact seem to enhance it.

In the suitability enquiry, a rational connection between the law and its purpose would need to be identified – or, in other words, that the means for which the law provides are capable of realising the purpose.[108] It is clearly the case that the privacy principles laid down in the Privacy Act are capable of realising the purpose of protecting individual privacy.

This then leaves the questions as to whether imposing privacy obligations on political parties and political acts and practices would be necessary and adequate in its balance. A restriction is generally not necessary if other, equally effective, means of achieving the statute's legitimate purpose which have a less restrictive effect on the freedom are available, obvious and compelling.[109]

In *Unions NSW v New South Wales*, members of the High Court reiterated that the onus of justification is on the supporter of the legislation[110] and made clear that, while it was Parliament's role to select the means to achieving the statutory purpose, it would not adopt a deferential approach to scrutinising the measures adopted.[111] In this context, it could be argued that the current, less restrictive regulatory framework provides sufficient protection to voter privacy. However, as discussed above, the rise of big data analytics and advanced communicative approaches, including micro-targeting, allows political parties to engage in potentially highly invasive data-handling practices. It is therefore increasingly difficult to

---

107 Victorian Law Reform Commission, *Surveillance in Public Places* (Final Report, 2010) para 4.78, citing Daniel Solove, *Understanding Privacy* (Harvard University Press 2008) 80. See also Charles Raab, 'Privacy, Democracy, Information' in Brian Loader (ed), *The Governance of Cyberspace: Politics, Technology and Global Restructuring* (Routledge 1997) 157.

108 *Unions NSW v New South Wales* [2013] HCA 58, (2013) 252 CLR 530, 557–558, para 50–55 (French CJ, Hayne, Crennan, Kiefel and Bell JJ); 561, para 64 (French CJ, Kiefel, Bell and Keane JJ); 579, para 140–141 (Keane J); *McCloy v New South Wales* [2015] HCA 34; (2015) 257 CLR 178, 217, para 80 (French CJ, Kiefel, Bell and Keane JJ).

109 *McCloy v New South Wales* [2015] HCA 34; (2015) 257 CLR 178, 217, para 57–58 (French CJ, Kiefel, Bell and Keane JJ).

110 *Unions NSW v New South Wales* [2019] HCA 1, (2019) 363 ALR 1, para 93–96 (Gageler J), 118 (Nettle J), 151 (Gordon J).

111 *Unions NSW v New South Wales* [2019] HCA 1, (2019) 363 ALR 1, para 47–53 (Kiefel CJ, Bell and Keane JJ), 146 (Gordon J).

argue that leaving the protection of voter privacy to the discretion of political parties and political actors is as effective in protecting informational privacy as a system of regulatory oversight on the basis of the Privacy Act.

The final step in the proportionality testing is to examine whether the restriction is adequate in its balance. When it was introduced, the exemption was justified by reference to the importance of the freedom of political communication to Australia's democratic process. In the Second Reading Speech, it was posited that the exemption was 'designed to encourage that freedom and enhance the operation of the electoral and political process in Australia'.[112] In light of the newly emerging practices of data-driven campaigning, it must now be doubted whether this rationale continues to stack up. At the balancing stage, the Court will have particular regard to the purpose of and benefit sought to be achieved by legislative provisions and the effect of restrictions imposed on the freedom of political communication.[113]

In *McCloy v New South Wales*,[114] the High Court upheld the validity of provisions contained in the Election Funding, Expenditures and Disclosures Act 1981 (NSW) that introduced general caps on political donations in an election cycle and a prohibition of political donations by property developers. A majority decided that these provisions did not impermissibly burden the implied freedom of political communication. Referring to the Court's own earlier jurisprudence, the plurality affirmed that equal opportunity of political participation is an aspect of the representative democracy guaranteed in the Australian Constitution.[115] Interestingly, the High Court did not consider that equality of opportunity to participate required formal freedom from discrimination. In the circumstances, the various caps and prohibitions on donations had different effects on the various constituents. In particular, they discriminated against those who would have been wealthy enough to contribute more than permitted under the legislation or who belonged to the group of property developers. However, the caps and prohibition on political donations in issue were held to be a proportionate measure to create a level playing field, in which wealthy voices could not drown out others, and as such permissible, despite their effect on the exercise of freedom of political communication. The plurality stated:

> The provisions do not affect the ability of any person to communicate with another about matters of politics and government nor to seek access to or to influence politicians in ways other than those involving the payment of substantial sums of money. The effect on the freedom is indirect. By reducing the funds available to election campaigns there may be some restriction on communication by political parties and candidates to the public. On the other

112 Australian Commonwealth House of Representatives, *Parliamentary Debates* (12 April 2000) 15749 (D Williams, Attorney-General), 15753.
113 *McCloy v New South Wales* [2015] HCA 34; (2015) 257 CLR 178, 217, para 89–93 (French CJ, Kiefel, Bell and Keane JJ).
114 *McCloy v New South Wales* [2015] HCA 34, (2015) 257 CLR 178.
115 Ibid para 45 (French CJ, Kiefel, Bell and Keane JJ); see also para 271 (Nettle J).

hand, the public interest in removing the risk and perception of corruption is evident. These are provisions which support and enhance equality of access to government, and the system of representative government which the freedom protects. The restriction on the freedom is more than balanced by the benefits sought to be achieved.[116]

This reasoning is almost directly applicable to the imposition of privacy obligations on political parties and other political actors. The practical effect of extending the Privacy Act to these political actors would be to require them to comply with a set of privacy principles. It would not curtail the ability of political parties and other actors to communicate with certain sectors of the electorate about matters of politics and government. The effect on the freedom would merely be indirect, and impose some restrictions on current practices. It is important to note that the privacy principles are open-textured and have been adapted to promote a further objective of the Act, which is 'to recognise that the protection of the privacy of individuals is balanced with the interests of entities in carrying out their functions or activities'.[117] This is reflected, for example, in the collection limitation principle, which does not generally mandate consent (except in relation to specific categories of sensitive information); instead, its main limitation is that information must be collected 'only by lawful and fair means'[118] and must generally be collected only from the individual unless 'it is unreasonable or impracticable to do so'.[119] The Privacy Act does not provide absolute protection for privacy but rather provides for a set of fair information-handling principles which are designed to protect privacy while still enabling the entities which are required to comply with it to carry out their functions and activities. This balance protects the personal autonomy which is necessary for the operation of a democratic system without unreasonably undermining the ability of political parties to communicate with voters. It follows therefore that the Privacy Act already has built in a number of mechanisms to ensure that the restrictions it imposes are reasonably adapted and appropriate, or proportional, to the ends it pursues. In addition, it can be argued that these protections help to create a level playing field between political parties and between political actors, because they impose certain general standards that all organisations need to adhere to in their political communications with voters, regardless of their financial resources or technical expertise.

In *Brown v Tasmania*, Nettle J held that the 'implied freedom of political communication is a freedom to communicate ideas to those who are willing to listen, not a right to force an unwanted message on those who do not wish to hear it'.[120] Certainly to the extent that privacy laws provide individuals with protection

116 Ibid para 93 (French CJ, Kiefel, Bell and Keane JJ).
117 Privacy Act 1988 (Cth) s 2A(b).
118 Ibid Australian Privacy Principle 3.5.
119 Ibid Australian Privacy Principle 3.6.
120 *Brown v Tasmania* [2017] HCA 43, (2017) 261 CLR 328, para 196 (Nettle J); see also
       Adelaide City Corporation [2013] HCA 3; (2013) 249 CLR 1, 37, para 54 (French CJ).

from being targeted against their will, these protections would be unlikely to be disproportionate curtailment of the freedom of political communication.[121]

This brief examination of recent jurisprudence of the High Court suggests that the removal of the exemption for political parties and political acts would be unlikely to be incompatible with the implied freedom of political communication as currently defined and that it is not strictly necessary to include a saving provision to ensure the constitutional validity of the required amendments to the Act. However, it is possible that the APPs may be updated at some stage and that these may affect the analysis of validity. To cater for this eventuality, we would support the inclusion of a saving provision along the lines of that suggested by the ALRC, as discussed above.

VII. Conclusion

In 2004 van Onselen and Errington noted the privacy issues arising from the use of political databases and that such databases were not subject either to the access or amendment provisions in Freedom of Information legislation:

> Political parties can therefore log information about voters without their consent, yet they cannot be made to disclose what information has in fact been logged, nor can they be made to correct it in the event it is inaccurate. Clearly this state of affairs prevents the checks and balances on which our representative democracy prides itself.[122]

Apart from providing access and correction rights, the provisions in the Privacy Act also require that data handlers follow fair information practices in relation to the collection, use and security of personal information, and give affected individuals a right of complaint to the Privacy Commissioner. Even at the time of its introduction, the blanket exemption from compliance with the Privacy Act was contentious. Recurring calls for removal of the exemption have fallen on the deaf ears of successive governments, who preferred to maintain the status quo, which enables political parties to avoid regulatory scrutiny of their data-handling practices.

The advent of big data, data-driven campaigning and political micro-targeting has created new threats to the privacy of personal information, making the case for reform even stronger. It is self-serving and ultimately short-sighted of Australia's main political parties to claim for themselves an immunity from following the same data protection practices and principles that apply to the wider community. Political parties intent on stemming further erosion of trust in political representation and campaigning would do well to no longer resist reforms that would bring

---

121 See also *Monis* [2013] HCA 4, (2013) 249 CLR 92, 206–207, para 324 (Crennan, Kiefel and Bell JJ).
122 van Onselen and Errington (n 68, 2005) 29.

Australian privacy laws into line with international best practice, which requires as a minimum the removal of the political exemption.

The above analysis of the implied freedom of political communication suggests that implementing the ALRC's recommendations would not conflict with the freedom of political communication. Any lingering doubt could be addressed through a saving provision that the Privacy Act does not apply to the extent, if any, that it would infringe any constitutional doctrine of implied freedom of political communication or parliamentary privilege, as it is currently already in place for other legislation.

Chapter 10

Big Data and the electoral process in the United States

Constitutional constraint and limited data privacy regulations

Ronald J. Krotoszynski Jr

I. Introduction: Some preliminary thoughts on the challenges of conducting free and fair elections in the era of Big Data

Big Data increasingly poses significant challenges for the practice of democratic self-government in the United States. The problems that manipulation of voters' personal data currently exacerbate are many and varied. To provide two salient examples, the use of sophisticated data analysis facilitates drawing rigged electoral districts that deny voters a meaningful choice in the general election, and with the possession of sufficient information about a particular voter, efforts to trick her into a supporting a candidate (or perhaps not voting at all) can be targeted with maximum effectiveness.

Of course, in this relatively brief chapter, it is not feasible to offer a comprehensive program of reform that sets forth a clear and detailed way forward. Instead, I will seek to offer more modest suggestions for improvement. In particular, I will attempt to identify some of the larger framing principles that might help to inform specific government interventions that could do more good than harm in controlling and constraining the most untoward effects of Big Data in contemporary American democracy.

At least initially, two potential routes to reform seem promising. First, structural reforms aimed at increasing the competitiveness of elections could help because they would create an incentive for more voters to actively engage in the process of democratic deliberation. Such structural reforms in the electoral process also would likely avoid the First Amendment pitfalls that regulating the collection, storage, and use of data would present.

Second, the government could adopt regulations that limit, or even proscribe entirely, the collection, analysis, and manipulation of voters' personal data. Despite the existence of good arguments in favor of stronger federal privacy laws, I am considerably less optimistic about the possibility of direct regulations of the use of voters' personal data to influence electoral choices. Such regulations would arguably be subject to strict judicial scrutiny – and would likely fail to survive judicial review under the First Amendment. Structural reforms, unlike privacy regulations, would not be as easily attacked on First Amendment grounds.

However, a preliminary question arises that must be asked and answered: Should we even care about the potential for Big Data to disrupt the U.S. electoral process? Even if the collection and analysis of vast quantities of voters' data in the United States facilitates the creation of rigged electoral districts (at all levels of government) and the use of highly questionable electoral practices – such as push polling and targeted dissemination of 'fake news' – does this represent a new problem? One could argue that the advent of Big Data analytics in contemporary politics is just another, more sophisticated, version of political business as usual. Politics in the United States, particularly at the federal level of government, has been a blood sport since the days when George Washington, John Adams, and Thomas Jefferson were standing for elected office.

Potentially distortionary practices – made possible through the use of Big Data – do matter. Indeed, they threaten to undermine the efficacy of regular elections in the United States as a means of conveying popular legitimacy on the institutions of government. To provide a concrete example, if incumbent state legislators can use sophisticated data analytics to permit a minority of a state's voters to control permanently a majority of the seats, precisely what is the point in even bothering to conduct the general election at all? Democracy in the United States can and should be more than a mere Potemkin village.

In the United States – and for that matter, in other democratic polities – a widely prevailing constitutional commitment is the notion that democratic institutions, whether in a presidential or parliamentary system,[1] derive their legitimacy from the regular conduct of free and fair elections in which all adult citizens may participate on an equal basis.[2] At the federal level of government, members of the House of Representatives must seek and obtain re-election every two years,[3] the President and Vice-President every four years (with a lifetime two-term limit on the President),[4] and members of the Senate every six years.[5] In other democracies,

---

1   See generally Bruce Ackerman, 'The New Separation of Powers' (2000) 113(3) Harvard Law Review 634, 639–52, 688–90 (discussing characteristics of the parliamentary and presidential systems and noting that, as an empirical matter, parliamentary systems, because of the fusion of executive and legislative powers, have been more stable over time).

2   See John Hart Ely, *Democracy and Distrust: A Theory of Judicial Review* (Harvard University Press 1980); Alexander Bickel, *The Least Dangerous Branch: The Supreme Court at the Bar of Politics* (Bobbs-Merrill 1962).

3   US Constitution, art I, § 2, cl 1: 'The House of Representatives shall be composed of members chosen every second year by the people of the several states, and the electors in each state shall have the qualifications requisite for electors of the most numerous branch of the state legislature.'

4   Ibid art II, § 1, cl 1: 'The executive Power shall be vested in a President of the United States of America. He shall hold his Office during the Term of four Years, and, together with the Vice President, chosen for the same Term, be elected, as follows'; ibid amend. XXII, § 1: 'No person shall be elected to the office of the President more than twice, and no person who has held the office of President, or acted as President, for more than two years of a term to which some other person was elected President shall be elected to the office of the President more than once.'

5   Ibid art I, § 3, cl 1: 'The Senate of the United States shall be composed of two Senators from each State, chosen by the Legislature thereof, for six years; and each

general elections take place every three, four, or five years. The precise timing of elections is obviously less important than the requirement that they must take place on a regular basis.

For elections to confer legitimacy, however, certain preconditions must be met; in the absence of these conditions, elections constitute something of a Potemkin village – a mere sham used to justify the arbitrary exercise of governmental power (meaning the exercise of governing powers without the consent of the governed, freely given). Perhaps the most central requirements for elections to be meaningful are that their conduct be free and fair, that candidates may freely stand for office, and that a process of ongoing democratic deliberation within the body politic exists to inform the casting of ballots.[6]

The Russian Federation, for example, holds regular elections, but they are not conducted freely and fairly.[7] In contemporary Russia, candidates may not freely stand for election and democratic deliberation takes place within strictly enforced limits.[8] The government exercises almost plenary control over the mass media and press outlets, which effectively serve as propaganda organs of the state. In sum, Russia provides an example of a pantomime of democracy. However, the Russian Federation is hardly unique. Even in member states of the European Union, serious questions have arisen about the fairness and legitimacy of elections.

In Hungary, for example, where the state exercises substantial control over the mass media, the current ruling party, Fidesz, has debased the electoral process by encouraging sham parties and candidates to splinter an already disorganized political opposition.[9] One might expect such behavior in places like China, Cuba, or

Senator shall have one Vote'; ibid amend. XVII, § 1: 'The Senate of the United States shall be composed of two Senators from each State, elected by the people thereof, for six years; and each Senator shall have one vote. The electors in each State shall have the qualifications requisite for electors of the most numerous branch of the State legislatures.'

6   See generally Alexander Meiklejohn, *Free Speech and Its Relation to Self-Government* (Harper and Brothers 1948) 22–27, 89–91. In this regard, meaningful constitutional protections of both privacy and speech constitute essential background conditions for the process of democratic deliberation to function. See Ronald J Krotoszynski, Jr., *Privacy Revisited: A Global Perspective on the Right to Be Left Alone* (Oxford University Press 2016) 173–88.

7   See Neil MacFarquhar, 'Putin Wins Fourth Term in Russian Election, and Broad Mandate to Pursue Policies' *The New York Times* (18 March 2018) A8; Neil MacFarquhar, 'Putin, After Thinning Candidates' Ranks, Wants Crowds at the Polls' *The New York Times* (25 January 2018) A4 [hereinafter MacFarquhar 'Thinning Candidates' Ranks'].

8   See MacFarquhar, 'Thinning Candidates' Ranks' (n 7) A4.

9   See James McAuley, 'Hungary Votes to Keep Prime Minister and Right Wing in Power' *The Washington Post* (9 April 2018) A9 ('In the past eight years in power, Orban – in two consecutive terms as prime minister – has enacted drastic changes to Hungary's constitution, attempted to dismantle its system of checks and balances, and sought to silence his critics, notably in the Hungarian media.'). For a general discussion of Hungary's hard turn toward illiberal democracy, see Kim Lane Scheppele, 'Autocratic Legalism' (2018) 85(2) University of Chicago Law Review 545.

Venezuela – places that do not really make even the pretense of practicing democratic self-government. In a post-Soviet bloc nation like Hungary, however, this sort of ham-fisted effort to tilt the political playing field is both surprising and depressing given the country's not-so-distant past with radically undemocratic governance.

It would be both comforting and highly convenient to assume that systematic failures of the democratic process are only a problem for less developed nations that lack long-standing, deeply entrenched democratic traditions. It would be both comforting and highly convenient to posit that elections in the United States are entirely free and fair – and therefore reliably convey democratic legitimacy on the governing institutions of the United States. In the era of Big Data, whether in the United States, or in other democratic polities, such as Australia, Canada, France, and Germany, we should pause to consider whether, in point of fact, democratic elections are free and fair in both theory and practice.[10] One should also exercise some care in identifying the principal threats to the democratic process presented by Big Data and the exploitation of metadata through the micro-targeting of voters.[11]

More specifically, in the United States, we tend to think of the government itself as the principal threat to free and fair elections. After all, incumbent politicians have both the motive and the means to skew the political playing field in their favor – to distort the democratic process in order to benefit themselves.[12] One need not embrace with brio all the claims of the law and economics crowd, and in particular public choice theory, to accept the proposition that politicians usually do not voluntarily give up their offices and will be tempted to use whatever means are near to hand to preserve them.

To be sure, government efforts to manipulate the electoral process constitute an important problem – for example, the ability to use sophisticated data analytics in systems that assign legislative seats by district opens up a vast opportunity to obtain more seats in legislative bodies than would be possible in a system using

10   Andrew Guthrie Ferguson, 'The Big Data Jury' (2016) 91(3) Notre Dame Law Review 935, 967 (positing that '[t]he rise of political microtargeting has demonstrated that big data can impact the outcomes of elections').

11   It bears noting that it was the Obama Campaign, in 2008 but particularly in 2012, that pioneered the use of micro-targeting voters through sophisticated analysis of available voter metadata. See Ira S Rubinstein, 'Voter Privacy in the Age of Big Data' [2014] Wisconsin Law Review 861, 865–68, 874–79; see also Michael S Kang, 'From Broadcasting to Narrowcasting: The Emerging Challenge for Campaign Finance Law' (2005) 73(5–6) George Washington Law Review 1070, 1075–80 (defining and explaining the concept of micro-targeting voters and noting that the approach involves finding and persuading 'the libertarian white male in Cobb County, Georgia, who would swing their way if approached appropriately' as well as 'the socially conservative African American on the South Side of Chicago who might vote for a Republican').

12   Malapportionment of legislative seats in polities that conduct elections on a districted basis provides a highly salient example. See *Reynolds v Sims*, 377 US 533 (1964); *Baker v Carr*, 369 US 186 (1962); see also Ely (n 2) 102–22; 180–84.

proportional representation to allocate legislative power. This is so because such data allows those who draw electoral districts to 'pack' and 'crack' voters who oppose the party holding political power at the state level. This involves creating a small number of districts that concentrate the opposition party's support, creating a high proportion of 'wasted' votes (votes in excess of those needed for the disfavored party's candidate to receive a majority) and rendering other opposition party voters irrelevant in 'cracked' electoral districts because the electoral district's lines are drawn to make it virtually impossible for the disfavored party's candidate to secure a majority of the votes cast.

The troubling Cambridge Analytica disclosures suggest that voter manipulation, using purloined Facebook users' data, could have materially affected the outcomes of both the 2016 U.S. presidential election and Brexit vote.[13] If true, these are certainly distressing revelations that require some sort of regulatory response. However, we must take care to ensure that the cure is not worse than the disease; if the ability to use Big Data to manipulate voters comes to serve as a basis for government control, or censorship, of data flows, the dangers associated with such regulatory controls could well be as bad, if not worse, than the private misuse of such data to influence (manipulate) voters and elections. A vast difference separates legitimate efforts to persuade voters to support particular candidates and policies through reasoned arguments and nefarious efforts to trick voters into sitting out an election (by convincing them that their votes do not matter or that the system is rigged against them) or to use subconscious efforts to push voters to support or oppose particular candidates.[14]

As one researcher in the field of predictive technology explains, 'Are we developing the tools for sci-fi-style mind reading? Not quite, but close enough for certain commercial purposes and soon perhaps for legal proceedings.'[15] New technologies that allow for very accurate assessments of an individual's thoughts and beliefs will 'raise [...] deep questions about the nature of our minds, consciousness and free will'[16] and '[o]ur legal system, institutions, rights and customs will struggle to adapt to a world in which our most intimate thoughts may be subject to a search warrant or become a matter of public record'.[17] If political operatives know where our buttons are located, it will be possible for them to push them in opaque ways that we may not fully recognize or appreciate. This is not persuasion – it borders on brainwashing. If voters want to provide their personal data in order to facilitate such efforts, that is one thing. But it is quite

13   Matthew Rosenberg, Nicholas Confessore and Caroline Cadwalladr, 'Firm That Assisted Trump Exploited Data of Millions' *The New York Times* (18 March 2018) A1.

14   The state of neuroscience and computer data processing capacity is rapidly reaching the point where it will be possible to quite literally 'read the mind' of a voter. See Jerry Kaplan, 'These Machines Will Read Your Mind' *The Wall Street Journal* (6–7 April 2019) C1–C2.

15   Ibid C2.

16   Ibid.

17   Ibid.

another for political parties to amass such data without effective notice or meaningful consent.

Professor Owen Fiss – albeit writing in the context of freedom of expression and the concentration of control over the mass media and institutional press rather than privacy – warned that the principal threat to freedom of speech might not be the abuse of governmental power to censor speech and suppress a free press. He posited that the undue accumulation of private power over the marketplace of ideas, meaning the ability to control, or even censor, the flow of information and ideas to the body politic, could constitute a greater threat to the process of democratic deliberation needed for democracy to function than state interventions in speech markets.[18] Fiss cogently argued that the state might need to intervene in private speech markets in order to check undue concentrations of private power to manipulate (or even control) the marketplace of ideas. He explained, 'In another world, things might be different, but in this one, we will need the state.'[19]

These arguments, about safeguarding the speech rights of citizens, seem highly relevant to thinking about how to protect voters' privacy and agency. Professor Fiss's concerns should help to inform whether, and how, to address the ability of companies like Facebook, Twitter, and Google to amass large quantities of personal data that could be weaponized to influence, and perhaps even control, electoral outcomes.[20] Moreover, private interventions in the political marketplace of ideas are likely to be non-transparent, making their efficacy in prefixing voters' choices very difficult, if not impossible, to assess.

Unlike the famous 'Daisy' political advertisement aired by Lyndon Baines Johnson in his 1964 presidential campaign against Senator Barry Goldwater (R-AZ), in the age of the internet, attempts to influence (manipulate) voters today will not be quite so direct and transparent. This spot, at the time, was innovative precisely because it did not directly attack Senator Goldwater by name or state directly that he would bring about a nuclear war. Instead, the ad merely implied that the election of Senator Goldwater would lead to a nuclear holocaust[21] – a concern that struck many voters as a serious risk after the Cuban missile crisis of 16–28 October 1962.[22]

---

18 Owen M Fiss, 'Free Speech and Social Structure' (1986) 71(5) Iowa Law Review 1405, 1412–16; Owen M Fiss, 'Silence on the Street Corner' (1992) 26(1) Suffolk University Law Review 1, 1–3; Owen M Fiss, 'Why the State?' (1987) 100(4) Harvard Law Review 781, 787–91 [hereinafter Fiss, 'Why the State?']. Professor Fiss posits that '[t]he state should be allowed to intervene, and sometimes even required to do so [...] to correct for the market': Fiss, 'Why the State?' 791.
19 Fiss, 'Why the State?' (n 18) 794.
20 See Kaplan (n 14) C1–C2.
21 Robert Mann, *Daisy Petals and Mushroom Clouds: LBJ, Barry Goldwater, and the Ad That Changed American Politics* (Louisiana State University Press 2011) 81–83.
22 Robert F Kennedy, *Thirteen Days: A Memoir of the Cuban Missile Crisis* (McCall 1968).

Senator Goldwater had famously – and quite foolishly – quipped that he would like nothing better than to drop a nuclear bomb in the Kremlin men's room and would 'make sure I hit it'.[23] In the Johnson campaign's political spot, a young girl is playing with a flower – a daisy – and counting down the petals as she pulls each one from the center. As the count approaches zero, the video image shifts to a mushroom cloud and the audio changes to a rocket-launch countdown.[24] Professor Robert Mann observes that the ad's 'message was that a vote for Johnson's unnamed opponent was a vote for nuclear annihilation'.[25]

The 'Daisy' spot received tremendous media attention.[26] It constituted a brilliant, and psychologically effective, attack on Barry Goldwater's temperament and character – and fundamentally changed the nature, function, and modality of political advertising in the United States.[27] The spot inaugurated the era of the attack ad – as well as the use of subliminal advertising to push voters away from a candidate without ever directly mentioning the candidate by name.

The truth is that both attack ads and subliminal political advertising work. Moreover, in the era of Big Data, efforts to influence particular pockets of voters can be sufficiently targeted so as to fly below the radar.[28] Cambridge Analytica's use of Facebook users' data to influence elections in 2016 provides an illustrative example. We should also expect that political parties and political operatives alike will not hesitate to weaponize personal data in order to enhance their prospects for electoral success – indeed, failing to mine voter data with alacrity when your opposition is doing it would constitute professional malpractice for a politician, political party, or hired-gun political consultant working for a particular candidate or party.

Big Data presents vast opportunities for attempting to influence (manipulate) voters in ways that are carefully targeted, highly effective, and remarkably cost-efficient. Relatively modest investments could, in theory, yield rather handsome electoral dividends because of the ability to use Big Data to engage in micro-targeting of persuadable voters.[29] Modern advertising techniques have always attempted to play on the hopes and fears of consumers – and of both the conscious and unconscious stripes. In some ways, Big Data and voter influence are simply a new variant of an old game. But they raise serious questions about the integrity of our electoral process because these new forms of intervention are completely non-transparent and potentially highly effective. It is one thing to attempt to influence voters through open argument – this is the essence of

23   Mann (n 21) 16.
24   Daisy Attack Political Spot, www.youtube.com/watch? v=dDTBnsqxZ3k, accessed on 10 April 2019.
25   Mann (n 21) xi.
26   Ibid 65 (noting that '*Time* featured an image of the Daisy Girl on the September 25 over of a special "Nuclear Issue"').
27   See ibid 81–90, 108–11.
28   See Kang (n 11) 1075–80; Rubinstein (n 11) 865–79.
29   Kang (n 11) 1077–80.

democratic deliberation and participatory politics. It is another to attempt to misuse personal data to trick voters into supporting or opposing particular candidates for political office.

The standard argument for an unregulated marketplace of political ideas relies on John Milton's *Aeropagitica*. Milton famously uses the metaphor of Truth and Falsity wrestling in a free and open competition.[30] In the contemporary marketplace of ideas, the apt metaphor would be that Falsity poisons Truth before the wrestling match ever begins – and Truth succumbs to Falsity's treachery. People believe falsehoods even when reputable news sources publish the truth, and actually hold false beliefs more intensely after traditional journalistic sources expose blatant lies and untruths.[31] A recent study of fake news propagated on Twitter found that '[b]y every common metric, falsehood consistently dominates truth on Twitter'.[32]

It would be naïve – dangerous, in fact – to assume that in an unregulated marketplace of political ideas, the weight of public opinion will come to embrace candidates and policies supported by objective truth. The question that we must ask and answer, then, is this: In a marketplace of ideas that is subject to opaque forms of manipulation, what role should government play in ensuring that voters have access to truthful, accurate information about matters related to the project of collective self-government?[33]

It is easy to posit an active role for government – but, at the risk of undue repetition, we must take care to ensure that the cure is not worse than the disease itself. It is far from clear that ceding to the government a broad power to censor speech – to declare what is objectively true and what is objectively false – would do more to enhance than to degrade the political marketplace of ideas. Accordingly, in thinking

30 John Milton, *Areopagitica* (Richard C. Jebb ed, Cambridge University Press 1918) (1644) 58: 'Let her [Truth] and Falsehood grapple; who ever knew Truth put to the wors, in a free and open encounter. Her confuting is the best and surest suppressing.' Alas, the lessons of 2016, in both the United States and the United Kingdom, teach that Milton might have been unduly optimistic about Truth's ability to best Falsehood in a 'free and open encounter'.

31 See Robinson Meyer, 'The Grim Conclusion of the Largest-Ever Study of False News' *The Atlantic* (8 March 2018) www.theatlantic.com/technology/archive/ 2018/03/ largest-study-ever-fake-news-mit-twitter/555104, accessed 30 March 2019.

32 Ibid; see also Andrew Guess, Brendan Nyhan and Jason Reifler, 'Selective Exposure to Misinformation: Evidence from the consumption of fake news during the 2016 US presidential Campaign' (9 January 2018) www.dartmouth.edu/~nyhan/ fake-news-2016. pdf, accessed 4 April 2019.

33 Even relatively absolutist scholars of the First Amendment, such as William Van Alstyne, have granted the point that unregulated private control over the modalities and channels of communication could do more to harm First Amendment values than to enhance them. See William W Van Alsytne, *Interpretations of the First Amendment* (Duke University Press 1984) 88: 'In a society where the effective speech-rights of all are already by no means equal (to the extent that they obviously depend significantly upon one's "speech-property" holdings), it is not obvious that *the* freedom of speech would be appropriately enhanced by exclusive reliance upon a private-property system that would literally drive out all those unable to compete effectively with dollars.'

about regulatory responses, we must distinguish between legitimate efforts to secure data users' privacy, empowering them to control the collection and use of their personal data, and self-serving efforts by governments – or major political parties – to reserve for themselves control over citizens' data.

In the specific context of voters' personal data, we must consider carefully what, if anything, should be done about the potential weaponization of this private information to manipulate voters into supporting or opposing particular candidates and policies through tactics that appeal to fear and prejudice rather than to reason and enlightened self-interest. Moreover, is the U.S. federal government likely to do *anything* to better secure the voters' personal data when the potential electoral dividends of mining and exploiting it are so vast and the practices themselves are often completely opaque? The metaphor of the fox guarding the henhouse comes immediately to mind – and when foxes guard henhouses, things usually turn out poorly for the hens (in this case, voters). Moreover, in the United States, even if Congress passed and the President signed a comprehensive privacy law that regulated the collection and exploitation of voters' personal data, the Supreme Court would be highly likely to invalidate such legislation on First Amendment grounds.[34]

We should also keep in mind that politicians have sought to move voters through manipulation and 'fake news' since the time of the Roman Republic.[35] In the age of the internet, voter manipulation techniques have undoubtedly become more sophisticated and more effective. But the problem of disseminating false information to deceive voters has a long, deep history in most industrial democracies.

The work of Karl Rove, and his allies, for George W. Bush provides a salient example. During the Republican Party's 2000 South Carolina presidential primary campaign, false stories circulated widely claiming that John McCain had fathered an African-American child out of wedlock. This grotesque, and blatantly racist, political hit job sought to play on the racism of South Carolina GOP primary voters; its dissemination proved highly effective at undermining Senator McCain's candidacy.[36] The false story clearly impacted the outcome of the election – and

34   *Sorrell v IMS Health, Inc.*, 564 US 552 (2011); see Jane Bambauer, 'Is Data Speech?' (2014) 66 Stanford Law Review 57, 60–63, 70–83 (arguing that data collection, processing, and manipulation constitutes a form of speech activity, namely knowledge creation, that merits robust protection under the First Amendment).

35   The great orator, and elected consul, Marcus Tullius Cicero, participated in a Roman electoral process characterized by mass campaigns of lies, chicanery, and open bribery. Mary Beard, *SPQR: A History of Ancient Rome* (Liveright Publishing 2015) 27–29. As Professor Beard explains, '[e]lectioneering at Rome could be a costly business' and in the time of Cicero 'it required the kind of lavish generosity that is not always easy to distinguish from bribery' (ibid 28).

36   Ann Banks, 'Dirty Tricks, South Carolina and John McCain' *The Nation* (14 January 2008) www.thenation.com/article/dirty-tricks-south-carolina-and-john-mccain, accessed 7 June 2018. Karl Rove's minions – both Rove and the candidate himself repeatedly denied personal knowledge or responsibility for this racist dirty campaign trick – initiated a whisper campaign with push-polling that asked likely South Carolina GOP voters: '"Would you be more or less likely to vote for John McCain [...] if you knew he had

that primary decisively affected the outcome of the 2000 Republican presidential nominating contest.[37]

Unfortunately, the advent of Big Data and fake news do not admit of any easy or obvious solutions; no single legal or policy response constitutes a silver bullet that will instantly solve the problem. Moreover, government responses, if they are to do more good than harm, must be carefully calibrated to avoid themselves distorting the deliberative process that is necessary for democracy to function. Finally, and as noted earlier, efforts to limit the collection, analysis, and manipulation of data, including voters' personal data, are subject to serious First Amendment objections.[38]

The best potential responses to efforts to dupe voters via the targeted dissemination of fake news should probably include serious efforts to facilitate the availability of accurate information (rather than active government efforts to suppress false information). Although enhanced government support of traditional media might present one way forward,[39] the use of collective citizen action through non-governmental, civil-society entities might present a better way forward. In sum, the risk of voter manipulation influencing elections is not a new problem – it is a problem as old as elections themselves. The advent of Big Data, however, makes the potential scope of the problem considerably more acute.

This chapter proceeds in five main parts. Part II considers the difficulties in the United States associated with defining 'voter manipulation' and adopting constitutionally permissible legislation to address such behavior. Part III focuses on how Big Data has greatly exacerbated the ill-effects of partisan gerrymanders in the United States – and argues that, despite the recent setback in the United States Supreme Court,[40] the federal courts must step in to stop this noxious practice (a practice that can and does render general elections meaningless).

fathered an illegitimate black child?"' (ibid). Moreover, as Banks explains, '[t]his was no random slur' because 'McCain was at the time campaigning with his dark-skinned daughter, Bridget, adopted from Bangladesh'.

37 See ibid: 'It worked.' See also Jean Edward Smith, *Bush* (Simon & Schuster 2016) 106–07 (describing the 2000 South Carolina primary as 'ugly', reporting on the widespread use of the false claim that McCain had fathered an illegitimate African-American child, and noting that, in the end, George W Bush prevailed over John McCain by a margin of 305,998 votes for Bush to 239,984 for McCain).

38 See n 34.

39 See Lili Levi, 'Social Media and the Press' (2012) 90(5) North Carolina Law Review 1531, 1542–44, 1590–96 (discussing serious proposals for potential government and non-profit financial support mechanisms for traditional investigative journalism in addition to other reform proposals that would help to sustain the newsgathering capacity and credibility of the traditional press). Professor Levi posits that '[w]hatever the benefits of social media for journalism, multiple models must be developed that will support the kind of press work that democracy needs' (ibid 1595). She is surely correct to argue that a free press capable of doing serious investigative journalistic work is an essential condition for democratic self-government to function.

40 See *Rucho v Common Cause*, 139 S. Ct. 2484 (2019) (holding that even the most extreme partisan gerrymanders present non-justiciable political questions because no

In Part IV, I discuss the limited prospects for the enactment of federal legislation that would safeguard voters' personal data – and the equally bleak prospects that targeted voter privacy protections would face in the contemporary federal courts. Part V offers some broader – and bolder – potential electoral system reforms that could mitigate the incentives for and also the adverse effects of efforts to amass and manipulate voters' personal data. Finally, Part VI provides a brief overview of this chapter and some concluding thoughts about the political and constitutional difficulties of protecting voters' personal data in the United States.

II. The need to define 'voter manipulation' with care and precision to avoid constitutional problems

For privacy regulations to stand any chance of surviving judicial review incident to a First Amendment challenge, the reform legislation would, at a minimum, need to define 'manipulation' with great specificity and care. If a federal privacy law defines the term very broadly, to encompass traditional forms of political advocacy, it will surely be invalidated by the federal courts.[41] It bears noting that many kinds of political arguments and claims are arguably deceptive. However, the Supreme Court of the United States has rejected laws that restrict speech, even when the speech is arguably false, misleading, or both.

Consider, for example, the claim that 'The 2017 tax reform legislation will benefit the middle and working classes significantly'. The truth or falsity of this statement is not self-evident. My own view is that the claim is patently false – but my view is informed by a strongly dyspeptic view of 'trickle down' theories of addressing wealth inequality, coupled with an equally deep skepticism of supply-side (aka 'voodoo') economics to inform fiscal policy.

Can it be said that characterizing Donald Trump's tax cuts as primarily bene-fitting the middle and working classes is empirically false? And even if this is arguably so, should the *government* be permitted to issue such a declaration and proscribe the dissemination of this message within the body politic? If one is intellectually honest and committed to the freedom of political speech, the answer to both queries should be 'no'.

Simply put, the effects of the Trump tax reform bill are a matter of political opinion, not empirically verifiable fact (at least for now). More to the point, the Supreme Court has held that 'there is no such thing as a false idea',[42] and, in the United States, 'we depend [for the] correction [of false ideas] not on the con-science of a judge and juries, but on the competition of other ideas'.[43] In the United States, even outrageous false speech often enjoys significant constitutional

sufficiently objective judicial standards exist to determine when a partisan districting exercise becomes too partisan).

41   See *Citizens United v Fed. Elec. Comm'n*, 558 US 310, 339–41 (2010).
42   *Gertz v Robert Welch, Inc.*, 418 US 323, 339 (1974).
43   Ibid 339–40.

protection.[44] In light of these constitutional commitments, creating a power to censor matters of political belief or to create legal liability for disseminating political opinions would be constitutionally difficult. The federal courts would likely view such efforts as inhibiting the process of democratic deliberation and denying willing listeners the ability to hear and receive speech that they would be highly likely to find persuasive.

Thus, in the United States, any policy response aimed at curbing voter manipulation must define 'voter manipulation' in the narrowest possible terms to avoid having this unintended effect. Potential liability for political speech would have a serious, and unfortunate, chilling effect on democratic deliberation. Because of this, regulatory responses to the risk of misuse of voters' personal data to target them for political messaging must be narrowly drawn to regulate the worst and most obvious practices of electoral distortion.

Consider another example: 'Hillary Clinton funds her campaign by selling access to child sex slaves in the basement of a pizzeria in Washington, DC.' This claim, unlike the earlier example, is demonstrably, and objectively, false. It also happens to be defamatory – even under the highly demanding standards for establishing liability for libel against a media defendant set forth in the Supreme Court's landmark *New York Times Company v Sullivan*[45] decision. This particular false statement contributes little, if anything, to the process of democratic deliberation and the purpose of the statement is to induce voters to cast ballots premised on an objectively false statement of fact. Although the Supreme Court of the United States has held that the First Amendment protects intentionally false statements in the absence of some sort of demonstrated social harm,[46] government may regulate false statements that cause social harm.[47] At least arguably, attempting to trick voters into casting ballots based on false information constitutes the kind of social harm that government should have the constitutional power to prevent.

Thus, the First Amendment prohibits the government from declaring political truth with respect to matters of opinion. However, it does not necessarily follow that it also precludes creating liability rules for intentionally false statements of fact that could distort the process of democratic deliberation. To be sure, fake news constitutes a freestanding problem. But the advent of Big Data makes it much easier, and more efficacious, to weaponize fake news to drive voters toward or away from candidates, parties, and ideas. The more carefully tailored a law that seeks to regulate deceptive political advertising, the better the odds will be that the law might survive judicial review.

44 *Snyder v Phelps*, 562 US 433 (2011); see *US v Alvarez*, 567 US 709, 719–22 (2012) (holding that the First Amendment protects intentionally false speech about the receipt of military honors).
45 376 US 254, 279–80 (1964): 'The constitutional guarantees require, we think, a federal rule that prohibits a public official from recovering damages for a defamatory falsehood relating to his official conduct unless he proves that the statement was made with "actual malice" – that is, with knowledge that it was false or with reckless disregard of whether it was false or not.'
46 *US v Alvarez*, 567 US 709, 718 (2012) ('Absent from those few categories where the law allows content-based regulation of speech is any general exception to the First Amendment for false statements.').
47 Ibid 718–22.

In particular, the standards of liability will, at a minimum, have to include a *scienter* requirement (meaning that the distribution of false information to influence voters must be both intentional and deliberate). The Supreme Court of the United States has invalidated a federal law that imposed liability on third parties who redistributed unlawfully recorded private cell phone conversations.[48] The Justices reasoned that the process of democratic deliberation would unduly suffer if the media could not report truthful information despite the information being obtained unlawfully.[49] Consistent with this precedent, it would be possible to impose liability on the person who unlawfully records a private cell phone conversation.[50] However, this will be of precious little consolation to the participants to the conversation that has now been broadcast to the general public.

This same reasoning would mean that even if the government could constitutionally regulate, or proscribe, the intentional and knowing distribution of false information to voters, the redistribution of fake news stories by innocent third-party media entities could not be proscribed or criminalized. This First Amendment–based rule would seriously limit the efficacy of efforts to create liability rules that could limit the distribution of fake news – at least by entities other than those that knowingly propagate such messages.

In sum, constitutionally-permissible proscriptions against the intentional distribution of objectively false election-related information might impede, to some extent, the dissemination of fake news – weaponized through the use of Big Data – to target, manipulate, and deceive voters. At the end of the day, in the United States, eradicating entirely deceptive electoral practices would prove at best very difficult and probably impossible.

III. A constitutionally permissible alternative: Structural reforms in the electoral process itself

Big Data also facilitates a different kind of democratic harm – the use of partisan gerrymanders to render the votes of those supporting the party out of power in the state legislature largely useless and nugatory. To be sure, since the early days of our Republic, incumbent politicians have engaged in efforts to use the power to draw district lines to tilt the electoral playing field to their advantage. In fact, the term 'gerrymander' relates back to a political cartoon that parodied a salamander-shaped electoral district in Massachusetts drawn up by Governor Elbridge Gerry – hence, a 'gerrymander'.[51]

---

48   See *Bartnicki v Vopper*, 532 US 514 (2001).
49   Ibid 527–30.
50   Ibid 529–32.
51   Gary W Cox and Jonathan N Katz, *Elbridge Gerry's Salamander: The Electoral Consequences of Reapportionment Reform* (Cambridge University Press 2002) 3; see Reid J Epstein and Madeline Marshall, 'Dear America, We All Say "Gerrymander" Wrong' *The Wall Street Journal* (25 May 2018) A1, A9 (discussing Elbridge Gerry's use of districting to maximize the electoral prospects of his fellow Democratic-Republicans and to marginalize Federalist candidates and their political supporters).

The problem of exploiting districting to deny a political majority a majority of seats in a state legislature or in the state's U.S. House of Representatives delegation is not a new one. Even so, it surely is a rapidly growing one. This is because Big Data and computers have greatly expanded the ability to draw districts in ways that deny a political majority the ability to elect candidates of their choice.[52] We are rapidly approaching a point in the United States where in many places a serious risk exists that data-driven partisan gerrymandering will permanently deny a political majority within the state the ability to elect either a majority of the members of the state legislature or the state's delegation to the U.S. House of Representatives.

To date, the federal courts have cast a blind eye on this pernicious political habit and have refused to arrest the growing use of partisan gerrymanders to render elections if not entirely meaningless, then significantly less meaningful than they could be as a method for securing government accountability. To be sure, the Supreme Court initially held that partisan gerrymanders constituted a constitutional violation if they permanently denied a political majority a majority of seats in the state legislature.[53] However, in the very same decision, the Justices comprising the majority held that the plaintiffs' evidence was insufficient to establish a valid constitutional claim.[54]

Almost 20 years later, in 2004, a plurality of the Supreme Court held that the partisan composition of electoral districts constituted a political question because no clear judicial standards existed against which to determine whether a particular partisan gerrymander went too far.[55] Justice Anthony M. Kennedy, although concurring in the result, expressly held open the possibility that, at some future point in time, feasible judicial standards for enforcing limits on partisan gerrymanders might be discovered.[56]

---

52 See Tom Davis, Martin Frost and Richard E Cohen, *The Partisan Divide: Congress in Crisis* (Fast Pencil Premiere 2014) 275–77 (providing a comprehensive and thoughtful critique of the contemporary effects of partisan gerrymandering on the ability of Congress to legislate effectively). Interestingly, Hungarian Prime Minister Viktor Orban, and his Fidesz party, have used gerrymandering as a successful technique to maximize their electoral advantage in Hungarian parliamentary elections. See James McAuley, 'Viktor Orban Is Likely to Win Hungary's Election. But What Happens Next?' *The Washington Post* (7 April 2018) A8 (noting that '[t]here is still the concern of gerrymandering' and reporting that in 2011 'the administration drastically redrew Hungary's electoral map' by combining 176 existing districts into only 106 districts, in order to reduce the ability of opposition parties to win elections). Thus, gerrymandering is hardly a phenomenon limited to the United States.

53 See *Davis v Bandemer*, 478 US 109 (1986).

54 Ibid 132–33 (holding that 'unconstitutional discrimination occurs only when the electoral system is arranged in a manner that will consistently degrade a voter's or a group of voters' influence on the political process as a whole').

55 *Vieth v Jubelirer*, 541 US 267 (2004).

56 See ibid 306 (Kennedy J, concurring): 'While agreeing with the plurality that the complaint the appellants filed in the District Court must be dismissed, and while understanding that great caution is necessary when approaching this subject, I would not foreclose all possibility of judicial relief if some limited and precise rationale were

In 2018, the Supreme Court again punted the question of whether a partisan gerrymander can go too far and violate the Constitution. Despite agreeing to hear cases from Wisconsin and Maryland that squarely presented the question of whether either the First Amendment (freedom of association and the freedom of speech) or the Fourteenth Amendment (the constitutional guarantee of equal protection of the laws) impose limits on partisan gerrymanders, the Justices dodged the merits and dismissed both cases on narrow technical grounds.[57]

However, in June 2019, with Justice Brett Kavanaugh replacing Justice Kennedy, the other shoe dropped in *Rucho v Common Cause*.[58] Writing for a 5–4 majority, Chief Justice John G. Roberts, Jr. held that, no matter how extreme, partisan gerrymanders present non-justiciable 'political' questions that the federal courts may not address on the merits. He posited that no objective metrics for partisan 'fairness' in districting exist for judges to identify and enforce; instead, defining a particular understanding of fairness in this context 'poses basic questions that are political, not legal'.[59]

More specifically, Roberts opined that 'no legal standards discernible in the Constitution [exist] for making such judgments, let alone limited and precise standards that are clear, manageable, and politically neutral'.[60] In consequence, '[a]ny judicial decision on what is "fair" in this context would be an "unmoored determination" of the sort characteristic of a political question beyond the competence of the federal courts'.[61] In sum, the federal courts 'have no commission to allocate political power and influence in the absence of a constitutional directive or legal standards to guide us in the exercise of such authority'.[62]

Despite the emphatic, confident tone of Chief Justice Roberts's majority opinion in *Rucho*, one should bear in mind that multiple lower federal court judges –

---

found to correct an established violation of the Constitution in some redistricting cases.'

57   *Benisek v Lamone*, 138 S Ct 1942, 1944–45 (2018) (affirming trial court's denial of a preliminary injunction and requiring plaintiffs' constitutional claims to go trial on the merits before being considered ripe for review); *Gill v Whitford*, 138 S Ct 1916, 1931–34 (2018) (dismissing constitutional challenges to state-wide partisan gerrymandered legislative districts because all the plaintiffs lacked Article III standing).

58   139 S. Ct. 2484 (2019).

59   Ibid at 2500.

60   Ibid.

61   Ibid (internal citation omitted). Chief Justice Roberts, in an effort to prove his point, raised a number of rhetorical questions: 'At what point does permissible partisanship become unconstitutional? If compliance with traditional districting criteria is the fairness touchstone, for example, how much deviation from those criteria is constitutionally acceptable and how should map drawers prioritize competing criteria?' Ibid at 2501. The dissenting members of the Supreme Court had answers to *all* of these questions and few (if any) qualms about a judicial intervention in the democratic process to arrest what they viewed as a grotesque perversion of it. See ibid. at 2519-24 (Kagan, J., dissenting).

62   Ibid at 2508.

appointed by Presidents of both political parties and having widely disparate over-arching judicial philosophies – were able to identify and apply standards that would determine how much partisanship is too much. Moreover, four members of the Supreme Court – albeit in dissent – also believed that reasonably objective and 'clear, manageable, and politically neutral' criteria for assessing extreme partisan gerry-manders existed and would not lead to unseemly judicial entanglements with partisan electoral politics. Justice Elena Kagan, writing for the four dissenting Justices, lamented that '[o]f all times to abandon the Court's duty to declare the law, this was not the one'.[63] In her view, '[t]he practices challenged in these cases imperil our system of government'[64] and 'the Court's role in that system is to defend its foundations'.[65]

Even if Justice Kagan is entirely correct to posit that, of these institutional and political foundations, '[n]one is more important than free and fair elections', until a future Supreme Court musters five votes to overturn the holding in *Rucho*, the federal courts have essentially exited the field of policing partisan gerrymanders completely. State legislators may gerrymander to their hearts' content. In most states, any remedy for such behavior must arise from the very political institutions that most directly benefit from this practice (namely the state legislatures and the federal House of Representatives). Because of this, waiting for serious reforms at the federal level of government to check extreme partisan gerrymanders will be akin to waiting for Godot.

Despite the Supreme Court's unfortunate (and misguided) holding in *Rucho*, the problem of partisan gerrymandering and Big Data is not going to go away. In fact, in thinking about practices facilitated by Big Data that have the potential to erode the democratic process, partisan gerrymanders, aided by metadata analytics, should appear at or near the very top of the list. As one academic observer has argued, 'Given the volume, velocity, variety, and value of voter data, there is little doubt that American presidential campaigns have entered the world of big data.'[66] What is true of presidential campaigns is doubly true of congressional and state legislative campaigns.

With sophisticated metadata techniques, coupled with the micro-targeting of voters, it is possible to engineer the political DNA of electoral districts with such precision that the outcome of general elections will be a foregone conclusion. If the design of an electoral district may be used to render voting in the general election for candidates for that seat essentially meaningless, elections and voting as a means of seeking and obtaining a mandate to govern lose their legitimating force. An election can convey democratic legitimacy on governing institutions only if the electoral process is free and fair. Using districts designed to preclude

---

63   Ibid at 2525 (Kagan, J., dissenting).
64   Ibid.
65   Ibid.
66   Rubinstein (n 11) 879.

meaningful electoral competition between candidates of different parties has the effect, essentially, of rigging the outcome of the contest before it has even been held.

Again, this problem is a not a new one – but the advances in predicting voter behavior, based on Big Data and metadata, are such that we must reconsider whether elections conducted using optimally rigged districts will still convey legitimacy on our elected government institutions. Given the stakes, it is imperative that the Supreme Court step in and limit the ability of elected officials to use Big Data to gerrymander districts in such a way as to deprive voters of meaningful electoral choices among general election candidates. Moreover, this is a structural problem – one that elected representatives will almost certainly never agree to address voluntarily. Much like malapportioned electoral districts, in which some voters enjoy greater voting strength than others because fewer votes are needed to secure a majority, gerrymandered districts benefit the party in power and convey an advantage that a rational politician in the current majority will never voluntarily give up. On the other hand, however, unlike efforts to regulate who may use voters' personal data or the purposes for which it may be used, structural reform efforts would not raise serious First Amendment issues because such reforms would be content- and viewpoint-neutral.

To borrow Professor Ely's turn of phrase, partisan gerrymanders present a problem requiring judges to deploy the Bill of Rights and Fourteenth Amendment to promote 'representation-reinforcing' principles – that is, to ensure that the political process is fundamentally fair and open to all on equal terms.[67] To be sure, there are alternative mechanisms to bypass legislative bodies in some states; it would be possible to use the initiative and referendum process to require the use of neutral districting principles. But it is not so in *all* states – nor is it possible at the federal level of government with respect to gerrymandered U.S. House of Representatives electoral districts.

Although we should be cautious in seeking and adopting quick fixes, structural reforms in the electoral process could help to reduce, but not entirely eliminate, some of the worst excesses that use of voters' personal data can facilitate. Indeed, rather than using voters' data to create non-competitive electoral districts, such data could be deployed to make more districts competitive. Some states, such as California, already have moved to non-partisan districting commissions to prevent partisan gerrymanders. This suggests that, at least in some jurisdictions in the United States, reforms in several critical aspects of the electoral process would be enhanced and accelerated if the federal courts were to hold that partisan gerrymanders violate the First and Fourteenth Amendments.

It is easy to identify the evils associated with partisan gerrymanders. The use of partisan gerrymanders on a national basis has led to a hopelessly polarized

---

67   See Ely (n 2) 87, 102–04, 118–21, 181–82; see also John H Ely, 'Toward a Representation-reinforcing Mode of Judicial Review' (1978) 37(3) Maryland Law Review 451.

Congress, particularly in the House of Representatives, that functions poorly because the greater electoral threat to an incumbent member comes from the primary election, rather than the general election.[68] This forces members to take positions pleasing to the base of their own party, rather than to seek compromises that advance the project of effective self-governance.[69]

Banning, or even merely reducing, the use of partisan gerrymanders would be a logical and entirely desirable political reform. The problem was serious in the advent of the internet age – it has grown to intolerable levels today. If the legitimacy of our governing institutions rests on a popular mandate, the electoral process itself must permit meaningful competition between general election candidates for the allegiance of the voters. Moreover, addressing a structural problem of this sort should be much easier than endeavoring to regulate political speech that attempts to mislead or dupe voters.

In fact, democratic polities that seek to ensure free and fair elections in the era of Big Data should arguably consider abandoning the use of districting completely – in favor of systems of proportional representation that generally prevent any citizen's vote from being irrelevant. Proportional representation also makes securing a bare majority of votes far less relevant than in a first-past-the-post system of elections.[70] My point is that structural innovations might be the best regulatory response to the risks that Big Data and voter micro-targeting present to the vibrancy and legitimacy of the electoral process in the United States.

IV. Incumbent politicians will almost certainly seek to use Big Data to their electoral advantage

Serious and troubling questions arise regarding the incentives Big Data creates for dominant political parties to behave badly. Given that micro-targeting of voters can pay very handsome electoral dividends for a relatively modest investment (particularly in electoral systems that use districts and follow the first-past-the-post rule), the aggregation and manipulation of voters' personal data will prove to be an irresistible temptation. Any political consultant worth her salt will seek to locate, mine, and target potential supporters using whatever personal data can be obtained. Given the Supreme Court's holding that the gathering and mining of data constitutes 'speech', any legislative efforts to rein in such practices will have to survive strict judicial scrutiny.

In the United States, both the Democratic Party and Republican Party are engaged in a voter data arms race. Moreover, even within party structures, data collection can create unusual fissures – for example, a dispute exists within the

---

68   See Davis, Frost and Cohen (n 52) 276–76.
69   ibid 70–72.
70   See Sanford Levinson and Jack M Balkin, *Democracy and Dysfunction* (University of Chicago Press 2019) 31 (advocating the abolition of the statutory districts requirement for seats in the US House of Representatives).

Democratic Party between the national party's control of the party's voter data-base and the ability of state party organizations to access and use this data. Control of voter data obviously provides a powerful lever of control for the national party over its state affiliates. And, as noted earlier, this activity probably enjoys robust protection under the First Amendment.[71]

Writing in *Sorrell*, Justice Anthony M. Kennedy characterized a Vermont law that protected patients' prescription data from disclosure for marketing purposes as both a 'content-based' and 'speaker-based'[72] restriction of speech that triggered strict scrutiny.[73] So long as this precedent remains on the books, laws that attempt to limit data collection or use based on the purpose for which data is used or the identity of the entity using the data are likely unconstitutional and hence void.[74]

In some sense, of course, collecting and exploiting information about voters is not new. Parties and politicians have always tried to identify and rally their supporters – and perhaps also demoralize and disorganize their opponents. Thus, in the early years of the U.S. federal government, the Federalists (led by John Adams) and the Democratic Republicans (led by Thomas Jefferson) regularly engaged in opposition research and attempted to persuade voters that their political opponents lacked wisdom, virtue, or both. Sometimes the nefarious stories, such as reportage on Thomas Jefferson's relationship with Sally Hemmings, happened to be true. In other instances, however, they were not. Thus, political parties in the United States have always sought to weaponize information to push voters toward one party and set of candidates and away from another. The Supreme Court has been highly skeptical of efforts to impose content-based civility norms either as general matter[75] or with respect to public officials and public figures.[76] As Chief Justice William H. Rehnquist explained in *Falwell*, 'in the world of public affairs, many things done with motives that are less than admirable are protected by the First Amendment'.[77]

The problem of efforts to manipulate voters, however, has taken on a new cast in the era of Big Data. The conjunction of Big Data with fake news greatly enhances the potential political efficacy of targeted efforts to deceive voters with false information, even as it has made it possible to micro-target voters in non-transparent ways very likely to keep nefarious efforts at voter persuasion below the radar.[78] False stories published in Federalist and Anti-Federalist newspapers in the early nineteenth century might have misled voters – but it was possible to answer charges in the public forum. With targeted tweets and Facebook advertising buys,

71   Bambauer (n 34) 86–105.
72   *Sorrell*, 564 US 563–64.
73   Ibid 564–71.
74   See Ashutosh Bhagwat, '*Sorrell v IMS Health*: Details, Detailing, and the Death of Privacy' (2012) 36(4) Vermont Law Review 855.
75   *Cohen v California*, 403 US 15 (1971).
76   *Hustler Magazine, Inc. v Falwell*, 485 US 46 (1988).
77   Ibid 53.
78   See Rubinstein (n 11) 865–82.

it is much more difficult to know when efforts to propagandize voters are taking place – and, accordingly, much more difficult for competing candidates and campaigns to attempt to counter them effectively.

Voters also tend not to know who is out there – watching, amassing data, and seeking to push them toward one party (or candidate). Simply put, most ordinary voters are very unsophisticated about what the political parties know about them and their preferences – including ideology, but extending to preferred retail vendors, method of shopping, and favorite laundry detergent. Social science research suggests that we are rapidly reaching a point where it will be possible to predict, with a remarkable degree of confidence, what a voter thinks and how to make her change her mind.[79] Thus, the lack of transparency regarding the micro-targeting of voters presents a set of problems that should be addressed through more robust disclosure and transparency requirements. But whether such reforms would survive constitutional review remains very much an open question.[80]

As Professor Ash Bhagwat has observed, 'the odds certainly seem stacked against data-disclosure restrictions under current law'.[81] He adds, on an even more pessimistic note, that 'few laws preventing data disclosure to protect privacy are likely to survive the "compelling interest" requirement of the traditional strict scrutiny test'.[82] Thus, in the United States, interests in dignity and privacy often give way to the imperatives of the First Amendment, and no good reasons exist to believe that this general approach will not apply in the context of laws designed to protect the privacy of voters' personal data (even assuming that Congress could be persuaded to enact such a statute).[83]

Of course, if voters had more comprehensive information about the kind of information available to candidates and political parties, and how that information gets used to persuade (manipulate) them, at least some voters would be more skeptical of sneaky efforts to push them toward supporting or opposing particular candidates for elective public office. It is also possible that transparency requirements, as opposed to bans on the collection, use, or transfer of voters' personal data, might survive a First Amendment challenge.[84]

The problem, of course, is that enactment of greater government regulations would require the political parties to act altruistically – which seems very improbable. Why would a rational and self-interested political operator cede any ground that she does not have to concede? Thus, even if limited regulations imposing

79   See Kaplan (n 14) C2.
80   Bhagwat (n 74) 868–874.
81   Ibid 871.
82   Ibid 873.
83   See *Falwell*, 485 US 53–55.
84   See *Citizens United v Fed. Elec. Comm'n*, 558 US 310, 319 (2010): 'Government may regulate corporate political speech through disclaimer and disclosure requirements, but may not suppress that speech altogether.'; see also ibid 371 (finding 'no constitutional impediment to the application of the BCRA's [Bipartisan Campaign Reform Act's] disclaimer and disclosure requirements to a corporate political speaker').

transparency and disclosure obligations would survive a First Amendment challenge, it is doubtful that Congress would enact such regulations in the first place. For example, when the Federal Trade Commission created a do-not-call registry that banned the unconsented to use of robo-calls to private homes, the regulations expressly excluded robo-calls placed by candidates for political office (as well as by charities).[85] Thus, even when federal regulatory agencies have adopted regulations aimed at promoting privacy, these regulations have specifically exempted politicians. Despite this exclusion, and an exclusion for charitable fundraisers, the lower federal courts sustained the do-not-call registry against First Amendment–based challenges.[86] This is because regulations of commercial speech receive only intermediate, rather than strict, scrutiny.[87]

V. Structural reforms – not content-based regulations against the use of data – clearly present the best way forward

We need to maintain some perspective about the nature and extent of the problems that confront the electoral process in the age of the internet. These problems have been with us since the use of elections to select the officers of government. The ability to make highly accurate predictive judgments about voters' behavior, however, through the use of sophisticated metadata analytics, makes the potential scope of these problems significantly greater today than they have ever been.[88] As noted earlier, empowering federal courts to scrutinize partisan gerrymanders would be a good first step and would help to limit the potential

85   See 16 CFR § 310.4(b)(1)(iii)(B) (FTC rule); 47 CFR § 64.1200(c)(2) (FCC rule); see also *Mainstream Marketing Services v Fed. Comm. Comm'n*, 358 F 3d 1228 (10th Cir 2004), cert. denied, 543 US 812 (2004). As the US Court of Appeals for the Tenth Circuit explained, '[t]he national do-not-call registry's restrictions apply only to telemarketing calls made by or on behalf of sellers of goods or services, and not to charitable or political fundraising calls' (ibid 1234).

86   See ibid 1250–51.

87   Ibid: 'We hold that 1) the do-not-call list is a valid commercial speech regulation under *Central Hudson* because it directly advances substantial governmental interests and is narrowly tailored; 2) the registry fees telemarketers must pay to access the list are a permissible measure designed to defray the cost of legitimate government regulation; 3) it was not arbitrary and capricious for the FCC to adopt the established business relationship exception; and 4) the FTC has statutory authority to establish and implement the national do-not-call registry'; see also *National Federation of the Blind v Fed. Trade Comm'n*, 420 F3d 331, 351 (4th Cir 2005), cert. denied, 547 US 1128 (2006) (sustaining the do-not-call registry against a First Amendment challenge). Consistent with the Tenth Circuit's reasoning, the US Court of Appeals for the Fourth Circuit found that '[o]ur Constitution does not prevent the democratic process from affording the American family some small respite and sense of surcease' and held that 'the FTC was authorized by Congress to promulgate the TSR, and we find that the rule is consistent with the First Amendment' (ibid). Again, because the do-not-call registry regulated only commercial speech, it was subject to a less demanding standard of judicial review than a regulation of political speech would face.

88   Kaplan (n 14) C1–C2.

damage to democracy that rigging electoral districts to prefigure electoral outcomes causes. But we might consider even bigger, bolder solutions.

For example, perhaps the use of districts is itself problematic in the age of the internet and metadata analytics. If we are not confident about the ability of government to regulate the use of metadata to skew elections, one potential regulatory response would be to alter the electoral process to reduce the ability of those who own or control such data to weaponize it. At-large, multiple-place elections, in which all voters may cast ballots for each place, might be less susceptible to manipulation. Districted, first-past-the-post elections, coupled with gerrymandered districts, create powerful incentives not to vote. This, in turn, exacerbates the ill-effects of using Big Data to draw districts. If every voter could potentially secure representation, voters who support the minority party candidate – or even a third-party candidate – would still have good reason to vote. Proportional representation systems, with multiple-place elections, that permit a voter to assign more than one vote to a candidate, as is the case with most corporate elections, will ensure that minorities (of whatever stripe) are able to elect candidates of their choice, even if they are far short of comprising a political majority within a state.

Once upon a time, U.S. senators had a much higher re-election rate than members of the U.S. House of Representatives.[89] This, however, is no longer the case. State-wide senatorial electoral contests, even in the reddest and bluest of states, are far more competitive than 90% of races for seats in the U.S. House of Representatives. This is because elections for the Senate do not use districts; they are conducted state-wide, and it not possible for U.S. senators to micro-engineer their electorates. As a potential reform, a return to multi-place elections, perhaps with cumulative voting, would be a logical response to the risks presented by clever manipulation of metadata to create electoral districts. As a practical matter, however, it is highly doubtful that the Supreme Court would order at-large elections for seats in the U.S. House of Representatives. Such a reform, if it is to occur, would have to come from Congress – a highly unlikely proposition.

On the other hand, we might encourage greater experimentation at the state and local level with the use of multi-seat, at-large elections with cumulative voting. The mechanism seems to work very well for elections to the boards of directors for publicly traded companies in the United States. It also reliably provides a mechanism for minority shareholders to obtain a seat at the table. Professor Lani Guinier proposed adopting corporate voting procedures in federal and state elections in the late 1980s and early 1990s;[90] her proposals for reforming the electoral process helped to derail her nomination for a senior post in the U.S. Department

89   Keene Lipsitz, *Competitive Elections and the American Voter* (University of Pennsylvania Press 2011) 35–36, 71–76; Jonathan S Krasno, *Challenges, Competition, and Reelection: Comparing Senate and House Elections* (Yale University Press 1994).
90   See e.g. Lani Guinier, 'The Representation of Minority Interests: The Question of Single-Member Districts' (1993) 14(5) Cardozo Law Review 1135; Lani Guinier, 'No Two Seats: The Elusive Quest for Political Equality' (1991) 77(8) Virginia Law

of Justice under President Bill Clinton. It is time to revisit Professor Guinier's very practical, and quite sensible, suggestions for adopting structural reforms that would enhance and promote the vibrancy of our nation's electoral contests.[91]

Alternatively, the use of proportional representation systems, rather than districts, could substantially reduce the potential for using Big Data and micro-targeting to trick voters into supporting or opposing particular candidates for office. The point is a relatively simple one: the design of the electoral process in the United States currently exacerbates, rather than reduces, the risk of voter manipulation. Structural reforms of the electoral process itself would be both constitutional – such reforms would not implicate the First Amendment at all – and they could be very effective at making every vote count. Such reforms would also have the salutary effect of reducing incentives to engage in Big Data–based chicanery to obtain the last marginal vote required to secure a majority within a single member district.

With regard to substantive regulations to limit or check the manipulation of Big Data and metadata to influence elections, the situation is considerably more complex – as well as constitutionally dubious.[92] *Sorrell* makes content-based or speaker-based restrictions on the collection, analysis, and use of voters' data if not quite legally impossible, then very difficult. Such active government censorship of political speech would create its own pathologies – and the federal courts probably would not permit such an experiment to take place in any event.[93] On the other hand, however, transparency and disclosure rules, as noted earlier, would stand on much firmer constitutional ground.[94]

As the Supreme Court explained in *Citizens United*, '[t]he First Amendment protects speech and speaker, and the ideas that flow from each'.[95] The Supreme Court has also held that data constitutes speech; it applied this principle and invalidated a Vermont law that limited the sale of physicians' prescribing data for marketing purposes. In light of these precedents, the government's ability to regulate the use of data to influence elections would seem to be quite limited – and all such reforms would have to survive strict judicial scrutiny (which, more often than not, proves fatal to laws and regulations subjected to it). For example, a flat ban on collecting or using such data for political purposes would be 'content-based' and arguably 'speaker-based', and the government would have to show a

Review 1413; Lani Guinier, 'The Triumph of Tokenism: The Voting Rights Act and the Theory of Black Electoral Success' (1991) 89(5) Michigan Law Review 1077.

91   The broadest exposition of these practical suggestions for structural reforms of the electoral process to better and more reliably empower political minorities appear in Lani Guinier, *The Tyranny of the Majority: Fundamental Fairness in Representative Democracy* (The Free Press 1994).

92   Bhagwat (n 74) 868–80.

93   See *Citizens United v Fed. Elec. Comm'n*, 558 US 310, 339–41 (2010).

94   Ibid 366–72.

95   Ibid 341.

compelling government interest and narrow tailoring to avoid the law's invalidation in federal court.[96]

It is easy to tick off the constitutional infirmities of direct government efforts to censor speech by regulating the use of data to influence voters. What regulatory responses might work? Self-restraint is the answer that the data hoarders have proposed. Facebook's Mark Zuckerberg has gone on a charm offensive, in the United States and Europe, seeking to assure lawmakers on both sides of the Atlantic that Facebook can be trusted to self-regulate to prevent both mass data breaches and also the dissemination of fake news.[97] Certainly, private companies may engage in self-regulation to address the problems laid bare by the 2016 presidential election and Brexit votes.

On the other hand, however, it might be wise to consider whether reliance on self-regulation constitutes a sufficient and reliable response. Even if government itself cannot be trusted to censor social media or secure personal data held by private companies,[98] one could posit a meaningful role for government. For example, government could attempt to regulate the storage and transfer of personal data controlled by companies such as Google, Facebook, and Twitter to ensure that it is secure. Such a regulation would not be content-based or speaker-based.

The General Data Protection Regulation,[99] which entered into force on 25 May 2018, demonstrates clearly that it is possible for government to regulate effectively the collection, storage, and transfer of personal data without actually taking control of the personal data itself. But, again, in the United States even carefully crafted government regulations on data storage and transfer would be subject to a formidable constitutional attack on First Amendment grounds because gathering, analyzing, and manipulating data constitute 'speech'. In Europe, by way of contrast, advancing privacy values routinely takes precedence over expressive freedoms.[100]

We could also consider adopting programs of government support for journalists who wish to engage in traditional journalistic activities and who are committed to observing journalistic ethics. Professor Lili Levi, of the University of Miami

---

96   *Sorrell*, 564 US 563–66; see Bhagwat (n 74) 871–74 (discussing the compelling government interest and narrow tailoring requirements in the context of a data privacy enactment).

97   See Natalia Drozdiak, Valentina Pop and Sam Schechner, 'Facebook CEO Dodges Tough EU Questions' *The Wall Street Journal* (23 May 2018) B1.

98   And, again, legislation of this sort would face a very heavy burden of justification before the current Supreme Court; government efforts to limit political speech, directly or indirectly, are almost reflexively invalidated on First Amendment grounds. See *Citizens United*, 558 US 339–42.

99   Regulation (EU) 2016/679 of the European Parliament and of the Council of 27 April 2016 on the protection of natural persons with regard to the processing of personal data and on the free movement of such data, and repealing Directive 95/46/EC (General Data Protection Regulation) [2016] OJ L 119, 1.

100   See Krotoszynski (n 6) 143–60, 171–72.

School of Law, has argued that the survival of local and regional newspapers that generate original content, through investigative journalism, might require support with public funds.[101] Professor Levi fears that in the absence of public subsidies, local and regional investigative journalism will continue its ongoing death spiral. As she observes, '[s]everal different public support models – including direct and indirect government subsidies – have been discussed',[102] but she cautions that 'to the extent that nonprofit news organizations receive their funding from one or a few funding sources – whether private or public – there is a significant concern that their editors could feel constrained by the wishes of the principal funders'.[103] If the government uses its largesse to essentially capture and control the free press through targeted subsidies, the cure will be worse than the disease.

Government subsidies can often come with significant strings – and we should be mindful of the risks that might be associated with government subsidies of local and regional journalism. As the saying goes, he who pays the piper calls the tune. On the other hand, however, examples exist of government-subsidized journalism without the loss of journalistic independence or integrity – the BBC provides a salient example, and NPR provides yet another. This is not to say that subsidies could not be linked to problematic government-imposed editorial controls. It is to say, however, that such subsidies do not inevitably lead to government censorship of journalists and their work.

Of course, a program of this sort would do little, if anything, to safeguard the security of voters' personal data. It could help to address the problem of 'fake news' and its distortionary effects, but a program to support serious journalism would not advance privacy as such in any appreciable way. If we are thinking broadly about the use of data analytics, however, to manipulate voters, the problem of fake news merits at least some consideration. Moreover, given the toxic effects of fake news on the process of democratic deliberation, and the use of sophisticated data analytics and micro-targeting of voters who might take the click bait if offered it via social media platforms such as Facebook and Twitter, or via search engines such as Google and Bing, the problem of fake news clearly relates to more general issues associated with Big Data and the electoral process.

VI. Conclusion

Sometimes old problems require new solutions. The ability to weaponize metadata to distort the process of democratic deliberation will require governments in democratic polities to consider adopting new policies. In an ideal world, these policies would include both substantive regulations designed to limit the potential abuse of metadata to manipulate voters and structural reforms in the electoral process itself. Reforms of both stripes could, at least potentially, help to ensure

101 Levi (n 39) 1542–44.
102 Ibid 1542 n 59.
103 Ibid 1544.

that elections remain free and fair. But we do not live in an ideal world – and in the United States the First Amendment imposes strict limits on the ability of the federal government to regulate the collection, analysis, and use of data for political communications. On the other hand, however, structural reforms in the electoral process would probably *not* be subject to serious First Amendment–based objections.

Because incumbent politicians are not well known for engaging in acts of electoral altruism, structural reforms in the United States will likely have to be the product of judicial, rather than legislative, action. As with the malapportionment of legislative seats in the 1960s, federal judges could deploy the First Amendment, the Equal Protection Clause of the Fourteenth Amendment, or both to limit the use of partisan gerrymanders to render voting and voters if not entirely irrelevant, then significantly less relevant. Moreover, there is at least some cause for hope that, at some point in the future, the Supreme Court will lift its self-imposed ban on judicial consideration of partisan gerrymanders and do its job to protect the free and fair operation of democratic politics in the United States. Perhaps, one day, a majority of the Justices will come to reject *Rucho* in favor of embracing the commonsense idea that judicial intervention is unavoidable in order to correct a structural defect in the democratic process that elected officials will never voluntarily agree to fix.

Limits on the use of personal data to target voters present a much harder case. The political economy of new legislation seeking to limit the micro-targeting of voters is complex and difficult to predict. On one hand, deceptive and opaque efforts to drive voters toward, or away from, particular political parties or candidates could benefit – or harm – both major U.S. political parties in equal measure. In the absence of a clear partisan advantage, elected politicians are unlikely to act. On the other hand, however, the absence of a clear partisan advantage might make it easier, rather than more difficult, to enact regulations addressing efforts to manipulate or trick voters.

It cannot be denied that mandatory transparency and disclosure regulations that put voters on fair notice that their personal data is being collected and will be used for political purposes would be both desirable and constitutional. Such regulations would not be subject to strict judicial scrutiny. Accordingly, if the problems associated with the political economy of their adoption could be overcome, such reforms would not face uncertain prospects in the federal courts if challenged on First Amendment grounds.

Of course, the internet does have potentially positive contributions to make to the functioning of the electoral process. The ability to reach a mass audience for a relatively modest investment of time, energy, and money has never been greater; the body politic has never been more readily accessible, at least in theory, to persons of ordinary means.[104] Moreover, the internet provides a vast repository of

104 See Lyrissa B Lidsky, 'Public Forum 2.0' (2011) 91(6) Boston University Law Review 1975.

truthful, and entirely accurate, news and information that can and does help to inform the process of deliberative democracy. In fact, the ability of voters to inform themselves about candidates and issues of the day is astonishingly vast.

The ability to use sophisticated, data-driven analytics both to micro-target voters and to rig electoral districts so that the results of elections are usually pre-ordained raises serious questions about the integrity of the electoral process itself. In particular, the utter lack of transparency associated with most micro-targeting of voters ought to be a matter of widespread and serious concern because it threatens to undermine the legitimacy of voter choice (and, hence, the ability of an election to confer legitimacy on the institutions of government). Absent struc-tural reforms to check the use of data-driven partisan gerrymanders, a non-trivial risk exists that general elections will cease to serve as a universally accepted means of securing a legitimate democratic imprimatur for our governing institutions.

Because the politicians and the political parties are self-interested and have little incentive to engage in a unilateral surrender of the potential electoral advantages that the effective use of Big Data and micro-targeting practices can confer on their candidates, effective reform efforts will likely have to be the product of either judicial action (as was the case with the pervasive use of badly malapportioned electoral districts[105]) or flow from citizen-organized reforms in states that observe the initiative and referendum process (which has been used in many states to require non-partisan districting by independent commissions[106]).

In sum, when foxes guard hen houses, the birds usually do not flourish. Unfortunately, what holds true of poultry also holds true for ordinary voters as well. Regulatory responses that impose transparency and accountability require-ments – and perhaps also require consent to the mining of voters' personal data by political parties or candidates for office – would help to reduce the growing risks to the integrity and legitimacy of our electoral process. Despite being plainly needed to ensure continued public confidence in the process of democratic self-

---

105 See *Reynolds v Sims*, 377 US 533 (1964); *Gray v Sanders*, 372 US 368 (1963); *Baker v Carr*, 369 US 186 (1962). The Supreme Court's emphatic rejection of malappor-tioned legislative districts helped to make the concept of equal citizenship more than empty rhetoric. See *Gray*, 372 US 381: 'The conception of political equality from the Declaration of Independence, to Lincoln's Gettysburg Address, to the Fifteenth, Seventeenth, and Nineteenth Amendments can mean only one thing – one person, one vote.' An equally strong and emphatic judicial response is needed to check the growing and problematic use of partisan gerrymandering to make general elections if not entirely meaningless then certainly far less meaningful as a source of securing government accountability than they otherwise would be. How is it consistent with a concept of 'one person, one vote' if the votes of a cognizable number of citizens are invariably meaningless because the electoral district has, quite literally, been rigged?

106 See *Arizona State Legislature v Arizona Indep. Redist. Comm'n*, 135 S Ct 2652, 2652–54, 2677 (2015) (discussing the adoption of non-partisan redistricting via initiative and referendum and upholding the constitutionality of this process against a constitutional challenge claiming that only the state legislature can draw district lines for US House seats).

government, greater transparency and accountability will be very difficult to secure through ordinary legislation because of the lobbying power and financial where-withal of companies such as Facebook and Google (that have a vested interest in strongly opposing such legislation). Finally, structural reforms in the voting pro-cess itself could certainly reduce, if not eliminate, the risk of weaponized Big Data being used to steal elections through efforts to deceive and manipulate voters.

Chapter 11

Data and political campaigning in the era of big data – the UK experience[1]

Stephanie Hankey, Ravi Naik and Gary Wright

Much has by now been written about the course of events surrounding the Cambridge Analytica and Facebook revelations and the potential impact of the misuse of private data on democratic participation. A number of broad investigations and enquiries by UK regulatory and parliamentary bodies[2] have highlighted some of the broader issues surrounding the use of personal information in political campaigning as well as the existing regulatory deficits.

This chapter seeks to explore the manner in which personal data has taken an increasingly prominent role in political campaigning in the United Kingdom. It also critically assesses the effectiveness of the current regulations underpinning the collection, processing, retention and other use of personal data in such campaigning, and comments on the reforms that have been proposed in the United Kingdom in the wake of the 2018 Cambridge Analytica/Facebook revelations.

The chapter commences with a brief discussion of the origins of political advertising and the rise of digital marketing during campaigns. The chapter continues with a discussion of the relevance of personal data in modern political campaigning, the analytical tools made available to political actors by Facebook and others, the rising significance of digital advertising in the UK and the role of data in the Brexit referendum. It also calls for greater public accountability on the part of the data-brokering industry and their services in the political process

---

1   This chapter has been adapted and updated from the report *Data and Democracy in the Digital Age* (10 July 2018), written by Stephanie Hankey, Julianne Kerr Morrison and Ravi Naik for the Constitution Society. That report is available at https://consoc. org.uk/publications/data-and-democracy-in-the-digital-age. All websites referred to in this chapter were accessed on 5 July 2019 unless otherwise stated.

2   UK Parliament, Digital, Culture, Media and Sport Committee, *Disinformation and 'fake news': Final Report* (HC 2017–19, 1791); UK Parliament, Digital, Culture, Media and Sport Committee, *Disinformation and 'fake news': Interim Report* (HC 2017–19, 363); Information Commissioner's Office, 'Investigation into the use of data analytics in political campaigns: A report to Parliament' (6 November 2018) http s://ico.org.uk/media/action-weve-taken/2260271/investigation-into-the-use-of-da ta-analytics-in-political-campaigns-final-20181105.pdf; Information Commissioner's Office, 'Democracy disrupted? Personal information and political influence' (11 July 2018) https://ico.org.uk/media/2259369/democracy-disrupted-110718.pdf.

because of their increasing impact on democracy across the globe. The final part of the chapter explores the current regulatory framework in the UK, giving particular attention to the gaps in it that give rise to concern, and comments on the proposals made by the Information Commissioner's Office and the Digital, Culture, Media and Sport (DCMS) Select Committee of the UK House of Commons.

I. The modern political campaign

In modern political campaigns, data on voters is an essential asset. Used effectively, data can help a party better understand the concerns of voters, more efficiently use its resources and directly speak to citizens on the issues that matter to them the most. The collection, analysis and use of personal data by political actors is now therefore not only an inevitable part of the democratic process but, where used appropriately, also has the potential to bring significant benefits by increasing citizens' participation in our political processes.

The history of political campaigning shows how data has become increasingly critical to voter information and activation. It also contributes to our understanding of how the regulatory landscape has developed in order to meet the challenges posed by the increased use of individual data, and of the gaps that have emerged as regulation has failed to keep step with technological change.

The American approach to political campaigns reflects a style that promotes the celebrity of the politician, where candidates are sold in the same way as 'washing powder' or other consumer goods. Behavioural manipulation methods were used in political campaigns in the US as early as the 1920s, when the pioneer of public relations, Edward Bernays, used them to soften President Coolidge's image.[3] Since the 1930s, advertising executives have used the same techniques as they used to sell consumer products to get politicians elected, such as playing on 'fear' factors in advertising to motivate people to act. In time the techniques of the advertising sector became commonplace in US politics and gradually inspired political actors in other countries to use them.

The history and style of election campaigning in the UK has consisted of a combination of polling, value-led marketing and developments in voter databases. Opinion polls have been undertaken by Gallop since the 1940s, with a range of companies emerging in their wake. In 1983 the Conservative Party hired Chris Lawson as a full-time director of marketing. Lawson worked with Saatchi and Saatchi 'to design a campaign which relied to a greater extent than ever before on US-style value research and "psychographics"'.[4] Similarly, the use of individual data in political campaigns has steadily developed in step with changes in data-driven technologies, including via initiatives to increase voter turnout,

3   Edward L Bernays, 'Putting Politics on the Market' *The Independent* (19 May 1928), 470.
4   Brian McNair, *An Introduction to Political Communication* (Routledge 2011) 101.

improvements to party membership databases and experiments with a range of political marketing tools, from opinion polls to canvassing.

These developments make clear that the use of data for individual targeting and the practice of appealing to voters based on their values are not new phenomena in political campaigning. What, then, is new about the digitisation of these techniques?

Unprecedented scale and granularity of personal information

The evolution of political data is hallmarked by the subjectivity and scale of digital messaging. The scope of political campaigning, its personalisation and its dynamism are unprecedented. The increased digitisation of personal lives makes it possible for political parties to monitor and target voters continuously and in depth, utilising methods intricately linked with and drawn from the commercial sector. The most significant factor is the pervasive collection and analysis of individual data. Massive investments by the commercial digital marketing and advertising sector, combined with the ubiquitous use of technology by citizens, have created an environment where personal data is collected and processed at scale, depth and speed. Innovations in data collection over the past decade have led to the growth of a multi-billion-dollar industry in which thousands of highly tuned methods and tools are used to collect, track, profile and target individuals, with the aim of changing their behaviour. The granularity of the data collected on individuals, combined with the scope of its use, is exceptional. In short, without the collection, processing and selling of vast amounts of personal data, the use of personal data for political influence would not be possible.

As personal data cascades around a developing ecosystem, researchers are taking steps to understand its value. It has been of particular use to psychologists, who have realised that social media platforms are a trove of information and a valuable source of data on individuals' personalities. Those platforms have been designed to retrieve and collect personal data and store it indefinitely. As a consequence, personal data is now available at a scale, with a degree of granularity and at a lower cost than was previously imaginable.

The value of the data has also been recognised in the political arena. Ideas that have been developing for the last century about the value of personal data and its potential for influence are finally being realised. This raises new questions when such techniques are put to use to influence the electorate. There are three dimensions to the use of individual data in the context of contemporary elections and campaigning:

- **Data as a political asset:** data collected on potential voters, accumulated by parties, exchanged between political candidates, acquired from national repositories, and sold or exposed by those who want to leverage them, such as voter data, consumer data and data processed from the open internet.

- **Data as political intelligence:** data on individuals collected and interpreted by political campaigns to learn about voters' political preferences, to inform campaign strategies and to test and adapt campaign messaging, such as 'digital listening'[5] tools for monitoring social media discussions and extensive 'A/B testing'[6] for honing and testing thousands of different messages.
- **Data as political influence:** data on individuals analysed and used to target and reach potential voters, with the aim of influencing their views or votes via methods such as micro-targeting (tailored advertising to the individual level), geo-fencing (dynamically targeting citizens based on their location) and 'search influence'.

These categories are a helpful guide to understanding the impact of modern political campaigning on democratic participation.

Micro-targeting: How political parties use the platforms

The ability and strategies of marketing companies to micro-target specific segments of the electorate are developing at a rapid rate and are becoming ever more sophisticated, spurred on in particular by finer and smaller audience targeting, location-based data analysis and sheer quantity data collection by data brokers and data exchanges.[7] Platforms such as Facebook and Google make a range of the services available to their advertising clients. We highlight three inter-related commercial services that are sold to political parties.

First, Facebook promotes the 'Custom Audience' feature that allows an organisation to upload their existing customer or client database, which can, in turn, be used to match against the Facebook user database to see if any of those particular people are also signed up to Facebook.[8] If they are on Facebook, then the advertiser may target them directly through Facebook by using the feature. Just as this is a way of allowing commercial entities to reach their existing customers, it also is a way of enabling political parties to reach individual supporters who are on their database.

Second, political parties can then combine 'Custom Audience' with a feature called 'Audience Insights'. This is a way for advertisers to increase their knowledge

---

5   'Digital listening' is a term used by companies selling services to political parties that enables them to get analysis of public sentiment regarding different issues through collecting and analysing information found on social media and the open internet.

6   A/B testing is the marketing term used for the practice of creating different versions of an advert or message and testing it on an audience to decide which one to use based on what best resonates with the target audience. In digital A/B testing several thousand messages can be dynamically tested and iterated on audiences.

7   Jamie Bartlett, Josh Smith and Rose Acton, 'The Future of Political Campaigning' (DEMOS, July 2018) https://demosuk.wpengine.com/wp-content/uploads/2018/07/The-Future-of-Political-Campaigning.pdf.

8   Facebook Business, 'Custom Audience: Reach your customers and contacts on Facebook' www.facebook.com/business/a/custom-audiences.

of their target audience, with analysis of personal traits such as 'relationship status' and 'frequency of activities', combined with third-party data showing other information, such as 'online purchases', 'household income' and 'home market value'.[9]

Third, there is an expansive feature called 'Lookalike Audiences', which gives the advertiser the ability to reach other Facebook members whose profiles 'look similar' to those uploaded in the Custom Audience database.[10] Facebook is not alone in offering such services. Google, for example, has a competitive product called Customer Match, which enables advertisers to reach customers across 'Search, Shopping, Gmail, and YouTube'.[11]

Facebook had previously posted political case studies of these technologies in action in its 'Facebook Business – Success Stories'. The whole category of these success stories named 'Government and Politics' has since been removed but is available in web archives.[12] These case studies document a series of campaigns directly using these features, including the use of the 'Custom Audience' feature by the Scottish National Party in the 2015 UK general election and the 'Lookalike Audience' feature in Trudeau's 2015 Canadian election campaign.

These private companies hold vast amounts of deeply personal data, make highly developed analytical tools available to their advertisers and provide them with access to a large proportion of the population. This gives political advertisers – and political campaigners – much greater capacity to influence behaviour than in the past. That, in turn, gives the platforms a unique potential to impact the democratic process. Whether this ability to exercise political power was intentionally designed is irrelevant. The fact remains that the power exists and has been used in ways that the public is only now beginning to understand.

Digital spending: The political zeitgeist

The data analytics methods used by Cambridge Analytica are considered relatively standard in both the commercial digital advertising and political campaigning sectors. It is therefore important to understand the context for the Cambridge Analytica story – in terms of both the methods used by data analytics companies and the broader issues of how this industry uses data in political campaigns. Some of these techniques have been driven by the broader digital advertising industry, a sector made up of thousands of companies worldwide which specialise in collecting, buying and selling data on individuals and in using that data to infer and

9   Facebook Business, 'About Audience insights' www.facebook.com/business/help/304781119678235.
10 Facebook Business, 'Lookalike audiences' www.facebook.com/business/help/231114077092092?helpref=faq_content#.
11 Google Ads Help, 'About Customer Match' https://support.google.com/adwords/answer/6379332?hl=en.
12 Tactical Tech, 'Tools of the Influence Industry' https://ourdataourselves.tacticaltech.org/posts/methods-and-practices.

interpret what may motivate individuals to act. It is these techniques and this logic that have been gradually adopted by political campaigns.

In 2018 a combination of media attention, the investigation of the Information Commissioner's Office,[13] legal claims[14] as well as the hearings and reports of the DCMS Select Committee in the UK[15] put the spotlight on Cambridge Analytica. There are, however, over 350 companies operating worldwide that specialise in the use of individual data in political campaigns.[16] These include a range of data brokers: those who politically interpret, re-package and sell a wide range of commercial data; companies that make tools for 'digital listening' and for tracking voters as they move across devices; and political campaign strategists who advise political parties on when and where to spend their digital budgets in a campaign and how to get the most out of a range of data-related techniques. Some of these companies are politically aligned and some of them are non-partisan.

A wide range of companies that specialise in the use of individual data in elections have worked in UK referendums and elections. These are predominantly North American companies and include, but are not limited to:

- Aristotle International, which reportedly owned a '35-million-person database for the UK, that was used by at least one candidate in London's [2004] mayoral race';[17]
- Nation Builder, a tool and set of services which has been used by most political parties in the UK in recent elections and referendums, including UKIP in the 2015 elections and SNP in the Scottish referendum;[18]
- Blue State Digital, which was used by the Labour party in 2015;[19] and
- Jim Messina and the Messina Group, who were hired by the Conservative Party in the 2017 snap election.[20]

13   Information Commissioner's Office (n 2).
14   Ravi Naik, 'We're taking on Cambridge Analytica in a legal fight for data rights' *The Guardian* (23 March 2018) www.theguardian.com/commentisfree/2018/mar/23/ suing-cambridge-analytica-data-rights-regulators-silicon-valley-tech.
15   UK Parliament, Digital, Culture, Media and Sport Committee (n 2).
16   Varoon Bashyakarla, Stephanie Hankey, Amber Macintyre, Raquel Rennó and Gary Wright, 'Personal Data: Political Persuasion: Inside the Influence Industry. How It Works.' (Tactical Tech, March 2019), https://tacticaltech.org/media/Personal-Data -Political-Persuasion-How-it-works.pdf.
17   James Verini, 'Big Brother Inc.' *Vanity Fair* (12 December 2007) www.vanityfair. com/news/2007/12/aristotle200712.
18   Ben Borland, '"Utterly hypocritical" SNP have been harvesting voters social media data for SEVEN years' *Scottish Express* (26 March 2018) www.express.co.uk/scotla nd/936592/Facebook-data-row-SNP-harvesting-data-controversy-social-media.
19   Blue State Digital, 'Labour Party: How do you transform the way a party organises offline, online?' www.bluestatedigital.com/our-work/labour-party.
20   Henry Mance and Jim Pickard, 'Conservatives hire James Messina for UK general election' *The Financial Times* (24 April 2017) www.ft.com/content/006e4a 74-28df-11e7-bc4b-5528796fe35c.

Even based on the limited information we have to date, British political parties have spent vast sums on these companies. Spending by parties on digital advertising increases each year and can vary widely. In 2015, the first year in which digital spending was reported separately by the Electoral Commission, around 23% of the total spend was digital, with the majority of this being spent on Facebook.[21] Spending on the digital platforms now significantly exceeds spending on national and regional traditional media.[22] For example, for the 2017 campaign, Facebook received: £2,118,045.95 from the Conservative Party, £577,542.19 from Labour, and £412,329.31 from the Liberal Democrats. Google received £562,000 from the Conservatives, £255,000 from Labour and £204,000 from the Liberal Democrats.[23] This is a significant increase from the 2015 elections when the Conservative Party spent less than half that amount and spending by Labour and the Liberal Democrats was less than 10% of that in the 2017 election. UK political campaign spending, however, is relatively small compared with the US Presidential elections, where the Trump campaign was said to have spent over $300 million on digital and advertising in the last three months of the elections.

Brexit and data

It has been suggested that Cambridge Analytica was also employed by Leave.EU in the Brexit referendum.[24] However, the company denied having carried out any tangible data analysis for Leave.EU, instead suggesting that its involvement in the referendum was limited to pitching for work with Leave.EU.[25] That position has been contested by former employees before the DCMS Committee. It has been speculated that this confusion may be attributed to the fact that Cambridge Analytica did conduct some work, but they were never paid for it.[26] Ultimately, the Information Commissioner's Office investigation into this specific question found

21   Damian Tambini, 'Social Media Power and Election Legitimacy' in Damian Tambini and Martin Moor (eds) *Digital Dominance: The Power of Google, Amazon, Facebook, and Apple* (Oxford University Press 2018) 265, 271.
22   The UK's seven major political parties spent £4 million on advertising with US tech giants during the 2017 snap general election campaign and just £239,000 on traditional news media: Freddy Mayhew and Arun Kakar, 'UK political parties spent 17 times more on advertising with US tech giants during 2017 election campaign than with traditional media' *Press Gazette* (23 March 2018) https://pressgazette.co.uk/uk-political-parties-spent-17-times-more-on-advertising-with-us-tech-giants-during-2017-election-campaign-than-with-traditional-media.
23   Alan Martin, 'The 2017 Election Spend Shows Our Fear of the Cambridge Analytica Saga Can Easily Be Overstated' *Alphr* (20 March 2018) http://alphr.com/go/1008864.
24   Paul Lewis and Paul Hilder, 'Cambridge Analytica Misled MPs over Work for Leave. EU, Says Ex-Director' *The Guardian* (23 March 2018) www.theguardian.com/news/2018/mar/23/cambridge-analytica-misled-mps-over-work-for-leave-eu-says-ex-director-brittany-kaiser.
25   Ibid.
26   Ibid.

that initial contact between Cambridge Analytica and Leave.EU did take place but that it did not move forward into a fully fledged working relationship.[27] However, there remain unanswered questions in regard to payments made by Leave.EU to Cambridge Analytica for its work on UKIP membership data in 2015. After drawn out challenges and appeals, an appeals tribunal found in April 2019 that UKIP had not adequately complied with the ICO investigation into political data services and ordered it to fully disclose its spending and data practices.[28] The case remains ongoing at the time of writing.

Cambridge Analytica's involvement, or lack of, in the Brexit referendum is only one aspect of the questions that have arisen with regard to the use of data-driven technologies and digital campaigning in the referendum. There are several other actors and alleged activities that warrant attention and will be briefly discussed below. These matters are important in the context of Brexit but also serve to illustrate the breadth of the challenges at hand and the kinds of questions that will need to be navigated for increased transparency and regulation in the future.

A hitherto little-known Canadian data analytics and digital marketing company, AggregateIQ (AIQ), was involved in the Brexit referendum as a service provider. In April 2018, AggregateIQ told a Canadian House of Commons committee on ethics, access to information and privacy that they are not a 'big data company' but a company who places online ads for clients and builds software that enables political campaigns to organise their contacts with voters.[29] While the wording has now been changed, in 2018 their website described them as a company providing 'digital advertising, web and software development' services.[30] AIQ is alleged to have worked in the Brexit referendum for four Leave-related entities: Vote Leave, BeLeave, Veterans for Britain and the Democratic Unionist Party.[31]

AIQ's significance stems in part from the complex relationship with Cambridge Analytica and Cambridge Analytica's parent company SCL. As the findings of the ICO state, there was a very close working relationship between these entities and several of its staff members. Yet the ICO Report determined that despite this uncommon arrangement, AIQ remained in a contractual relationship with Cambridge Analytica/SCL and found no evidence that the latter were involved in the Brexit referendum via AIQ. However, in its 2019 findings the DCMS suggests that there are still unresolved questions when it comes to the close proximity of

27   Information Commissioner's Office (n 2), 44.
28   Robert Verkaik and Emma Graham-Harrison, 'Judge Orders Ukip to Reveal Brexit Referendum Data Use' *The Observer* (14 April 2019) www.theguardian.com/politics/2019/apr/14/judge-orders-ukip-reveal-brexit-referendum-data-use.
29   Aaron Wherry, 'Canadian company linked to data scandal pushes back at whistle-blower's claims' *CBC News* (24 April 2018) www.cbc.ca/news/politics/aggregate-iq-mps-cambridge-wylie-brexit-1.4633388.
30   AggregateIQ, https://aggregateiq.com.
31   Information Commissioner's Office, 'Investigation into the use of data analytics in political campaigns: Investigation Update' (11 July 2018) https://ico.org.uk/media/action-weve-taken/2259371/investigation-into-data-analytics-for-political-purposes-update.pdf, 8.

these companies, particularly with regard to how data was handled and shared. The report states that while it agrees with the ICO that 'there was certainly a contractual relationship', it believes that, based on the data repository analysis by security researcher Chris Vickery, the relationship 'would imply something closer, with data exchanged between both AIQ and SCL, as well as between AIQ and Cambridge Analytica'.[32]

An investigation by the Electoral Commission found that AIQ received £2.7 million from Vote Leave, and an additional £675,315 from BeLeave.[33] Both Vote Leave and BeLeave were found to have exceeded their spending limits and produced inaccurate spending returns. Vote Leave was issued a fine of £61,000, while Darren Grimes, the founder of the BeLeave campaign group, was issued with the maximum individual fine of £20,000.[34] Furthermore, both entities were referred to the Metropolitan Police in relation to false declarations of campaign spending and possible other related offences which lie outside of the Commission's remit.[35]

The above examples serve to highlight the complex web between political data strategists, parties and campaign groups, and digital marketing and data analysts in the already highly controversial EU Referendum. Allegations and suspicions were met with counter-allegations, triggering numerous investigations into digital campaigning practices and their effects on democratic processes.

Irrespective of the role of these particular companies, the power of data was writ large over the referendum. In one telling example, Dominic Cummings stated that the Vote Leave campaign spent 98% of its budget on digital,[36] which gives an indication of how important those planning the campaigns thought that digital channels were. In a blog post about his experience working on the campaign he explained that they decided to

> put almost all our money into digital (~98%) [...] [We decided to] hold the vast majority of our budget back and drop it all right at the end with money spent on those adverts that experiments had shown were most effective (internal code name 'Waterloo').[37]

Media reports suggest that an overall £5 million was spent in total by all Leave-related campaign groups on digital and data, whereas £1 million is estimated to

32   UK Parliament, Digital, Culture, Media and Sport Committee, *Disinformation and 'fake news': Final Report* (n 2) [166].
33   The Electoral Commission, 'Vote Leave fined and referred to the police for breaking electoral law' (17 July 2018) www.electoralcommission.org.uk/i-am-a/journalist/electoral-commission-media-centre/party-and-election-finance-to-keep/vote-leave-fined-and-referred-to-the-police-for-breaking-electoral-law.
34   Ibid.
35   Ibid.
36   Dominic Cummings, 'Dominic Cummings: how the Brexit referendum was won' *The Spectator* (9 January 2017) https://blogs.spectator.co.uk/2017/01/dominic-cummings-brexit-referendum-won.
37   Ibid.

have been spent by 'Remain' campaign groups. Even with the Electoral Commission's spending reports on hand, such spending is difficult to trace. Nevertheless, questions arise as to whether such spending is significant in the context of a 2% margin in the vote to leave the EU.

There is very little evidence at this point as to the efficacy of data techniques. Christopher Wylie, the whistleblower who brought Cambridge Analytica to the attention of the media, claimed in his testimony to the DCMS Select Committee, however, that the 'conversion rates' of the digital advertisements placed by the Leave campaigns were unusually high.[38] Conversion rates are the feedback mechanism for helping digital advertisers understand how many and which of their advertisements lead to a significant action, such as a donation, signing up for a group or attending an event, rather than just a click. In his testimony, Wylie claimed that the 'normal' conversion rate for a digital advertisement would be around 1 or 2%, whereas Leave-related conversion rates were reportedly in the 5–10% range. In addition, Dominic Cummings claimed that it was one of the reasons why the Leave vote won and that in the official ten-week campaign they 'served about one billion targeted digital adverts'.[39]

A different aspect of the Brexit referendum which is currently under the spotlight is the question of where the data on citizens came from. In her testimony to the DCMS Select Committee, another Cambridge Analytica whistleblower, Brittany Kaiser, stated that she believed that the data was bought from companies like Experian on aspects such as citizens' credit rating.[40] How much data was bought is unknown and how it was utilised remains subject to speculation. The significance here lies in the fact that it is a case in point of how deep campaigns will go to source data on the electorate. Experian is a major aggregator and broker of vast quantities of hyper-detailed consumer data which is becoming increasingly valuable in campaigning. In her oral and written testimony, Ms Kaiser claimed that she was asked to devise a strategy for UKIP, Leave.EU and Eldon Insurance/GoSkippy data.[41] Eldon Insurance is one of Arron Banks' insurance companies. Mr Banks is the key funder behind Leave.EU and Leave.EU's campaign activities, which operate from the offices of Eldon Insurance.[42] The interplay and interlinking between commercial data entities and political

38 UK Parliament, Digital, Culture, Media and Sport Committee (27 March 2018) https://parliamentlive.tv/Event/Index/28e9cccd-face-47c4-92b3-7f2626cd818e.

39 Dominic Cummings's Blog, 'On the referendum #20: the campaign, physics and data science – Vote Leave's "Voter Intention Collection System" (VICS) now available for all' (29 October 2016) https://dominiccummings.com/2016/10/29/on-the-refer endum-20-the-campaign-physics-and-data-science-vote-leaves-voter-intention-collection-system-vics-now-available-for-all.

40 UK Parliament, Digital, Culture, Media and Sport Committee (17 April 2018) www. parliamentlive.tv/Event/Index/e5ae6255-c88e-4e62-bbf4-9c0c18ba7b6b.

41 UK Parliament, Digital, Culture, Media and Sport Committee, 'Written evidence submitted by Brittany Kaiser' http://data.parliament.uk/writtenevidence/committeeevi dence.svc/evidencedocument/digital-culture-media-and-sport-committee/fake-news/ written/81556.html.

42 At the time of writing the Leave.EU website and Eldon Insurance website gave the same contact address in Bristol.

campaigning in the digital age are becoming increasingly difficult to untangle and strategies to deal with opacity by using 'follow the money' strategies would be served by expanding the notion to include 'follow the data'.

In her testimony, Ms Kaiser raised the concern that data on customers of Eldon Insurance and data on people who had made queries to Eldon Insurance and their affiliated companies may have been used in the Brexit campaign. She stated in her written evidence that she had reason to believe that 'misuse of data was rife among the businesses and campaigns of Arron Banks'.[43] Indeed, the DCMS Select Committee found a 'porous relationship'[44] between Mr Banks' Eldon Insurance and Leave.EU and that systems for keeping data of insurance customers separate from that of political subscribers were ineffective. Both entities have been issued with a total of £120,000 worth in fines and are facing audits of their data protection practices. It should also be noted that Eldon Insurance claims in its annual report that it holds data on 24.9 million people in Britain.[45] The implications of such a vast data trove – and its political use – could be significant.[46] Overall, while it took considerable effort and engagement at the political level, illegal activities in the uses of citizen data were ascertained successfully and sanctions handed down. This case shows that while data-driven campaigning can be highly opaque, there is still room for legal frameworks to have a meaningful impact on illicit activities.

II. Hiding in plain sight: Public knowledge and steps towards accountability

There has been mass coverage and public discussion of the Cambridge Analytica/ Facebook revelations. That coverage and discussion has focused on a number of issues, including the impact of the advertising techniques and the power of personal data. The business model of companies such as Facebook has been subject to regulatory scrutiny on both sides of the Atlantic, with widespread concerns about the apparent pitfalls of a model built on data profiling and the 'attention economy'. It is remarkable that the actions of these companies proceeded for a number of years

43 UK Parliament, Digital, Culture, Media and Sport Committee, 'Written evidence submitted by Brittany Kaiser' (n 41).

44 UK Parliament, Digital, Culture, Media and Sport Committee, *Disinformation and 'fake news': Final Report* (n 2) [16], [146].

45 Carole Cadwalladr, 'Arron Banks, the insurers and my strange data trail' *The Guardian* (21 April 2018) www.theguardian.com/technology/2018/apr/21/arron-ba nks-insurance-personal-data-leave-eu.

46 The questions of broad data collection by Eldon Insurance and its possible misuse was further queried by journalist Carole Cadwalladr, who submitted a Subject Access Request to Eldon Insurance. The information she received showed that despite not being a customer of Eldon Insurance they did have her data on file (including her name, email address, address and family member details) due to insurance she took out through the website Moneysupermarket.com: Carole Cadwalladr, 'Arron Banks, the insurers and my strange data trail' *The Guardian* (21 April 2018) www.theguardia n.com/technology/2018/apr/21/arron-banks-insurance-personal-data-leave-eu.

without sanction or accountability. Indeed, when the companies were forced to account for their actions, they treated their own regulators with an attitude bordering on disdain.[47] The fact that the companies were able to operate with such indifference to any consequences shows not just a lack of regulation but also a lack of respect for the regulations that do exist – and an obvious gap in enforcement.

While the Cambridge Analytica scandal focused much public attention on the US Trump election and the UK Brexit referendum, the revelations also exposed the extent of data-driven micro-targeting and attempts to use digital manipulation in elections elsewhere in the world.[48] The recent scandals have hit public consciousness in a way that may lead to demands for transparency and control over personal data in a greater way than was the case with the Snowden revelations. While Edward Snowden revealed the extent of state surveillance carried out under the auspices of national security, the more recent events have shone a light on the potential for misuse of data on social media and collected by the private sector for political gain.

The Cambridge Analytica/Facebook scandal broke at around the same time as the arrival of the General Data Protection Regulation (GDPR)[49] into UK law. This coincidence has had the effect of launching data regulations into mainstream consciousness, as both a force for good and a regulation with effect. Indeed, such has been the clamour for change that US legislators, lawyers and consumers have begun to ask questions as to why they are not protected by regulations similar to the GDPR.[50] The next part of this chapter will explore the current regulatory framework of online political campaigning in some detail.

III. The existing framework and the absence of specific regulation for online political campaigning

Electoral law has the function of creating a level playing field between the various actors, while simultaneously allowing for accountability regarding campaigning

47   In the enforcement notice from the ICO to Cambridge Analytica, the ICO revealed that Cambridge Analytica and its parent companies wrote to the ICO that they did 'not expect to be further harassed with this sort of correspondence': Information Commissioner's Office, 'ICO serves Enforcement Notice on SCL Elections Ltd over inadequate response to subject access request' (5 May 2018) https://ico.org.uk/about-the-ico/news-and-e vents/news-and-blogs/2018/05/ico-serves-enforcement-notice-on-scl-elections-ltd.

48   Allegations have been made that Cambridge Analytica also sold similar techniques through partners, consultants and affiliated entities in elections in a number of other countries, including Brazil, India, Kenya, Nigeria and Mexico. This has broader implications for the democratic process, social stability and security in a variety of contexts.

49   Regulation (EU) 2016/679 of the European Parliament and of the Council of 27 April 2016 on the protection of natural persons with regard to the processing of personal data and on the free movement of such data, and repealing Directive 95/46/EC (General Data Protection Regulation) [2016] OJ L 119, 1.

50   See e.g. Trevor Butterworth, 'Europe's tough new digital privacy law should be a model for US policymakers' Vox (23 May 2018) www.vox.com/the-big-idea/2018/3/26/17164022/gdpr-europe-privacy-rules-facebook-data-protection-eu-cambridge.

practices. The focus of electoral law for these purposes is on (a) imposing spending limits (and at least some transparency and reporting obligations) and (b) controlling the use of television for political campaigning. The ability of electoral law to combat the problems of misuse of personal data is, however, limited. That is because it was designed with a different aim and in a different era – that is, the pre-big-data world.

Printed campaign material must indicate who is behind the campaign and who created the materials. Beyond these requirements, the content of the material is not regulated. No such requirements currently apply to online campaign material. Political campaigning is also exempt, for example, from the Advertising Code (sometimes referred to as the CAP Code), which is written by the Committee of Advertising Practice (CAP) and administered by the Advertising Standards Authority (ASA). The UK has adopted a self-regulatory model for non-broadcast advertising, including newspapers, posters, websites, social media, cinema, emails, leaflets and billboards. TV and radio advertising is governed by a co-regulatory regime that is administered by the ASA in an arrangement with the communications regulator, Ofcom. This form of regulation, which is funded by the advertising industry, imposes at least some control on the types of advertising to which it applies.

Following the 1997 General Election, however, CAP decided to exclude political advertising from the ASA's remit because of a number of factors that risked bringing regulation in general into disrepute. The factors included:

- There was a likelihood that complaints subject to ASA investigation would be ruled upon after an election has taken place because of the short, fixed timeframes over which elections run.
- There was no consensus between the Labour, Conservative and Liberal Democrat Parties to bring political advertising wholly within the scope of the Code. This played a part in CAP taking the decision to exclude all of it, as partial regulation poses its own problems.
- There were concerns about the implications of the introduction of the Human Rights Act 1998. In particular, concerns were raised that the application of the Code could be contrary to the rights of freedom of speech around democratic elections and referendums.

Thus the focus of the statutory regulation in place, and that of the Electoral Commission, is on (a) restraining the expenditure of parties on campaigning and (b) regulating strictly the access of parties or political groups to broadcast media. There is no regulation designed to generally restrain the political campaigning and advertising activities of political parties or the activities of those acting on their behalf or in support of them. At best, spending limits can provide an indirect means of controlling advertising, profiling or other data processing – and this was at least part of the purpose of introducing such controls. But in the new digital age, such indirect controls are incapable of having a significant effect – not least in relation to activities of third parties on platforms such as Facebook.

As outlined above, freedom of expression concerns were relied upon, in part, in justifying a decision to preclude regulation of political advertising (beyond the restrictions on the use of broadcasting services). However, given that freedom of speech is not an absolute right and that other legitimate interests are at stake where political advertising peddles falsehoods or is distorted, the better approach would involve the introduction of regulation that adopts proportionate means for the purpose of achieving a legitimate aim.

The Electoral Commission, among others, points to the Information Commissioner and data protection law as a key part of the regulatory answer to the problems posed. To understand why data protection law can only be part and not the complete answer, it is necessary to understand its background and current reach.

IV. Data protection and regulations on communications

This section outlines the history and rationale of data protection legislation. The data protection regime is enjoying a new level of prominence, but it has been developing for some time. We also outline a less well-known but equally important suite of provisions, forming part of the overall data protection regime, namely the Privacy and Electronic Communications Regulations 2003 (PECR). An overview of the new data protection regime introduced by the GDPR is set out first, followed by a review of the complementary provisions.

Background and rationale

In 1980 the Organisation for Economic Co-operation and Development (OECD) issued Guidelines on the Protection of Privacy and Trans-border Flows of Personal Data (the 'Guidelines').[51] Those Guidelines were intended to harmonise and enhance the regulation of data protection in light of technological developments, without creating any undue barriers to trade. The broad aim of the Guidelines was said to be striking a balance between protecting the privacy and the rights of individuals, while simultaneously allowing the uninterrupted flow of personal data across national frontiers in jurisdictions that subscribed to a broadly similar level of data protection.

In 1981 the Council of Europe adopted the Convention for the Protection of Individuals with regard to Automatic Processing of Personal Data (Convention 108).[52] However, the Convention merely identified minimum standards, and, accordingly, a diverse set of regimes began to develop, even within the European Community. The European Commission was concerned to ensure harmonisation

---

51   Organisation for Economic Co-operation and Development (OECD), OECD Guidelines on the Protection of Privacy and Transborder Flows of Data (Paris, 23 September 1980).
52   Council of Europe Convention for the Protection of Individuals with regard to Automatic Processing of Personal Data [1981] ETS 108.

and accordingly developed a more robust and developed framework, culminating in Directive 95/46 'on the protection of individuals with regard to the processing of personal data and on the free movement of such data', also known as the Data Protection Directive (the Directive).[53]

The Directive built on the Guidelines, listing eight data protection principles and how they should be protected. The method of implementation of the Directive was left to each member state. In the United Kingdom, the Directive was incorporated into the Data Protection Act 1998 (UK) (the DPA 1998). The DPA 1998 included the eight data protection principles in Schedule 1.

From 23 May 2018, the Directive was replaced by the GDPR, as supplemented by the current Data Protection Act 2018 (UK). The data protection principles have been modernised and strengthened but continue to represent the framework around which data protection is developed. The principles seek to enshrine personal autonomy and dignity over personal data by providing a class of rights over that data.

Data protection, meanwhile, has become not just an aspect of the right to respect for private life but a distinct human right of its own, at least in the EU Charter of Fundamental Rights. The Charter became legally binding EU primary law with the coming into force of the Lisbon Treaty on 1 December 2009.

The General Data Protection Regulation

The GDPR puts in place a detailed regime governing the processing of personal data, building on the existing regime under the prior Data Protection Directive. The Data Protection Act 2018 (UK), which came into force on 23 May 2018, includes additional provisions relating to the application of the GDPR.

Article 5 GDPR sets out the data protection principles. The most relevant principles in the present context are those which require personal data to be:

- Processed lawfully, fairly and in a transparent manner in relation to the data subject (the first data protection principle);
- Collected for specified, explicit and legitimate purposes and not further processed in a manner that is incompatible with those purposes (the second data protection principle);
- Accurate, and, where necessary, kept up to date; every reasonable step must be taken to ensure that personal data that are inaccurate, having regard to the purposes for which they are processed, are erased or rectified without delay (the fourth data protection principle); and

---

53 Directive 95/46/EC of the European Parliament and of the Council of 24 October 1995 on the protection of individuals with regard to the processing of personal data and on the free movement of such data [1995] OJ L 281, 31.

- Processed in a manner that ensures appropriate security of the personal data, including protection against unauthorised or unlawful processing and against accidental loss, destruction or damage, using appropriate technical or organisational measures (sixth data protection principle).

The GDPR also sets out a number of fundamental rights, including, in particular:

- The right to information (arts 12–13) – essentially a transparency obligation requiring notices to be given of the types of processing a controller will engage in.
- The right to information where data is obtained from a third party (art 14) – a similar right as outlined directly above, but applied in situations of data sharing.
- The right to object (art. 21) – the right to object to processing carried out in reliance on an official authority or the legitimate interests of the controller or others, in particular processing involving profiling. Data subjects also have the right to object to processing for direct marketing purposes, including profiling.
- The right of subject access (art. 15) – the most well-known data subject right. It is the key gateway to the exercise of the other data protection rights in many cases. Without knowledge of and compliance with this right, it is often nigh on impossible for data subjects to know whether and, if so, what data is being processed.
- The right to rectification (art. 16) – this right allows data subjects to demand the correction of inaccuracies, etc.
- The right to erasure (art. 17) – this is essentially the right to be forgotten.
- The right to restriction of processing (art. 18) – this arises where (a) the accuracy of the data is contested (so that the dispute may be resolved), the processing is unlawful but the data subject does not want the data to be erased, (b) the data are required by the data subject to establish a legal claim or defence of a claim, and (c) the data subject has objected to processing under art. 21, pending verification of whether the interests of the controller can override the objections of the data subject.
- The right to data portability (art. 20).

These important rights assist individuals in controlling how their data is used and protect them from data processing in breach of their data and privacy rights. Data subjects can go to court or complain to the Information Commissioner about: (a) any failure to comply with the above rights; or (b) any unlawful processing they discover as a result of the exercise of those rights (arts 77–79). The GDPR also introduces joint and several liability for controllers and processors involved in the same processing, in an effort to make it easier for data subjects to bring damages claims (art. 82).

The Data Protection Act 2018

Member States may introduce restrictions to the rights granted to data subjects (art. 23). Many restrictions are included in the new Data Protection Act 2018 (the DPA 2018). Member States may also impose specific conditions that controllers can rely upon to justify processing special category data. Taken together, such restrictions or special conditions can provide a defence for problematic processing.

Article 85 of the GDPR requires Member States to ensure that the rights of protection for personal data and freedom of expression are reconciled, including processing for journalistic purposes and the purposes of academic, artistic or literary expression. The DPA 2018 contains a variety of provisions protecting journalistic activity (e.g. Para 13 of Part 2 of Schedule 1 and Part 5 of Schedule 2).

Importantly, the DPA 2018 creates protections to political parties' processing that limits the new regime's ability to combat misuse of data. Paragraph 22, Part 2, of Schedule 1 provides political parties with a specific substantial public interest condition for the processing of special categories of personal data. It provides that:

1. This condition is met if the processing—
   a. is of personal data revealing political opinions,
   b. is carried out by a person or organisation included in the register maintained under section 23 of the Political Parties, Elections and Referendums Act 2000, and
   c. is necessary for the purposes of the person's or organisation's political activities, subject to the exceptions in sub-paragraphs (2) and (3).
2. Processing does not meet the condition in sub-paragraph (1) if it is likely to cause substantial damage or substantial distress to a person.
3. Processing does not meet the condition in sub-paragraph (1) if—
   a. an individual who is the data subject (or one of the data subjects) has given notice in writing to the controller requiring the controller not to process personal data in respect of which the individual is the data subject (and has not given notice in writing withdrawing that requirement),
   b. the notice gave the controller a reasonable period in which to stop processing such data, and
   c. that period has ended.
4. In this paragraph, 'activities' include campaigning, fund-raising, political surveys and case-work.

The processing of special category data, such as data revealing political opinion, is generally prohibited by art. 9(1) of the GDPR, unless the controller can rely on a condition in art. 9(2). Part 2 of Schedule 1 of the new Act outlines the situations that fall within art. 9(2) GDPR.

The protections to political parties' processing in the DPA 2018 quoted above are designed to give effect to art. 9(2) by allowing for processing of 'special category' data, namely, data revealing political opinions. However, this basis for special category processing does not remove individual data rights, and political parties should be aware of and give effect to individual data protection rights.

Scope and limitations of data protection rules

The GDPR marks a considerable step forward in the drive to ensure protection for personal data and privacy. However, it has its limitations in relation to political processing of data and targeted marketing.

An important limitation is that data protection laws apply only to data qualifying as personal data. Data is not 'personal' if it does not relate to an identified or identifiable individual. If data is stored, used or shared in aggregate or anonymised form, the DPA 2018 and the GDPR do not apply at all.

This is problematic because it can be very difficult to know when and if personal data is being processed because of the ability of new technologies and techniques to allow data to be re-identified. Data may not identify any 'individual' in the hands of one controller but becomes personal data once included in a database operated by another. This makes it very difficult for individuals, and the Information Commissioner, to keep track of personal data and how it is being used across many different types of companies.

Second, the data protection provisions cannot help tackle the problem of inaccurate or fake news. The means by which individuals or groups of individuals are profiled or targeted may be covered by the Act, but the content of political advertising itself is unlikely to be regulated by the GDPR or Data Protection Act.

The third problem is that the controls exerted by data subjects, whether *ex poste* or *ex ante*, depend on two things: (a) information; and (b) resources. Most of the time data subjects do not know whether and what data relating to them are being processed. Privacy notices, the requirement for explicit consent and other GDPR measures may help with this. In reality, however, the complicated web of companies involved in compiling and processing data makes it very difficult for any individual to exert real control.

If a data subject knows or reasonably suspects that their data is being processed unlawfully, a complaint can be made to the Information Commissioner, but she does not have the resources or the wider public mandate to act on every case of breach. Further, and in any event, individual case-by-case enforcement is likely to have only a limited impact on the practices of major platforms such as Facebook – even if such a well-resourced defendant could be realistically targeted by many data subjects. Much of the success of the regime therefore depends on the Information Commissioner being in a position to be effective. That requires a significant budget and the right resources to be available.

All of these problems apply in general. With respect to political campaigning on forums such as Facebook, the problem is that individualised targeted messaging may not be recognised as such by individuals – or be transparent to a regulator. The *ex ante* obligations on data controllers, and the threat of enforcement, might be hoped to provide a disincentive to bad practice, but given the scale of activities discussed above, data protection alone is insufficient to ensure lawful and appropriate behaviour which does not undermine democratic values.

The data protection regime described above focuses on the protection of personal data. In contrast to first-generation rights, which necessarily are tied to the individual, these rights adhere to the data itself. Accordingly, jurisdiction follows the data and is inevitably extraterritorial, as data crosses borders at will. As a result, individuals based in third countries such as the US can have rights over their data processed in the United Kingdom.

The element of extraterritoriality is illustrated in the context of Cambridge Analytica's activities when a US citizen, Professor David Carroll, was able to assert his rights over his personal data processed in the United Kingdom. Cambridge Analytica disputed that jurisdiction could flow in this way and refused to provide Professor Carroll with full and complete disclosure of his file.[54] The Information Commissioner disagreed and served an Enforcement Notice on the company on 4 May 2018. The company failed to comply and, on 9 January 2019, pleaded guilty to an offence for failing to comply with the Enforcement Notice.[55] It was fined £15,000 for breaching s 47 (1) of the DPA 1998.[56]

The battle to impose EU norms on foreign data controllers thus dominates many of the current data protection reform controversies, including the 'right to be forgotten', the requirements for the legality of data exports, and the question of how overseas cloud providers should respond to state demands for access to data in the name of national security.

The Privacy and Electronic Communications Regulations

The Privacy and Electronic Communications Regulations 2003 (PECR) implement Directive 2002/58/EC concerning the processing of personal data and the protection of privacy in the electronic communications sector (the 2002 ePrivacy Directive).[57] The Directive was introduced to supplement the Data Protection Directive, which preceded the GDPR.

---

54   In their answer to the Information Commissioner, the company stated that Professor Carroll was 'no more entitled to make a subject access request under the DPA "… than a member of the Taliban sitting in a cave in the remotest corner of Afghanistan"': Information Commissioner's Office, 'Enforcement Notice to SCL Elections Ltd' https://ico.org.uk/media/action-weve-taken/enforcement-notices/2258812/en-scl-elections-20180504.pdf.

55   David Pegg, 'Cambridge Analytica owner fined £15,000 for ignoring data request' *The Guardian* (9 January 2019) www.theguardian.com/uk-news/2019/jan/09/cambridge-analytica-owner-scl-elections-fined-ignoring-data-request.

56   Information Commissioner's Office, 'SCL Elections prosecuted for failing to comply with enforcement notice' (9 January 2019) https://ico.org.uk/about-the-ico/news-and-events/news-and-blogs/2019/01/scl-elections-prosecuted-for-failing-to-comply-with-enforcement-notice.

57   Directive 2002/58/EC, [2002] OJ L 201, 37.

Subject to narrow and specific exceptions, the 2002 ePrivacy Directive and the PECR require specific consent[58] to be obtained before the following direct marketing communications can be executed:

- automated calls;[59]
- faxes;[60] and
- emails/other electronic mail systems.[61]

The Information Commissioner has long held the position that the PECR apply to direct marketing by political parties. The Information Tribunal upheld this view in *Scottish National Party v the Information Commissioner*. [62] The ICO has published detailed guidance on conducting political campaigns in accordance with the PECR and the GDPR.[63]

The limitations of the PECR are, however, twofold. First, they address specifically identified forms of direct marketing only. There are many forms of political advertisements, targeted to various degrees, over platforms such as Facebook. It is not clear to what extent any such forms of advertising are caught by the PECR. Second, the PECR regime is reliant primarily on the Information Commissioner and her resources to enforce it. Some examples of such enforcement activities are as follows:

- The Information Commissioner fined David Lammy MP £5,000 for making nuisance calls by playing a recorded message urging people to support his campaign to be the Mayor of London.[64]
- The Information Commissioner issued an unofficial warning to the Conservative Party, and other parties generally, concerning the need to ensure that campaign research calls should not stray into direct marketing.[65]
- The Information Commissioner took multiple actions following its investigation into the uses of data during the EU Referendum (see above).

58   From 25 May 2018, the standard of consent required is that prescribed by the GDPR.
59   2002 ePrivacy Directive, art. 1, PECR, Regulation 19.
60   2002 ePrivacy Directive, art. 13; PECR, Regulation 20.
61   2002 ePrivacy Directive, art. 13; PECR, Regulation 22.
62   [2006] UKIT EA_2005_0021.
63   Information Commissioner's Office, 'Guidance on political campaigning' (2018) http s://ico.org.uk/media/for-organisations/documents/1589/promotion_of_a_politica l_party.pdf.
64   Rajeev Syal, 'David Lammy fined over mayoral bid nuisance calls' *The Guardian* (10 March 2016) www.theguardian.com/politics/2016/mar/10/david-lammy-fined-o ver-mayoral-bid-nuisance-calls.
65   Lydia Smith, 'Conservative Party receives warning from Information commissioner over secretive election campaign call centre' *Independent* (23 October 2017) www. independent.co.uk/news/uk/home-news/conservative-party-warned-secretive-election-campaign-call-centre-blue-telecoms-neath-a8016176.html.

However, it is essential that the Information Commissioner is well resourced if she is to be able to enforce not only the PECR but also the data protection regime more generally, including the GDPR.

V. Further rights or better enforcement of data rights

Data is an asset for those who control it, both in terms of its commodity value and the uses to which it can be put. For this reason, data acquisition by political parties is ongoing and likely to increase. The cumulative effect may be the creation of inequities in terms of possession of data on voters and the electoral insights it provides. As data is considered to be such a key asset, it also has the potential to attract investment and donations.

For the individuals, however, the financial value of their own personal data could be negligible. Financial redress for data collection cannot therefore balance the continuing need for data rights and protection. Indeed, arguments based solely on data commoditisation miss the mark, and such perspectives offer a convenient way for data controllers to dispose of the broader issues of data misuse, without balancing the rights of the data subject.

The real asset for the individual is the value that is intrinsic in our humanity. Much as was the case with first-generation rights, once individuals understand the value of their rights, they will be able to assert more control over them. At the same time, however, given the power that can be derived from controlling huge databases of personal data, it is essential that regulators and regimes are in place to ensure that the regime is enforceable at a collective, as well as individual, level. This is especially true in relation to major platforms.

Data rights are the next generation of human rights. They are a new-world expression of the traditional right to privacy. Unlike their more established forefathers, the mischief these rights seek to grapple with is difficult to pin down. Technology is advancing and evolving at a faster pace than it is possible for legislation to keep up with. And anything without shape is difficult to contain. However, the existing data protection regime offers the primary solution to the problems caused by data misuse, which is to protect individual rights over their data. The regime is currently reflected in the GDPR. The framework is detailed and evolved over many years, across many jurisdictions, to respond to, and to keep up with, rapid technological progress. It therefore offers an established answer to the problems caused by the ever-fluid developments of technology.

The results of that regime have been positive, through both the legal precedents set and the effect on data subjects. While there have been criticisms that the evolution of the framework has been slow to react to new problems and challenges, this was also true of first-generation rights at their embryonic stages. However, those first-generation rights are now embedded in our law and the public consciousness. It follows therefore that the real shift required is cultural, rather than a new and different digital charter of rights. Such a charter exists in all but name; it just needs to be respected on an *ex ante* basis, as well as being enforceable on an *ex poste* basis.

In its final report on its investigation into disinformation and 'fake news', the House of Commons DCMS Select Committee offered a number of recommendations for tackling the current problems of opacity in the uses of personal data in political processes. Electoral laws need to reflect a deeper understanding of the tools and commercial ecosystems that drive digital political advertising and data-driven political campaigning, and the DCMS Select Committee's recommendations for better definitions of what constitutes conventional and non-conventional political advertising are well founded.

VI. Conclusions

There are many companies working in the political digital space that are similar to Cambridge Analytica.[66] They are buying and processing personal data, using several different profiling and micro-targeting techniques, and working on multiple elections and referendums across borders. In practice, the difference between Cambridge Analytica and many of the other companies in the sector is how far they are willing to go and how they navigate the ethical and legal dilemmas that present themselves in using individual data for political influence. Cambridge Analytica was in many respects an outlier, which had garnered it a negative reputation within established political circles for some time.

While Cambridge Analytica is an extreme example, its story shows what can happen if the actors utilising these techniques put profit before respect for an open and fair democratic process. Moreover, it points to a need for action to ensure that all operators offering such services, and the political actors purchasing them, are aware of their potential impact and comply with a sufficiently robust and enforced regulatory regime.

The issues created by the activities of Cambridge Analytica also raise questions as to what checks and balances need to be put in place to prevent such practices from getting out of hand in the future, both in the UK and internationally. Given the potential impact of these practices on democratic processes, this question is both urgent and in need of determined resolution.

The revelations of the practices employed by Cambridge Analytica, and their associated potential for exploitation and manipulation, have caused political shockwaves around the globe, but it remains to be seen which consequences will flow from the numerous official enquiries and reports in the UK, Canada and elsewhere. The answers will not lie in wholesale legal change or reductive arguments about the loss of value in data rights. They will instead rest in understanding the role of personal data in politics, the importance of respecting and enforcing the regulations that exist and in finding workable and effective additional or amended solutions to make rights over personal data real and effective.

---

66 At the time of writing, Cambridge Analytica and its parent companies, SCL Elections and SCL Group, have appointed administrators and commenced insolvency proceedings.

Index

accountability 175, 176, 212–213, 214–215, 224–226; democratic control and 80–81, 82–83, 84

Adams, John 204

advertising 2, 27, 35, 36–38, 47, 60, 73, 76, 170, 217–218; attack ads 192; Canada 149–150, 157, 159; Code of Conduct 111; conversion rates of digital 223; elements of democracy 82–83; ePrivacy Regulation, draft 132, 133, 137; Facebook dark posts 77–78, 83; General Data Protection Regulation (GDPR) 120, 134, 231; subliminal 192; UK: Privacy and Electronic Communications Regulations 2003 (PECR) 233; UK Advertising Code 226; UK co-regulatory regime for TV and radio 226; UK DCMS Select Committee 235; UK self-regulation for non-broadcast 226; United States 191–192, 204–205, 215

age: of children in household 149; Facebook 'likes' 61; location check-ins 62; search query histories 62; social media postings 61; tailoring messages 59

AggregateIQ (AIQ) 221–222

Alexander, Keith 75

Alphabet 73

Amazon 73

Anderson, B 6, 19, 25–26, 34–35

Anderson, C 37–38

appearance of candidate 54–55

apps on mobile phone 62, 149

Arendt, H 65

Aristotle International 219

artificial intelligence (AI) 29, 68, 169

association, freedom of 66, 91, 92, 134, 200

Australia 13, 164–185, 174, 189; big data and micro-targeting 169–170, 181–182; compulsory voting 175; Constitution 177–178, 182; Do Not Call Register Act 2006 168; Facebook data matching 165–166; implied freedom of political communication 167, 176–184, 185; Law Reform Commission (ALRC) 166; Law Reform Commission (Victoria) 180–181; political communication and democracy 174–176; political exemptions in Privacy Act 166–169; political micro-targeting, issue of 170–174; Privacy Charter 79; Privacy Commissioner 165, 184; Spam Act 2003 168–169; unsolicited calls or faxes or messaging 168–169

authoritarianism (personality trait) 56

autonomy 47, 52, 63–64, 65, 79, 135, 180, 183, 228

Bailenson, J N 55

Balibar, E 35

'bandwagon' effect 55–56

Banks, Arron 223–224

Barendt, E 174

Bartlett, J 36

BBC 100, 210

Becker, G S 38

behavioural tracking online and big data analytics 60–63, 73, 76, 102

behaviourism, neoliberalism and giant tech companies 35, 36–38

Bennett, C 10, 114, 127

Berlusconi, Silvio 109

Bernays, E L 51–52, 215

Bernstein, J M 24, 26, 30–31

Bessi, A 66

Bhagwat, A 205
biases 19, 51–52, 57
big data analytics 60–63, 73, 76, 102, 169–170, 187–196; consent 119, 120, 170
Bing 210
Bird, Jeremy 148
Black Lives Matter 76
Blackstone, W 39
bloggers and private postings 109–110
Blue State Digital 219
Boehme-Neßler, V 180
Borgesius, F J Z 21, 173
botnets 102
bots 2, 4, 13, 66, 75–76, 102–103, 173–174, 179; amplifier 103; from mass to automated media 28–29, 32–33; shit storms 103
Brandeis, L 63
Brexit referendum 1–2, 34, 46, 102, 103, 105, 120, 170, 190, 209, 220–224, 233
broadcasting 53, 83, 99, 100–101, 210; Europe: political ads during elections 82; Italian elections in 1994 109; UK co-regulatory regime for TV and radio advertising 226, 227; US: Radio Act 1927 66–67
Brown, W 29–30
Bush, George W 57, 194

Cambridge Analytica 1–3, 5, 13, 34, 38, 66, 73, 74, 77–78, 98, 102, 156, 162, 172, 190, 192, 225, 235; anonymity 81; Australian political parties 174; consent 120, 122; democratic participation, right to 88, 93, 105; direct marketing 77; elements of democracy 81, 82–83; extraterritoriality 232; methodology 171, 218; Ocean Score 77, 89; privacy 89, 90, 92, 93; public interest and processing of personal data 122; sources of data 223; states: duty to protect own elections 88; transparency 127; United Kingdom 1–3, 34, 102, 120, 218, 219, 220–223, 224, 225, 235
Canada 10, 13, 141–163, 189, 218, 221, 235; Communications Security Establishment (CSE) 161; Conflict of Interest Code for Members of the House of Commons 159; consent 155, 156–157, 158, 159, 163; constitutional protections for political parties 150–151;

data breaches 160–161; data brokers 148, 156; data-driven elections in 146–150; effective representation, right to 150–151; election law, voters lists and personal privacy protection 151–154; Elections Act 151, 152, 153–154; hacking 161; Information and Privacy Commissioner Ontario 161; Office of the Information and Privacy Commissioner of BC 156–157, 158, 159, 160, 161, 162–163; Office of the Privacy Commissioner of Canada 153, 155; petitions 158, 159; political arena 142–146; privacy law: application to political parties 155–157, 162; privacy risks: personal data and political parties 157–161; profiling 148, 157, 159, 160; Quebec independence referendum 57; regulatory gaps 154, 156, 158; robocalls 154–155, 158; rules and protections 150–157; unsolicited communications, rules for 154–155; voter relationship management (VRM) platforms 141, 146–148, 149, 154, 158, 161
capitalism 40–41
Cate, F H 119
Chambers, S 31
China: 50 Cent Army 103; National Military Strategy 84–85; Social Credit System 72
choice architecture 51–53, 63
class 13, 34, 37, 196
Clinton, Bill 208
Clinton, Hillary 75, 76, 77, 197
Code of Practice on Disinformation 104, 111
cognitive heuristics 50–51
Cohen, J E 63–64
Coleman, J 41–42, 46
communication and Spinoza's philosophy 35–36, 42–46
confirmation bias 19, 57
Conflict of Interest Code for Members of the House of Commons (Canada) 159
conscience, freedom of 64
consent 170, 190–191, 212; Canada 155, 156–157, 158, 159, 163; complexity of data processing and 119; engineering of 51–52; ePrivacy Directive 131–132, 233; ePrivacy Regulation, draft 132–133; General Data Protection Regulation (GDPR) 89, 118–120, 122,

124, 125, 126, 135, 136, 231; nudging 52; photos 108; take-it-or-leave-it 119; UK: Privacy and Electronic Communications Regulations 2003 (PECR) 233; US: do-not-call registry and robo-calls 206
consumerism 22–23, 24, 31
contract(s) 40–41, 43; social 39
Coolidge, Calvin 215
Council of Europe: Convention 108 on personal data 88, 227
Court of Justice of the European Union (CJEU) 78–79; *Google Spain* 78, 87; right to be forgotten 87
Covenant on Civil and Political Rights (CCPR): Arts 17 and 23(1): right to private life 88, 91; Art 19: freedom of expression 88, 92; Art 21: freedom of assembly 91, 92; Art 22: freedom of association 91, 92; Art 25: democratic participation 87–88, 91, 92, 97
criminal law 109, 112
Cruz, Ted 77
Culnan, M J 65
Cummings, Dominic 222, 223
cybersafety 5

dark posts 34–35, 73, 77–78, 83
Data & Society Research Institute 17
data mining 60–63, 73, 169, 192, 194, 203
data protection: Australia 166–169; Canada 141, 155, 157–158, 162; EU: GDPR *see* General Data Protection Regulation; EU Data Protection Directive 87, 90, 115, 228, 232; United Kingdom 89–90, 224, 225, 227–234; United States 209
definitions: big data 74, 169; democracy 79–80; direct marketing 131, 132, 133, 137; electoral activities 116; political micro-targeting 4, 47, 59–60, 171; profiling 133–134; recommendations for better 235; voter manipulation 196–198
democracy 187–195; acceptance of majority's decision 81, 82, 83; algorithms: black box 83; anonymity 80, 81, 83; democratic control and accountability 80–81, 82–83, 84; electorate's freedom of forming political will 80, 82, 83–84; elite theory 175, 176; filter bubbles, conceptions of self and 6–7, 34–36; international law and new challenges to *see separate entry*;

openness of discourse 80, 83, 84; participatory theory 175, 176; pluralism 81, 82, 83, 84; political communication and 174–184; protective theory 175, 176; seven elements of 78–84; transparency 81, 82–83; voter preference and micro-targeted information: implications for 63–67, 68
democracy, filter bubbles and conceptions of self 6–7, 34–46; actively taking part in decision-making 41; continuum, democracy as 41; Foucault: *homo œconomicus* and *homo juridicus* 38–40, 46; Locke: property in the person and 'private' individual 35, 40–42; neo-liberalism, behaviourism and giant tech companies 35, 36–38; Spinoza, the passions and their political implications 35–36, 42–46; subordination 40–41, 44–46
discourse ethics 17–18
discrimination 170, 182; *see also* racism; sexism
domestic violence 41
Downs, A 49–50
due diligence principle 93, 94
due process 170

economic inequality 22
economics 38
education 17, 52; location check-ins 62; universities 37, 39
Elaboration Likelihood Model 53–54
Eldon Insurance 223–224
election, right to stand for 106
electoral commissions 83; Australia 164; United Kingdom 220, 222–223, 226, 227
email and consent: Canada 155; ePrivacy Directive 131–132; ePrivacy Regulation, draft 132–133
email release: US Democratic National Committee 75
employment contract 40–41
epistemological injustice 44–45
erasure or to be forgotten, right to 87, 128, 229, 232
Errington, W 174, 184
espionage 95
ethnicity: Canada: parties collecting information on 149, 158; General Data Protection Regulation (GDPR) 116, 117n20, 119n33; *see also* race

European Commission 227–228; data brokers and data analytics companies: processing of data 122; data controllers and data processors 116; online disinformation 104, 111; political parties and processing of data 121; special categories of data 125; transparency 127

European Convention on Human Rights (ECHR): Art 8: private life 88, 110; Art 10: freedom of expression 88, 104, 107–110, 111; democratic society, needs of 91, 92; Additional Protocol No. 1, Art 3: free elections 88, 97, 105–107

European Court of Human Rights (ECtHR) 80; bloggers and private postings 109–110; democracy 79, 105–106, 116; electoral period 116; European Parliament 105; margin of appreciation 106; proportionality 106, 110; public-watchdogs 99–100, 107–108; state's duty to protect 87; surveillance 79; territorial basis and cyberspace 86

European Data Protection Supervisor 116

European Union: Charter of Fundamental Rights 88, 91, 92, 104, 115, 123, 228; Code of Practice on Disinformation 104, 111; Commission see European Commission; Court of Justice of the 78–79, 87; Data Protection Directive 87, 90, 115, 228, 232; democracy: foundational value of 91, 92; Electronic Commerce Directive 83; ePrivacy Directive 131–132, 232, 233; ePrivacy Regulation, draft 132–133, 137, 138; General Data Protection Regulation (GDPR) see separate entry; Parliament 102, 105; privacy 40, 87; Treaty on the (TEU) 91, 92; Works Council Directive 41

expression, freedom of see freedom of speech and expression

extraterritoriality 86, 115, 232

extraverts 56, 61, 77

face recognition 72

Facebook 14, 17, 18, 34, 35, 36, 73, 78, 92, 191, 209, 210; accountability 224–225; 'Audience Insights' 217–218; Australia 165–166; business model 224; Cambridge Analytica 1–3, 66, 73, 74, 77–78, 82–83, 102, 120, 171, 190, 192, 224; Canada 149, 156, 157, 159–160, 218; case studies, political 218; Code of Practice on Disinformation 111; consent 120; 'Custom Audience' feature 165–166, 217–218; dark posts 73, 77–78; empirical work on effects of political messaging 172; fake accounts 73, 76, 83; fines 3, 90; 'likes' and private characteristics 61, 77; 'liking' a political party 159–160; lobbying power 213; local groups on 27; 'Lookalike Audiences' 159, 218; privacy 3, 89–90, 92; reluctance to view itself as publisher 27; Russian social bots 76; Russian troll farms 74, 76, 81, 103, storage and transfer of personal data, regulation of 209; terms and conditions 83, 89; transparency, lack of 82–83, 90, 204–205; UK: Privacy and Electronic Communications Regulations 2003 (PECR) 233; UK: spending by political parties 220, 226; UK data protection 231

fact-checking 17, 18–19, 104

facts: and political opinion 196–197; and value judgments 49, 108

fake news 2, 4, 13, 14, 17, 82, 101, 102, 173, 209; civil society 195; conjunction of big data and 204–205; freedom of the press 108, 109; politicised entertainment 18; Roman Republic 194; UK data protection 231; US: 2000 South Carolina presidential primary 194–195; US: defining voter manipulation 196–198; US: support for local and regional newspapers 210

Fassino, Piero 109

feminism 44–45

Ferrara, E 66

filter bubbles 4–6, 17–23; anti-pluralistic 82, 83; beyond content 22–24; democracy, conceptions of self and 34–46; finding 20–22; from mass to automated media 24–29; glut chamber 31–33; neoliberal sociality 29–31; transparency, lack of 83

fines 112, 222, 224, 232, 233; Facebook 3, 90

first impressions 54, 57

Fiss, O M 191

Flaxman, S 21

Fletcher, R 21

forgotten or to erasure, right to be 87, 128, 229, 232
Foucault: *homo œconomicus* and *homo juridicus* 38–40, 46
Fox News 53, 100
fragmentation 83; of body politic 20–24, 66
France 111, 189; bots in 2017 presidential election 173–174; Commission Nationale de l'Informatique et Libertés (CNIL) 127, 162
freedom of political communication, implied (Australia) 167, 176–184, 185
freedom of speech and expression 9, 14, 45, 64, 92, 99–101, 209; bloggers and private postings 109–110; Code of Practice on Disinformation 104, 111; ECHR: Art 10 88, 104, 107–110, 111; ECHR Additional Protocol No. 1, Art 3: free elections 88, 97, 105–107; EU Charter of Fundamental Rights: Art 11 88, 104, 115; EU Commission: online disinformation 104; French legislation 111; General Data Protection Regulation (GDPR) 123, 130, 136, 137, 138, 230; German legislation 112; ICCPR Art 19 88, 92; old-fashioned media vs internet 101–102; press, freedom of the 107–109, 175, 210; private power over marketplace of ideas 191; UK Advertising Code 226, 227; US: defining voter manipulation 196–198; *see also* Constitution: First Amendment *under* United States

Gallant, Cheryl 159
Gavison, R 63
gender 13, 34, 41, 44–45, 54; 'bandwagon' effect 55; Canada: parties collecting information on 158; Facebook 'likes' 61; location check-ins 62; search query histories 62; social media postings 61; tailoring messages 59
General Data Protection Regulation (GDPR) 9–10, 87, 114–138, 209, 225, 228–229, 230, 231, 233, 234; access, right of subject 229; Art 6(1)(e) base for processing data: public interest 120–122, 129, 138; Art 6(1)(f) base for processing data: legitimate interests 120, 122–124, 129–130; Charter of Fundamental Rights (CFEU) 115, 123; consent 89, 118–120, 122, 124, 125, 126, 135, 136, 231;

consent, explicit 119, 124, 135, 136, 231; consent, right to withdraw 118–119; data controllers 116–117, 118, 119, 121, 122–124, 126, 128, 129–130, 135, 229, 231–232; data processors 116–117, 122, 126, 229; derogations under 135–136; differences across Member States 125, 126, 132–133, 135–136, 137, 138; direct marketing, right to object to (Art 21(2)) 130–133, 137; joint and several liability 229; lawful processing provisions and processing of special categories of data: arts 6 and 9 117–127, 230–231; legitimate interests 120, 122–124, 128, 129, 135; meaning of electoral activities 116; object, general right to (Art 21(1)) 129–130, 137, 229; object to direct marketing, right to (Art 21(2)) 130–133, 137, 229; platforms, data brokers and analytics companies 116, 121, 122, 125, 126, 136–137; political parties 115, 116, 118, 121–122, 125–127, 131–133, 135, 137, 138; principles 117, 228–229; privacy by design 89; proportionality 121, 123, 124–125, 128, 135–136, 137; public interest 120–122, 123, 124–125, 128, 129, 136, 138; rectification, right to 229; restriction on automated decision making and profiling: Art 22 133–135, 137–138; special categories of data: Art 9 exceptions 117–118, 124–127, 138, 230–231; transfer of data outside EEA 128; transparency: Arts 13 and 14 127–129, 137, 138
geo-fencing 217
Germany 189; face recognition 72; Federal Constitutional Court 79, 80, 82, 101; Network Enforcement Act 2017 112; participation in decision-making and majority rule 80; privacy and democracy 79; public and private broadcasting 101
Goldfarb, Florine 18
Goldwater, Barry 191–192
Google 29, 35, 73, 191, 210; Code of Practice on Disinformation 111; Customer Match 218; *Google Spain* case (CJEU) 78, 87; lobbying power 213; storage and transfer of personal data, regulation of 209; UK: spending by political parties 220
Guinier, Lani 207–208

Habermas, J 13, 24
hacking 4–5, 161; Russian 66, 75
health care 29, 30; health communication 57
heuristics 50–51
homosexuality 45, 61–62
Howard, P N 103
human rights 14, 177; data rights 234; EU
    Charter of Fundamental Rights 88, 91,
    92, 104, 115, 123, 228; European
    Convention on Human Rights (ECHR)
    see separate entry; European Court of
    Human Rights (ECtHR) *see separate
    entry*; freedom of association 66, 91,
    92, 134, 200; freedom of speech
    and expression *see separate entry*;
    International Covenant on Civil and
    Political Rights (ICCPR) *see separate
    entry*; privacy 14, 88–93, 98, 110, 115,
    123, 130, 234; and protection of
    democracy 85–93
human rights and protection of democracy
    85–93; democratic participation, right to
    87–88, 93, 105; limitation clauses
    90–93; non-state actors and democracy
    as legitimate aim 91–92, 93; privacy,
    right to 88–93, 98; proportionality
    90–91, 92, 93; state's duty to protect
    86–87, 88, 92; territorial basis 86
Hume, D 39
Hungary 188–189

ideas, marketplace of 64, 66–67, 100–101,
    191, 193
imagined community 6, 19–20, 25–27,
    34–35
immigration 44, 76
immunity, sovereign 94
individualism 23, 24, 30–31
inequality 22, 196
influence industry 13–14, 219–220
information environment 51, 53, 63
information overload 51
Instagram 76; Canada 150
International Court of Justice (ICJ) 96
International Covenant on Civil and
    Political Rights (ICCPR): Arts 17 and
    23(1): right to private life 88, 91; Art
    19: freedom of expression 88, 92; Art
    21: freedom of assembly 91, 92; Art
    22: freedom of association 91, 92; Art
    25: democratic participation 87–88, 91,
    92, 97

International Law Commission (ILC) 97
international law and new challenges to
    democracy 8–9, 71–98; ability of
    international law to protect democracy
    84–98; application of international law
    to cyberspace 84–85; big-data based
    threats to democracy 71–74, 172–174;
    human rights and protection of
    democracy 85–93; non-intervention
    principle 93–98; power of
    big-data-based cyber operations 74–78;
    seven elements of democracy 78–84
introverts 56
Israel, J 35–36
Italian elections in 1994 109

Jefferson, Thomas 204
Jesse, J 52
John, P 53
Johnson, L B 191–192
joint and several liability 229
journalism 13, 100, 101, 111, 113, 136,
    193, 209–210, 230; EU Commission
    104; facts and value-judgments 108;
    freedom of the press 107–109, 175,
    210; good faith 108; subsidies 210

Kant, I 13, 65
Kenner, Jason 159
Kerr, I 52
Kollanyi, B 103
Kosinski, M 61, 62
Kuklinski, J H 50–51

law and economics 189
Levi, L 209–210
literacy, media and information 111
location check-ins 62
lock-in, social 119
Locke, J 38–39; property in the person and
    'private' individual 40–42
Lovelace, Ada 36

McCain, John 194
McCarthy, T 23
machine learning 28, 68, 169
mailing lists, campaign 65
Mantelero, A 119
marital status: location check-ins 62
marketplace of ideas 64, 66–67, 100–101,
    191, 193
marriage 40, 41

mass media 20, 25–27, 32, 99–100, 109,
188, 191, 195; old-fashioned media vs
internet 101–102; to automated media
6, 17–33; *see also* broadcasting; freedom
of speech and expression; journalism;
newspapers
mass surveillance 66, 71–72, 74–75, 78,
79, 225; anonymity 81; elements of
democracy 81, 83–84; human rights 89,
90–91, 93, 98; non-intervention
principle 95; proportionality 90–91
mass to automated media 6, 17–33;
always-on media 27; beyond content
22–24; bots 28–29, 32–33; civic
disposition 6, 19–20, 22, 23–24, 26;
deficit of sociality 27–28; everyone's got
their goons 18–19; finding filter bubbles
20–22; from 24–29; glut chamber
31–33; interdependence 30, 33;
neoliberal sociality 29–31; shared
informational space of mass media 25;
trust and recognition 30; violence 31
*Mathieu-Mohin and Clerfayt v
Belgium* 106
Mayer-Schönberger, V 119
media bias, perceptions of 22
media deregulation 22
Messina Group 219
Milton, John 193
misogyny 44
mobile phones 62, 149, 157
Mueller, Robert 73, 75

NationBuilder 146, 159, 219
neoliberalism 46; behaviourism, giant tech
companies and 35, 36–38; Foucault:
homo œconomicus and *homo juridicus*
38–40; Locke: property in the person
and 'private' individual 35, 40–42;
sociality 29–31; statist 19, 24, 29
newspapers 25–27, 34–35, 36, 67, 99–101,
210; freedom of the press 107–109,
175, 210
Nielsen, R K 21
no-harm principle 93, 94
non-intervention principle 93–98; object of
protection: will of states to decide and
act freely 95; prohibited means of
intervention: coercion 95–98
novels 25
nudging 37, 52–53, 57, 63, 64;
hypernudge 52

Obama, Barack 147, 170, 189n11
OECD (Organisation for Economic
Co-operation and Development):
Guidelines on the Protection of Privacy
and Trans-border Flows of Personal
Data 227
one-issue voting 48, 68
O'Neil, C 37
online behavioural tracking and big data
analytics 60–63, 73, 76, 102
openness (personality trait): Facebook
'likes' and predicting 61
opinion polls 55, 215–216
outrage and sensationalism 21

panoptic sorting 66
parental status 77; apps on mobile
phone 62
Pariser, E 20, 22–24, 29, 34
parliamentary systems and political
parties 48
Pateman, C 40–41, 46
Patmore, G 175
Pentikäinen v Finland 108–109
personal data, right to protection of 87–89,
115, 123, 232
personalisation of messages 59
personality 56, 59, 123, 216; Facebook
'likes' and predicting openness trait
61; Facebook quiz 1; photos and
photo-related activities 62; social media
and online behavioural tracking
information 61
petitions 158, 159
Pitfield, Tom 148–149
political polarisation 22, 32; Canada 145;
United States 21–22, 202–203
political views/opinions/affiliations 47,
217; Australia 169; Canada 147, 149,
160, 161; data mining 60–61; General
Data Protection Regulation (GDPR)
117n20, 119n33, 126; search query
histories 62; United Kingdom 230
Posner, R A 40
power imbalances 119
Pratte, R 22
predictive technology 190
presidential systems and political parties 48,
187–188
Prigozhin, Yevgeniy Viktorovich 75
privacy 2, 3, 4, 5, 13, 47, 67, 78–79, 113,
209; Australia 13, 79, 164–185;

autonomous individual 63–64; bloggers and private postings 110; Canada 13, 141–142, 143, 152–153, 155–163; forgotten, right to be 87, 128, 229, 232; freedom of the press 107–108; General Data Protection Regulation (GDPR) 123, 130; information that would perpetuate subordination 45–46; neoliberalism 40; nudging 52; OECD Guidelines 227; online behavioural tracking and big data analytics 60–63; right to 14, 88–93, 98, 110, 115, 123, 130, 234; Spinoza's analysis of the passions 45–46; to generate spaces necessary to promote democratic self-rule 64–65; United States 3, 13, 68, 186, 191, 194, 196, 205–206, 210

private postings and bloggers 109–110
privatisation of public space 28n48
Prodi, Romano 109
profiling 2, 4, 47, 114, 115–116, 171, 224, 235; Australia 165; Canada 148, 157, 159, 160; ePrivacy Regulation, draft 133; Facebook's 'Lookalike' audience tool 159; General Data Protection Regulation (GDPR) 123, 129, 130, 133–135, 137–138, 229; online behavioural tracking and big data analytics 60–63, 73, 76, 102; sources of information 60, 62; transparency 128; see also Cambridge Analytica

property, right to 92
proportional representation 190, 203, 207, 208
proportionality 14, 90–91, 92, 93, 106, 110, 227; Australia 180–184; General Data Protection Regulation (GDPR) 121, 123, 124–125, 128, 135–136, 137
psychology 55–56, 58; insights on voter behaviour 50–54
public choice theory 189
public interest 13, 29–30; Australia 183; General Data Protection Regulation (GDPR) 120–122, 123, 124–125, 128, 129, 136, 138; United Kingdom 230
Putin, Vladimir 75

Quirk, P J 50–51

race 13, 126; and epistemological injustice 44–45; Facebook 'likes' and predicting 61; General Data Protection Regulation

(GDPR) 117n20, 119n33; see also ethnicity
racism 35, 45, 194–195
rational voter model 49–50
Rawls, J 65
rectification, right to 128, 229
Regan, P M 52, 65, 180
register, electoral 123; Canada 151–152, 154
relationship status 116, 218; apps on mobile phone 62
religion 84; apps on mobile phone 62; Canada: parties collecting information on 158; Facebook 'likes' 61; General Data Protection Regulation (GDPR) 117n20, 119n33; search query histories 62
robocalls 154–155, 158, 206
Rössler, B 64–65
Rousseau, J-J 41
Rove, Karl 194
Russia 17, 18, 66, 171, 188; hacking 66, 75; hacks and email release: US Democratic National Committee 75; non-intervention principle 95–97; Project Lakhta 75–76, 88, 90, 93, 95, 96–98; social media bots 66, 75–76, 103, 174; states: duty to protect own elections 88; troll farms 73, 74, 75–76, 81, 82–83, 88, 90, 93, 95, 96–98, 103

Schwartz, P 64–65
self-censorship 84
self-determination 63–65; collective 79–80, 93, 94, 98; right to 90n128, 93, 94
self-monitoring 56
self-regulation 17, 99, 111, 209, 226
selfhood 63–64; democracy, filter bubbles and conceptions of self see separate entry
semantic web 169
sensationalism 21
sexism 44, 45
sexual orientation: Facebook 'likes' and predicting 61; General Data Protection Regulation (GDPR) 117n20, 119n33; social media profile pictures 62
signalling 58
Simon, H A 50
single-issue voting 48, 68
Skinner, B F 36–37
slavery 42
Slovic, P 47, 53, 64
Snowden, E 71, 225

social contract 39
social lock-in 119
social media bots *see* bots
social norms 54
social welfare 29
socially constructed self 63–64
socio-economic status 48
sockpuppets 102
Sorochan, C 30
sovereign equality 94
sovereignty, state 93–94
Spinoza, B 39; the passions and their
    political implications 35–36, 42–46
spying 95
standard business terms 119
subordination 45–46; communication and
    44–45; contracts and 40–41
subsidies 210
suicide 42
Sunstein, C R 20, 22–25, 29, 52
surveillance, mass 66, 71–72, 74–75, 78,
    79, 225; anonymity 81; elements of
    democracy 81, 83–84; human rights 89,
    90–91, 93, 98; non-intervention
    principle 95; proportionality 90–91
swing voters 57–58

Tapson, M 52
taxation 30, 196
tech giants, neoliberalism and behaviourism
    35, 36–38
television advertising *see* broadcasting
terrorism 90, 91
text messages and consent: ePrivacy
    Directive 131–132; ePrivacy Regulation,
    draft 132–133
texting 28
Thaler, R H 52
transparency 81, 82–83, 90, 111, 112, 113,
    173, 225, 228, 229; Australia 164;
    Canada 156–157; General Data
    Protection Regulation: Arts 13 and 14
    127–129, 137, 138; United Kingdom
    225, 226, 231; United States 191, 192,
    204–206, 208, 211–213
Trudeau, Justin 218
Trump, Donald 1–2, 29, 37, 46, 73,
    75–77, 84, 170, 173–174, 196,
    220, 225
Tufekci, Z 53
Turing, Alan 36
Turkle, S 27–28, 29

turnout in elections 49, 144–145, 215
Turow, J 58
Twitter 14, 74, 82–83, 92, 191, 210; bots
    66, 76, 103, 173; Canada 150; Code of
    Practice on Disinformation 111; fake
    accounts 73, 76, 83; political affiliation
    62; reluctance to view itself as publisher
    27; Russian bots 66, 76; Russian troll
    farms 74, 81; storage and transfer of
    personal data, regulation of 209; study
    of fake news propagated on 193;
    transparency, lack of 82–83, 204–205

United Kingdom 12–13, 214–235; 2015
    elections 218, 219; 2017 general
    election 66, 219; AggregateIQ (AIQ)
    221–222; BBC 100, 210; Brexit
    referendum 1–2, 34, 46, 102, 103, 105,
    120, 170, 190, 209, 220–224, 233;
    Cambridge Analytica 1–3, 34, 102, 120,
    164–165, 218, 219, 220–223, 224, 225,
    235; competition law 2; Data Protection
    Act 1998 89–90, 228, 232; Data
    Protection Act 2018 228, 230–231;
    data protection and regulations on
    communications 227–234; Eldon
    Insurance 223–224; existing framework
    and absence of specific legislation for
    online political campaigning 225–227;
    fines 3, 90, 222, 224, 232, 233; further
    rights or better enforcement of data
    rights 234–235; House of Commons
    DCMS Committee 2, 3, 164, 219, 220,
    221–222, 223, 235; Information
    Commissioner's Office (ICO) 2–3, 90,
    120, 121–122, 127, 131, 135, 162,
    164, 219, 220–222, 231–234; modern
    political campaign 215–224; privacy 2,
    3, 89–90; Privacy and Electronic
    Communications Regulations 2003
    (PECR) 227, 232–234; public
    knowledge and steps towards
    accountability 224–225; scale and
    granularity of personal information
    216–217; Scottish referendum 219;
    spending in Brexit referendum, digital
    222–223; spending by political parties,
    digital 218–220; transparency 225,
    226, 231
United Nations: Charter 94, 95; Human
    Rights Committee (UNHRC) 80, 86,
    87, 88; Special Rapporteur 14

United States 11–12, 14, 27, 84, 171,
173, 186–213, 215, 225; 1964
presidential election 191–192; 2000
presidential election 57; 2000 South
Carolina presidential primary 194–195;
2016 presidential election 1–2, 18, 34,
37, 46, 66, 73, 75–78, 102, 103,
172, 173–174, 190, 197, 209, 220,
225; approach to political campaigns
215; Bill of Rights 202; Cambridge
Analytica 1–2, 3, 34, 38, 66, 73,
77–78, 102, 190, 192, 225; challenges
on conducting free and fair elections
186–196; consent 190–191, 206, 212;
Constitution: First Amendment 186,
194, 195, 196–198, 200, 202, 204,
205–206, 208–209, 211; Constitution:
Fourteenth Amendment 200, 202,
211; defamation 197; electoral
districts, rigged 186, 189–190,
198–203, 206–207, 211, 212; face
recognition and demonstrations 72;
Facebook 1–2, 3, 18, 27, 66, 73, 76,
81, 190, 191, 192, 204–205, 209,
210, 213; Federal Trade Commission
3, 68, 206; fines 3; Florida 76; fox
guarding the henhouse 194, 212;
Fox News 53, 100; free speech threat:
private power over marketplace of ideas
191; gerrymandering 186, 189–190,
198–203, 206–207, 211, 212; House
of Representatives 187, 199, 201–203,
207; incumbent politicians and big
data 203–206, 211, 212; indictments
against Russians by Mueller 73, 75;
individuality 30–31; judicial review
194, 196–203, 203–206, 206–210,
211–212; libel 197; manipulation,
defining voter 196–198; National
Security Agency (NSA) 71–72, 74–75,
78, 81, 90, 98; NPR 210; one-issue
voting 48; political opinion 196–197;
political parties in presidential systems
48; political polarisation 21–22,
202–203; privacy 3, 13, 68, 186, 191,
194, 196, 205, 206, 210; proportional
representation 190, 203, 207, 208;
Radio Act 1927 66–67; reforms of
electoral process, potential structural
186, 198–203, 206–208, 210–211,
212, 213; reforms, potential personal
data 186, 190–191, 193–194, 195,
196–198, 205, 208–213; Schrems
case 78; Senate 187, 207; social
welfare 29; Sorrell 194n34, 204, 208;
'speech': gathering and mining of data
194n34, 203, 208–209; spending,
digital 220; surveillance 71–72, 74–75,
78, 81, 84, 90, 98; taxation 196;
transparency 191, 192, 204–206, 208,
211, 212–213; Twitter 62, 73, 81,
173, 191, 193, 204–205, 209, 210;
Twitter data and political affiliation
62; universities, for-profit 37;
VoteBuilder (NGP VAN) 147;
Voter Vault software 146
universities 39; recruiting manual: for-profit
US 37
unsolicited: calls or faxes or messaging
(Australia) 168–169; communications
(Canada) 154–155; ePrivacy Directive:
electronic mail and text messages
131–132; ePrivacy Regulation
(draft): direct marketing
communications 132

value-judgments 49, 108
Van Onselen, P 174, 184
Vienna Convention on the Law of
Diplomatic Relations 97
violence 31, 42
Von Hannover v Germany (No 1)
107–108
Von Hannover v Germany (No 2) 108
vote, right to 106, 134, 150
voter preference and micro-targeted
information 7–8, 47–68; appearance
54–55; constructing political choice
54–58; democracy, implications
for 63–67, 68; enhanced voter files
60; micro-targeting: targeting to and
tailoring for individual voters 58–63;
psychology 50–54, 55–56, 58;
traditional political science
theories about political behaviour
48–50
voting, compulsory 37, 49,
58, 175

Wang, Y 62
Warren, S 63
Watson, J B 36–37
women 44–45, 54; 'bandwagon' effect
55; Facebook 'likes' and predicting

private traits 61; traditional marriage
contract 41

Yeung, K 52
YouTube 103, 218

Zhong, Y 62
Zittrain, J 53, 60
Žižek, S 19
Zuckerberg, Mark 209

Printed in the United States
By Bookmasters